MODERNIZING ISI

JOHN L. ESPOSITO
FRANÇOIS BURGAT

editors

Modernizing Islam

*Religion in the Public Sphere
in the Middle East and Europe*

RUTGERS UNIVERSITY PRESS
NEW BRUNSWICK NEW JERSEY

First published in the United States 2003
by Rutgers University Press, New Brunswick, New Jersey
First published in Great Britain 2003
by C. Hurst & Company (Publishers) Ltd., London
Copyright © 2003 John L. Esposito and François Burgat
All rights reserved

Library of Congress Cataloging-in-Publication Data and British Library Cataloguing-in-Publication Data are available upon request.

ISBN 0-8135-3197-7 (cloth)
ISBN 0-8135-3198-5 (paper)

Set in Times New Roman by Bookcraft Ltd, Stroud, Gloucestershire
Printed in Great Britain

CONTENTS

ACKNOWLEDGMENTS

This volume was a collaborative effort and thus we would like to thank all of our colleagues who patiently wrote and revised their manuscripts. We are especially grateful to all those in the Muslim world who have been so responsive in establishing the kind of dialogue that enables scholars to continue to do research at a time when too often there has been a lack of bilateral understanding. Finally, Natana DeLong-Bas played an invaluable role in preparing the mansucript for final submission and publication.

September 2002   JOHN L. ESPOSITO AND FRANÇOIS BURGAT

THE CONTRIBUTORS

Fariba Adelkhah is Lecturer in the political sociology of Shiism at INALCO (National Institute of Oriental Languages) and Researcher at the National Foundation of Political Science, Center of International Studies and Research (CERI), both in Paris. Her publications include *La Révolution sous le voile. Femmes islamiques d'Iran* and *Being Modern in Iran*.

François Burgat is Director of the French Center for Yemeni Studies in Sanaa, Yemen, and specialist on political and ideological dynamics, particularly Islamic movements, in the Middle East and North Africa. His most recent publications include *The Islamic Movement in North Africa* and *L'Islamisme en face*.

Jocelyne Cesari is Senior Research Fellow at the National Center for Scientific Research (CNRS-EPHE-La Sorbonne) and Visiting Professor at Harvard University. She has written extensively on Islam and ethnicity in France and Europe. She is currently carrying out research on Muslim minorities in Europe and in the USA. Her most recent publications include *Musulmans et Républicains: les jeunes, l'islam et la France*, "Islam in European Cities," in Sophie Body-Gendrot and Marco Martiniello (eds.) *Minorities in European Cities. The Dynamics of Social Integration and Exclusion at the Neighbourhood Level*; "The Re-Islamization of Muslim Immigration in Europe," in Gema Martin-Munoz (ed.), *Islam, Modernism and the West*; "Islam in France: The Shaping of a Religious Minority," in Yvonne Yazbek-Haddad (ed.), *Muslims in the West: From Sojourners to Citizens*, and "Global Multiculturalism: The Challenge of Heterogeneity," *Alternatives*, 27, 2002.

Oussama Cherribi was elected as a member of the Dutch Parliament in 1994 and is currently serving his second four-year term. He also represents the Netherlands in the Assemblies of the Council of Europe and the West European Union. He received his Ph.D. in the social sciences from the University of Amsterdam and is an associate member of the University of California's Berkeley Center of Globalization and Information Technology.

Connie Carøe Christiansen has a Master's degree in Cultural Sociology and a Ph.D. in Anthropology from the University of Copenhagen. Her Ph.D. thesis, "Self and Social Process in Women's Islamic Activism: Claims for Recognition", was accepted in 1999, and since then she has published several articles on Islamism and on transnationalism. She is currently employed at the Danish National Institute of Social Research.

Baudouin Dupret is Research Fellow at the French Centre National de la Recherche Scientifique (CNRS) and is affiliated with the Centre d'Etudes et de Documentation Economique, Juridique and Sociale (CEDEJ) in Cairo. His recent publications include *Au nom de quel droit? Répertoires juridiques et référence religieuse dans la société égyptienne musulmane contemporaine*; *Pluralism in the Arab World* (co-edited with Maurits Berger and Laila Al-Zwaini); and *Egypt and its Laws* (co-edited with Nathalie Bernard-Maugiron).

John L. Esposito is University Professor as well as Professor of Religion and International Affairs and of Islamic Studies at Georgetown University. Founding Director of the Center for Muslim-Christian Understanding in the Walsh School of Foreign Service, he has served as President of the Middle East Studies Association of North America and of the American Council for the Study of Islamic Societies as well as a consultant to governments, multinational corporations, and the media. Editor-in-Chief of the *Oxford Encyclopedia of the Modern Islamic World* and the *Oxford History of Islam*, his more than 25 books include *Unholy War: Terror in the Name of Islam*; *The Islamic Threat: Myth or Reality?*, *Islam: The Straight Path*; *Islam and Politics, Islam and Democracy* and *Makers of Contemporary Islam* (with John Voll), *Political Islam: Radicalism, Revolution or Reform? Iran at the Crossroads* (with R. K. Ramazani); *Islam, Gender and Social Change* (with Yvonne Haddad); and *Women in Muslim Family Law*.

Linda Herrera received her B.A. from UC Berkeley in Middle East Studies (1986), her M.A. from the American University in Cairo (AUC) in Anthropology/Sociology (1992), and her Ph.D. from Columbia University in Comparative Education (2000). She has worked extensively in the fields of development and social science research in the Middle East Region. She is currently an education consultant and lecturer in the Department of Sociology/ Anthropology at AUC.

Dilwar Hussain graduated from King's College, London, in 1992. He currently works as a Research Fellow at the Islamic Foundation, Leicestershire, England where he conducts research on Muslim communities in Europe. He is on the editorial boards of the journals *The Muslim World Book Review* (quarterly), and *Encounters: Journal of Inter-Cultural Perspectives* (bi-annual). He regularly speaks, trains and writes on issues such as Muslim identity, Muslims in Europe/Britain, Islam in the modern world and Islamophobia.

Bjørn Olav Utvik is Associate Professor of Middle East History and head of the Department of East European and Oriental Studies at the University of Oslo. His main research interest is the economic discourse of Egypt's Islamist opposition. In addition, he has written articles on Egyptian politics and the Islamist movement in Egypt, and translated short stories and a novel from Arabic into Norwegian.

MODERNIZING ISLAM AND RE-ISLAMIZATION IN GLOBAL PERSPECTIVE

John L. Esposito

The tragedy of September 11, 2001, sparked increased questioning about Islam as a global force. Perhaps more than any other religion, Islam is often associated with the violent acts of extremists, terrorism and the oppression of women. And, perhaps more than any other religion, the combination of the lack of information and a plethora of distorted information are responsible for Western ignorance about Islam and Muslims and perceptions of Islam as a threat to Western civilization. The reality is far more complex. While a minority of extremists focus on revolution in their own countries and abroad, others concentrate on more peaceful political and social "revolutions" and reforms dedicated to the incorporation and expression of Islamic values in both the public and private spheres.

During the last three decades, Islam has become a more visible presence and force in Muslim politics and societies from North Africa and the Middle East to Central, South, and Southeast Asia. Greater attention to religious observance (prayer, fasting, dress, pilgrimage) has accompanied the creation of new institutions (Islamic banks, finance houses, insurance companies, schools, clinics, and hospitals). New Islamic republics have emerged in Iran, Afghanistan, and Sudan; religiously inspired social and political movements have proliferated. Islam has inspired revolution in Iran as well as reform, resistance, and opposition movements in countries as diverse as Tunisia, Algeria, Lebanon, Jordan, Egypt, Pakistan, Afghanistan, Kashmir, Malaysia, and Indonesia. If some governments and rulers (Saudi Arabia, Pakistan, Iran, Sudan, and Afghanistan) have appealed to Islam to enhance their legitimacy and mobilize popular support, others in Tunisia, Algeria, and Turkey have attempted to control or repress religion in public space.

At the same time, increased Muslim migration (emigration) has resulted in a changing religious landscape in Europe and America in which Islam is the second or third largest religion. Only a few decades ago, Muslims were a small invisible presence at best. Today, mosques and Islamic centers may be found in Western cities and towns; Muslims are visible in the professions and labor force, as military and prison chaplains, mayors, lawyers, professors,

1

engineers, businessmen, scientists, and judges. A list of major Muslim cities and populations today must not only include Cairo, Tunis, Damascus, Islamabad, Kuala Lumpur, or Jakarta, but also Paris, Marseilles, London, Manchester, Bonn, Amsterdam, New York, and Detroit. This global presence of Islam and Muslims today requires that we speak not only of Islam and the West but also Islam in the West.

However different the experiences, many Muslims are engaged in a process of Islamization or re-Islamization, the application of Islamic principles and values to personal and public life. Islam has always been a visible and dynamic force in Muslim life and societies. Yet, in recent decades, Islam has reemerged as a major religious, political, and social force in public as well as personal life in response to the multiple experiences of Muslims: the failures of modern states and societies, social dislocation due to rapid development and urbanization, the desire to reaffirm and retain faith and identity in the midst of Western-oriented modernizing societies. Issues of faith and identity, assimilation or integration, are faced by Muslims in many urban centers in Muslim countries as well as Muslim minority communities living in non-Muslim societies. In both cases, the prevailing elite culture and ethos is based upon a Western, secular worldview and set of values. Islamization has had an impact on states, societies, and communities—on politics, economics, law, education, women, and minorities.

Islam remains a persistent and powerful discourse and force in contemporary Muslim politics and societies. Many have chosen to monitor and chronicle its development in terms of political power: to what extent has Islamism come to power, what governments does it control, is it strong or weak, etc.? Although some speak of the failure of political Islam, a more widespread and significant reality exists. Throughout much of the Muslim world, Muslim societies and communities have become more Islamized both politically and socially. Islam as a religion, source or component of identity, a system of values has become more pervasive. Its influence cuts across geographic and ethnic boundaries, social class, and gender. The Islamization of society from below can be seen not only in individual lives, but also in the institutions and organizations of societies. This volume speaks to the significance of this phenomenon: its origins, scope, influence, and impact as well as its implications for the future. *Modernizing Islam: Religion in the Public Sphere in the Middle East and Europe* provides a perspective on the significance and impact of re-Islamization in the Muslim world and the West. Case studies from North Africa, the Middle East, and Europe will exemplify the diverse ways in which Islam has reemerged in Muslim politics and society, and focus on the political, social, and legal implications.

The challenge of political Islam

The most visible manifestation of Islamization has been Islamism or Islamic political activism (often popularly referred to as Islamic fundamentalism or political Islam). The nature, challenge, or threat of political Islam has been the most controversial and contested issue in Muslim domestic politics and in international relations between the Muslim world and the West. Fear of political Islam, a post-Cold War tendency to demonize Islamic activism and movements, often projecting it as a new global threat, has been a major factor in international politics.[1] Memories of the Iranian revolution and its anti-Western rhetoric and actions, Shii anti-government protests in Saudi Arabia, Kuwait, and Bahrain, the assassination of Egypt's Anwar Sadat, and the taking of hostages and other acts of terrorism in the Middle East fed concerns about the spread of radical Islamic fundamentalism. The international community and many Muslim governments feared "other Irans" during the 1980s, worried about Islamic activists coming to power through revolution. Most maintained that Islamic movements were marginal groups that lacked any significant constituency and would be rejected by the people in open elections. However, few authoritarian governments were anxious to test their hypothesis. In the late 1980s and early 1990s, many stood traumatized as they witnessed the power of activists in electoral politics. Islamic activism demonstrated its diversity, complexity, and appeal as a social and political movement. It quickly became evident that Islamism had a broad-based appeal, that it was now an alternative force in mainstream society. Economic failures led many countries (Egypt, Jordan, Tunisia, Algeria) to hold elections and to allow Islamists to run for office. Islamic political parties and individuals participated in elections and emerged as the leading opposition. However, the Islamic Salvation Front's sweep of municipal and parliamentary elections in Algeria set off an alarm among many Muslim governments in the region and in Western capitals, particularly France and the United States. For many, Islam was seen as incompatible with modernity, in particular with democratization and modernization.

Issues and trends in global re-Islamization

The reassertion of Islam in Muslim politics challenged the presuppositions and expectations of modernization and development theory that was predicated on the belief that modernization required the progressive secularization and westernization of society. Thus, many have questioned whether Islam is compatible with modernity, democracy, civil society and pluralism.

---

[1] Samuel P. Huntingdon, "The Clash of Civilizations," *Foreign Affairs*, Summer 1993; Bernard Lewis, "The Roots of Muslim Rage," *The Atlantic Monthly* 226:3, September 1990; and Daniel Pipes, "The New Global Threat," *Jerusalem Post*, April 11, 2001.

As François Burgat notes in Chapter 1, "Veils and Obscuring Lenses," the West (French even more than Anglo-Saxons) dismisses the use of an Islamic idiom as incompatible with modernity because it is "religious." The result, as Burgat puts it, is that the West "fails more and more to realize the banality but also the seriousness, legitimacy, and often the urgency of all or part of the claims carried by the Islamist political generation." Yet, being attentive to Islamist concerns and to the role of fundamentalism in politics can sometimes lead to a glossing over of the complex causes of conflicts. Real political differences and grievances are often ignored or dismissed by simply attributing conflict and violence to religious fundamentalism(s) as can be seen in Algeria and Israel/Palestine. Appreciation of issues of North-South differences, authoritarian and repressive Muslim regimes, and Western states that find easy answers to complex situations by attributing them to an "Islamic threat" are, as Burgat reminds us, critical to our understanding of the dynamics of Muslim politics today. The diversity of Islamization is revealed in the many Islamic discourses, orientations, and strategies that impact on Muslim politics and societies today, from right to left, mainstream and extremist, social and political, government and opposition. This awareness and perspective is critical to an appreciation of the strength and dynamics of Islamization in the 21st century.

The reassertion of Islam in contemporary Muslim politics led many to assert that Muslims were faced with a choice between Mecca and mechanization. For more than a century, the question of whether or not Islam is compatible or incompatible with modernity and modernization has been a point of contention between and among Muslims and non-Muslims alike. The Islamic modernist movement in the Middle East and South Asia in the late 19th and early 20th centuries addressed this issue intellectually, socially, and politically. The relationship of revelation and reason, religion and science/technology, the status and rights of women and minorities, the nature and function of Islam in the modern state have been and continue to be debated. Although the founders of Islamic movements like the Muslim Brotherhood and the Jamaat-i Islami saw themselves as providing an Islamic response to modernity, for others the rise of fundamentalism provided living proof of Islam's revolt against modernity and modernization. This belief has been used by many governments in the Muslim world to discredit and repress Islamist groups, by others (in the West) especially to warn of a clash of civilizations between Islam and the West, and by governments in Europe and America to implement anti-terrorism legislation that often targets Muslims and Muslim organizations.

Bjorn Olav Utvik's "The Modernizing Force of Islamism" (Chapter 2) argues that contrary to conventional wisdom, Islamism, although critical of the excesses of modernity, is not anti-modern: "From the time of Hasan al-Banna, Islamists have been unequivocal advocates of bringing their societies up to the technological level of modern industrial society. The most fertile recruiting ground for Islamist organizations has been students in technological and natural science subjects. If any one vocation is typical for an Islamist, it is that of the engineer." Indeed, Islamists are often more modern than their authoritarian counterparts and provide a bridge between tradition and modernity for many in their societies.

The ideologies, institutions, and goals of many Islamist groups reflect their modern orientation, character, and agendas. Islamist discourse, while sometimes at odds with secular counterparts, is modern and rational; it promotes developments that are conducive to individualization, social mobilization, and economic development. It is less anti dependency on the West and anti-Western intervention. As Utvik notes, a primary concern for many activists is a cultural authenticity and cultural nationalism that sepa-rates and frees it from the West. The track record of Islamist movements in recent years demonstrates the extent to which many promote attitudes and values that are conducive to change and the development of modern states and societies, from popular sovereignty, civil society, and political pluralism to science and technology. They are among the most prominent advocates of political, economic, and technological development. Utvik argues that rather than preventing, Islamism is, in fact, speeding up the process of modernization and acclimating populations to modern ideas. At the same time, emphasis is placed upon the moral regeneration of society as a prerequisite to material development. Islamists are vocal critics of corrup-tion, particularly in government and in land speculation and other economic practices, as well as proponents of individual freedom and responsibility, promotion based upon merit rather than government or family connec-tions. Utvik notes that even the call for implementation of the Shariah (Islamic law) by groups such as the Muslim Brotherhood is modern in orientation since it calls for the codification of the Shariah into modern legal texts by elected assemblies and its application by modern state judi-ciaries rather than *ulama/qadi* (religious scholars/judges) courts.

An integral part of the re-Islamization of society in the late 20th and early 21st centuries has been the creation or Islamization of civil society. Islamic movements and activists in countries from Egypt, Algeria, Tunisia, Turkey, and Jordan to Iran, Pakistan, Malaysia, and Indonesia have created both an alternative vision and alternative non-governmental institutions from schools, hospitals, and clinics to legal, social, and welfare services and professional associations. In Chapter 3, "Islam and Civil Society," I discuss the diverse ways in which Islamic activists have sought to Islamize politics and society through the creation of political parties and profes-sional associations as well as social welfare agencies and projects. As case studies from Tunisia, Algeria, Egypt, and Jordan demonstrate, authori-tarian and secularly oriented regimes have perceived these developments as a threat.

In many parts of the Muslim world, civil society and democratization are under siege or in retreat. If some blame Islamic governments (Sudan, Afghanistan, and, until recently, Iran) and Islamist movements, others cite the intransigence of authoritarian states and the military (Algeria, Turkey, Tunisia, and Egypt) to tolerate and abide by the results of open electoral politics. At the same time, some political analysts and policymakers legitimate those who speak of an incompatibility of Islam and democracy or Islam and civil society. They emphasize an underlying clash of civilizational values between Islam and the West. However, Iran, long regarded as a terrorist threat, has in fact provided a major example of the mobilizing power of an appeal to democratization and civil society. The election of President Khatami, his civil society agenda, and current power struggles within Iran are often framed within the context of civil society and democratization issues.

Re-Islamization in the public sphere

Islamization in the public sphere in the 20th and 21st centuries has been most evident in calls for the establishment of Islamic states, the emphasis on the political and public dimension of Islam, the re-implementation of the Shariah as the law of the land, the debate over women's rights in both private and public life, and the battle for control over education.

The primary example most often cited of Islamization of politics and the public sphere is revolutionary Iran. For many, the Islamic Republic of Iran has been the test case for contemporary Islamization of politics and society. The Iranian revolution stunned Middle East governments and Western policymakers alike. It signaled the contemporary reassertion of Islam in politics and society. At the same time, it set in motion a cycle of mutual satanization as Iran and Western governments (and indeed some Muslim governments) condemned and denounced each other. The fallout from the impact of the seizure of the American embassy during the revolution and hostage-taking, purges and export of revolution, the Iran-Iraq war, Western-backed sanctions against Iran and its labeling as a terrorist state are with us today.

The election of President Mohammed Khatami as President of Iran stunned both Iran's militant conservative leadership and Western governments. Khatami's overwhelming victory signaled a new stage in Iran's post-revolutionary history. As Fariba Adelkhah notes in Chapter 4, "Islam and the Common Mortal," it signaled a restructuring of the regime rather than its end. Adelkhah analyzes the new forces unleashed by Khatami's election and the ensuing struggle in domestic politics between Khatami and his allies and supporters of the Supreme Guide, Ali Khamenei. Despite the concentration of power in the hands of the Supreme Guide, a transformation is perceptible in Iranian society. Khatami's support for civil society, the rule of law, and democratization, though not imposed, has become part of the political culture and debate within Iran. Although conservative forces have been able to arrest and imprison liberal supporters of Khatami, their actions have become contested in public space. The actions of ministries, courts, and police have been the subjects of public criticism and demonstrations. Clerically dominated institutions, from the Supreme Guide and the Council of Experts to the parliament, have been publicly examined and criticized, their powers questioned and challenged.

Another way to observe the changes in post-revolutionary Iran is to study the extent to which social and political boundaries in public space are being redrawn. While much attention has been given to the bureaucratization and rationalization of the state as well as clergy-laity and gender relations, Adelkhah discusses the ways in which dying (funeral ceremonies, sanctuaries, and the commemoration of saints and the deceased), a universal and definitive calendar marker in Iranian society, has played a significant role in the redrawing of social and political space. Religious rituals like the Ashura processions were redefined. The Iraq-Iran war and the deaths of many due to terrorist acts of the Mojahedin Movement produced a cult of martyrs that became a national liturgy. Behesit-e Zahra cemetery and Imam Khomeini's mausoleum became the object of daily visits, and family rituals and funerals became the site of political demonstrations as well as speeches by political leaders. At the same time, as death rituals were transformed, they not only became a political but also a middle class activity, a source of expenditure and land speculation, reflecting the creation of a bourgeois, consumer society.

Integral to the desire or demands for Islamization in many Muslim societies is the call for introduction of the Shariah. Historically, Islamic law provided the ideal blueprint for the good society. Based upon the Quran and Sunnah (example) of the Prophet Muhammad as well as human interpretation, Islamic law sought to provide comprehensive guidelines for worship (*ibadat*) and social life or relations (*muamalat*). Thus, it governed not only prayer and fasting, but also marriage, divorce, inheritance, issues of war and peace, and commercial relations. While most modernizing Muslim states tended to adopt or adapt Western legal codes in creating modern states, since the 1970s, the Islamic resurgence has witnessed the introduction or reintroduction of Islamic laws in countries like Pakistan, Iran, Sudan, and Afghanistan and the demand by many Islamists in other countries, such as Egypt, that Shariah be the only law of the state or that its presence and influence be expanded. Egypt, a Muslim country that incorporated Western political, legal, and educational models for development, served as an example to other Arab countries of modernization. In recent decades, it has also been a prime area for Islamic activism and calls for the re-Islamization of law and society. Although their tactics have differed sharply (violent versus non-violent), both mainstream (the Muslim

Brotherhood) and extremist Islamic organizations (the Gamaa Islamiyya and Jamaat al-Jihad) have challenged the Islamic character and legitimacy of the state and called for the creation of an Islamic order. Baudouin Dupret's "A Return to the Shariah? Egyptian Judges and Referring to Islam" (Chapter 5) examines whether the struggle and debate over Shariah has been over implementation of a legal model as much as an ideological discourse that uses the Islamic idiom for political purposes. Dupret examines Egyptian law (criminal, constitutional, civil) and identifies those areas where Islam is present and/or contested. While Islam is present especially in civil law, its more influential impact has come less from the law itself than from the interpretations of judges and jurists. Egyptian judges have appealed to Islamic law not only to legitimate but also to challenge or invalidate statute law.

The central issues in the Shariah debates in Egypt can be seen most clearly in the legal profession and decisions of the judiciary. As elections in Egyptian professional associations have shown, Islamically oriented lawyers are an important component in the legal profession; similar comments can be made regarding the judiciary. Dupret's interviews with lawyers reflect the plurality of views within the legal establishment regarding the role of Islam in Egyptian law. If some believe that the bulk of Egyptian law does not contradict the Shariah, others identify many areas in which current laws are incompatible with the it. Those who fear the downfall of the state counter others who believe that introduction of Shariah or greater Islamization of the Egyptian legal system will strengthen state and society.

Major legal cases also reflect the struggle within Egyptian society today, the extent to which Islam and calls for Islamization are as much about ideological discourse and direction as legal models or codes. Dupret selects three cases that reflect central issues: (1) a challenge against the Ministry of Education's attempt to exclude female students who wear a full or face veil (*niqab*) from public schools; (2) the Abu Zayd case in which an Egyptian professor was taken to court by Islamists who accused him of apostasy and therefore demanded that the court issue a divorce (against the will of Abu Zayd and his wife) or nullify their marriage; and (3) an inheritance case involving a trans-sexual. Dupret maintains that these three cases reflect a broader phenomenon in Egypt today in which Shariah rulings are not so much about the application of a specific prescription or law as about using the Shariah as an ideological resource/ discourse within which judges fashion rulings. Thus, he concludes, "the so-called return to the Shariah should be viewed as the invention of a new Shariah in the contemporary political, legal, and judicial setting."

The contemporary resurgence of Islam and attempts to re-Islamize have heightened concerns about women's progress and development of women *vis-à-vis* the reforms made in the 20th century in education, employment, and gender relations. Women and gender relations have been central to Islamic law and Muslim society. The family is the basic unit of the Islamic community, long regarded as the locus for the training of the next generation of believers. Thus, women's status and role have been of central concerns and issues throughout Islamic history. Their significance is reflected in Quranic texts, Prophetic traditions, and Islamic law, in particular family laws (marriage, divorce, and inheritance). The tendency of some who wish to Islamize or re-Islamize society to immediately call for the veiling and seclusion of women or their restricted access to education and employment has been the subject of debate and confrontation in some Muslim societies and of concern and condemnation by human rights and women's organizations. The impact of Islamization on women in Pakistan, Iran, and Sudan and the policies of the former Taliban regime in Afghanistan epitomized for some the dangers and threat of Islamization.

Yet, there is another picture as well. In many Muslim societies, women have found Islam offers alternative paths to empowerment and liberation. Many women have become more religiously observant, attend mosque, study and recite the Quran, participate more fully in society, and choose to wear modern forms of Islamic dress as a sign of their modesty and independence. They are students and professionals who are fully involved in their societies as well as in their families, engaged in political and social activism and reform. Thus, Islamization has been both a source of oppression and a source of empowerment.

Connie Carøe Christiansen's "Women's Islamic Activism: Between Self-Practices and Social Reform Efforts" (Chapter 6) demonstrates the impact of Islamism on Moroccan women, and their increasing engagement and empowerment individually and collectively. Her study draws heavily upon social science theory and surveys conducted of Islamically oriented women and men. Christiansen discusses how for these women in particular their turn to Islam, the Islamization of their personal lives, has enhanced their skills, knowledge, competencies, and sense of self. Many women have become more politically and socially active. In contrast to experiences where women are marginalized, Moroccan Islamists, emphasizing education and human development, have produced individuals who are strong, assertive, coherent, and organized, who combine an interest in personal piety, spiritual development, wisdom, and the next life with social reform in the present. Islam has become a means for young women's mobilization in politics. It is a vehicle and mode that Christiansen believes is more accessible and attractive to a larger segment of the population when compared to Western feminism's primary appeal to elite women. She presents a series of statements from interviews, the voices of Islamist women, with analysis to demonstrate the ways in which Moroccan women are responding to and finding an alternative path to empowerment in their Islamic faith and heritage.

The impact of Islamism is also apparent in the ongoing battle for control over both private and public education. Egypt is a case in point. Although the state maintains official control over school curricula and texts, it has not always successfully maintained control over the political, cultural, and economic transformations resulting from the politicization of Islam. Furthermore, the state has little control over the interplay between itself, non-state actors, youth, and the market.

Linda Herrera's "Islamization and Education in Egypt: Between Politics, Culture, and the Market" (Chapter 7) explores the impact of Islamization on both private and public schools in Egypt, studying the ways in which Islam is both adapted to and transformed by modern institutions. She notes that, despite the apparent tight control of the Egyptian state over the school system, Islamists have managed to exert so much influence over the educational system that the Minister of Education, Dr. Kamal Baha Eddin, has characterized Egyptian schools as "factories of terrorism." His proposed solution to the problem was to emphasize education as a component of national security. Because of the perceived need to protect the nation's youth from "dangerous" or "extremist" elements, he engaged in a strategy of purging Islamist educators, administrators, and materials from schools and restricting "Islamic" school uniforms, particularly for girls. However, this policy has not proven to be particularly successful given that Islamists already exert significant power in social and cultural life in Egypt.

Perhaps nowhere is the cultural politics of education more visible than in the crisis of moral authority over appropriate dress for Egyptian schoolgirls. At issue is the question of whether the state or the parents should decide how their children, particularly their daughters, are dressed. Although Ministerial Order 113 of 1994 forbade girls in grades 1–5 from wearing the *hijab* (headscarf), permitted it for girls in grades 6–8 only via written permission from a guardian, and prohibited the wearing of the *niqab* (full veil) at all educational levels, school communities, particularly parents, have refused to obey such orders. Rather than having the desired effect of depoliticizing girls' dress, this Order caused many to reassert the right of the parents, rather than the state, to determine how their children should be dressed. As a result, numerous lawsuits were filed and the matter of Islamic dress remains a highly divisive issue.

Herrera also notes that private Islamic schools do not necessarily cater to the poor and orphans. Instead, a parallel series of institutions servicing the educated and wealthy has also arisen in response to market demands, rendering education a commercial commodity like many others. Such schools seek to marry technical expertise and knowledge of the English language with religious orientation and values so that Muslim students are prepared not only to engage modernity, but also to shape it morally and ethically, preparing a new generation of leaders.

Re-Islamization in Europe

Islamization today is occurring not only in the Muslim world but also in the West. In Europe and America, societies whose histories, religious traditions, and values are rooted in a Judeo-Christian past as well as a secular heritage now face a new and major addition to their societies. In contrast to many other immigrants that they have welcomed in the past, Islam and Muslims represent a very different "other," a religio-political force that has engaged the West for centuries with a legacy of major confrontations and conflicts, from the early Arab conquests to European and American colonialism. France provides a major example of these challenges, past and present, and the extent to which ideology and perceived national interest affect both domestic and international politics. Burgat (Chapter 1) surveys issues from the integration of Muslims into French society to France's support for the Algerian junta and Algeria's recent civil war, noting the extent to which secularism has become an "anti-religious device" and "anti-culture of the Other." Too often in France and Western countries, in general under the guise of the war against terrorism, repressive regimes in Muslim countries have been supported uncritically and Islam and Muslims have been reduced to a monolithic "other" and threat.

Part of the challenge to Islam and Muslims in the 21st century is their major presence in Europe and America resulting from the globalization of Islam. There are more Muslims living in Muslim minority communities than at any time in past history and many, if not most, will remain permanent communities. In fact, by the year 2050, Muslims are expected to outnumber non-Muslims. Where the growth in Muslim communities in Europe and the United States has been accompanied by the increased visibility of Islam in public space and the political mobilization of Muslims.

In Chapter 8, "The Growing Islamization of Europe," Oussama Cherribi has identified three main developments for Muslims in Europe: the institutionalization of the establishment of Islam, as seen in the proliferation of mosques, schools, and Islamic centers; the emergence of religious leaders as the voice of the community (as opposed to the leftists of the past); and the re-Islamization of Muslims as seen through the resurgence of religious identity among Muslims, regardless of their country of origin. He notes the challenges facing Muslims as they struggle to decide whether to assimilate, integrate, or remain apart from mainstream European society at the same time that they are changing the face of Europe. Muslims daily confront issues ranging from discrimination and prejudice at both the official and personal levels to more private concerns, such as the desire to maintain a *halal* diet and avoid pork products. At the same time, they are concerned by their socio-economic status as largely an "underclass" in European societies, representing the lowest incomes and largest families statistically.

Cherribi further notes an increase in feelings of marginalization, rejection, and discrimination since the September 11, 2001 attacks in the United States, as Muslims have been singled out for physical and verbal harassment and abuse. Almost daily reports of connections of Muslims in Europe to the al-Qaida network have led to a resurgence of concerns about "the Islamic threat" from within. The result has been that Muslims, although previously trusted and accepted in their various communities, have once again become outsiders who are "increasingly isolated and stigmatized, as opposed to integrated and respected." One of the major challenges ahead for European Muslims will be the recovery of the recognition and respect they had previously achieved.

Dilwar Hussain expands on the discussion of the Muslim presence in Europe by examining their representation in and relationship to the state in Chapter 9, "The Holy Grail of Muslims in Western Europe: Representation and Relationship with the State." Generally speaking, Muslims in Europe have the right to observe their major practices, seek knowledge of their faith, found organizations, form representative bodies, and appeal to the law. However, there are several different models for the relationship between Islam and the state, including recognition, indifference, tolerance, and hostile separation. European countries remain guided by their historical experiences with Islam, including the colonial eras, the period of Ottoman expansion, and the Crusades. The resultant stereotypes have perpetuated negative images of Islam and Muslims which have led European countries to continue to view Islam as "a threat and a problem."

Hussain notes that one major change in Muslim migrants since the 1960s has been that many of the Muslim migrants of today are political refugees, rather than work-related migrants. He identifies three main ways of dealing with these new migrants: the Guestworker model, which assumes that migrant presence is temporary (prominent in Germany, Austria and Switzerland); the assimilation model, which encourages individual integration into the national culture and discourages the formation of migrant communities (France); and the ethnic minorities model, which allows for the institutionalization of some degree of pluralism and the preservation of cultural identity (the United Kingdom and Scandinavian countries). While all of these models have their shortcomings, Hussain points to the ethnic minorities model as being the most successful in terms of institutionalizing religious pluralism and multiculturalism.

Muslim communities have also grown sufficiently strong in presence to pursue different goals. Initially, the major issues of concern were to build mosques, appropriate spaces for prayer, provide educational facilities for their children, and seek *halal* food. These goals were local in orientation, although they also served over time to build bridges between communities. Muslim communities today are seeking a more prominent voice, up through and including at the national level. This has necessitated the development of broader institutions and organizations capable of working with mainstream European institutions. Various umbrella organizations have consequently been established in different countries to coordinate the goals of local organizations and seek official recognition of Islam as a religion, thereby making Muslims eligible for the kinds of state subsidies and protection available to other religions, and make the Muslim voice heard at the national level. The major question that remains to be addressed is "What do Muslims want in Europe and from Europe?" now that they have achieved recognition and participation within the state.

Another major issue facing Muslims in Europe is the divide between the older generation of migrants from the original home country and the younger generation born and raised in Europe. More than the older generation, the younger generation is struggling with the question of whether to adapt or adopt itself to the realities of new homelands. For many the challenge is to distinguish between faith and cultural traditions. This often pits Muslim youth against their elders. The older generation, born and raised in Muslim countries, in its desire to preserve its Islamic faith in new environments and concerned about passing on its faith to its children, too easily identifies cultural practices dealing with piety, dress, and social mores with Islamic faith rather than with their homeland traditions. In Chapter 10, "Muslim Minorities in Europe: The Silent Revolution," Jocelyne Cesari analyzes the situation in France where Muslim youth seek to distinguish between the faith of their fathers and mothers and cultural trappings and superstitions as they try to construct an Islam that is cohesive with French society. They are engaged in a process of negotiating their identity, attempting to bridge the gap between ethnic identity and multiculturalism. Belonging to a religious tradition whose ideal is that Muslims live in Muslim societies and coming from backgrounds in which they were a majority, they attempt to redefine their identity as a minority in a non-Muslim majority context so that it can be inclusive of their past and present realities and lives.

Muslims in France, like Muslims throughout Europe and North America, are engaged in discussions and debates about new relationships between religion and politics, and religion and society within the more secular contexts of the West. As Cesari notes, "Muslims" or "Muslim youths" who struggle against total assimilation by negotiating and reconstructing their identities multiculturally also affect their host countries. France and indeed other Western countries will continue to be challenged not only by their new citizens' desire to live in a multicultural, not a unicultural, society, but also by the need to broaden their understanding of the sources and foundations of their society and culture, their notions of religious pluralism and civil society.

At the beginning of the 21st century, Islam remains a dynamic and expansive presence and force globally. Many regard Islam, the second largest of the world's religions, as also the fastest growing in geographic areas as diverse as Africa and Europe and America. Many in Muslim countries who believe that Islam is a comprehensive way of life will continue to press for a re-Islamization of their societies. Others who live in the West will seek to define their Islamic identities in non-Muslim societies and to shatter the negative images and stereotypes that have proliferated since September 11, 2001. For all, the challenge will be to articulate processes of re-Islamization that effectively respond to the challenges of contemporary life, that demonstrate the extent to which Islam is compatible with modern life and society, and that project a pluralistic vision that is not seen as a threat to other sectors of their societies.

Part I

ISSUES AND TRENDS IN GLOBAL RE-ISLAMIZATION

1

VEILS AND OBSCURING LENSES

François Burgat

"Our policy makers ought to restrain from using the word 'Islam' or 'fundamentalism' to label or to evaluate political dynamics in the Middle East." (Paris, June 1997, an analyst for the French Ministry of Foreign Affairs)

Does the use of cultural and religious terms such as "Islam," "Islamism," and more so that of "secularism," their supposed antidote, describe most accurately the dynamics of our Muslim political surroundings or do they carry a subjective and emotional dimension having above all an obscuring effect?

Islamist political opposition movements stem from historical factors common to the whole Arab world and also from a certain degree of specificity linked to their own national histories. Firstly, all these movements are part of a process of an essentially reactive and identity-led nature through which, in the societies of the West's former colonial periphery, the categories and vocabulary of Muslim culture—that for a while were marginalized to the benefit of their Western counterparts—are making a comeback in the perception pattern in general and in political discourse in particular. Secondly, this ideological phenomenon is linked to internal oppositional struggles or to regional conflicts in ways which vary significantly from one country to another.

Nowhere is it possible to explain the rise in visibility of the Islamists by referring only to a terminology describing social or political pathologies. The Islamist impulse is most probably a reactive, but not necessarily or not exclusively a pathological episode in the contemporary history of the Arab world. It represents the rearticulation of the discourse of secular Arabism with that of Muslim religion and culture to express all kinds of aspirations, either internal, regional, international, social or political, revolutionary or legalist, nationalist or linked to identity, of a large portion of the actors of this region of the world. For a number of reasons linked to its history, today the West—the French more than the Anglo-Saxons—tends to consider any discourse using the Islamic idiom as incompatible, because it is "religious," with the culture of its modernity. This being so, the West fails more and more to realize the commonality, but also the seriousness, legitimacy, and often the urgency of all or part of the claims carried by the Islamist political generation.

ISLAM AND REASON

On the northern shore of the Mediterranean, the perception of the nature (and role) of the Islamic factor in political dynamics, and consequently of its impact on internal and/or diplomatic behavior is shaped by two broad categories of causes. The first, more structural, results from the long-term historical process of European identity building in which, as we know, Islam has always played the central role of "partner-foil." The second stems more conjuncturally from the negative image that the Islamist trends have inherited, first in Iran and then during the 1990s, more particularly in Egypt, Algeria, and in Palestine. The rational assessment of the "Islamist factor" by France—as a Mediterranean political actor and a nation including a considerable number of Muslims—requires taking into account a number of distorting effects that prompt the observers more than the actors to separate Islam and Reason.

In 1997, after much polemical debate, the international experts on the Islamist phenomenon finally agreed on many crucial issues. The quantitative relevance of Islamist trends and their centrality within the ideological spectrum of Arab opposition movements are hardly questioned anymore.[1] The time—not so far away—is gone when the social basis of "political Islam" was reduced by external observers to the few extremist groups of its radical fringe. The capacity of militant cells to rally the support of a broad moderate electorate has been shown. The experts also tend to acknowledge almost unanimously the fact that if really open and free elections were held today, it is most probably the Islamists (taken as a whole) who would win them.

But the second and probably the most important point of agreement is that, given its relative, plural, and reactive character, Islamism is now perceived as a differentiated and variegated phenomenon subject to powerful internal dynamics, and this to a degree that may seriously put into question the relevance of the concept itself.[2] In *The Islamic Movement*

---

[1] Basma Kodmany Darwish and May Chartouni DuBarry, *Les Etats arabes face à la contestation islamique* (IFRI, Paris: Armand Colin, 1997). "Within 20 years, religious-based political protest, that is Islamism, became the sole idiom of social protest and of opposition to the incumbent regimes in most of the Muslim Arab world[.]"

[2] Ibid. "We must pay attention to the diversity and heterogeneity of national settings regarding the relationship between the state and Islamists. This is only possible by acknowledging on the one hand the variegated nature of the Islamic idiom and its use by

in North Africa,[3] I came to the conclusion that one uniform conceptualiza-
tion of Islamism was unable to reflect the great diversity of situations and
contexts. I also argued against undertaking too accurate a social territoriali-
zation of the phenomenon, and against linking in too strict a fashion the
vocabulary of political opponents in the Arab world to their economic and
social status. For a long time now, it has been possible to see that the
Islamists indeed use a wide variety of strategies and action patterns, ranging
from fascist-type populism to the most legalist of parliamentarisms and that
they are active in all the socio-professional strata of the societies under
study. Today, no serious observer can any longer hold that they form a politically, ideologically, and socially homogeneous whole:

Today, the Islamist label covers greatly varying projects, ranging from the most
obvious of legalisms to the overthrow of incumbent regimes, where some use the
mosque and others assassinate, where some advocate the moral regeneration of the
Muslim while others advocate the establishment of the Islamic City.[4]

To reflect actual reality, any talk of "the strategy of Islamist actors" must
be preceded by a patient and quasi-exhaustive survey of the oppositional
and social dynamics prevailing in a very wide region of the world; and this
because in Western collective images, as reflected in the realm of politics
as well as in that of the media, the concept of the "Islamist threat" is still
used in an artificially and perniciously homogeneous fashion. The
Western political elite and public opinion still cheer the victories that,
through a subtle mixture of counter-ideological measures here, constitutional takeovers there, and police terror and manipulation of the media
everywhere, the secular elites in power in the Arab world have achieved
over an everlasting "fundamentalist threat." In this way, Europe is playing
a role in blocking the processes of political liberalization and elite change
in its close political surroundings. Whether with regard to General
Mubarak, General Zeroual, Colonel Qadhafi, or General Ben-Ali, the
"successes" of military regimes over the "Islamist threat" come down
more and more clearly to the clampdown on any type of democratic
opening or even to the rejection of any institutionalised regulation of the
political sphere.

Asked by the cultural commission of the European Parliament[5] to
answer in too little time questions too various in nature on "Europe and

---

many actors seeking legitimacy or power, and on the other hand the discrepancy between
the words and deeds of the actors in the religious realm."

[3] François Burgat and William Dowell, *The Islamic Movement in North Africa*, 2nd edn.
(Austin, TX: Center for Middle Eastern Studies, University of Texas at Austin, 1997).

[4] Darwish and DuBarry, *Les Etats arabes*.

[5] "L'Islam et l'Europe," Hearing before the Cultural Commission of the European Parliament, Brussels, January 1997.

Islam," I chose to present my answer(s) in the form of two short essays that could also serve as guiding posts here:

1.   "Islam is only what the majority of today's Muslims want to make out of it."

The aim here is to restate in a strong fashion that no essentialism can account in a scientific way for the role of the Islamic factor in the evolution of the societies or individuals who claim a link to Islam. Against the joint claims of (or at least part of) the actors as well as the observers, "Islam" is in no way an intangible or timeless barrier or dogmatic rampart, impervious to sociological inquiry, that would block the course of the social and political history of the societies which claim a link to it, or of the communities with whom we share a destiny at the national level. Like all dogmas, whether secular or religious, Islam becomes a worldly reality only through its social expression. This social expression itself can only become a reality through a strictly human intervention. This human intervention, while respecting the symbolic relation to the founding texts, may well bring changes and adaptations to them.

2.   "The Muslims of tomorrow's France will be those we will have taken part in shaping."

The action patterns of all opposition movements, whether in the Arab region or in the rest of the world, are shaped mostly by the behavior towards them of those wielding power. This reactive aspect is certainly valid concerning the behavior of the international community towards the Islamists. In an environment where the balance of power at the economic, political, and military level is largely in favor of the northern shore of the Mediterranean, the European political elites make decisions that have a direct impact on the status of the political actors in the south.

In this sense, Europe partakes in shaping the behavior of whole blocks of its "Islamist" political surroundings. The assistance it provides to regimes lacking popular support directly contributes to the emergence of this Islamist "threat" from which, with the legitimate concern for defending both its "principles" and its "interests," it thinks it is thereby protecting itself.

   This study seeks to emphasize the need for France, every time its foreign diplomatic activity is involved in the internal oppositional dynamics of the Southern Mediterranean countries, to make decisions only on the least ideological bases possible. If only in order to seem credible when condemning the—very real—excesses of some of the Islamists, France must remain able to assess in the same detached and critical manner the endeavors of their (more political than ideological) opponents who hold power. In order to have an ideology-free analysis, criteria must be set regarding the description of the actors involved in oppositional struggles and regional conflicts, and these criteria must then be applied universally.

What is at stake today is our ability to maintain, between the rising generations on both shores of the Mediterranean, a common language that will not tomorrow be reduced to that of confrontation.

THE ISLAMIC REFERENCE BETWEEN POPULAR PERCEPTIONS AND STATE STRATEGIES

Islam and national identity

The presence of the Islamic reference at the center of the French identity system creates an obstacle for the rational management of relations with the "Other."

Islam, or the religious culture of a too close "Other". From a French perspective, Islam is first and foremost the identity marker of the "Other's" culture and thus simply of the Other. Reflecting on Islam, and all the more so on Islamism, its militant outgrowth, is *par excellence* talking about the Other. But as we know, talking about the Other is in many ways talking about ourselves. It is indeed the Other who tells us who we are, what space we take up in the world, and for many what role we play in it. Identity is only the result of the encounter with otherness. It is the second one to reach the top of the mountain or the shores of the desert island who determines the main part of the first occupant's ego, whether male or female, black or white, intellectual or manual laborer, fat or skinny. It is on the Other that our "relativity" depends and we will thus identify ourselves with or against him.

In the case of the relation to Islam, the propensity of the Other to affect the always fine internal balance of our individual or collective (notably national) ego is high since it is not just "any Other." He does not come from Planet Mars. He does not live in a setting devoid of cross-perceptions. On the contrary, he is mostly (at the level of perceptions, but for once also at that of statistics) from a doubly near North Africa, with regard to the narrowness of the Straits of Gibraltar and to a largely common (for lack of having been really "shared") history. To this long face-to-face encounter strewn with Andalusians and Crusaders, colonists and fellaghas, repatriates and immigrants:

bear witness not only to the events and their wounds, not always healed, or the names of fruits and vegetables, of sciences or stars, the artistic, literary, technical, and conceptual transfers, but also the fantasies, the phobias or attractions that only too often still make attempts at cultural encounter difficult.[6]

---

[6] Jean Michot, *Musulman en Europe. Réflexions sur les chemin de Dieu, 1990–1998* (Paris: Editions Jeunesse sans Frontières, 2001).

It is a telling fact that the relation to the Other's culture in its Chinese or Indian version, which somehow is just as necessary to set the frontiers of the realm of identity, is not as traumatizing as is the case with the Muslim Arab neighbor. At Morvan, the green heart of the French countryside, on the road that leads him to the Imam Training Center (of Château Chinon) whose creation has fed so many fantasies in the media, the astonished visitor discovers a Buddhist temple with a frontage inlaid with gold and scarlet that underlines the architecture's thundering exoticism. Contrary to the smallest mosque of our suburbs, this temple of another "religion of the Other" has not worried the watchful guardians of our national "identity." The Muslim Other does not come from Vietnam either, a country that went through the colonial storm, just like Algeria, but whose distance escapes memory and dissolves apprehension. In time as well as in space, the Muslim is thus doubly (too) near. He is also so with regard to the religious realm, since for a good part we claim the same Holy Scriptures. Our old and too near neighbor is thus logically the actor who is most involved in the construction of our collective identity, either at the linguistic (his references are not Latin), ethnic (he does not want Gauls for ancestors), or, of course, religious level (his Prophet is little known to us and he rejects above all the secular character of our modernity). It is in relation to the Saracen or to the Moor that part of our ethnic and political identity was built, in relation to the Muhammadan that (without forgetting our own wars of religion) we wanted to remain Christians first, then lay people.

To increase this proximity of the references comes the trauma of the spatial "re-territorialization" of the encounter between neighbors. The perception of Islam is surely still partly shaped on the Other's territory, through—as we will discuss further on—the information that crosses the sea so quickly but so awkwardly. But its shaping takes place more and more often in the intimate realm of our public spaces, within our own society. We no longer build our cathedrals on Africa's hills: we discover with astonishment mosques in our own suburbs. We are no longer "welcomed" by the Other but, as an expected result firstly of the legacy of colonialism, then as the deliberate product of our industrial strategies, it is the Other who today lives among us. The dear distance is further abolished. Finally, let us mention the sociological specificity—inherited from the post-colonial relation—of the human factor of Islam: even if today it is changing rapidly, it is made up of more manual workers than figures of the technical or artistic intelligentsia.

Islam in a doubly disenchanted country. Islam is the culture of our closest neighbor at a time when the great imbalance stemming from the colonial relationship is fading, even if only very slowly, to the benefit of the southern shore and thus, subjectively, at the expense of the northern shore.

In 1930, the year of the colonial zenith, Islam, despite the fact that it was already the culture of the "Other-close neighbor" who was already settled in France, did not disturb then as much as it does now in our suburbs of the 21st century. At the time, France's national identity sat well with the folklorized Islam of the great colonial exhibition marking the "100 years of the conquest of Algeria." Has Muhammad changed his message since? Certainly not. But the sociological setting of the Other's religion has irresistibly freed itself from the constraining colonial framework. The "blessed era" of a totally one-way relation is over. At the beginning of the 21st century, and as unequal as it may have remained, the relation between the two shores leaves the North with the vague (and not totally unfounded) feeling that the time of its political hegemony has ended.

France's disenchantment is not only the result of the reassuring colonial paradigm. With regard to development, the triumph of economic rationality has surely shown its quantitative potential. But with it also came its contradictions and qualitative limits: a high ecological price, a weakening of the social bond, a loss of ethical references. Hidden for a time by technological progress, the crisis with regard to values is worsening as growth is slowing down and unemployment is on the rise.

Even though the fact that (most of) the followers of the "new" religion (i.e. Islam) are ethnically of foreign origin contributes to an increase in the tension stemming from the assertion of Islam,[7] this is to a great extent a tension which would be prompted by any religious assertion whichever it may be, since Western societies are in fact, strictly speaking, not so much "secular" as "de-Christianized." Islam must not only overcome its status as a "religion of the Other," but also overcome the reserves that are prompted by its status as a religion. Behind the banner of secularism, it is indeed more the decline of the religious realm than its separation from the public one that left its mark on the century of Jules Ferry's successors. The "Islamic tension" then is less a reflection of the competition between two (divine) revelations than that of the stir created by the stating of a demand for spirituality in a society that thought it had moved beyond any need for public intervention regarding the sacred realm.

Islam, Christendom, Judaism: three fundamentalisms? The analogical construction of "three fundamentalisms" is feeding the "over-ideologization" of the reading of political tensions in the Mediterranean.

The distorting lens of the three fundamentalisms. To make sense out of the political upheavals in the Muslim world, comparing (between "re-Islamization," "re-Judaization," and "re-Christianization") may prove

---

[7] Let us note here that for now the native French who converted to Islam only play a very marginal role in its representation.

enlightening. But the strictly analogical perspective on the "three fundamentalisms" to which it all too often leads works as a distorting lens that is as pernicious as it is reassuring. In particular, it serves to obscure the most powerful actors' main share of responsibility and their refusal to take into account claims and resistances that are actually less religious or ideo-logical than simply political.

"Tel Aviv-Algiers: a common struggle against the fanatics of God," was the title of an article published in a French magazine on the day fol-lowing the assassination of Prime Minister Itzhak Rabin by a young "fun-damentalist." What do we really "explain" when we compare a privileged student from a rich and democratic country who is hostile to any territorial compromise with the radicalized fringe of a powerful popular movement opposing an "undebunkable" dictatorship?

What speaking out in an undifferentiated way against "fundamentalisms" often does is, in fact, to conceal the refusal to take into account more complex situations and claims far more legitimate than their reading through a religious lens may suggest. Used for the three monotheistic reli-gions, this illusory comparison obscures the major impact of the conflictual imbalance between the "Judeo-Christian" North and the "Muslim" South and the various domination effects that come with it. It also hides the struc-tural differences between the political settings of the "Muslim," "Chris-tian," and "Jewish" protagonists. It thereby masks the whole secular aspect of an Islamist mobilization that is too quickly locked up in its sole religious dimension while it actually serves to carry more widely cultural, but also political (nationalist or even "democratic") claims. By over-ideologizing the reading of socio-political upheavals in the Muslim world, the comparison perpetuates the age-old essentialist and theologico-centrist bias of the Orientalist perspective.

Thus, the rise of the "fundamentalist danger" remains the only factor used to explain the Algerian civil war, at the expense of any other secular explanation of the origin of violence and of the means to put an end to it. The competition between the two fundamentalisms, both the Jewish and the Muslim one, is still put forth to "explain" the failures of the Israeli-Palestinian peace process, at the expense of the essential political factor that is the continuation of the military occupation of one side by the other. The near similarity in the means of action between these two extremes thus allows an avoidance of the question of their respective causes. In Algiers, it allows at best the placing of instigators and victims of a military coup, and of the large-scale repression and manipulation of information that followed, in the same category, and at worst to purely and simply invert the blame.

The Islamist generation, whose scope of activities is much wider than violence, plays a role within the internal (Arab) and regional (Arab-Israeli conflict) order that is not only larger, but also very different from that of the "re-Christianization" or "re-Judaization" movements. It does so in national and regional settings that are very different from those of the actors of the North—differences which are denied by the "three fundamentalisms" theory. The common factor among the political contexts where Islamists are found is the absence of any possibility for a change of political elite by institutional means, or even only for serious parliamentary participation. Also, the Islamists are part of a geopolitical block that, within the "new order" at a regional and world level, is on the losing side; on the other hand, "born-again Christians" and Jewish Orthodox "men in black" are active within democratic and liberal political systems, and at a regional and world level are on the "winning side."

After closer examination, it is not surprising to observe that today, most of the Mediterranean state leaders are brandishing the "fundamentalist threat." The outlawing of those who—in every Arab country as well as in the regional or world political order—are often on the front line of protest movements serves as a means to reduce to the emotional and irrational realm all oppositions and resistances, as legitimate as they may be, to those wielding power in the national, regional, and international political order. If you are the Arab leader of a military junta that has mastered the art of manipulation through terror, you may present yourself as a "bulwark against fundamentalism." You will thereby immediately gain the unbounded trust of international financial institutions, and you will be able to fill your jails and your ballot boxes and to put down effectively any alternative to your own autocratic rule, even if it is made up of a very wide front including secular forces, in the way of the Algerian signatories to the Treaty of Rome. If you are an Israeli and can make your opponent appear as a "fundamentalist," you will be able to de-legitimize the large number of Palestinians disappointed with the Oslo Agreement[8] and to further strengthen your arrogant military and media supremacy. Finally, if you are a Western (i.e. French) "republican" leader or thinking of becoming one, you know that, as the present and future National Front supporters are there to periodically remind you, using the "fundamentalist threat" can turn your fellow citizens' distress in the face of general powerlessness regarding the economic crisis into valuable electoral gains. Here we are definitely far from a universal "return to God."

Harmful state cooperation.   While in Western public opinion the first reason for the emotional detraction of the role of the Islamic factor stems from fears intensified by a long and conflictual history, during the 1990s other more conjunctural factors emerged on both shores of the Mediterranean. In the early 1990s, almost everywhere the Islamists became those at the forefront of the main political struggles. Indeed, in the wars of

---

[8]   Which leads to granting international legitimacy to the military occupation by Israel of more than 90 percent of the Palestinian territories occupied since 1967.

succession linked to the natural weakening of the post-Independence regimes and also in the resistance to the "new regional order" that, in the Arab-Israeli conflict, the American-Israeli coalition was able to impose (owing to the disappearance of the Soviet counterweight), Islamists today rank first regarding protest. Conjuncturally, the difficulty of rationally assessing the role of the Islamic factor in politics thus stems partly from the joint media and political battle that the southern as well as the northern state leaders (the Arab regimes as well as the Israeli leadership and its Western supporters) are waging against this new generation of protesters.

The signing of the Oslo agreement, a reflection of the willingness of the historical representatives of the Palestinian resistance and, after them, of a majority of Arab states to drop armed violence in favor of diplomatic efforts resulted in leaving an important part of nationalist assets on the shelves. Even if they were not the only ones, the Islamists thus found themselves able to take up the heritage of the first generation of the Palestine Liberation Organization's "secular" nationalists. In Palestine as well as in Lebanon (but also in the rest of the Near East, particularly in Jordan or in Egypt), with the support of secular—indeed Christian—parts of the population,[9] they became the spearhead of the criticism against the flagrant contradictions of the Oslo peace agreement even more than of a rejection of normalization with Israel. The Islamic Resistance Movement (Hamas) has partly succeeded the PLO, and in Lebanon it is the Hizbollah that has lifted the torch of armed struggle against the occupation of the southern part of the country.

Furthermore, on every national political scene, and even despite a reduced visibility due to repression, the Islamists have reached first rank as opposition forces everywhere. This accession to the double frontline of political order protests at both the internal (demands for participation) and regional level (Arab-Israeli conflict), or of this "new international order" has led to a conjunctural meeting of interests between the northern and southern state leaders in discrediting their common opponents.

On March 13, 1996, a series of bomb attacks were carried out in Israel by two factions of the Palestinian Islamist trend.[10] Within the context of guerilla war and waves of repression shaking Egypt as well as Algeria or Saudi Arabia, the Sharm al-Shaykh summit meeting held the day after in a sense made explicit and reinforced the bipolarization which designates and consecrates the Islamists in the role of contestants simultaneously against the internal Arab political order and against the international order—an order fixed in the cement of Israeli-American policy. Even if

---

[9] The DFLP and PFLP leaders opposed to the Oslo agreement are Christian. The Coptic Pope Chenouda III supported the Hamas suicide attacks as "acts of self defense," only regretting the fact that not "all Arabs" participated in them. (See his statements reprinted in *Al-Quds* or *Al-Hayat*, London, Apr. 1997.)

[10] Hamas and Jihad.

the process was attenuated somewhat after the hardening of the Israeli stance following the election of Benyamin Netanyahu (with the Arab state actors marking their distance to the evident contradictions of this process), the holy communion at Sharm al-Shaykh, uniting the representatives of the Arab, Israeli, and Western political establishments in a common denunciation of the entire Islamist generation, signified the institutionalization of the "anti-Islamist" security and media cooperation of the states from both sides. In a very significant way, the most media-covered Algerian proponent of "eradication" had come to Israel a few days earlier, sending out a "call to the free world" to "fight" the sole enemy of the day— terrorism, a term referring at once to all forms of armed resistance to the repressive campaign launched in Algeria in January 1992 against the party that won the 1990 and 1991 elections; and those from the Palestinian resistance movement who used violence to counter the Israeli occupier's use of violence against the population of the (more than ever) occupied territories. The Sharm al-Shaykh meeting somehow crystallized the view which, in a very reductionist manner, tends to put all the blame for political tensions on the "Islamic" idiom opposing the Arab state leaderships on the one hand, and the Israeli-American international order on the other hand.

As could be expected from this apparent coalition of state actors from all sides, at least one tendency within the Islamist trend (in Algeria, in Egypt, but also in Libya and in Saudi Arabia) is adopting both a strategy of a total breakaway from the internal and international institutional frameworks, and ways and means for action whose extremist nature in turn feeds the endless cycle of mutual violence.

The Arab political formula of the 1990s. From Cairo to Algiers, including Tunis, in addition to Israeli political intransigence, it is a spreading identical "Arab institutional model" that should be held responsible for a large part of the so-called Islamic violence. In this model, from which the Algerian military had unwisely strayed in the early 1990s and with which they are now falling into line through elections and referendums, the real political forces have no access whatsoever to legal political competition. Thus, the elections are not meant to designate the rulers but only the quality and the number of the opponents that these rulers intend to tolerate for the sake of a purely make-believe democratization process ("for the Yankees to see"[11]). This hollow pluralism complacently sanctioned by the West is used to hide the locking-up of the institutional system and the standardization of a very high level of repression. This pernicious mixture feeds a double radicalization, at once ideological and political, of the opposition, and inevitably a certain level of armed violence or counter-violence towards the regime and its local or foreign supporters. This so-called "terrorist" violence allows the regime to amalgamate the actions of that

---

[11]   Nazih Ayubi, *Overstating the Arab State* (London: I. B. Tauris, 1995).

fringe of its opponents that it itself contributed in radicalizing with the entire legalist opposition, thus justifying in the eyes of its Western partners the perpetual postponing of any democratic opening.

The essential cooperation between the partners of tomorrow's political Mediterranean will have to overcome the obstacle of the "over-ideologization" of national and regional political tensions. Behind the rise of "fundamentalisms" and other forms of "terrorism," the northern shore will gradually have to come to see social and democratic claims more simply here, nationalist ones elsewhere (e.g. in Palestine), and whatever the idiom used by the authors of these claims or whatever the weight of the stakes involved may be, to consider addressing these claims as one of the pre-requisites for any future cooperation.

Islamism, Sufism, Ulema: the obscuring lens of the "three Islams"

The socio-educational profile of the leader of Tanzim al-Jihad, the most revolutionary Islamist group, shows better than long speeches the danger of the everlasting "economic" reading of the Islamist phenomenon. A surgeon by training and married to a philosopher, Ayman al-Zawahiri is the son of a faculty dean and of a university professor. But recalling the family ancestry of the leader of the organization that assassinated Anwar Sadat (with the support of Omar Abdurrahman, an *'alim* from al-Azhar), and who became famous as the closer companion of Osama bin Laden, further underlines the limits of the use in politics of an otherwise often useful distinction between the "Islams," whether Sufi, Islamist, or that of the Ulema. Through his father, the Islamist Ayman al-Zawahiri is the grandson of a Shaykh al-Azhar (Rab'i al-Zawahiri) and through his mother (daughter of Abdelwahab Azzam), of a rector of Cairo University, an ambassador, but especially a shaykh of a Sufi brotherhood!

Moving boundaries. In Egypt or anywhere else, the category of "Islamist" creates the everlasting problem of definition with regard to describing the relations between society, politics, and religion. In the Western outlook, and not only through the media, it remains only negatively connoted, which is far from being the case in Arab societies. Furthermore, it tends to strengthen the idea that Islamists are the only ones using—in a static and "a-historical" way—religion for political purposes, and this would distinguish them from all other forms of belief. According to the set framework in which they are defined, Islamists are indeed those who, because development policies have forgotten them, use Islam to oppose the prevailing political order. They supposedly do so on the basis of an interpretation of the religious message that is wrong, and thus antithetical to the social modernization and the political liberalization process that "modernizing" regimes and/or "secular" intellectuals, sometimes with the support of the guardians of Islamic orthodoxy would be desperately advocating.

In the Arab world, the ruling groups are more simply trying to establish the existence of an "apolitical" Islam—that is, "non-oppositional." This is one that would justify their support and that of the international community to better distinguish it from a political Islam, one necessarily reactionary, intolerant, indeed terrorist, and, in any case, anti-modern that the forces working for good all over the world would naturally be called on to fight. The media representation of the Egyptian religious scene has thus for a long time shown an "institutional" Islam (al-Azhar University, the Mufti of the Republic, but also renowned official "TV preachers") in the role of non-oppositional, if not apolitical guardian of an Islamic orthodoxy that is tolerant and modernist, alongside Sufi brotherhoods that are themselves as much apolitical as ideologically hostile to the ideas of the "political" and "reactionary" Islam of the Islamists.

A closer look at the various, changing, and often unexpected links by which the different Islams actually partake of oppositional dynamics, but also of the social or political modernization process, shows a more complex situation. The line separating al-Azhar, the brotherhoods, and the Islamist generation, long considered as the basic division for any theoretical work on the relationship between religion and politics, tends to fade away.

Depicting the Islamists as the sole users of religion for political purposes implies indeed ignoring the fact that monarchic or "secular and republican" regimes are doing just the same, and in a not necessarily less traditionalist or conservative manner than that of their Islamist challengers. This reductionist view also leads to minimizing or ignoring the fact that the institutions (such as brotherhoods or al-Azhar) also have tense relations with the regime or are involved in their own process of ideological or political radicalization. These institutions' relations with the Islamist trend are complex and cannot be construed as being based on mutual exclusion. At times a conflictual setting, but also a recruiting ground (for the brotherhoods), an ideological sounding board, and a referential source (al-Azhar), after examination these institutions appear more as means for the legitimation and rooting of "oppositional Islam" than as tools for a certain ideological counter-attack, as the media, and sometimes in the past academia, have tended to picture them. That was when the "Islamist tree claiming the shari'a" was accused of "hiding the forest" of good and tolerant Sufism or that of the orthodoxy of a reassuring age-old civilizational Islam.

However, we have known for a long time now that the apolitical nature of Sufi brotherhoods is very relative,[12] and that their always circumstantial support to incumbent regimes is based more on clientelist and tactical reasons than on ethical or ideological ones. In Egypt, as just about

---

[12] For a contrasted reading of the political role of brotherhoods in Egypt, see Rachida Chih, "Soufis et confréries mystiques dans l'Egypte contemporaine" (Ph.D. thesis in History, Aix-en-Provence, France, 1996), and Pierre-Jean Luizard, "Le rôle des confréries soufies dans le système politique égyptien," *Maghreb-Machreq*, 131, Jan.–Mar. 1991, p. 26.

everywhere else in the Arab world, brotherhoods remain one of the favorite recruiting grounds of the Islamist generation, with whom they have (in Sudan in particular) very differentiated political relations. In countries where Islamists are repressed, many members of security forces (police and justice) are said to join a brotherhood solely as a mean to bypass the interdiction of having another type of religious commitment. The so-called tolerance of Sufi brotherhoods must be qualified in light of the fact that most of their members call for the application of the Shariah (etc.), just as any of their Islamist (or Azharite) neighbors do. The same caution should be applied towards the supposed "moderation" of the Ulema, since the regime repeatedly makes concessions to the most conservative of them in order to buy their political allegiance. Thus, the "liberal" Tantawi, former mufti of the Republic and successor of Gad al-Haq Ali Gad al-Haq at the head of al-Azhar, otherwise so quick to support the economic policy of the regime when the latter is in need of a bold *fatwa* on financial or banking matters, had an extremely "classic" attitude when the condemnation of a scholar (Nasr Hamid Abu Zayd) to be separated from his (Muslim) wife was confirmed by an appeals court. It was confirmed on the pretext that his allegedly materialistic interpretation of the status of the Quranic revelation made him an apostate. This apolitical nature of the Azharite institution seems illusory, considering the life path of many of its graduates or (at a more structural level) its reluctant stance towards the instructions or the leaders that the regime has forced upon it since its "harnessing."[13] The "guardian of orthodox Islam" has repeatedly supported the suicide attacks of the Palestinian Hamas and, at an altogether different level, has strongly condemned the works of the French Orientalist Jacques Berque and his translation of the Quran. While the widely media-covered Nasr Hamid Abu Zayd case strengthens the idea of the "secular intellectual" being prevented by "the Islamists" from implementing his project for the modernization of thought, that of Hasan Hanafi, much less covered by the French media, puts these categories into question. Those who prevent the secularization of Muslim thought are no longer the Islamists but the "official guardians" of "the great al-Azhar University"; and Hasan Hanafi, the impertinent "modernizer," duly honored by the French Sorbonne, who in the early 1980s founded an "Islamic Leftist" trend (and journal), is also one of the leading figures of the contemporary Islamist movement.

The affront of Islamist ballot boxes. The mainstream perspective on the Islamic scene is often biased with regard to the relation of Islamism to

---

[13] On the links or convergences between Al-Azhar and the Islamist mobilization, see Malika Zghal, *Gardiens de l'Islam: les Oulemas d'Al-Azhar dans l'Egypte contemporaine* (Paris: Presses de Sciences Po, 1996), p. 328 ff; on the "harnessing" of al-Azhar, see also Pierre-Jean Luizard, "Al-Azhar, institution sunnite réformée" (paper presented at the conference on "La Réforme sociale en Egypte," CEDEJ-IFAO, Cairo, Dec. 10–13, 1993).

the process of political liberalization and social modernization. Here again, the Islamist trends, whose bases of support range from the lumpenproletariat to the high bourgeoisie and the army, including the entire spectrum of the middle classes, do play complex and changing roles in the political and social modernization process, but these roles cannot be reduced to the everlasting "rejection of modernity," as external observers have done. I have tried to show in another study[14] the ideological nature of any attempt to deny that the Islamist impulse is partaking in the complex modernization and political liberalization process currently taking place in Egypt as well as in the Arab world. Indeed, very often, under the demonized label of Islamism, simply only the most serious opponents to the incumbent regimes are to be found, opponents who are themselves very active in the emergent civil societies and who are fully involved in various processes oriented towards progress. In Egypt, one of the criteria for differentiating between these powerful challengers to the prevailing order is their stance (legalist or revolutionary) towards the institutional system.

On May 27, 1997, the Iranian presidential elections brought to power a candidate known to be hostile to the line defended by his predecessors.[15] The day after the elections, analysts quickly concluded that this expressed a failure—indeed "the end"—of the Islamic regime. It had just been rebuffed, widely disavowed by a people that had "required and obtained a thorough reorientation." And so a regime unanimously described as a monolithic and "undebunkable" dictatorship would apparently have authorized its ballot boxes to radically shift its course.

Thus, "under the Islamic veil," the slow and difficult political liberalization process in Iran has continued to make its long way. Of the Tunisian government, that not long ago topped the list of Western political references (it was described as "an exemplary case of modernization" by the French Head of State during his 1996 visit to Tunisia), or of the Algerian political leadership that "protects secularism," which of them has, for now, allowed such an affront to happen?

FRANCE'S "MUSLIM POLICY"

The issue of Islam and/or of Islamism in France, or the presence and the growing visibility of Muslims and the politicization of all or part of this component of the national community is prompting obvious concerns. For most of the French, as was mentioned earlier, over and above being a religion different from theirs, Islam is the marker of the identity of "the

---

[14] François Burgat, *L'Islamisme en face*, 2nd edn. (Paris: La Découverte, 1996), or "Islamisme et Modernité," in *L'Islamisme* (Paris: La Découverte [Les Dossiers], 1995).

[15] Fariba Adelkhah, *Iran. Vers un espace public confessionnel* (Paris: FSNP, Les Etudes du CERI, Jun. 27, 1997), and *Être moderne en Iran* (Paris: Karthala, 1998).

Other's culture," and thus of simply the "Other." The thinking about our relation to Islam in France thus revolves around a logically recurrent question in the collective images of our fellow citizens: which compromises can the Nation or the Republic, without "losing their soul," make to these ideological newcomers that are Muslims?

In France, for a very long time a good Muslim was one that was not such anymore, expect maybe for the pointy-tipped slippers that he sometimes wore at home at night, or for his hardly British way of making tea. A good Muslim was in a way one that at prayer time would never have had the strange idea of declining an invitation to drink *pastis*. It was the time of integration-disintegration, the integration by "disappearance" or "dissolution." Today, at least part of the Muslim community is trying to get the idea through that a Muslim, although he may be French, can be someone who at *pastis* time goes to pray. Does this mean the end of all forms of socialization at the national level? The whole problem is that in France, the Muslim is referred to not as a "practicing" believer as we would say of a Christian, nor even as an "Orthodox" believer as is said of a Jew, although he may really be an extremist, but as a "fundamentalist" or an "Islamist." We can certainly agree on the fact that this change in our close surroundings is somehow disturbing. Some like to see in it the limit to the Republic's "integrative" capacity that seems to be drifting towards the British "communitarian" model. We can agree with the view that it reflects the limits of this model (even if there are still a large number of "sociologically-defined" Muslims that do not perform religious rituals). We can also agree that it is a sign that it is no longer the only model found in France, and that growing numbers feel that it is time to close the chapter of "integration-disappearance" of the Muslim community. If "losing our soul" is to accept the evolution of the images of the French Republic of 1930, then maybe we will just have to lose a little bit of our soul to make possible the integration of a considerable Muslim community that will probably sometime soon include a significant number of "native French" individuals. This presence will "affect," "transform," or partake in the transformation of a number of aspects of France's institutional, legal, cultural, political, and religious landscape.

If it has not already taken place, some of the social customs and legal practices will thus inevitably have to evolve in order to meet the requirements of this new historical phase of the national community efficiently and functionally. Settling in France, after a long period in which the return to the native land had remained a future prospect for a whole generation of Muslim immigrants, also requires on the part of Muslim individuals that they keep in mind that they live in an environment where Islam is in a minority status and where the clear separation between public and private, state and religion is part and parcel of the landscape. By putting them in a situation where they have to position themselves with regard to changes that often have not yet affected their own native community or the one they refer to, the settlement in France prompts them, more than in their native land, to innovate at the legal and doctrinal level. The more the cutting of the umbilical cord to foreign states is facilitated for them, the more they will find themselves in a state of "weight-lessness" that is very conducive to such innovation and doctrinal renewal. This does not imply putting up with an ostentatious proselytism nor with fundamentalist behavior, unless they do not go beyond the low level that is reached by all the other religions in France. But then we must agree on the terms used. In other words, we must determine as accurately as possible what is and is not fundamentalist behavior.

The tendency to ostracize the Muslim community that claims a mini-mum visibility is aggravated by a kind of French tradition of meddling with the (by definition fragile) representation system of this community. To see the rise of modernist and progressive Muslim elites likely to ease the integration of the whole community is the highly legitimate aim of many officials from the Ministry of Interior. It is the means employed to reach this end which can be questioned. Through a device similar to that used to nominate "bachagas" and other "aghas" of the colonial administra-tion, the Ministry of Interior and Cults often seems to want to create from above French Muslim elites by authoritarian means that it would not use for other denominational groups. One day government intervention is for or against this or that country, another day for or against this or that national "chapel." This administrative intervention, as praiseworthy as its intentions may be, is of limited use since it tends to underestimate the number of people these institutions of "Islam in France" leave out (if only because they mostly remain assimilated with the Algerian regime) and who, in the near future, will inevitably be tempted to build their own out-side the national realm at the cost, in some cases, of other allegiances.

Restructuring the link to religion and sharing modernity

For the non-Muslims in France, accepting the increasing visibility of an Islam that refuses to totally dissolve itself in the prevailing symbolic order definitely has a cost at the symbolic level that presents a double challenge. The first, which is not necessarily the most difficult one, is to assess the actual meaning of secularism in a realistic way.[16] The tension stemming from the rise in visi-bility of Islam is a result in large part of the "non-native" aspect of its human component, but also of the reaction prompted by any religious assertion in a

[16] On the useful distinction between "combat secularism" and "broadened secularism," see Farhad Khosrokhavar: "Combat secularism ... holds that French citizenship is secular by excluding any religious reference from public space; on the other hand, broadened secularism ... states that the Republic is tolerant towards religion or any other type of specificity even in public space, under certain conditions, which are always defined according to the social context and in a spirit reflecting a willingness to compromise," in *L'Islam des jeunes* (Paris: Flammarion, 1997).

society that is quickly losing any religious sense—de-Christianized and in certain ways anti-religious more than it is, strictly speaking, secular. The reticence of the non-Muslim community is thus, as stated earlier, less the reflection of the competition between two revelations than that of the disturbance caused by the demand for spirituality in a society that thought it had moved away from the need to intervene publicly regarding the realm of the sacred. In the course of the 20th century, the idea of secularism has much too often been limited first to a kind of anti-religious device, and more recently to an anti-"culture of the Other." This type of secularism, which is very far from the original and real meaning of the term (as the State Council periodically recalls) does indeed create a problem of coexistence, not only with the Muslim believers but even with the "sociologically-defined" Muslims. And this because these Muslims understandably feel provoked when the prevailing aggressiveness of the media (and sometimes of the political circles) moves beyond the religious realm to affect the symbolic markers or codes of part of their culture which is important since remoteness (from the native land) has given it a mostly mythical dimension.

The second challenge, even more basic since the West is facing it at a global level, is being able to distinguish between the contents of the reference to values—which it is legitimate to want to defend by all means—and the symbolic system that serves to legitimate these values in the individual and collective minds. What is asked of the host community is to accept that a plurality, not of values but of symbolic means to express these values, can coexist within the national realm, and it is urgent that these values be seen on the whole as common to both Muslims and non-Muslims.

If we take the now classic example of the wearing of the veil, we can agree that republican law must forbid the wearing of a clothing apparel whose thickness and cut make it impossible for those wearing it to hear the teacher's voice, to see his/her face, to read their math book, or even to run in the schoolyard. Along similar lines, republican law should oppose any endeavor to boycott course teachings (in natural or other sciences) that would supposedly run counter to religious convictions, etc. But if the clothing apparel in question is really not a problem (that is, when it does not run against the values inherent to the existence of the school and the way it is managed), secular republican law must not interfere with the will of those who want to wear it, granted that, furthermore, it is very easy to see that they wear it voluntarily, often even against the family's will.

THE KHELKHAL SYNDROME

The "Khaled Khelkhal" story has often been taken as evidence that there are implications far more radical than wearing the veil. What is the exact meaning of this particularly widely media-covered event? In the turmoil of the Algerian civil war and in conditions not yet totally clarified (if only because the individual who gave out the orders has never been clearly identified and let alone arrested), a few dozen French Muslim youths (of whom a small number were French-born) identified with the struggle of the Algerian Islamist opposition to the extent that they took up subversive activities on its behalf with regard to the country in which they lived. Let us first put things in perspective: the events involved a very tiny fringe of the Muslim community. But let us not underestimate them and recognize that they made explicit an uneasiness that is felt today, although in less extreme forms, by part of the Muslim community.[17] This uneasiness has also been felt by a small number of non-Muslims partaking in the Algerian crisis, either when watching news reports or most of the popular news programs. It stems from the dichotomy between the perception of a conflict in which an actor feels involved (as an actor in the proper sense of the word for some, and as simply a privileged observer for others) and the representation and management of this crisis by the surroundings. A number of Maghrebi students, who were not particularly fundamentalist, often mentioned getting "sore fingers from constantly zapping" in order to avoid having to bear the contents of news programs on Algeria or on a number of conflicts involving Muslims. A good number of external observers have felt in France the same painful uneasiness towards what must be seen as dishonesty, and towards the extent of the dubious means used to support a too often one-sided and much biased perspective on "Algerian" violence. The same unease is felt towards those means used to present the heavily Manichean reading of this or that oppositional process, in Tunisia, in Egypt, or even in Sudan, by playing with the fear of the Other where the old anti-Arab ethnic racism has been replaced by its anti-Muslim ideological and denominational avatar.

The essential struggle against terrorism has constantly led to ignoring the violence that is suffered by the thousands of those targeted by ascription by our public safety programs (e.g. "vigi-pirates") and their unavoidable spillovers. Instances of this include the aggressive search for information that a specialist in criminology was noisily calling for in December 1996, within the group of "50,000 fundamentalists" that a former Minister of Interior claimed to have identified; those "kicks in the Islamist anthill" that involve thorough searches where copies of the Quran are waved in front of the television cameras as incriminating evidence; those public calls to use "the means that the law forsakes to fight terrorism which forsakes the law."

In his criticism of the constant excesses of a number of French audio-visual media dealing with current affairs in the Muslim world, Jean-François Legrain (CNRS, Maison de l'Orient) came up with an analogy of

---

[17] See "La Recette du poseur de bombes," in *Libération (Rebonds)*, Oct. 30, 1995.

which the "special envoys" of our national television networks too often irresistibly remind us:

The djellaba, the skullcap and the beard have replaced the crooked nose, the frock coat and the hat, while the unavoidable bomb with the lit match takes the place of bloody incisor teeth and crooked fingers. The (Islamist) gangrene is only the new version of the (Jewish) plague while the filthy squid continues to squeeze the civilized world in its tentacles.[18]

The particularly symbolic series shown in February 1997 on a French public television channel and dealing with the Islamist networks in Europe could well be said to qualify, in the true etymological sense of the word, as anti-Semitic.

In the monolithic and a-historical world of these "envoys" trailing the "terrorist" or "Islamist networks," there is simply no room for sociology, history, culture, and nuance. Conflation and accusations rule. The program's strategy was actually to eliminate one by one all the representatives of the Muslim community, or more generally all those who were able to offer an articulate view on the issue at hand, that is, who were able to evoke, and to explain in a rational manner (which does not mean to justify), how and why a tiny portion of the members of the Muslim community who are involved in the opppositional struggles tearing the Arab world apart became radicalized. The program looked for and selected only the most unpolished speakers guaranteed to have an off-putting effect, and whose words would inevitably be understood as a discourse of rupture and separation, even if this required meticulous selection during editing. Thus, the part devoted to Great Britain, for example, allowed the most credible representatives of the Islamist diaspora only to show their faces (or the tip of their beards) and certainly not to present the less disturbing content of their analyses and the information they hold on the real ins and outs of "Islamic terrorism" in Europe. FR2's privileged speaker was, on the other hand, unsurprisingly an individual whom 90 percent of London's Arab Islamist movement repeatedly criticized. The cautious analysis of the (complex) oppositional dynamics in the Arab world and of their effects on the changing status of the Muslim communities in Europe was thus left to a (former?) member of a extreme rightist group boasting merely the label of "criminological" scientist and totally ignorant of the linguistic, cultural, religious, and political characteristics of the communities and countries reputed to be sources of terrorist activity. One may wonder what would happen to a program from the same French television channel that tried to present as credible a debate on the possible annoyance of the French Jewish community vis-à-vis the Arab-Israeli conflict by a specialist in "criminology" who, furthermore, would be totally ignorant of the history, culture, or languages of the communities or country in question. By

[18]   J.-F. Legrain, in *Le Monde*, Mar. 13, 1996.

which—oh how legitimate—reactions would not the editor's offices, the legal chancelleries, and the ministerial cabinets be assailed?[19]

French television's coverage of current political events involving Muslims in fact regularly increases the rifts and the tensions, and on occasion, the small number of reactive excesses that it seeks to denounce. It thus, all too often, irresponsibly contributes to the creation of self-fulfilling prophecies. When, after having wrapped their fears ("Islamists are trouble makers!") in prophetic garb ("they will push us to war"), some media or political figures seeking to support their "analyses" actively participate in making them realities, they behave as irresponsible "firemen-pyromaniacs." The danger with such an approach made up of conflations, short cuts, and ignorance is that it feeds fears and other fantasies on which the ideologies of exclusion that it paradoxically claims to be fighting will then be able to grow, from Vitrolles[20] to Algiers.

All that is left then is for other unruffled "special envoys" to show up in another high-profile program to speak out noisily against the political havoc resulting from the fears that they themselves partook in prompting.

FRANCE'S MUSLIM POLICY DEFYING UNIVERSALITY

Although leading in infinitely small proportion to disruptive conduct towards the national community, the junction between the reconstructive "re-Islamization" that a small portion of second-generation immigrants[21]

---

[19] Libel action was taken against the FR2 corporation by Imam Larbi Kechat of the socio-cultural center on Tanger street. What is there to do when, in the interview with this "dangerous fundamentalist" of the Tanger street mosque, the editors are unable to isolate at least part of a sentence with an ambiguous meaning, and when the looks of the interviewee, his tie and the setting sun behind him helping, remain desperately credible and sympathetic? The solution comes then from a voice-over that is required to ruin the credibility of a speaker who is too polite to be honest. Larbi Kechat never denied the existence of extremist conduct; he explains their cause very rationally, thus referring to the most efficient way to fight them: extremism "is the result of frustration, of despair," etc. The way he expresses himself in front of the cameras clearly carries a condemnation of violence. A categorical comment thus becomes necessary to make the television viewer believe that what he has in front of him is a dangerous advocate of terrorism: "Once again," says the peremptory voice of the commentator, "no condemnation of violence." But what violence in such a procedure!

[20] A town in France where the rightist National Front led by Jean-Marie Le Pen first won local elections on Jun. 11, 1995.

[21] Khosrokhavar, *L'Islam des jeunes*. On the emergence of a radical Islamist trend in French society, Farhad Khosrokhavar writes: "Certain conducts that we tend to consider as Islamist, or even as radical Islamist are in fact reactions to a social, economic, and cultural reality that is moving further and further away from the norms set by the republican ideal. ... Part of the defiant stance of the Islamic youth who transgress the norms of public space stems from the difference in status that society ascribed to them before they, in return, asserted it and amplified it through a conspicuous use of religion. 'Provocative' Islam then is a means to protect oneself against racism and all the other types of

is undertaking and the militant involvement for "foreign causes" (the international conflicts of Palestine, Afghanistan, Bosnia, and Chechnya, or the support for Islamist opposition movements all over the Arab world) does not necessarily stem from a pathological tendency. The solely security-oriented or even solely "social"[22] approach to what is today perceived only through the lens of "religious radicalization" cannot justify that we not proceed to a realistic assessment of the issues brought up by the reactions to certain aspects of France's foreign policy. The country that, in 1996, celebrated the courage of the "international brigades," which André Malraux joined to fight fascism, seems on the other hand unable to assess the current conflicts in the Muslim world according to criteria reflecting a minimum of universality. In today's former Soviet Russia, an entire generation of soldiers is suffering from the "Afghan syndrome," that is, the difficulty of moving beyond the devastating memory of the bestial and totally useless repression of the civilian populations of this country that the fading USSR had invaded. Outside the Russian realm however, the young Muslims who voluntarily joined the struggle against one of the most bloody post-colonial episodes (and furthermore, that did so with the push and support of the CIA, at a time when the Western press referred to them as noble "fighters of the faith") are now the target of a demonization campaign that is as systematic as it is instinctive. Making any form of sympathy towards the Algerian Islamic Salvation Front (FIS) a crime stems from a similar blindness. Can we really consider as a "bad French citizen" the person who supports the wide opposition front to an Algerian regime that even the leader of the most politically correct (in the eyes of the French democrats) "secular" group (Saad Saadi, leader of the Constitutional Democratic Assembly (RCD)) has (finally) accepted to acknowledge as "being behind more terrorism than the Islamists are"?

Is a young "Beur" (French-born Arab) who is up in arms against the Iraqi embargo a "bad French citizen"? Is a young Muslim who is revolting against television programs' constantly one-sided view on the Israeli-Palestinian conflict or on the Algerian civil war necessarily putting the Republic in danger? Could not the distress signals that some of the French Muslims are sending us (those who dare to do it, since it is so easy to find oneself in Folembray![23]) also be considered as valuable warning signs? Had they been heard earlier, maybe they could have prevented the

---

ostracism that the youth put up with in everyday life; fed up, in the name of a difference that is now considered as sacred, they can choose a reversed form of racism towards society, fighting the racism of the dominant by that of the dominated, this time in the name of the religious people."

[22] Which is mostly based on an assumption that is not totally wrong but nevertheless remains very far from being true: "Khelkhal wouldn't have done this if he had a job."

[23] A French town where individuals are placed under house arrest.

Republic from locking itself up in what one day will inevitably be seen as the costly deadlock of our support to the Algerian junta.

ISLAM SOLUBLE IN EMPLOYMENT?

The French state's response to certain irritations felt by part of its Muslim community sometimes indeed takes the same short cuts and in many ways falls into the same pitfalls as does the Arab states' response to the impulse of their Islamist opponents. The economic reading of the Islamist thrust in the Arab world and the solely repressive nature of the states' responses to the often totally legitimate issues that it raises have already been denounced.[24] Following the same perilous logic, it seems that a large part of the French political elite is also dreaming of a sort of economic treatment for the Islamic issue, which would somehow be "soluble in employment." But since money or only the generosity and the altruism that would make it possible to reduce the deficiencies (very real after all, even if they do not explain everything) usefully disclosed by the economic approach are lacking anyway, the response unavoidably tends to stick to the old security options. Islam is thus said to be soluble in employment but inevitably ends up being bludgeoned.

Many of the successive options of French foreign policy in the Arab world (from its participation in the Gulf War to its unwavering support to the ruling junta in Algeria) have considerably reduced the gains made during the time of President De Gaulle. In the Palestinian conflict, but also more generally in the management of the Libyan, Iranian, Iraqi, and Sudanese crises, President Chirac's diplomatic endeavors have definitely helped the country to gain back some of its lost autonomy and credibility. Paris's position during the April 1996 Israeli attack of South Lebanon set the trend. Its reservations towards stepping up France's military involvement during Bill Clinton's "electoral strikes" against Iraq confirmed it, as well as its relatively moderate stance towards Libya under UN embargo or terrorist Sudan. But this fortunate change of position still has its limits since Paris refuses to learn from all of its lessons. French foreign policy officials admit that part of the irritation felt by such Islamist groups as the Palestinian Hamas (Islamic Resistance Movement) or the Lebanese Hizbollah is not totally unfounded in light of Israeli political and military intransigence. But, for the time being, they refuse to extend this logic and to gradually accept the idea that elsewhere in the Arab world there just may be members of the Islamist generation who also hold legitimate political yearnings that should be seen as acceptable by the international community.

The constant temptation to withdraw (out of suspicion and for security reasons) in the face of the Islamic factor thus corrupts whole blocks of

---

[24] Burgat, *L'Islamisme.*

France's "Muslim policy," inside as well as outside its borders. If it was only the passive expression of our existential fears, the strictly patholo-gical representation of the future of our relation to the Muslim Other would not be as worrisome. But the "security first" option that character-izes the response to the "fundamentalist threat" prompts not only a suspi-cious attitude and one of inner withdrawal of the national ego. In a more detrimental way, it also feeds many "pre-emptive" initiatives (at the internal level as well as in so-called "foreign" affairs) that partake in ostracizing and radicalizing a whole part of our environment or of our national community, with whom, on the contrary, everything should be done to improve relations.

In Algeria, we have not always been able to dissociate ourselves in a credible manner from the sanctioning (even if covered by hypocritical dis-cretion) of the "eradicating" option. Closing its eyes on the fact that the relative decrease in visibility of a political trend with a large popular sup-port base is simply the result of both an unprecedented level of political violence and impudent electoral manipulation, France is about to acquire the particularly harmful image of regional leader of the anti-Islamist strug-gle just about everywhere in the Arab world. Thus it becomes assimilated with the blind support to regimes that are more and more clearly discred-ited because more and more systematically repressive, and thus with the opposition to any process of political liberalization.

Clearly reflecting the Algerian and Tunisian case, this analytical pat-tern can be used for many other national settings since Maghrebi or Arab politics are unfortunately not the only ones concerned. "Why do we sup-port all the African despots?" asked the young confused hero not long ago of President Chirac in a cartoon published in the French newspaper *Le Canard Enchaîné*. "Their peoples do not want to do it anymore," replied the Head of State unwaveringly, "and so someone's got to do it!" The way customs and immigration officers treat tourism and business coming from this part of the world completes the picture of debasement:

Today in French Africa, the commercial networks are seeking to make up for a very restrictive French policy regarding getting a visa: the procedures are increas-ingly longer, costlier, and thus more uncertain. Also, visits to France will bring many administrative and police problems. Often corruption is necessary to get the right form, ... racism and hostility is the norm regarding relations with most French public servants: today this description has become too common for any need to dwell further on the issue.[25]

The not too distant future will tell us if French support of the Algerian junta will have really helped to save democracy and human rights or those of women, and with them the cultural, economic, and political interests of

---

[25] Rolland Marchal, *Doubaï. Le développement d'une cité entrepôt dans le Golfe* (Paris: FNSP, Les Etudes du CERI, Jun. 27, 1997), p. 16.

the Republic (which was, save for a few details, the agenda of the French intelligentsia and political elite when they mobilized to prevent the fellaghas of the National Liberation Front (FLN) in the 1950s from coming to power) or if instead it will have contributed to blocking the process of political and social modernization in that country.

Although we can easily agree that this suggestion is much more ambitious, an efficient response to the "Islamic threat" requires not so much supporting Arab military dictatorships, the illusory locking-up of the Internet, the indiscriminate slandering of French Muslim charitable organizations, or stepping up all types of security measures at our borders, but rather, limiting here as well as there the arrogant domination of one side or political generation over the other. At the Mediterranean level, it implies the acceptance of a credible and honorable peace by Israel in the eyes of a great majority of Palestinians, that which the Oslo framework, and not only its distortion by the right-wing Likud when it came to power, was very far from achieving. It also implies an opening-up of Arab political systems, that is, the holding of genuinely free elections (whatever the expected results may be), open to all the real political forces, and on the basis of electoral programs similar, for example, to those put up by the real pioneers of Algerian anti-terrorism that were the Algerian signatories to the National Program of Sant Egidio in February 1995 in Rome.

2

THE MODERNIZING FORCE OF ISLAM

Bjørn Olav Utvik

By lumping Islamism into one category with present-day Christian "fundamentalisms" or "integrisms" in the US, France or Italy, writers like Bruce
Lawrence and Gilles Kepel came to the conclusion that Islamists are part
of a world-wide "revolt against the modern age."[1] But in these kinds of
analyses too much of the dynamic relationship of the respective religious
movements to their socio-political environment gets lost in the process of
comparative abstraction. My contention is that contemporary Islamism in
the Middle East and North Africa should rather be seen as part of the
breakthrough for the "modern age" in Muslim societies.

Islamist advocacy of catching up with the West in economic and technological development is explicit. But beyond that, a study focusing on the relationship of the Islamist movements to their context would show them to be
promoting at the social and political level a number of developments otherwise
considered as tied to the transition from "traditional" to "modern" society:

(a) Individualization, as can be seen in the development of the ideal of the
true believer as engaged in a constant *jihad* (holy war) for good against
evil, in the fight against corruption and for the impersonalization of politics and business, in the Islamic work ethic propagated by Islamists, and in
the individual life projects of Islamist youth.
(b) Social mobilization, as evinced by the drawing of people from the
lower, and especially the lower middle, classes into the circuit of politics.
On this level Islamism could also be seen to prepare the grounds for mass
democracy.
(c) The centrality of the state, in that political Islamism envisages the
state as a major agent in creating a true Islamic society, and that the
"Shariah Islamist-style" would be made up of modern legal codes enacted

---

[1] Gilles Kepel, *La Revanche de Dieu. Chrétiens, juifs et musulmans à la reconquête du
monde* (Paris: Seuil, 1991). Bruce B. Lawrence, *Defenders of God: The Fundamentalist
Revolt against the Modern Age* (London: I. B. Tauris, 1990).

by an elected assembly, rather than working through the interpretations of the traditional scholars.

On this basis, Islamism should properly be seen not only as a product of the changes and conflicts wrought by modernizing economic and social processes, but not least as an important modernizing agent within current Middle Eastern society.

The Middle East in the throes of change

For the purposes of this chapter, modernization is understood to refer to:

(a) historic processes of technological and economic change under way in some areas of Europe since the 16th century and in the Middle East from the 19th, producing a society where market relations dominate production and exchange, where the cities contain the bulk of the population, and where industry is the dominant branch of production; and

(b) the attendant processes of social and political change: at a social level, the break-up of tightly-knit traditional units dominated by family and patron-client relations within urban quarter, village, or kinship group; at a political level, the increased mobilization of the population and the rapid growth and centralization of the state apparatus.

When it is stated in the following that a certain characteristic of the Islamist movement is "modernizing," it is meant to suggest that it tends to speed up the processes outlined here, or at least to accommodate the population to them.

From the time when modern Islamism emerged in Egypt with the creation of Hasan al-Banna's Society of Muslim Brothers and until today, Islamism has been part of Middle Eastern societies undergoing rapid change of the nature defined as modernizing above, and on a comprehensive scale. Processes of urbanization, commercialization, and to a certain extent industrialization were cutting large groups loose from their traditional position and from the social control of their traditional environment. At the same time, the growth of a centralized state bureaucracy, and increased literacy connected with expanded education, were increasing the strain on old parochial social and political loyal-ties and creating new social groups with an increased awareness.

There are some who would argue that the Middle East has been "modern" since the 19th century. Of course, it is true that by, say, 1880, the region had been irreversibly changed as a result of the confrontation with modernizing Western Europe. Unmistakably "modern" phenomena like newspapers and railways were a fact of life in some areas. But a tramway in Cairo does not change the world. In no way had the processes referred to above worked themselves out on any comprehensive scale. By 1900, only 15 percent of the population of the Middle East lived in urban centers with more than 10,000 inhabitants. In 1920, in, admittedly backward, Iran, the journey from Teheran to the Gulf took more than a month to accomplish. By the 1940s, modern industry was still limited to some recently established textile mills in Egypt and a few other places, and, although a lot has happened, the industrial base is still weak today compared to most regions outside Africa. In the 1990s, a large majority of the Egyptian population remain functionally illiterate. The fact that the processes of modernization could be felt in Istanbul, Beirut, Cairo, and Alexandria by 1880 should not lead to the false assumption that they were at all nearing completion. They still are not.

Obscurantists with cellular phones?

Nonetheless, rapid socio-economic change has remained a central feature of the environment for the growth of Islamism in our century. The idea that Islamism might represent a revolt against this "onslaught of the modern age" would immediately seem to fly in the face of the evidence if we look at attitudes towards modern technology and towards economic development. For one thing, it is generally acknowledged that Islamists are extremely apt at utilizing in their organizational work the most modern means of communication and propaganda. For another, all the way back to the founding father of modern Islamism Hasan al-Banna, the Muslim Brothers and other Islamist movements have explicitly argued that the moral regeneration they sought was a prerequisite for Muslim societies to be able to catch up with the West in material development. And in their programs the Islamists have strongly emphasized the need for comprehensive and rapid economic development; indeed, the Muslim Brothers in the 1940s called for the "immediate industrialization" of Egypt.

Bruce Lawrence and others have acknowledged these facts, but they hasten to distinguish between modernity and modernism, admitting that what they call the "fundamentalists" do not oppose the technological aspects of modern life. Lawrence sees fundamentalism rather as a revolt against modernism, understood as the rationalist, scientific way of thinking propagated by the Enlightenment, and a defense of Absolute Truth as preserved in the Holy Scriptures. It is certainly beyond question that Islamists defend the idea that Absolute Truth has been revealed to us through the Quran and the Sunnah (example) of the Prophet, and that this truth should guide our individual and collective behavior. But this does not necessarily imply that their political discourse in general has a non-rationalist character.[2]

Let us look for instance at Islamist discourse on economic questions, as it is found with the two main constituents of Egypt's Islamist movement, the Muslim Brothers and the Labor Party.[3] We will look at the ideological

[2] Bjørn Olav Utvik, "Islamism: Digesting Modernity the Islamic Way," *Forum for Development Studies* 2, 1993.

[3] For a thorough documentation and discussion, see Bjørn Olav Utvik, "Independence and Development in the Name of God: The Economic Discourse of Egypt's Islamist

content of this discourse below, but does its style of argument represent a move away from rationalism? There is not one answer to this. It is true that Islamist economics is in many respects a moral discourse. And it is true that there is a tendency, as Samir Amin has argued, especially in the writings of the Muslim Brothers, to provide justification for particular positions by a paraphrase of the text of the Quran and Sunnah, rather than by substantial argument.[4] The style is often apologetic rather than probing.

On the other hand, there need hardly be a contradiction between a moral discourse and a rational one. If we consider the proponents of a "scientific" economic thinking in the 18th century (and certainly in later centuries) it is not difficult (in most cases at least) to discern that the morals and/or interests of certain classes determined the angle from which their "neutral, objective" observations were made. This did not in the least reduce their importance as pioneers of a rationalist approach to economic questions.

If we look at the level of intellectual approach, broadly speaking the Islamist discourse on Islamic economics, or on how economic problems would be solved by an Islamic state, fall into two categories. One is found among writers associated with the Muslim Brothers, Sayyid Qutb in the 1950s, and Yusuf Kamal, Husayn Shahhata, and Abd al-Hamid al-Ghazali from the 1980s onward.[5] Here there is a tendency to proceed from Quranic and Sunnah injunctions on economic matters and discuss their superiority to capitalist and socialist solutions. The emphasis is on a show of orthodoxy, as illustrated by the frequent references to the Quran, Sunnah, and the viewpoints of exegeter and experts on jurisprudence down through the centuries. For although it is a general Islamist belief that the door of *ijtihad* (original interpretation and thought) is open (given certain conditions), in many of the theoretical writings on an Islamic economic alternative produced by the Muslim Brothers considerable deference is shown to the old masters, like the founders of the four legal schools. This tendency is explicitly apologetic in that it takes the economic elements of the Shariah as given and proceeds to a rational argumentation for their superiority in producing a stable, prospering, and just society. In both these aspects this is reminiscent of the

---

Opposition 1984-90" (dissertation for the Dr. Art. degree, University of Oslo, 2000).

4 Samir Amin, *Delinking* (London: Zed Books, 1990), p. 181.

5 Our presentation of the views of these writers is based mainly on the followings works: Sayyid Qutb, *Ma'rakat al-islam wal-ra'smaliyya [The struggle between Islam and capitalism]* (Cairo: Dar al-shuruq, 1987), and *Al-'adala al-ijtima'iyyah fi al-islam [Social justice in Islam]* (Cairo: Dar al-shuruq, 1989); Yusuf Kamal, *Al-islam wal-madhahib al-iqtisadiyyah al-mu'asirah [Islam and contemporary schools of economic thought]* (Mansura: Dar al-wafa, 1986), and *Fiqh al-iqtisad al-'amm [The fiqh of public economy]* (Cairo: Stabrus lil-tiba'a wal-nashr, 1990); and Husayn Shahhata, *Al-minhaj al-islami lil-amn wal-tanmiya [The Islamic road to security and development]* (10th of Ramadan City: Dar al-tawzi' wal-nashr al-islamiyya, 1990). The views of Abd al-Hamid al-Ghazali can be gleaned from, for instance, Hamdi al-Basir, "Al-insan wal-minhaj al-islami fi al-tanmiya al-iqtisadiyya [The people and the Islamic road to economic development]," *al-Nur*, Dec. 7, 1988.

discourse of Azhar scholars who from time to time deliver *fatwas* on economic issues in the Egyptian press.[6]

As against this, the other type of discourse, with Adil Husayn[7], the central ideologue of the Labor Party, as one of the foremost representatives, to a much greater extent proceeds on the one hand from an analysis of the actual situation of the economy, and on the other from general principles defined as Islamic, such as self-reliance. The Labor Party newspaper *al-Shaab* gives broad coverage to current economic issues. Islam is not seen so much as offering ready-made solutions, but as the moral force which will unite the population in enduring the effort and hardships of independent development, and as offering broad principles of social justice and harmony. Based on those principles the concrete strategies for progress are developed with reference to modern economic and political theory as formulated both by Westerners and by theorists from the Third World, more than with constant reference to the Quran or models from Islamic history. In fact, in its ideas about the conditions for development the Labor Party was quite close to the delinking strategy proposed by the radical Egyptian economist Samir Amin.[8]

Of course, it could be said that Husayn is atypical of Islamists in that the formative years of his political career were spent in the Communist movement and that he seems to have moved towards Islamism from the outside in search more of a source of political energy and legitimacy than in search of particular economic or other precepts. But also among some Muslim Brothers a change of style could be observed, especially from 1987 when the Brothers entered parliament with a sizeable group of representatives. Here we find that members of the younger generation, recruited from the student movement in the 1970s, like Isam al-Iryan and Mukhtar Nuh, discuss economic issues in a way that, both in style and content, is much closer to Adil Husayn than the old guard represented by Mamun al-Hudaybi who remain closer to the more conservative style described above. I would argue that, while appealing to the Quran and the Sunnah as sources of legitimacy for their policies, the Labor Party and the younger Muslim Brother leaders seem to represent a thoroughly modern form of political discourse, and a decidedly rationalist style in argument.

The two tendencies described here are, of course, not mutually exclusive. Individual writers will typically oscillate between the different styles

---

[6] See, for example, the series of articles in *al-Ahram al-iqtisadi* in August 1991 by the Mufti of Egypt, Muhammad Sayyid Tantawi, on the question of what constitutes *riba*.

[7] For Husayn's views see Adil Husayn, *Nahwa fikr 'arabi jadid: al-nasiriyya wal-tanmiya wal-dimuqratiyah [Towards a new Arab thinking: Nasserism, development and democracy]* (Cairo: Dar al-mustaqbal al-'arabi, 1985), and *Al-islam: din wa hadara—mashru' lil-mustaqbal [Islam: Religion and Civilization—a Project for the Future]* (Giza: Al-manar al-'arabi, 1990).

[8] Amin, *Delinking*, p. 41 ff.

of argument. But the difference in emphasis and in the manner of approaching the problematic is clear. An instance of this difference can be found concerning the question of *zakat* (an obligatory tax required of Muslims). Yusuf Kamal and Husayn Shahhata make the collection of *zakat* (or *jizyah* in the case of Christians and Jews) from every able citizen according to the rates established in classical *fiqh* (jurisprudence) an important task for the state, and the mainstay of public finances and of social security in an Islamic state. In contrast, Adil Husayn would prefer it to remain a voluntary contribution by the pious, while the state must construe an efficient and just system for securing the revenue necessary for the development effort, national security, and social redistribution. This should be according to the criterion of efficiency and guided by general Islamic principles of justice, but not bound by particular historic interpretations or implementations of those principles.

Even if we concentrate on Muslim Brother writers like Yusuf Kamal and Husayn Shahhata whom I have suggested as examples of the "scripturalist" category, the picture needs to be nuanced, and it is debatable indeed whether they could be said to represent an anti-rationalist trend. Apologetics is a hybrid genre in this regard. It is out to defend the correctness of the divine truth of the texts. But to do so it has to enter into a discussion of reality, and thereby comes to contain elements both of rationalist and non-rationalist exegesis of Scripture, although its *a priori* goals may blunt its critical edge. As importantly, it must be emphasized that even though the writers in question underpin their views with frequent quotations from the Quran and Sunnah and with references to classical *fiqh*, theirs is of course a selective reading of the divine texts and of the old masters. We might refer here to the near total absence of any reference to the issue of slavery which was regulated in classical interpretations of the Shariah, and to the way in which some writers emphasize strongly how the holy scriptures sanctify private property, while others stress the limits imposed on the enjoyment of such property through Quranic verses and sayings of the Prophet. In this context, the Quran-quoting may well be a way of obscuring the fact that the idea of an Islamic economy that one is about to develop is really something quite new, and that it is being constructed by people outside the corps of *ulama* (religious scholars).

Finally, also with Kamal and Shahhata, and *a fortiori* with Abd al-Hamid al-Ghazali, there is towards the end of the 1980s a discernible move away from the scripturalist approach. This is clearly visible in Kamal's book from 1990, *Fiqh al-iqtisad al-amm*, where there are extended excursions into the real problems of the current Egyptian economy, like the huge public debt, the crisis of the public sector, etc. Classical *fiqh* is used as a reference (though not the only one) in discussing these issues, but not as the starting point. In the same work Kamal clearly gives secular economic science the role of analyzing the workings of the economy, once the choice of guiding ideology is made by a society. The difference from Adil Husayn is then mainly in Kamal's use of mainstream liberal Western economic theory, versus Husayn's proximity to dependency theory and other critical trends. In the same vein, we may point to the criticism made by Shahhata and others of Islamic financial institutions, which reveal these authors to be more concerned with what is required to achieve economic progress for the country than with the subtleties of what constitutes the abominable "usury" (*riba*) forbidden according to classical *fiqh*. The remark by Abd al-Hamid al-Ghazali that God's will is found in that which serves the public interest is only the most pronounced expression of this tendency.[9] As for the Islamic principles supposed to guide the economy, Yusuf Kamal declares that his purpose is to "connect the present with the [sacred] text" in order to develop a contemporary interpretation through *ijtihad*.

Returning here for a moment to the discussion on whether Islamism is primarily to be seen as a defense of absolute truth, it would seem that for the tendency represented by the Labor Party and increasingly by a number of Muslim Brothers, Islam is seen as an absolute source of moral injunctions, but not as a provider of an infinite number of particular truths about how to organize society. Perhaps it could even be said that the important thing is the idea that one possesses so to speak a "domestic" source of absolute truth, more than the precise contents of this truth. It is not so hard to imagine how this could potentially serve as a tool for liberating oneself from the universalist claims of Western science and policy recommendations ostensibly built on it, in order to be able to criticize established Western truths and to ponder more freely the right course of action.

The tendency towards a more "free" Islamist thought is, however, to a certain extent contravened by another which strengthens the hold of the traditional *fiqh* of the *ulama* over Islamist thought. The Islamist movement may have narrowed somewhat the scope of interpretations of God's message by raising the slogan of the Shariah as their front issue. For even if the Islamists defend the right to fresh *ijtihad* on the basis of Scripture, they cannot avoid the weight of the historical traditions of *fiqh* scholarship. And this is true even if Adil Husayn, for instance, makes an interesting distinction between the Shariah as God's eternal guidance for mankind, and *fiqh* as the concrete human efforts at interpreting God's message in line with the changing circumstances of time and place.[10]

The *ulama*, originally more a target of attack from the Islamist movement than participating in it, have begun to seize the opportunity for regaining some of their lost status in society by capitalizing on their traditional role as the protectors and transmitters of the Shariah. "The Shariah," they say, "that is us!" And as they join the bandwagon of Islamic revival

---

[9] See the cited article by Hamdi al-Basir.

[10] Kari Vogt, *Islams hus. Verdensreligion pa fremmarsj* (Oslo: Cappelen, 1993), pp. 56–7.

they carry along the whole juggernaut of scholarly interpretations of the Law accumulated through the fourteen hundred-odd *Hijra* years (the Muslim era) that have passed, inducing by the same token a fair amount of conservatism to Islamist discourse, for instance on the question of property.

The Islamist movement never had a clear-cut attitude towards the role of the *ulama* in the true Islamic society they seek to create. On the one hand, we see them calling for the question of *riba* to be settled by trained *fuqaha* (jurists) and not by politicians, and demanding the convening of the Azhari Islamic Research Academy (*Majma' al-buhuth al-islamiyyah*) to pronounce on the issue. On the other hand, in practice the Islamist politicians and ideologues themselves are living examples of lay men venturing into the field of *ijtihad* and taking it upon themselves to proclaim how the sacred texts should properly be understood. And an analysis would show that the main thrust of their discourse is rationalist in style with regard to economic as well as other issues.

More importantly still, the focus on the perceived dichotomy in Islamist attitudes toward "the modern age," with a positive welcoming of new technology on the one hand, an unflinching defense of "Absolute Truth" on the other, tends to obscure the all-important analysis of the social and political effects of Islamist ideology and activity, and their relation to modernity.

Kindred spirit: Falwell or Cromwell?

A word about "fundamentalism studies" in this connection: comparison probably always has some value, but the desire to find common traits between the objects observed easily gains the upper hand. When cross-cultural studies of religio-political activism are undertaken with the aim of isolating a common essence pertaining to something *a priori* identified as a worldwide phenomenon of fundamentalism, the typical result one comes up with is that what the movements studied have in common is the defense of "Absolute Truth." All too quickly this is then identified as the essential feature of the movements in question. But then one has lost in the process of abstraction too much of the social dynamics that these various movements are a part of. The fundamentalism analyses really contribute nothing else than what was known all along, that there exists around the globe movements which seek to sanctify their political ideas by anchoring them in the sacred texts of their respective religions. So the circle is complete, since this observation was what triggered the comparative study in the first place. Thus, the whole exercise becomes about as valuable as undertaking to identify a common essence between the movements led by Lionel Jospin or Tony Blair and the Mexican *zapatistas*. One would surely find that they all talk of social justice, but whether one will have gained new insights worth the effort is rather doubtful.

If comparison is indeed called for, I would suggest that a potentially more fruitful effort would be to focus on the study of religio-political movements in countries undergoing similar processes of economic, social, and political change to the contemporary Middle East. In the case of Christian movements this would mean that instead of looking at the present day American Christian Right dominating the Republican Party or at the Italian *Comunione e liberazione*,[11] we should study the Protestant movements of early modern Europe, from the English Puritans to the Scandinavian revivalist movements of the 19th century. Elsewhere I have presented some suggestions as to where this approach might lead us,[12] but a summary of some salient points of similarity and of difference emerging from such a comparison might be in order.

There is a striking resemblance between the Christian activists of days gone by and current Islamists in the social composition of the active cadre, in the sense that in both cases we are talking about middle and lower middle class groups upwardly mobile through education and, to a certain extent, business endeavors. Ideologically there is an obvious agreement on the idea that the existence of religion as a moral discourse and norm is not sufficient, nor the individual's acceptance of its authority or even adherence to ritual. Rather, God's Kingdom on earth must be realized and it is the duty of the state to enforce the rule of God's will. In the Christian setting this means that the millennium foreseen in Holy Scripture is seen as an actual earthly kingdom;[13] among the Muslims the talk is more of a reenactment of the virtuous society of the Prophet and the four "rightly-guided" caliphs that followed him.

"Men have no allowance to be rulers where the Lord is not served," the Puritan preacher Perry wrote in 1588.[14] In the same vein contemporary Islamists insist that Muslim rulers are not legitimate if they do not secure the implementation of the Shariah in every sphere of life including state matters. Furthermore, for both Puritans and Islamists it is the duty of the individual to struggle for the kingdom of God at two levels: by being an example of a good Christian/Muslim, but also by striving for the dominance of God's will over state and society.

In the case of Calvinism and other Protestant movements there was a move away from the Catholic belief in the redeeming effect of good

---

11 Kepel, *La Revanche de Dieu*, pp. 94 ff.
12 Bjørn Olav Utvik, "'A pervasive seriousness invaded the country ... ' Islamism—Cromwell's Ghost in the Middle East," in *Between National Histories and Global History*, eds. Stein Tonnesson, Juhani Koponen, Niels Steensgaard, and Thommy Svensson (Helsinki: FHS, 1997). See also "Hasan al-Banna—ein muslimsk Oftedal?" *Midtosten Forum* 1/93.
13 See for instance Hanserd Knollys, "A Glimpse of Sion's Glory," (1641), in *The Puritan Revolution. A Documentary History*, ed. Stuart E. Prall (London: Routledge and Kegan Paul, 1968), p. 90.
14 Michael Walzer, *The Revolution of the Saints: A Study in the Origins of Radical Politics* (London: Weidenfeld and Nicolson, 1966), p. 263.

works, and towards the insistence that salvation was conditional on faith alone. But, perhaps paradoxically, this led to very harsh demands placed upon the individual Christian to lead a holy life, and to wage untiring war on evil. For if faith really had taken hold of one's heart and soul this would show in one's words and deeds (or if one believed in predestination, a pious life would be the sign that one belonged to the chosen few). Similarly, the Islamists envisage the life of the true believer as an unceasing battle against evil.

It is important to notice the way the Puritans and later the Islamists made political use of history and tradition, as precedence rather than as custom. The past is used not as a conservative defense of tradition but as a radical challenge to present practices. Historical examples, taken to represent the original, the God-intended, and just state of affairs are used to denounce current conditions as unjust and godless. Often it is implied, rightly or wrongly, that the just practice had reigned until recently, before the present dynasty or regime destroyed it. Thus John Milton described the right of Parliament to depose a king as both biblically attested and as the natural state of affairs, in his defense of the trial and execution of Charles I in 1648–49.[15] And thus the Islamists set the idealized rule of the God-given law, the Shariah, against current secularist regimes. At the same time, the Puritans in their day and the contemporary Islamists have in common a stress on the responsibility, and by the same token, albeit implicitly, the freedom, of the believing individual. Parallel to this duality there is in both cases a focus on the state as the enforcer of good, but also an effort at mobilizing the population into an active political stance. We will return in some more detail to these aspects of Islamism below.

A glance at Norwegian revivalist leaders like Hans Nielsen Hauge (1771–1824), condemned by conservative contemporaries such as the Norwegian Cromwell, and Lars Oftedal (1838–1900) would reveal many of the same traits common to early modern Protestant movements and current Islamism. Oftedal's movement resembled the Muslim Brothers and other Islamist movements not least in its strong emphasis on practical welfare work, providing health care and educational services where the state failed.

Why did religion and not some secular ideology deliver the vocabulary for the social and political assertion of the upstart groups mobilized by Puritans and Islamists respectively? Certainly, at the time of Cromwell there were no ideological options outside religion. In the case of the Islamists the dismal failure of competing nationalist and socialist movements has played an important role. But common to the context of both Puritans and Islamists is that the traditional societies, in which religion had provided moral legitimation to the existing order, were rapidly dissolving.

---

[15] John Milton, "The Tenure of Kings and Magistrates (1648)," in Prall, *The Puritan Revolution*, pp. 35ff.

A deep-felt dismay at the ensuing perceived chaos led to the reassertion of religious values, but in reformed shape, more fit to secure moral order in the new environment created by social change.

In the contemporary Middle East we may add that the Westernization and secularization of the current dominant social and political elites make Islamism a vehicle for the hundreds of thousands of first-generation university graduates from traditional backgrounds in their struggle for social ascendancy. For them Islamism is not least a fight for validating their own cultural capital, while devaluing that of the Westernizers.

Of course, there are a number of obvious differences between the two situations in question that could immediately be pointed out. While the Puritans emerged in the pre-industrial era and at a time when the emergence of world economic integration was in its early stages, the Islamist movement was the product of societies dominated by the industrialized West, integrated into the world economy in a subordinate position, and subject to cultural and intellectual influences from the post-Enlightenment Western world. One result of this is that, contrary to the situation of the Puritans, the Islamists are faced with fierce competition and opposition from established secularist tendencies inspired by the West, tendencies which have at present a history of at least eighty years in the Muslim region.

The competition, and the constant need to defend and justify their ideology in the face of criticism from world opinion and from secularists at home, influences Islamists. Therefore, more than was the case with the Puritans, there are wings of Islamism which have developed ideas of democracy, pluralism, power-sharing, and power rotation, etc. On the other hand, the fact of Western dominance also means that Islamism must be seen as a cultural nationalism of sorts, while the question of independence was at best marginal in the case of the English Calvinists (despite the anti-Pope and anti-Spanish agitation involved). Interestingly, while Calvinists and other Protestants clashed openly with the Pope, Islamists are often more hesitant in their conflict with tradition, for fear of laying themselves open to the charge of cultural treason.

We must indeed be clear about the boldness of the suggested comparison and keep in mind that on a number of issues there are great differences both in circumstances and in character between the two movements we are discussing. It should be emphasized that, even if our ideas turn out to be confirmed by more serious comparative research, it will never be said that the Puritans and the Islamists are identical in their social and political function in their respective societies. What it might do is to help clarify the discussion about the character of Islamism with regard to modernity. For if we say, as is broadly accepted, that the Puritans should be seen as part of the modern breakthrough in English politics and society, one would at the very least be hard put to argue that the Islamists are basically a reactionary force.

Economic development as a divinely imposed duty

Moving back to the investigation of Islamist attitudes toward modernity, if we look at the surface of things, as it were, at the level of programmatic statements, we find, as indicated above, that from the time of Hasan al-Banna, Islamists have been unequivocal advocates of bringing their societies up to the technological level of modern industrial society. The most fertile recruiting ground for Islamist organizations has been among students in technological and natural science subjects. If any one vocation is typical for an Islamist it is that of the engineer.

The need for technological and economic development has remained central in the political agenda of the Islamists up to the present. They devote a great deal of their political energy to criticizing the failure of the economic development effort, and emphasize the need for building an independent technological base in Muslim countries, in order to escape the total dependence on Western countries and Japan for advanced equipment. Through their press and as elected representatives, where they get access to such a luxury as elections, the Islamists keep calling for rapid industrialization, improved communications, upgrading basic infrastructure and services in the villages, etc. But not least, beyond the level of immediate questions of economic policy, the Islamist interpretation of the social message of Islam is much conducive to economic development, and reminiscent of the Protestant ethics that Max Weber saw as propitious to capitalist development in Europe.[16] This will be confirmed by a brief look at the set of values presented as those that should guide a true Islamic economic system by the Egyptian Islamist writers discussed above.

Based on their pronouncements, the building of a strong and technologically advanced economy emerges as a sacred duty. For Adil Husayn this is an integral part of the quest for independence which remains at the heart of his political and intellectual efforts, and Islam really enters the picture as a mobilizing force towards this end.[17] Kamal and Shahhata for their part state that the Shariah aims at comprehensive development in order to achieve strength and glory for the Muslim nation. They claim that mankind is entrusted with a sacred obligation to exploit natural resources to the full for the increase of the material wealth of society, and that economic development is a *fard kifayah*, a collective duty, to be secured by the state if individuals fail to promote it with sufficient force. The whole development effort is likened to a *jihad*, ironically reminding one of the decidedly non-Islamist Tunisian former leader Habib Bourguiba, who in the 1960s tried to exempt his people from the fast during Ramadan on

---

[16] Max Weber, *The Protestant Ethic and the Spirit of Capitalism* (London: HarperCollins, 1991), pp. 157ff.

[17] This is not to suggest that Husayn is insincere in his Islamism, merely that the goal of independent development is taken for granted and not deduced from Islamic teachings.

the grounds that they were engaged in a *jihad* for development. Both Kamal and Shahhata emphasize the centrality of the development effort in an Islamic system through stating that *zakat* revenue can be used for productive investment in order to further development. Shahhata states that work is to be considered an *'ibadah*, part of the worship of God. This implies that the perfection of one's work is a religious obligation equal in importance to the fulfillment of the ritual duties like prayer and fasting, and is reminiscent of the Protestant idea of work as a calling. The further-ance of public interest, *maslahah*, is held up as equal to fulfilling God's will, and in line with this the call for modernizing the economy is given priority over the formal fulfillment of tenets of *fiqh*, as in Islamist critique of "Islamic" investment companies and banks for not investing in projects which would contribute to the development of production. There is an old *fiqh* principle that in considering *maslahah* in the choice between possible interpretations of the Quran or Sunnah on a specific point of jurispru-dence, one should proceed according to a descending ladder of priorities: first necessities, *daruriyyat*, then needs, *hajiyyat*, then improvements, *tahsinat*. The Islamists take up this list of priorities and adopt it as "Islamic priorities for production and investment," so that Muslim society, and the Islamic state as its representative, must before anything else secure the sufficient allocation of resources for the procurement of basic necessities for the population. Even if the self-proclaimed Islamic financial institutions can be said to be operating without interest it does not make them Islamic in the eyes of the Islamists if they do not support this effort, but concentrate on financing trade and currency speculation.

There is common agreement among Islamist writers that private prop-erty is the basic principle in Islam and that this is necessary for stimulating men to exert their best efforts at developing and preserving wealth. None-theless, they all stress that public interest takes priority over private inter-ests. A central idea is that of man as "God's steward (*khalifah*) on earth." Every man has the right to private property, but it is limited by fundamen-tally being God's property. The individual is seen as holding property in trust from God and from society as God's deputy, as it were. Therefore, private property involves a social responsibility. It should be made to bear fruit in the service of society, and it should be preserved and developed for future generations. And others have claims on the property, that is, the return it brings, or even parts of the property itself may be needed to satisfy urgent needs of the wider community.

All the writers consider it a task for an Islamic state to secure a mini-mum of welfare to all members of society. This is to be realized through concentrating investment and production on the provision of basic neces-sities, and, centrally for Kamal and Shahhata, through the *zakat*. The Muslim Brother writers emphasize that the *zakat* should provide more than what is necessary for mere survival; every member of society should have the right to a certain degree of enjoyment of life. The ideal of the just Islamic society is not one of radical egalitarianism, but rather of balance, of Islam as a moderate third way avoiding the excesses of capitalism and communism. This implies that the ideal is to seek a harmonious balance between different social groups and between generations. Class conflict is seen as an evil which it is an imperative to avoid lest its divisive cancer split society into warring factions.

Over and above the general principles enunciated as guiding an Islamic economy, the Islamist writers emphasize the liberating force of faith in itself. Faith induces good behavior towards others and thereby creates a solid framework for social solidarity, says Kamal. Husayn stresses belief in a sacred doctrine as an indispensable prerequisite for the will to sacrifice without which any serious development effort is doomed to failure. More generally, this is linked to the idea that a true Muslim is involved in an unceasing battle for good against evil, and should use her or his measured time in this world in a disciplined and purposeful way. When the energy of the believer, through the values listed above, is directed towards the increase of material production, Islamist doctrine would seem to possess a substantial potential for economic mobilization. This is true not least since there is an emphasis not only on an Islamic state enforcing these values, but ultimately on them being internalized as natural instincts by believers.

"Renewal of self"—not Westernization

But while the Islamists can thus be seen to be open advocates of economic growth and development, they are far more hesitant when pronouncing on "modernization" as a general phenomenon. Typically they would oppose the use of this concept to describe their goals, on the grounds that it has become synonymous with Westernization. In the Arab countries they would discard the Arab translation for modernization, *tahdith*, in favor of *tajaddud dhati*, "self renewal," the implication being that modern Muslim society should evolve from indigenous culture and tradition rather than through imitation of the West. I would argue that behind the choice of term Islamists can be seen actually to promote a whole range of ideas and values with a Western heritage. But more importantly, in order to properly grasp the relationship between Islamism and modernity our analysis needs to move beyond the level of explicit ideology and rhetoric. We must move from what the Islamists say about modernization to how their words and actions are affecting the Muslim Middle Eastern societies in which they work.

Loyal to God only—the individualizing aspect of Islamism

In terms of social organizations, the processes of change outlined above and identified as "modernizing" are generally viewed as straining primordial ties of loyalty, like those tying the individual to his family, tribe, or village and placing him or her in a client relationship to a patron. Modernization then implies the increasing freedom of the individual, and "horizontal" ties of voluntary association replacing the old "vertical" and organic bonds of solidarity and loyalty. By the same token, it places far greater responsibility on the individual. So what has been the attitude of current Islamist movements in this regard? Certainly they cannot be seen to defend the old ways. Rather they try to reconstruct religion so that it may provide a guide and reassuring framework for acting under the novel circumstances.

As Andrea Rugh has pointed out, the tendency is to stress individual responsibility and accountability in realizing the values of Islamic society, in contrast to the traditional locating of responsibility for an individual's behavior in the primary groups of which they were a part. Rugh points out that for Islamists "the higher authority to which the individual is accountable is Allah, even when compliance with that authority requires that individuals take actions which contradict the guidance of mundane authorities."[18]

This focusing of the individual is visible in the increasingly central idea of the true believer as a *mujahid*, that is, one engaged in *jihad*, or struggle for the cause of God. Abd al-Salam Farag, ideologue of the group that killed President Sadat of Egypt in 1981, wrote of *jihad* as the forgotten sixth obligation of Islam, which should properly be added to the so-called five pillars of confession, prayer, alms, fasting, and pilgrimage.[19] For Farag, this duty of *jihad* implied taking up arms against a ruler who was only formally a Muslim. But also in the mainstream Islamist movements, like the Muslim Brothers, committed to a strategy of peaceful political work, there is the idea of the life of the true believer as a constant battle on all fronts against the forces of evil within oneself and within society. This fight may take many forms, from prayer via welfare work to political agitation and, should the situation demand it, military struggle.

It might seem contradictory to regard a duty to devote one's life to the struggle for a cause, in the interest of God and mankind, as linked to a process of individualization. But the crucial point here is that what is demanded is not a step backwards into some kind of primordial form of group identification, where the individual is subordinate to the perceived collective will of the group, but rather a step forward into a situation where the individual must constantly choose of his or her own free, conscious,

---

[18] Andrea B. Rugh, "Reshaping Personal Relations in Egypt," in *Fundamentalisms and Society: Reclaiming the Sciences, the Family, and Education*, ed. Martin E. Marty and R. Scott Appleby (University of Chicago Press, 1993), p. 176.

[19] Abd al-Salam Farag, *Al-farida al-gha'iba [The absent obligation]* (Cairo: n.p., n.d.).

and informed will to act for the cause. This freedom of individual choice becomes explicit with the most modernist and liberal wing of Islamism, like the Tunisian Ahmida Enneifer. "It is difficult to say that because my father was a Muslim, I should be one," Ennefeir says, and quotes the Prophet in favor of the view that people must be left to choose their religious affiliation based on their own convictions.[20] Similar views can be found in the Turkish Welfare Party.[21] But also, within more "orthodox" Islamist circles like the Muslim Brothers, the idea of a choice is inherent in the very idea that it is not enough just to be a Muslim by tradition or family, nor even to perform the ritual duties, but that the believer's whole life in all its aspects should be devoted to the struggle for God's cause. Implicit in this idea is the centrality of an active individual stance. "Islam is the solution," and therefore people must choose it.

That something in the nature of individualization is indeed involved is born out by some other aspects of the movements we are discussing. There is first of all the idea of work as a calling, that the life of the believer should be filled with serious work, not with idle pastime. Time should be used in a purposeful and effective way. "A pervasive seriousness invaded the country," wrote Michael Walzer of the English Puritans of the 16th and 17th centuries,[22] but he could as well have been referring to Cairo's Islamists in the 1940s and again in the 1980s and 1990s.

Secondly, central to the work of the Islamists is a call for the impersonalization of public life, and springing from it an intense fight against corruption. They deplore the role of private interests in politics, and hold the view that people in public life must divest themselves of all personal feeling and private connections. We see how the Islamists are in the forefront in the struggle against the corrupt practices and attitudes permeating their societies. The main target of attack is the misuse of public office to further personal interests or those of individuals or groups close to the office holder. The Islamists condemn officials taking bribes and illegitimate charges for exercising their duties. Above all, they criticize the misappropriation of funds for buying votes, for paying commissions to cronies of people in office, or in awarding public contracts to other than the one presenting the best tender. Here can also be seen a modernizing aspect, for in many of its aspects current corruption is a continuation of time-honored practices that, until recent times, were seen as quite legitimate: the duty of individuals who gain influence and control over material resources to use their position for the benefit of their relatives, neighbors, friends, clients, or patrons. Now the Islamists denounce such practices as a sin, and those who practice them as those "corrupters of the earth,"

---

[20] François Burgat and William Dowell, *The Islamic Movement in North Africa* (Austin, TX: Center for Middle Eastern Studies, University of Texas at Austin, 1993), pp. 214–5.
[21] Banned in January 1998 and resurrected as the Virtue Party.
[22] Walzer, *The Revolution of the Saints*, p. 245.

al-mufsidun fi al-ard, condemned by the Quran. One might perhaps say that corruption thrives in the confrontation between the age-old social structures based on the reciprocal solidaric obligations of kinship and client networks, and the institutions of a modern market and a modern state. The Islamists seem not only in their campaigning against corruption, but also to the extent that they are involved in business, to favor a detached impersonal style focused on economic efficiency.[23]

Thirdly, in line with this they argue for the establishment of merit as the prime or sole criterion for promotion to posts of responsibility within society. No more should rank be inherited. This was an important novel feature of the Muslim Brothers when they appeared on the Egyptian scene in the 1930s. Always clever tacticians, as they spread through Egyptian towns and villages in the 1930s, they created honorific committees where local notables sympathetic to the cause were accorded prominence, but in the real leadership structures promotion was always based on merit. In fact, part of the attraction of the Brothers in an Egypt still controlled by the landowning elite was the fact that its ever-growing organization offered an alternative career path for talented youngsters without the right family background and connections.

Together, these aspects of Islamism work to open the road for the idea of individual career, individual life projects. This has been shown to be a characteristic setting young Islamist students in the 1980s off from their parent generation.[24] It means that the choice of partner and line of work is something the young Islamists expect to do for themselves and not to be decided by the family or some other communal entity.

At the same time, the Islamist movements represent and promote new forms of association and relations of solidarity. They share a strong involvement in social and charitable activities. Since early in the 20th century, and especially in the last fifteen years or so, a plethora of Islamic organizations have provided health care, education, and disaster relief along with religious preaching to the increasing number of millions squeezed between economic processes destroying their traditional livelihood and government retrenchment, especially after the fall in the price of oil in the mid-1980s.

The recruitment to Islamist organizations has not come primarily from those groups made most miserable by the social changes underway. Rather, the cadres come from middle and aspiring groups with a triple anxiety: fear

---

[23] Nefissa N. A. Naguib, "Men of Commitment. An Anthropological Study about Top Norwegian Business Executives" (thesis for the Cand. Polit. Degree, University of Oslo, 1989), p. 105.

[24] Marit Tjomsland, " 'The Educated Way of Thinking': Individualisation and Islamism in Tunisia," in *State and Locality*, ed. Mette Masst, Thomas Hylland Eriksen, and Jo Helle-Valle (Oslo: Center for Development and the Environment, University of Oslo, 1994), p. 142.

of social chaos threatening their as yet precarious position and property, unsettledness at the new environment they are moving into through their social ascent, and anger at the obstacles presented by the power monopoly of the established culturally and politically dominant groups.

Religious associations are assuring brother (and sister) hood and religion as a political weapon to establish social order (also through the positive means of charity) and as a sword wielded against the decadent upper class. Some *ulama* played a role in these developments, but in the Middle East emerging from the colonial period in the 20th century, as well as in similar Christian movements in early modern Europe, the central factor was the new class of educated laymen. Michael Walzer wrote of 17th-century England:

Puritanism was … the religion of men newly come to the city, uneasy there, not yet urbane, not yet sharing the sophistication of the town dweller or courtier. Such men, disoriented and unsure of themselves responded to the intense moralism of the clerical saints: at the same time the congregational discipline taught them an urban style, provided new standards of order and a new routine, set them apart from the motley population of the expanding city, and eventually produced a new self-confidence.[25]

With the changing of a few words he could have been writing of the Egyptian cities in the 20th century, where an educational explosion thrust aspiring youth by the tens of thousands into the universities. Studies of Islamist organizations have shown that their main recruiting ground is found among students with lower middle-class backgrounds, often first or second-generation city dwellers.

Some have analyzed so-called religious fundamentalism in general and Islamism in particular as a reaction against the increasing differentiation of society brought on by modernization. As the number of distinct positions and vocations increases, social interaction becomes more complex, and the solid social and moral universe of traditional society is broken up. This creates fear and uncertainty, and "fundamentalism" is then supposedly an effort to reestablish a holistic order both on the ground and in heaven, as it were. This is hardly accurate. For one thing, one may discuss how free of fear the old social order really was. But more importantly, I would argue that if Islamism is a reaction it is a progressive one, a step forward into something new, not trying to reverse social developments, but rather to adapt religion so that it enables people to cope with the new realities. It promotes an Islam that does not try to remove the causes of the new fear, but to address them. For instance, the fact of women moving and working outside the home in an urban setting where they interact with men they are not related to was largely unknown in the old days. As women increasingly took up studies and work, especially in the expanding bureaucracies of the modernizing

---

[25] Walzer, *The Revolution of the Saints*, p. 243.

states, they were therefore open to criticism for un-Islamic and immoral behavior. This could conceivably be met in two ways: through an open break with religious tradition, or through a renewal from within the religious universe, through a rereading and reinterpretation of the Quran and Sunnah to create a new model of a pious working woman. The result can be observed in Middle Eastern cities and universities in the form of the ubiquitous *muhajjabat*, women, mostly young, covering their hair with a headscarf and dressing in loose robes designed to hide the contours of the body. They present themselves as decent women through their wearing of the *hijab* (headscarf), while insisting on their right to mobility, study, and work. Although they acknowledge that men and women are complementary rather than equal, and that men have a certain right of leadership within the family, they insist that ultimately their loyalty is to God only, thereby establishing for themselves a platform for independent action not part of the traditional image of the relationship between the sexes.

Politics for the many

Moving to the more directly political aspects of Islamist activity it is, of course, a moot question whether there is a necessary link between modernity and democracy. But modernity in the political sphere certainly has to do with increased mobilization of the population, with the drawing of wider circles into participation in the political process. This development takes place in interaction with the increasing centrality of the state and the reduction of autonomous power centers outside it. On these scores our Islamist activists also clearly come out on the modernizing side.

Modern mass politics is characterized by a number of new methods such as free assembly, mass petition, group pressure, appeal to public opinion, and not least the political association of men and women not connected by kinship or other primordial ties of loyalty for the purposive furtherance of political change. Although the Islamists might not be the very first to use such techniques in the Middle Eastern Muslim countries, it was certainly the Muslim Brothers in Egypt who in the 1930s and 1940s for the first time drew people by the hundreds of thousands and from the lower middle and working classes into this kind of political work. Thereby they clearly represented a break with politics as the business of alliances of big landowners with their entourage of intellectuals. For the first time, elements of the new literate groups produced by modern education emerged as a political force in their own right and as leaders of broad mass movements.

Closely related is the challenge Islamism has represented to social and clerical hierarchy. At times explicitly, but always implicitly, by force of their activity, Islamist movements made political and religious matters the responsibility of people outside the ruling classes. As in yesterday's European Protestant movements lay men (and some women) would read and interpret the holy texts in a manner hitherto unheard of. The Muslim Brothers launched their own interpretation of Islam, quite distinct from that held by the dominant theological institution of al-Azhar. In theory and practice they challenged the power monopoly of the established ruling classes.

For certain, to put it modestly, not all Islamists have been democrats and, still less, tolerant liberals. But too often we tend to think of the development of democracy, tolerance, and secularism in Western societies as a smooth process, which it was definitely not, and it cannot be expected to be so elsewhere. To the extent that the Islamists represent part of such a process, it is clear that in theory and above all in practice they have often tended to totalitarian and dictatorial views and practices.

Nevertheless, there is at present, significantly, a pronounced tendency within mainstream movements towards a principled advocacy of parliamentary democracy, political pluralism, and power rotation through popular elections. In 1994, the Muslim Brothers in Egypt published a declaration on the principle of *shura* (consultation in state matters), which goes a long way towards identifying this Quranic (and indeed pre-Islamic) term with popular sovereignty and representative democracy. The declaration states that "the people are the source of political power," and that they must elect through free and fair elections "a representative assembly possessing effective legislative and supervisory authority." For the purpose of creating a just system of government the people must decide upon a written constitution securing a balance between the different institutions of the state.

There are limits to this democracy in that the constitution must be built upon the Shariah. But the Brothers acknowledge that there is an act of human interpretation involved. The constitution, they say, must build first upon the unequivocal texts of the Quran and the Sunnah, thereafter on the "intentions and general principles of the Shariah." It is significant in this regard that the declaration emphasizes that questions of law and political decisions which are subject to human interpretation (*ijtihad*) or which fall within the scope of the permitted (*al-mubah*), that is, where the choice of a particular decision is neutral *vis-à-vis* the Shariah, will constitute the bulk of the affairs dealt with by the popular assembly. From this they draw the conclusion that disagreement and debate is not only natural, but also indispensable in order to reach the decision most socially beneficial, especially if the debate is characterized by "tolerance, breadth of vision, and the absence of fanaticism." This leads the Brothers to the view that the Islamic society needs to practice a multi-party system, and they oppose any conditions imposed by the future Islamic state on the free formation of parties and associations.[26]

---

[26] The Muslim Brothers, "Mujaz 'an al-shura fi al-islam [Brief statement on consultation in Islam]," *al-Shaab*, May 19, 1994. For similar views expressed by Islamists, cf. Rashid Ghannushi, "The Participation of Islamists in a non-Islamic Government," in *Power-sharing Islam?* ed. Azzam Tamimi (London: Liberty for Muslim World Publications, 1993), and 'Isam Al-'Iryan, "The Future of power-sharing in Egypt." Ibid.

At a deeper level, it could be argued that a prerequisite for a well-functioning democratic and pluralistic society is the internalization of social mores by individual citizens. Writing of England, Michael Walzer noted that according to the Puritans discipline was to be "voluntary but socially enforced," and that a tense mutual watchfulness characterized the saints and their followers. Nevertheless, Walzer stressed that the Puritans' insistence on the fostering of self-discipline was vitally conducive to the relatively peaceful development towards greater democracy in England:

The same fearfulness of social chaos felt by the Puritans ... set off the Hobbesian search for absolute power. ... Puritans searched instead for obedient and conscientious subjects ... and it was part of their success in finding such men that made Hobbesian power unnecessary in England.[27]

Where Hobbes thought that social order would have to be enforced from above by a despotic ruler, the Puritans sought to groom the conscience of the individual believer for this task.

The Puritan duality of law and conscience as enforcer of public morality is found also with the Islamists. According to Sayyid Qutb, for instance, Islam has a double approach to securing social justice: through refining the conscience of the individual, and through the constraints and directions of the Shariah. An example of this is the issue of almsgiving. Islam has fixed a tax, the *zakat*, to be paid from income and capital to the benefit of the poor, as one of the central duties of being a Muslim, one of the five pillars of Islam. Paying this tax is also in this way considered a part of the act of worship.[28] The *zakat* is a duty and the authorities have the legal power to enforce its payment, but the aim is to make it an act of conscience, or a thing that becomes natural.[29] Despite the dualism involved, according to Andrea Rugh, Islamism is significantly contributing to a shift in Muslim society "from external means of controlling individual morality to internal self-monitoring controls."[30] It is an explicit hope for Islamists that Islam should become that moral force needed to unite the people for the sustained effort and suffering without which the aspirations of economic development will remain unfulfilled, and indispensable in order to avoid social explosion in the process.

But certainly, part of the modernizing aspect of Islamism is also its emphasis on the state. Above we saw how Islamists and Puritans have in

---

27 Walzer, *The Revolution of the Saints*, p. 204.

28 When the Shariah is discussed it is common to draw a distinction between on the one hand the *'ibadat*, rules concerning the relations between human beings and their creator, that is, required acts of worship, and on the other, the *mu'amalat*, regulating the relations between human beings.

29 Sayyid Qutb, *Al-'adala al-ijtima'iyya fi al-islam [Social justice in Islam]* (Cairo: Dar al-Shuruq, 1989), pp. 87–8.

30 Rugh, "Reshaping Personal Relations in Egypt," p. 167.

common the view that hand in hand with the individual responsibility to fight for good against evil, there must go the responsibility of the state to enforce God's will. Islamists are certainly critical of the totalitarian power of the state. Nevertheless, it is a crucial feature of their ideology, setting them off from Islamic reform movements of earlier times, that the virtuous society they seek can only come about through the agency of an Islamic state. This becomes clear if we look at their central demand, which is for the reintroduction of the Islamic law, the Shariah, as supreme law. It is important to notice that for the Islamists this involves the codification of the Shariah into modern law texts by an elected assembly. This is something very different from the traditional situation where the Shariah was nothing but the Quran and the Sunnah (the example of the Prophet as recorded in collections of stories about his words and deeds) as interpreted by experts on religious law. The Islamist version of the Shariah ties it to the state and its judicial bureaucracy, and to the representatives of the people, rather than to the religious class, the *ulama*.

Even in the special case of Iran, where the Islamist revolution of 1979 brought the men of traditional religious learning into power, the same change is in evidence. For while the *ayatollahs* and *hojjatoleslams* were traditionally able to influence events through an autonomy based on control of local fiefs involving the income from huge tracts of land and networks of clients, in the new Islamic Iran they wield power only in so far as they have gained positions within the state. And they have continued the expansion of the centralized state begun under the Pahlavi shahs, to the effect of undermining any prospect of regaining their traditional autonomous position, as they are now gradually losing their grip on the levers of the state.

A modernizing force

If we try to place Islamism in historical perspective, we might then want to see it as a modernizing force on several counts.

Islamists have been insistent advocates of technological and economic development. But, as importantly, they have been actively promoting values and attitudes favorable to modernizing change. Not least important in this respect is their fight for the impersonalization of politics (and business) and their striving for the idea of work as a calling. This is closely related to the individualizing aspect of their ideology which I have pointed to, and which also represents a clear break with traditional society. They have contributed in important ways to make politics a business for people outside the old "political classes" of notables and *ulama* and outside the new state elites. This is a crucial democratizing step in and of itself, and it certainly works to prepare the ground for the development of democracy. The same can be said about their constant emphasis on the furthering of education, and their promotion of new political techniques, preparing the ground for mass politics. On the more immediate level, many Islamist movements are involved in a bitter struggle for the establishment of democratic rules in a region dominated by authoritarian regimes, and increasingly they move towards a principled defense of popular sovereignty and political pluralism legitimated by references to the holy scriptures of Islam.

Where is Islamism leading? Modernization in itself is neither good nor evil. Hitler's Nazi regime probably had as many modernizing aspects as post-war Scandinavian social democracy. Will Islamism be the mainstay of totalitarian dictatorship or will it speed a process towards pluralism or even secularism? Here speculation takes over, but some indications can be found by briefly considering a central aspect of Islamism that I have barely touched on above: its quest for cultural authenticity as a shield against Western domination. Having an arch-enemy may at times be a deadly relationship, but it is always a strong one, and long-time enemies often come to resemble one another; in particular the weaker part consciously or unconsciously tends to learn from the stronger. If Islamists insist (though not exclusively) on tapping the rich reservoir of the Islamic heritage for symbols and concepts to formulate their ideology, and dispensing with Western linguistic imports, their discourse is still structured by that of the enemy. Being the first modernizer, it is the West which has formulated answers to the challenges posed by modernity. And since Islamists do not intend to dismantle modernity but to Islamize it, to create an alternative modernity, as it were, they must answer the same challenges and provide alternative answers to those of the West. These are questions of economic development, of social welfare, of gender relations, of democracy, and of human rights. It is interesting then to notice that what often seems to be happening is that in important fields Islamist solutions come to resemble closely ideas known from Western societies, but expressed through an Islamic idiom and legitimized with references to the Quran and the Sunnah. To give but one example, the Quranic principle of consultation in state matters, known as *shura*, is now, as discussed above, interpreted by many Islamist groups as almost the equivalent of parliamentary democracy.

Indeed, despite their programmatic effort to establish distance from the West and Western ideas, the Islamist attitude is not unambiguous. A whole range of ideas and values propagated by the Islamists have a Western heritage, or at least a well-established Western counterpart, and more often than not aspects of Western society are used explicitly as positive models of emulation. Even the choice of alternative "Islamic" terms in discussing socio-economic issues is not consequent.

When the Islamists encourage the believers to a purposeful use of their time, they echo the Western ethos of work and efficiency with roots back to early-modern Christian Protestant movements. The call for impersonal relations to dominate in public and market affairs has the same resonance in the West. When Yusuf Kamal talks of the advantages of the free movement of supply and demand in order to set commodity prices he is spreading ideas of a Western origin, no less than Adil Husayn when he is discussing the vices of a dependent economic relation *vis-à-vis* the West.[31] Not least, the very focus on the need for rapid economic development has as its starting point a wish to emulate the West in this regard, to "join the developed world," as a leading figure in the Egyptian Labor party, Muhammad Hilmi Murad, once expressed it.[32]

More explicitly, Western society is praised for its strong emphasis on productivity and on education, and for the way the rich voluntarily contribute to social redistribution through the tax system, because they grasp that it is in their own interest to do so. Often Western economic theorists of diverse persuasions are quoted approvingly in support of one argument or another.

Finally, although Islamist discourse on economic questions is interspersed with positive and negative terms from the Quran, Sunnah, and more broadly from Islamic history (*riba, zakat, fasad* (wrongdoing, corruption), *muhtasib* (the powerful market inspector), etc.), overwhelmingly the conceptual apparatus consists of Arabic, Persian, or Turkish translations for the terminology used in Western (including Marxist) economic theory. Sometimes we may even see how distinctly Islamic terms with an original set of connotations are used by the Islamists in a manner that nearly reduces them to translations for modern Western-originated phenomena: witness how *riba* comes to mean interest.

We should remind ourselves here that, as Fouad Ajami has noted, when people struggling against Western domination are "busy trying to revalidate once-discredited traditions and revive once-forgotten symbols," they tend to simultaneously "embrace the dominant model for fear of being left behind and denounce it to affirm their uniqueness at the moment that they feel swept by the current."[33] Discussing "Orientalism-in-reverse," Mehrzad Boroujerdi writes that "even in their newly acquired capacity as speakers, authors and actors the 'Orientals' continue to be overdetermined by the occidental listener, text and audience."[34]

The contradictory situation of simultaneous rapid change and frenetic appeals to an "authentic" past is nicely portrayed in a passage from Karl Marx, who wrote that:

[just when people] seem engaged in revolutionising themselves and things, in creating something entirely new, precisely in such epochs of revolutionary crisis they

---

[31] Notwithstanding the important contribution of many non-Western scholars to the criticism of modernization theory.

[32] Muhammad Hilmi Murad, "Al-mashakil madrusa wal-hulul ma'rufa [The problems have been studied and the solutions are known]," *al-Shaab*, Jan. 20, 1987.

[33] Fouad Ajami, *The Arab Predicament: Arab Political Thought and Practice since 1967* (Cambridge University Press, 1992), p. 208.

[34] Mehrzad Boroujerdi, *Iranian Intellectuals and the West: The Tormented Triumph of Nativism* (Syracuse University Press, 1996), p. 13.

anxiously conjure up the spirits of the past to their service and borrow from them names, battle slogans and costumes in order to present the new scene of world history in this time-honoured disguise and this borrowed language. Thus Luther donned the mask of the Apostle Paul, the Revolution of 1789 to 1814 draped itself alternately as the Roman Republic and the Roman Empire, and the Revolution of 1848 knew nothing better to do than to parody, in turn, 1789 and the revolutionary tradition of 1793 to 1795. In like manner the beginner who is learning a new language always translates it back into his mother tongue[.][35]

Marx's comment may be overly disparaging in tone, but it grasps well how new ideas and practices are given legitimacy and positive value through being identified with known phenomena in a glorious past.

The very fact that the animosity exhibited by the Islamists towards the West and its intellectual products is not unambiguous may be taken as an indication that there are other things at stake here besides cultural nationalism. To put it in a more circumspect way, the struggle for national independence, whether at the economic, political, or cultural level, never takes place in a social vacuum. It is always intertwined with struggles that are internal to the society which seeks independence.

In the case of Islamism, I would argue that there is a strong socio-religious impulse behind it parallel to the politico-cultural one. It could be seen as a fight for empowering that part of the educated middle and lower middle classes fostered in an environment dominated by the indigenous symbolic universe of Islam. Islamism is in a sense the Islam of precisely these groups. As such it is an effort at creating a new moral order, not to stop the changes underway, but rather to promote them while at the same time subjecting them to a set of ethical rules. This effort may well be setting in motion processes of getting to grasp with the problems of the real world, hitherto impeded by the insulation of "tradition" from the realm of power and policymaking. Such processes would be accentuated and accelerated by the fact of Islamists actually acceding to power as in Iran since 1979, and they may well be seen to open up, as it were, the ideas of broad layers of the population to modernity.

My contention is that Islamism should be seen properly not only as a product of the changes and conflicts wrought by modernizing economic and social processes, but as an important modernizing agent within current Middle Eastern society. It is important to grasp the difference between a handful of landowners discussing liberal Western ideas in the 1930s while conducting politics in the time-honored ways of alliance and intrigue involving traditional clans and families, and, on the other hand, the current unpolished bearded activists calling for the reintroduction of the Shariah, but organizing their political work in thoroughly modern ways, and legitimating these ways with reference to the religion which is still the final criterion of good and evil for the broad millions. The former may *sound* modern, the latter *are* so.

[35] Karl Marx, "The Eighteenth Brumaire of Louis Bonaparte," quoted here from Ajami, *The Arab Predicament*, p. 214.

3

ISLAM AND CIVIL SOCIETY

John L. Esposito

The post-Cold War period has been one of civil disorder and of civil order. It has witnessed calls for a New World Order and signs of a New World Disorder. If Bosnia, Algeria, Chechnya, Afghanistan, Kosovo, Rwanda have reminded us of the breakdown of the state and of civil society, South Africa and the new democracies of Latin America have signaled that a true civil society with representative government can emerge in areas where once authoritarian governments with elaborate state security systems appeared to prove that "might made right." Yet, in many parts of the Muslim world, civil society and democratization are under siege or in retreat. If some blame Islamic governments (Sudan, Afghanistan, and until recently Iran) and Islamist movements, others cite the intransigence of authoritarian states and the military (Algeria, Turkey, Tunisia) to tolerate and abide by the results of open electoral politics. At the same time, some political analysts and policymakers legitimate those who speak of an incompatibility of Islam and democracy or Islam and civil society, rooted in a clash of civilizational values.

A "selective" headline or crisis-oriented approach to Muslim politics, which focuses on the acts of extremists, from hostages and kidnappings in the Middle East, New York's World Trade Center bombing, and Osama Bin Laden's support for global terrorism, has too often provided the lens through which Islam and Muslim politics have been regarded. Islam and all Islamic movements are identified with violence and religious extremism, leading some to speak of an Islamic Threat or a "clash of civilizations" between the Muslim world and the West.[1] This perspective has become the convenient excuse for some in the West to equate Islam and Muslim civilization with authoritarianism or to declare that Islam and

---

[1] For a discussion of this issue, see Bernard Lewis, "The Roots of Muslim Rage," *Atlantic Monthly* 226:3, Sept. 1990; Samuel P. Huntington, "The Clash of Civilizations," *Foreign Affairs*, Summer 1993; John L. Esposito, *The Islamic Threat: Myth or Reality?* 3rd edn. (New York: Oxford University Press, 1999), ch. 6, which has been a major source for this analysis.

democracy are incompatible. Some Muslim rulers in the post-Gulf War period have used the threat of religious extremism to renege on promises of greater political liberalization, to repress mainstream Islamic movements, and to limit the development of civil society.

Islam, democracy and civil society

At the dawn of the 21st century, democratization and civil society are common themes throughout much of the world. From the former Soviet Union and Eastern Europe to the Middle East, Asia, and Africa, voices have been raised that call for power-sharing (greater political participation, representation, and self-determination) and with it more emphasis on government accountability, the rule of law, and social justice. Non-state actors and organizations (NGOs), from political parties and trade unions to professional associations, educational, financial, and medical services, women's and human rights organizations, have become more visible.

Religion has been a significant factor in the reassertion of civil society in many Muslim societies. The creation of modern (and often authoritarian) states in the Muslim world, which extend governmental control over state and society and over religion and religious institutions, as well as the tendency to regard civil society as a modern construct, have often obscured the existence of civil society in Islam. Islamic history provides examples of many non-state actors, institutions, and organizations that served as intermediaries between the ruler/government and the people, between state and society. Religious endowments (*waqf,* pl. *awqaf*) supported schools, universities, hostels, hospitals, and social welfare activities. The development of Islamic law (*Shariah*) itself was often the product of private individuals or scholars (*ulama*) and schools (*madhab,* pl. *madhahib*) that were independent of the state and indeed initially sought to limit and curb the power of rulers. Sufi brotherhoods (*tariqahs*) and masters (*shaykhs* or *pirs*) provided not only spiritual guidance, but also significant educational and social services in Muslim societies. Finally, guilds played an important role in the economic and social life of Muslim cities. Professional groups or guilds were organized around trade and commerce. Their activities included "regulating the production of goods, maintaining a professional code of ethics, overseeing prices."[2] Guilds often relied upon religion and religious rituals for rites of initiation and celebration and to legitimate their origins and activities, such as that of the market supervisor (*muhtasib*) who was responsible for the enforcement (*hisbah*) of public morals.

---

[2] André Raymond, "Guilds," in *The Oxford Encyclopedia of the Modern Islamic World,* ed. John L. Esposito (New York: Oxford University Press, 1995), Vol. III, p. 73.

Contemporary Muslim politics

In the contemporary Muslim world, Islam has become closely associated with the emergence or expansion of civil society. While some Islamic activists and movements have sought to destroy or overthrow the state, many have commandeered or championed the institutions of civil society. Proclaiming Islam as the solution to the political and socio-economic ills of their societies, Islamists have often constituted both an ideological alternative and, on the ground, a state within the state. They have not only challenged but also concretely responded to the failures and inadequacies of governments and elites by creating alternative non-governmental political, economic, and social welfare associations and institutions. Across the Muslim world, Islamically oriented political parties, professional associations, social welfare agencies, and educational and financial institutions have proliferated in Egypt, Algeria, Lebanon, Jordan, Palestine, Turkey, Pakistan, India, Bangladesh, Malaysia, and Indonesia.

Given the historic significance and centrality of Islam in Muslim life and its continued presence and vitality in Muslim societies, the relationship of Islam to democratization and civil society is both a timely and an important issue.

Islam and the modern state

For decades, analysis and understanding of the development of societies has been seen in terms of the modern state: its boundaries, legitimacy, institutions, and functions. The modern state has been exemplified by its growing power, control, and centralization as the state absorbed or extended its power and influence to outlaw or control the institutions of civil society. Authoritarian rulers have used the modern state to control both politics and society.

In recent years, social scientists and political analysts have debated the future of the nation state. Modern states and rulers have been challenged by opposition movements. Many are states, relatively recently created (post-Second World War), with artificial boundaries, often a legacy of European colonialism, whose rulers have tenuous legitimacy and are dependent for their stability on their military and secret police. Religious (nationalist and sectarian), ethnic, and tribal warfare in Sudan, Bosnia-Herzegovina, Kosovo, Chechnya, Afghanistan, Pakistan, Kashmir, and the Central Asian republics have provided shocking examples of the fragility of the modern state.

Increasingly in recent years, analysis of Muslim societies, their problems and future, has been placed within the framework of civil society and democratization. The breakup of the Soviet Union and liberation of Eastern Europe and events within the Muslim world have led to a heated debate over the political future and possibilities of Muslim communities and societies. Both in the Muslim world and in the West, issues of the compatibility of Islam and democracy, of political participation, pluralism, women's rights, and tolerance are discussed and contested.

The challenge of Islamic revivalism

Despite significant differences, the resurgence of Islam as a significant socio-political alternative reveals common causes and concerns. Among the more significant are: the failure of secular nationalism (liberal nationalism, Arab nationalism, and socialism) to provide a strong sense of national identity; the need for independence from foreign influence and hegemony; and the ability to produce strong and prosperous societies. Governments (most of which are non-elected, authoritarian, "security states") have failed to establish or strengthen their political legitimacy. They have been criticized by opposition voices for a failure to achieve economic self-sufficiency or prosperity, to stem the growing gap between rich and poor, to halt widespread corruption, liberate Palestine, resist Western political and cultural hegemony. Both the political and religious establishments have been criticized: the former as a minority of western, secular elites more concerned with power and privilege, and, in the Sunni Muslim world, the latter (the ulama) as a religious leadership coopted by governments who often support and control mosques, religious universities and institutions.

Political Islam is in many ways the successor of failed nationalist programs. They included: the failure of Arab nationalism/socialism, signaled by the 1967 Six Day Arab-Israeli war, and of Muslim nationalism in the Pakistan-Bangladesh civil war of 1971; the shattering of the Lebanese confessional mosaic by its civil war (mid-1970s to 1990); and economic failures in North Africa, Egypt, Turkey, and Jordan in the late1980s and early 1990s. Many founders of Islamic movements were formerly participants in nationalist movements: the Egyptian Muslim Brotherhood's founder, Hasan al-Banna, Tunisia's Rashid Ghannoushi of the Renaissance Party (Ennahda), Algeria's Abbasi Madani of the Islamic Salvation Front (FIS), and Necmettin Erbakan of Turkey's Refah (Welfare) Party.

Islamic movements have offered an Islamic solution, a third alternative to capitalism and communism. They argue that a modern Western bias or orientation, secularism and dependence on Western models of development, have proven politically inadequate and socially corrosive, undermining the identity and moral fabric of Muslim societies. Islamists assert that Islam is not just a collection of beliefs and ritual actions, but a comprehensive ideology or framework for Muslim society. Islam embraces personal as well as public life. Islamists call for the implementation of Islamic law, the Shariah, as the comprehensive blueprint for society. While the majority seek to work within the system, to bring about change from within society, a small but significant minority believe that they have a mandate from God and that the rulers in the Muslim world are anti-Islamic. They seek to topple governments, seize power, and impose their vision or interpretation of Islam upon society.

Islamic movements have been particularly strong among the younger generation, university graduates and young professionals, and the lower middle class. They recruit from mosques and universities, finding fertile ground among the politically and economically disenfranchised or oppressed. Contrary to popular expectations, their strength is not in the religious faculties and humanities so much as in science, engineering, education, law, and medicine. Organizations like the Egyptian Muslim Brotherhood of Egypt, Jordan, Kuwait, and Sudan, Turkey's Refah (Welfare) Party (and now Virtue or Fazilet), Tunisia's Ennahda, South Asia's Jamaat-i-Islami, Malaysia's Islamic Youth Movement (ABIM), or Indonesia's Muhammadiya consist in great part of university graduates and professionals. Dr. Hassan al-Turabi, leader of Sudan's National Islamic Front, holds a doctorate in law from the Sorbonne. The senior leadership of Egypt's Muslim Brotherhood includes judges, lawyers, and physicians. The FIS's Abbasi Madani earned a doctorate in education from a British university. Seventy-six percent of the FIS candidates in municipal and parliamentary elections held post-graduate degrees. Dr. Necmettin Erbakan, leader of the now-suppressed Refah Party, is a German-trained engineer. Amien Rais, former leader of Indonesia's Muhammadiya and now Speaker of parliament, and Nurcholish Madjid, leader of Paramedina (an intellectual reform organization) hold doctorates from Cornell and the University of Chicago respectively. Similar comments could be made about the leadership of many other Islamic organizations.

In general, most Islamic movements are urban-based, and draw heavily from lower middle and middle classes. A major portion of their leadership and membership are middle-class professionals as well as the economically deprived. In the past, financial support has come from individuals within countries and from governments such as Saudi Arabia, Libya, Iran, and the Gulf States. In many Muslim countries and societies today, an alternative elite exists, modern educated but more self-consciously Islamically oriented and committed to social and political activism as a means for creating a more Islamic society or system of government. This social phenomenon is reflected in civil society by the presence and often dominance of Islamists in professional syndicates or associations of lawyers, engineers, professors, and physicians. Where permitted to live and participate in society, they are found in every sector of society: government, the professions, and even the military. Thus, they provide an avowedly "Islamic alternative" to the power and privilege of more secular elites.

Democracy and civil society in the Muslim world

As in many other parts of the world, including the former Soviet Union, Eastern Europe, Latin America, and Africa until recently, the history of the modern Muslim world reveals a majority of authoritarian regimes. The Muslim experience has been one of kings, military, and ex-military rulers possessing tenuous legitimacy and propped up by their military and security forces. Indeed, the states of the Middle East are commonly referred to as security (*mukhabarat*) states. At best, many have been authoritarian states with democratic facades; parliamentary institutions and political parties that existed at the sufferance of rulers. At the same time, militant Islamic movements have often projected a religious authoritarianism and political intolerance of divergent viewpoints which parallels that of secular authoritarianism. Yet, in recent years, the call for greater liberalization and democratization has become common and widespread. Throughout much of the Muslim world diverse sectors of society, secular and religious, leftist and rightist, educated and uneducated, increasingly use greater political participation or democratization as the litmus test by which to judge the legitimacy of governments and political movements alike.

Despite this reality, there are those who have increasingly charged that the absence of democracy is due to peculiar characteristics of Arab and Muslim culture. Some maintain that Arab culture and/or Islam are inherently authoritarian and thus incompatible with democracy. Others assert that the introduction of democracy is premature. Still others believe that democracy is a product of the Western experience that may well be inappropriate or non-transferable to other cultures.[3]

The movement for democratization in the Muslim world has raised widespread discussion about the future of democracy in the Muslim world and the creation or promotion of civil society. Many Muslim countries, in common with other developing societies, face serious obstacles to the creation of strong civil societies: authoritarian governments whose legitimacy and stability are often dependent upon security forces; economic underdevelopment (chronic unemployment, lack of adequate housing); ethnic and regional strife (often a legacy of the artificial borders created by colonial powers); weak institutions and infrastructures.

---

[3] For a sampling of these positions, see Bernard Lewis, "Islam and Liberal Democracy," *Atlantic Monthly*, Feb. 1993; Samuel Huntington, "Will More Countries Become Democratic," *Political Science Quarterly* 99:2, Sept. 1984; and Martin Kramer "Islam vs. Democracy," *Commentary*, Jan. 1993. For a critical analysis of many of these positions, see Yahya Sadowski, "The New Orientalism and the Democracy Debate," *Middle East Report*, Jul.–Aug. 1993.

The quiet revolution: Islam and civil society

The specter of "other Irans" or of extremist/terrorist groups were the dominant images of Muslim politics in the 1980s. However, in the late 1980s and 1990s the presence of a more nuanced, broader-based, diverse reality, became increasingly evident. Civic institutions such as associations of professionals (journalists, physicians, engineers, university professors), human rights and women's organizations, and political parties sprang up across the Muslim world. Beneath the radical monolithic facade, the world of small marginalized groups of extremists on the periphery of society, a quiet social and political revolution had taken place. While a militant rejectionist minority had sought to impose change from above through violent revolution or holy wars, many other Islamic activists actualized and institutionalized their faith through a bottom-up approach. They pursued a gradual transformation, Islamization or re-Islamization, of society through words and example, as well as social and political activism.

The comprehensive vision of Islamic renewal or reawakening, from its early trailblazers, Hasan al-Banna's Muslim Brotherhood and Mawlana Mawdudi's Jamaat-i Islami, to contemporary movements, is the desire to reassert Islam in cultural, social, and economic life. As a result, Islamic activists and organizations have in fact trained in the professions, participated in professional associations, and created educational, financial, cultural, and social institutions and associations. Thus, the majority of activists have not been trained in seminaries (*madrasas*) to be formal religious scholars (*ulama*) but are graduates of universities trained in the professions: from teaching, engineering, and law to medicine, mass communications, and computer science.

In many Muslim countries, Islamic organizations and associations have become part and parcel of the mainstream, institutional forces in civil society. They have attracted members from the middle and lower middle classes (businessmen, bureaucrats, doctors, engineers, lawyers, journalists) and revenue from non-governmental domestic sources, as well as members working in the oil rich countries of the Gulf and Iraq. They have engaged in a broad range of social and political activities, from the creation of Islamic charitable associations (*jamiyyat khayriyyah*) to participation in parliamentary and professional association elections. Their network of mosques, hospitals, clinics, day care centers, youth clubs, legal aid societies, foreign language schools, banks, drug rehabilitation programs, and publishing houses have multiplied. Islamic private volunteer organizations (PVOs) have filled a void and thus are, in some countries, an implicit critique of the government's ability to provide adequate services, in particular for the non-elite sectors of society. Their services provide an alternative to expensive private institutions or overcrowded public facilities. At the same time, they reinforce a sense of community identity as well as spiritual and moral renewal. Thus, for example, as will be discussed more extensively below, the educational and social programs of the Muslim Brotherhood in Egypt, the Islamic Salvation Front in Algeria and the Refah Party in Turkey were an integral part of their activities. They not only provided services, but also mobilized popular support and loyalty that could be translated into votes. Militant resistance movements such as Lebanon's Hezbollah and Hamas in Palestine strengthened their base of popular support and looked after the needs of their members and local citizens. Their combined political opposition and military action were augmented by substantial social services and charitable activities from education to housing and financial support for the families of members killed, wounded, or detained by authorities.

It is essential to note that many, if not most, Islamic organizations and NGOs are non-political and non-violent. Thus, in the West Bank and Gaza, hundreds of thousands of Palestinians have been the beneficiaries of services provided by Islamic social and economic institutions. Islamic associations have provided support for between 7,000–10,000 orphans, spending between $3–4 million annually for clothes, food, and school supplies, as well as services for approximately 5,000 families.[4] Hundreds of Islamic medical clinics in Egypt, ranging from two- to three-room clinics attached to a small mosque to major health care centers/hospitals such as the Mustapha Mahmud Islamic Clinic, have also been supported by religiously motivated individuals and organizations. Their primary concern has been the needs of Egypt's poor and middle class.

The creation of Islamically oriented institutions and the participation of religiously motivated Muslims (political and apolitical) in professional associations, private voluntary organizations, and corporate life have contributed to the gradual Islamization of society from below. A greater emphasis on Islamic discourse and symbolism as a source of legitimacy and authority is increasingly more evident throughout much of the Muslim world. This Islamization from below is not simply due to Islamist movements but also to the activity of Muslim professionals (physicians, psychiatrists, professors, lawyers, journalists, social workers), many of whom are apolitical, but committed to a more Islamically oriented community or society. Their support for religiously motivated projects (educational, medical, economic, social, and religio-cultural) is informed by faith not politics.

Social activism has also been accompanied by increased political participation. In Iran, Mehdi Bazargan, the Paris-educated engineer and intellectual who would go on to be Iran's first prime minister after the fall of the shah and return of Ayatollah Khomeini, had emphasized the Islamic character of his Association of Engineers and his Liberation Movement in

---

[4] Sara Roy, "Extremism and Civism," Grant Proposal, Appendix A, 14.

Iran. They joined with other professional associations, such as the Association of Iranian Journalists and National Organization of Physicians, as well as with clerical leaders to challenge the shah. In Tunisia and Algeria, the Islamic Tendency Movement (later renamed Ennahda) and the FIS moved from apolitical religio-cultural organizations to socio-political movements whose projects for the poor and disenfranchised won supporters from the poor and unemployed. Their promise of a more credible and effective alternative attracted the votes of those who simply wanted to register a vote against the policies of the ruling party. For many of the disenfranchised in Turkey, Refah's social programs in working class neighborhoods became reason enough to support it in municipal/local elections in 1994. Similarly, the effectiveness of Egypt's Muslim Brotherhood as a social and economic actor resulted in its emergence as a major social actor and opposition group in electoral politics. In the former Soviet Union, the Islamic Renaissance Party surfaced in the 1990s as a political opposition whose agenda included welfare services for the poor, private ownership of property, health programs, and ecological projects.[5]

Increased attention to social welfare has been incorporated into the redefinition or broadening of contemporary notions of *dawah*, religious propagation. The call (*dawah*) to Islam has increasingly become institutionalized, spawning modern organizations from Cairo to Kuala Lumpur. Moreover, many modern *dawah* organizations have not only called non-Muslims and Muslims to Islam but also become heavily involved in social welfare. ABIM in Malaysia, Diwan Dawat al-Islam in Indonesia, the World Assembly of Modern Youth (WAMY) in Saudi Arabia and the Ansar al-Islam in Nigeria reflect the combination of preaching with education, medical, and other social services. These organizations are transnational as well as national: among the more active are the World Muslim League and the International Islamic Council for Dawah and Relief, which has focused heavily on refugees.

Political participation and civil society

Throughout the 1980s, media images of radical Islamic fundamentalism had been accompanied by charges by many governments in the Muslim world that Islamic movements were simply violent revolutionaries, unrepresentative extremist organizations whose lack of popular support would be evident if elections were held. However, few governments proved willing to test that claim. When political systems were opened up and Islamic organizations were able to participate in elections, the results stunned many in the Muslim world and the West.

---

[5] Eden Naby, "Islamic Renaissance Party," in *The Oxford Encyclopedia of the Modern Islamic World*, vol. II, p. 311.

In the late 1980s and early 1990s, failed economies and mass demonstrations moved governments (Egypt, Algeria, Tunisia, Jordan) to hold elections. Islamic activists ran as candidates (Egypt and Tunisia refused to grant legal recognition as political parties to the Muslim Brotherhood and Ennahda respectively) and in some cases as political parties (Jordan and Algeria). In the post-Gulf War Kuwait and Yemen held elections and King Fahd of Saudi Arabia, after hesitant moves to create an appointed consultative council (*majlis al-shura*) to the king, continued to encounter demands for greater participation and government accountability.

The electoral track record of Islamic organizations and the diverse responses of governments to the emergence of Islamists as significant actors in civil society and in Muslim politics may be witnessed in a brief survey of Tunisia, Algeria, Turkey, Egypt, Iran, and the Gulf.

Tunisia. After seizing power from Bourghiba in 1987, Zein Abidine Ben Ali promised democratization and held parliamentary elections in April 1989. In early 1989, MTI had renamed itself Hizb al-Nahda (The Renaissance Party) in order to comply with Ben Ali's stated position that no single group should monopolize the claim to be Islamic since all Tunisians were Muslim. As one of its leaders had earlier declared, "[we] accepted the rules of the game ... we want to act within the framework of democracy."[6] Yet, in spite of this, the government did not permit it to participate as a legal political party. High inflation, growing unemployment, and increased poverty proved to be consequential: Islamic candidates won 14.5 percent of the vote nationwide and a stunning 30 percent in cities like Tunis, Gabes, and Sousse.

The Renaissance Party's early commitment to pluralist politics reflected the thinking of its leaders, in particular Rashid al-Ghannoushi. Al-Nahda's leaders combined the criteria of Islam with that of democracy to critique the Tunisian government and to serve as a platform in al-Nahda's appeal for popular support. For Ghannoushi, democracy, popular sovereignty and the role of the state multi-party elections, and constitutional law are all part of a "new Islamic thinking" whose roots and legitimacy are found in a fresh interpretation or reinterpretation of Islamic sources. He distinguished between God's sovereignty over the universe and the creation of the state, arguing that "The state is not something from God but from the people ... the state has to serve the benefit of the Muslims."[7]

Ghannoushi indicated his willingness to work within the legal framework to improve it by making it more democratic and pluralistic. He

---

[6] Interview with MTI member, July 21, 1989, Tunis.

[7] Interview with Rashid Ghannoushi, December 15, 1989, Wayland Mass. See also, Rashid Ghannoushi, *Fi al-mubadi al-Islamiyya li dimuqratiyya wa al-usul al-hukm al-Islamiyya* [The Islamic Principles of Democracy and Fundamentals of Islamic Government] (n.p. 1410/1990).

maintained that the parliamentary system was the legitimate means for universal participation in the political process through elections, one that fulfills the role of the Islamic institution of a consultative council (*majlis al-shura*).[8] Indeed he declared: "Islam, which enjoins the recourse to Shura (consultation) as a principle governing relations between political authority and the people, finds in democracy the appropriate instruments (elections, parliamentary system, separation of powers, etc.) to implement the Shura."[9] Ghannoushi maintained that the Quranic prescription or principle that there is no compulsion in religion was a sure basis for religious, cultural, political and ideological pluralism in Muslim society.[10]

In contrast to many other Islamic activists, Ghannoushi maintained that if the Tunisian people voted Nahda out of power in favor of even a communist or atheist government, then as good Muslims the party would have to accept the verdict of the people. He called upon the West to apply a similar standard of respect for the people's choice, chiding the West for not promoting its democratic ideals in the Muslim world: "While the West criticizes Islamic governments for not being democratic, it also supports governments who are not democratic and are keeping Islamic movements from developing their ideas.[11]

Algeria. Algeria, like Jordan, allowed Islamists to participate in electoral politics as political parties, not just as individual candidates. While the performance of Jordan's Muslim Brotherhood and other Islamists in winning 32 of 80 seats proved an unexpected surprise, the stunning electoral successes of Algeria's Islamic Salvation Front proved a decisive turning point.

Algeria had been dominated by a one party dictatorship, the National Liberation Front (FLN), for decades. Socialist and with a strong secular elite and feminist movement, few took Algeria's Islamic movement seriously. The government of Chadli Ben Jadid was faced with intractable economic difficulties, among them a 25 percent unemployment level, foreign debt of some $20 billion, and food shortages. Following bloody anti-government riots of October 1988, the government felt constrained to hold elections. Algeria, long regarded as one of the most monolithic, single-party political systems in the Arab world, held multi-party elections which included the FIS, North Africa's first legal Islamic political party, led by Shaykh Ali Abbasi al-Madani.

---

[8] Rashid Ghannoushi, "The Battle Against Islam," *Middle East Affairs Journal* 1:2, Winter 1992/1413, p. 5.

[9] Rashid Ghannoushi, "Islam and Democracy can be friends," *North African News*, Jan. 1992, p. 1 (excerpted from the *London Observer*, Jan. 19, 1992).

[10] Rashid Ghannoushi, "The Battle Against Islam," *Middle East Affairs Journal* 1:2, Winter 1992/1413, p. 7.

[11] Interview with Abdelfattah Mourou, July 23, 1989, Tunis.

Islamic groups had flourished as Algerian state socialism failed to resolve its social and economic problems. The FIS, with a national organization and an effective mosque and social welfare network, emerged as the largest of these groups and one of the strongest opposition parties. In the June 1990 municipal elections, the first multi-party election since independence in 1962, the FIS scored a stunning victory, capturing 54 percent of the vote, while the FLN garnered 34 percent. The victory of the FIS in municipal elections in 1990 sent a shock wave throughout the world. In the aftermath of elections, the government arrested FIS leaders, Abbasi Madani and Ali Belhadj, then cut off funds from the central government to municipalities which often crippled FIS officials' ability to provide services, and gerrymandered to redraw voting districts more favorably. Despite these precautions, the FLN failed to prevent the FIS from an even more stunning electoral sweep of parliamentary elections. Amidst the euphoria and celebration of Islamists within Algeria and across the Muslim world, the Algerian military intervened, forced the resignation of Algeria's president, arrested FIS leaders, imprisoned more than 10,000 in desert camps/prisons, and outlawed the FIS and seized its assets.

In the face of this repression much of the world stood silent. The conventional wisdom had been blind-sided. While most feared and were on their guard against "other Irans," the FIS victory in Algeria raised the specter of an Islamic movement coming to power not through violent revolution but through democratic elections. Ballots not bullets proved to be even more worrisome for many world leaders. The justification for acceptance of the Algerian military's seizure of power was the charge that the FIS merely wished to "hijack democracy;" that they really only believed in "One man, one vote, one time." The threat of violent revolutionary Islam was intensified by fear of the capture of power from within the political system.

Turkey. The seemingly inexplicable power of Islamists at the ballot box was reinforced in secular Turkey, long regarded as a paragon of Muslim secularism, the most secular of Muslim states. Refah won mayoral elections in 1994 in more than a dozen major cities, including Ankara and Istanbul. Refah had become an effective presence in civil society through its social service network, businesses, professional associations, and the media. As Turkish senior politicians squabbled and the West looked on, Refah, after winning 158 seats in the 550-seat National Assembly in parliamentary elections in December 1995, came to power at the head of a coalition government. Dr. Necmettin Erbakan become Turkey's first Islamist prime minister in its 45-year history.

Refah used democracy as a yardstick by which to judge the failures of Turkish secularism to be truly pluralistic, to respect the rights of all of its citizens, including their freedom of conscience or right to live according to their religious beliefs. Erbakan had maintained that true secularism (separation of religion from the state) should not only mean state autonomy but religious autonomy. That is, religion also has its autonomy that should be respected by and free from state interference. The state should not intervene in the religious sphere by attempting to regulate dress (the right of women to wear a headscarf or, for that matter, men to wear beards) or religious practice. Refah wished to add a new amendment regarding the definition of secularism to guarantee the right of all people to live in accordance with their religious beliefs. For Turkey's radical secularists, this stance was regarded as a direct threat: "The radical secularists, comprising the majority of the intelligentsia, including a number of leading journalists, believe this stand on the part of RP is a challenge to the secular premises of the state. They think that the RP is concealing its long-term intention to establish an Islamic state in Turkey."[12]

The successes of Refah were due to many factors: the failures of previous governments meant that it garnered the support of its members and of a crossover protest vote from disgruntled voters who would normally support other parties. The vote was as much, if not more, about politics and economics (double and triple-digit inflation, urban poverty, inadequate social services and health care, pollution, congestion, high employment, inadequate housing, crime, corruption) as about religion. Indeed, a 1994 survey found that only one-third of Refah's voters voted primarily because it was an Islamic party.[13] Refah's focus on voter issues like employment, pensions, health care, housing, and environment and its indictment of the failures of society reflected in its slogans of "clean politics" and a "just order," proved effective.

The reason for the successes of Refah mayors in many municipalities such as Istanbul and Ankara was widely acknowledged: "Refah Party mayors offered better services than their predecessors and worked hard to improve public services. They reduced corruption and nepotism in the municipalities and acted more professionally than other parties of the left and right."[14] The combined track records of many Refah municipal governments and of its workers in neighborhoods brought effective social change and made for a formidable force in electoral politics. At the same time, its support for private enterprise and economic liberalization drew support from small businessmen who resented the state's continued ownership of as much as 60 percent of the financial and manufacturing sector, its failure to curb the powers of big industrialists, and its dependence on European imports. Thus, Refah enjoyed the support of MUSIAD,

---

[12] Metin Heper, "Islam and Democracy in Turkey: Towards a Reconciliation," *Middle East Journal* 51:1, Winter 1997, pp. 43–4.

[13] Ibid., p. 35.

[14] M. Hakan Yavuz, "Turkey's 'Imagined Enemies': Kurds and Islamists," *The World Today*, Apr. 1996, p. 100.

a Muslim business association founded in 1990 that advocated full liberalization and privatization of the economy.

During Erbakan's brief tenure as prime minister, Refah encouraged the expanded role of religion in society: increasing the number of schools, religious foundations, businesses, banks, social services, and the media. Both secular Muslims and religious minorities such as Turkey's Alevi Muslim minority (perhaps 20 percent of its 98 percent Muslim population), despite the public assurances of Refah, were skeptical about its commitment to pluralism. They questioned whether the Refah's redefinition of the state would affect its ability to respect the rights of others—other (non-Refah) Muslims, non-believers and religious minorities. Cynics charged that Refah, like the FIS in Algeria, was using the democratic system to come to power in order to dismantle Turkey's democratic and secular state.

Erbakan's biggest obstacle proved predictably to be the military. Turkey's military has a long history of influence and intervention in domestic politics. Made up of staunch secularists, some might say militant secularists, with a low opinion of Turkey's politicians, it has consistently espoused the role of defenders of Kemalism and has had an allergic reaction to any form of religion in public life, from female students' right to wear a headscarf (*hijab*) to Islamist politics. Among the common justifications for previous coups was the claim that the government had betrayed Ataturk's principle of secularism. Thus, it took every occasion to signal its concerns about any compromising of Turkey's secular principles. It instituted a new purge of officers who were suspected of being Islamists. (Grounds could be the fact that an officer's wife wore a headscarf or that they prayed at a mosque.) In Spring 1997, the military presented the Erbakan government with a set of 18 demands, designed to stem an Islamist threat to the secular state. These included restrictions on the wearing of Islamic dress, measures to prevent Islamists from entering the military or government administration, and a mandate that the Imam-Hatep schools, religious schools, that it believed taught religious propaganda and served as a training ground for Islamists, be closed because of their anti-secular bias. At the same time, it demanded that compulsory secular education be increased from five to eight years. In April, General Cevik Bir publicly declared that the military's top priority, greater than that of its 10-year battle with Kurdish separatism, was the struggle against anti-secular Islamists.[15]

Erbakan and the Refah Party's brief government proved to be a lightning rod for militant secularists, contributing to the increased polarization of society. Turkey's radical secularists' (much of the military, civil service, and intelligentsia) secularism was not simply based on a belief in the separation of religion and the state but on an anti-religious secular ideology/

---

[15] Kelly Couturier, "Anti-Secularism Eclipses Insurgency as Army's No. 1 Concern," *Washington Post*, Apr. 5, 1997, p. A 22.

belief system, which was as rigid, militant and intolerant as it claimed "Islamic fundamentalism" was. The fear and charges of radical secularists led some to observe: "There is a neurotic edge to the way many secularists talk about the awkward, rather earnest, just-up-from-the-country sort of people who make up most of Mr. Erbakan's following."[16] As in Algeria, the secularist establishment was willing to compromise Turkey's commitment to democracy to prevent Islamists from participating in politics and society and to preserve their power, privilege, and lifestyle rather than allow voters to choose through free and open elections. It was unwilling to take the risk that democracy always involves, one that some leading Turkish secularists had believed possible, if not necessary, if democracy was to prevail: "A marriage between Islam and democracy in Turkey can be consummated if the radical secularists stop trying to impose their preferred life-style and set of values upon the Islamists, and if the latter do not attempt to undermine by word or deed the basic tenets of the secular democratic state in Turkey. A critical mediating role can be played by moderate secularists whose numbers are on the increase."[17] Ayse Kadiogl commented that the Republican elite, the political offspring/disciples of Ataturk, were moved by a "disgust" towards religion even if they sometimes resorted to religious symbols, paying lip service to religion.[18] Sherif Mardin's comparison of this Kemalist attitude to Voltaire's hatred of the Church goes a long way toward understanding the source and living legacy of militant secularism in Turkey. [19]

The military increased the intensity of its campaign in June by conducting briefings for judges, attorneys, and the media on the Islamist threat to the Turkish state. Finally, the Erbakan-Ciller coalition collapsed. Erbakan submitted his resignation on June 18, 1997. In February 1998, Turkey's Constitutional Court issued a court order which banned Refah. Erbakan was expelled from Parliament and barred from participation in the political process for five years. Refah's assets were seized. He and a number of other leaders were tried for sedition. In February 1998, a new law was passed requiring that children first complete eight years of secular education program before being permitted to take Quran classes. Weekend and summer Quran courses were banned. Female students and teachers in Islamic schools were barred from wearing the *hijab*, a ban that already existed in all other areas of education and in government departments.

---

[16] *The Economist*, Jul. 19, 1997, p. 23.

[17] Heper, "Islam and Democracy in Turkey," p. 45.

[18] Ayse Kadioglu, "Republican Epistemology and Islamic Discourses in Turkey in the 1990s," *Muslim World* 84:1, Jan. 1998, p. 11.

[19] For a discussion of this phenomenon, see Sherif Mardin, "Ideology and Religion in the Turkish Revolution," *International Journal of Middle East Studies* 2, 1971, especially pp. 208–9.

Egypt. In Egypt, the breathing space of the early Mubarak years had enabled Islamic political and social activism to grow more rapidly, to expand its institutions, and to become part of mainstream society. Perhaps the most significant development was the extent to which the Muslim Brotherhood and other voluntary (philanthropic) Islamic organizations became effective agents of social and political change, developing alternative socio-economic institutions and participating in the political process, demonstrating their strength in institution building and popular mobilization.

The Muslim Brothers and other Islamic activists became dominant voices in professional syndicates and democratic and voluntary associations of teachers, lawyers, doctors, engineers, and journalists, which have been pillars of Egyptian civil society. As Raymond Baker has observed regarding the Muslim Brotherhood: "Denied access to the political arena, they have made the professional syndicates perhaps the most vibrant institutions of Egyptian civil society."[20]

By the 1990s, the mainstreaming of Islamic activism had produced a professional class whose impact included election to leadership positions in professional associations or syndicates. In September 1992, the Brotherhood's winning of a majority of the board seats in Bar Association elections, long regarded as a bastion of liberalism, signaled this strength and influence. Muslim Brotherhood successes reflected the growing number of younger Islamist-oriented professionals, the appeal of the Brotherhood to professional classes as the only credible opposition, the indifference of many professionals about voting in association elections, and the ability of a well-organized, highly motivated minority to "get out the vote" and work with purpose and persistence.

The clearest testimony to the mainstreaming and institutionalization of Islamic revivalism or activism was the emergence of the Muslim Brotherhood as a political force in electoral politics. Operating within the political system, moderate activists such as the Muslim Brotherhood couched their criticisms and demands within the context of a call for greater democratization, political representation, social justice, and respect for human rights. At the same time, the Mubarak government continued to be a "presidential state." Mubarak won presidential elections with 94 percent of the vote in an election marred by voting irregularities and with no opposition candidate. The People's Assembly and the bureaucracy continued to be dominated by the Government's National Democratic Party. The government maintained absolute control over the creation and continued existence of political parties; thus, it refused legal recognition of the Muslim Brotherhood as a political party.

---

[20] Raymond William Baker, "Invidious Comparisons: Realism, Postmodernism, and Centrist Islamic Movements in Egypt," in *Political Islam: Revolution, Radicalism, or Reform?*, ed. John L. Esposito (Boulder, CO: Lynne Rienner Publishers, 1997), p. 124.

Radical violent alternatives, more silent in the early Mubarak period, boldly and directly challenged the regime and Egyptian society in the late 1980s and 1990s. Islamists in Assyut, Minya, Cairo, and Alexandria pressed for an Islamic revolution. Bent upon destabilizing the Egyptian economy and overthrowing the government, extremists attacked and murdered foreign tourists, Coptic Christians, and government officials, as well as bombing banks and government buildings.

Mubarak's flexible policy of the late 1980s gave way to a more aggressive response to the challenge of both religious extremists (those who advocate the violent overthrow of the government) and moderates (those who participate within the established political and legal framework). In the process the lines between radical and moderate Islamists, state security and the limits of state authority, prosecution of criminals and human rights have often been blurred. The government broadened its battle beyond the Gamaa Islamiyya, Jihad, and other radical groups, using harassment and imprisonment to curb also the growing strength and challenge of more moderate Islamist movements such as the Muslim Brotherhood. It attempted not only to eradicate violent extremism, but also increasingly to counter and control the legal institutionalization of Islamic activism politically and socially (professional associations, schools, and mosques) in Egyptian society. Its war against "terrorism" led to a broad government crackdown and massive arrests, not only of suspected extremists but also of moderate Islamists, in an attempt to silence all Islamic opposition. Thousands were held without charge; the Arab Human Rights Organization accused the government of routine torture.[21] The Mubarak government's extended war not just against the terrorism of the Gamaa Islamiyah but against Egypt's strongest legal opposition group, the Muslim Brotherhood. One prominent commentator observed that the government sought: "to curtail not only those movements that have carried out violent attacks, but also one that has come to dominate many municipalities, professional and labor associations and university faculties."[22]

The government crusade included legislation in February 1993 to counter the prominence of Islamists, particularly the Muslim Brotherhood, in democratic and voluntary associations of teachers, lawyers, physicians, engineers, and journalists. In a move widely seen as an attempt to weaken the influence of Islamists, the government-controlled People's Assembly passed a new educational law, Law 104, on May 31, without warning or consultation, which cancelled the right of Egyptian professors to elect their faculty deans and allows the rectors of universities to appoint them instead. Opponents charged that, despite the fact that the Brotherhood had not been

---

[21] Jane Freedman, "Democratic Winds Blow in Cairo," *Christian Science Monitor*, Jan. 17, 1990.

[22] Chris Hedges, "Egypt Begins Crackdown on Strongest Opposition Group," *New York Times*, Jun. 12, 1994, p. 3.

particularly active or successful in university faculties, the law is "one step in the government's attempt to eliminate any possibility of the Islamists capturing any more key positions ... [and that] If university professors are not to be trusted with electing their own representative, then there is no point in talking about democracy."[23]

The government also moved to control a breeding ground for Islamic opposition, Egypt's private mosques. The vast majority of Egypt's mosques were private (and thus independent in terms of their preachers, content of sermons, and activities) rather than state-controlled. However, the overwhelming majority were private mosques outside government control. Although both Sadat and later Mubarak (in 1985) announced plans to take control of private mosques, given the enormous number of mosques and limited resources, results had been limited. In October 1992, Mubarak's ministry of religious affairs announced that all sermons at state-controlled mosques would be subject to approval by government-appointed officials and that the building of private mosques would be curbed. On November 10, 1992, Mohammed Ali Mahgoub, the minister of religious affairs, announced that all private mosques would be brought under the control of the ministry.

The degree and extent of the Mubarak government's concerns about schools and universities as primary sources of Islamic militancy were reflected in a statement by Hussein Kamel Baha Eddin, Minister of Education: "Terrorism starts in the mind ... The fundamentalists are planning to brainwash our children to seize power."[24] The government designated education as an issue of national security and initiated a number of policies designed to counter its "Islamist threat." Teachers suspected of being Islamists or having Islamist sympathies were dismissed, retired, or transferred—many to clerical positions in remote areas. A national curriculum was imposed and, in a reversal of previous policy, an attempt was made to introduce the English language and Western secular values to provide a window on development as well as "a 'culture shock' to upset the wave of fundamentalism sweeping Egypt's schools."[25]

Iran and the Gulf. Iran and the Gulf provide their own distinctive experiences. Post-revolutionary Iran saw the suppression of political and religious dissent by militant clergy, from royalists to the Tudeh party, from secularist opposition to a variety of religiously oriented officials and leaders, senior ayatollahs like Mehdi Bazargan, the Islamic Republic's first Prime Minister and Ayatollah Shariatmadari. However, despite restrictions, parliamentary elections and heated parliamentary debate continued undisturbed and gradually during Hashemi Rafsanjani's

---

[23] "Professors can not choose," *Middle East Times*, June 6–12, 1992, p. 1.

[24] "Educating against extremism," *Middle East Times*, May 2–8, 1994, p. 1.

[25] "Ministering to the Satanic West," *Middle East Times*, May 2–8, 1994, p. 6.

presidency increased liberalization occurred amidst a struggle between more progressive/pragmatic forces (led by Rafsanjani) and militant ideologues (led by Khomeini's successor Ayatollah Khamenei).

The election of Mohammed Khatami as president by more than 70 percent of the population signaled the third phase of the Islamic Republic of Iran (Khomeini, Rafsanjani/Khamenei, and Khatami). Significant voter support came from women and younger people among others who desired a more open society. President Khatami has signaled his responsiveness by emphasizing two themes: civil society and civilizational dialogue. The former is equated with democratization, the rule of law, increased women's rights, and respect for human rights. The latter refers to attempts to reestablish or strengthen cultural and, in time, political relations with the United States and Europe.

Though final authority remains in the hands of Ayatollah Khamenei, often referred to as the "Supreme Leader," Khatami and his Minister of Culture and Islamic Guidance, Ataollah Mohajerani, institutionalized these issues through official statements, in speeches, and in national conferences such as the conference on Islam and Civil Society in January 1998. In several prominent cases involving attempts by more militant factions to silence critics like Ayatollah Montazeri, once designated as Khomeini's heir, and Ibrahim Yazdi, a former foreign minister during the early days of the Islamic Republic and leader of the Bazargan-founded Freedom Party, Khatami quietly pressed issues of civil society, particularly rule of law, to foster their release. While Iranians have experienced greater freedoms and "space," more militant factions in the government have fought back, arresting, trying, and imprisoning Khatami supporters like the former Mayor of Teheran and the Interior Minister. They have closed newspapers, encouraged confrontations on university campuses, and refused to approve the credentials of potential electoral candidates.

The situation in much of the Gulf has been quite different. In most countries, political and social organization and participation in society remain controlled by the state/ruling families. There is little non-state approved space/activity. In recent years, Saudi Arabia and Oman have created a *majlis* or consultative assembly, appointed by the ruler. Bahrain has resisted calls for a reopening of parliament and harshly suppressed voices of dissent. Only Kuwait and Yemen have held parliamentary elections. Few Gulf countries permit political parties, unions, professional associations, or a free press.

Government responses to civil society in the post-Gulf War period

The record of Islamic republics in Iran, Sudan, and Afghanistan reinforced for some old images and fears of the spread of religious authoritarianism. Muslim rulers pondered the challenge of the growing power of Islamism in the institutions of mainstream society and Europe faced the specter of an Islamist-led state in its midst in Turkey. Democratization became a major issue in Muslim politics. It led not only to political debate, but also to a military takeover and a virtual civil war in Algeria, the suppression of Islamists in Tunisia and Egypt, and a military/secular confrontation with Turkey's first Islamist prime minister which drove him out of office and led to the subsequent banning of the Refah Party. In its most extreme forms, the struggle sometimes appeared to be a battle between "secular fundamentalists" and "Islamic fundamentalists" which curtailed political participation and strictly limited, if not suppressed, the development of the culture and institutions of civil society.

Threat or challenge to civil society?

In contrast to other parts of the world, increased calls for greater political participation and democratization in the Middle East in the late 1990s were met by empty rhetoric or repression by many rulers and by strong ambivalence or silence in the West. The threat of "Islamic fundamentalism" increased authoritarianism and suppression of Islamic parties or groups in Tunisia, Algeria, Egypt, Saudi Arabia, Bahrain, and Turkey. Western governments and policymakers often stood by ambivalent, if not compliant.

Fear of fundamentalism, like responses to the communist threat, made strange bedfellows, providing a ready excuse for repression and the violation of human rights. Tunisia, Algeria, Egypt, Turkey, and Pakistan (under Benazir Bhutto), as well as Israel warned of a regional and international Islamic threat in a bid to curry Western aid or excuse their repression of Islamists. Moreover, as one observer noted, "Israel which for years won American and European backing as a bulwark against the spread of communism throughout the Middle East, is now projecting itself as the West's defense against militant Islam, a movement it is portraying as an even greater danger."[26] Prime Minister Yitzak Rabin justified the expulsion of 415 Palestinians:

Our struggle against murderous Islamic terror is also meant to awaken the world, which is lying in slumber. ... We call on all nations, all peoples to devote their attention to the greater danger inherent in Islamic fundamentalism ... This is a real and serious danger that threatens world peace in future years ... we stand on the line of fire against the danger of fundamentalist Islam.[27]

Equating Khomeiniism with a pan-Islamic threat and drawing parallels with communism, Shimon Peres declared, "Since the collapse of communism in the Soviet Union, we consider Khomeiniism the greatest danger

---

[26] *Association of Muslim Professionals Singapore Annual Report 1995/1996*, p. 48.
[27] Michael Parks, "Israel Sees Self Defending West Against Militants," *Los Angeles Times*, Jan. 2, 1993, p. A22.

the Middle East is facing—not only us but the Arabs as well ... it has many of the characteristics of communism. It is fanatic, it is ideological ... Most of all, it has the same inclination to export its ideas."[28]

Israel and its Arab neighbors warned that a resurgent Iran exported revolution throughout much of the Muslim world, Sudan, the West Bank and Gaza, Algeria, Central Asia, as well as Europe and America. Indeed, Egypt's Hosni Mubarak called for a "global alliance" against this menace.[29] Many pointed to the World Trade Center bombing in New York City and subsequent arrests of Muslim fundamentalists for conspiracy to set off other bombs as further proof of the international and anti-Western nature of the threat.

A triple threat?

Islam is often portrayed as a triple threat: political, civilizational, and demographic. Fear of Iran's export of the revolution in the 1980s was succeeded by fears of a monolithic, international pan-Islamic movement, at the heart of which is an Iranian-Sudanese axis: "The fear is of the militant brand of Islam being espoused by Iran, practiced in Sudan and spread by organizations like the Muslim Brotherhood in and from countries that have turned a blind eye to their activities."[30] In the 1990s, despite Iran's relative failure in exporting revolution, talk of a global Islamic threat increased, combining fear of violent revolution with that of Algerian-style electoral victories. France's Raymond Aron's warning in the 1980s of an Islamic revolutionary wave generated by the fanaticism of the prophet and Cyrus Vance's concern about an "Islamic-Western war" were succeeded by Charles Krauthammer's assertion of a global Islamic threat of "fundamentalist Koran-waving Khomeniism,"[31] led by the new commintern, Iran.[32]

The Ayatollah Khomeini's condemnation to death of Salman Rushdie combined with Saddam Hussein's call for an Islamic holy war against the West during the Gulf War reinforced fears of a political and cultural confrontation. This was magnified by some who reduced contemporary realities to the playing out of ancient rivalries, political confrontations rooted in a clash of civilizations.

It should now be clear that we are facing a mood and a movement far transcending the level of issues and policies and the governments that pursue them. This is no less than a clash of civilizations—perhaps irrational but surely historic reaction of

---

[28] Ibid. See also, Clyde Haberman, "Gunfire Stops Arab Deportees from Going Back to Israeli Zone," *New York Times*, Dec. 22, 1992, p. A1.

[29] Ibid.

[30] *The Economist*, p. 49.

[31] Charles Krauthammer, "The New Crescent of Crisis: Global Intifada," *Washington Post*, Feb. 16, 1993.

[32] Charles Krauthammer, "Iran: Orchestrator of Disorder," *Washington Post*, Jan. 1, 1993, p. A19.

an ancient rival against our Judeo-Christian heritage, our secular present, and the worldwide expansion of both.[33]

Muslim-Western relations and conflicts have often been placed within the context of an historical confrontation in which Islam is again pitted against the West, against "our Judeo-Christian and secular West," rather than specific political and socio-economic grievances. Thus, what can the West really do to respond to what is obviously primarily emotional and "irrational," an assault upon the West by peoples who are peculiarly driven by their passions and hatred? As James Piscatori, in explaining this phenomenon, observed:

Whether it was the Ottoman attempt to thwart Christian nationalists or the Muslim attempt to gain independence from the West, Islam was fanatical because it ran counter to imperial interests. But it was the converse formulation that became the standard explanation of Muslim conduct: Islam was hostile to the West because it was fanatical ... Consequently, Muslims came to be seen as a uniformly emotional and sometimes illogical race that moved as one body and spoke with one voice.[34]

The growth of Muslim populations in Europe and America has resulted in Islam becoming the second largest religion in Germany, France and Italy as well as the third largest in Britain and America. Disputes over Muslim minority rights, demonstrations and clashes during the Salman Rushdie affair, the World Trade Center and conviction of Shaykh Omar Abd al-Rahman and others of plotting to blow up major sites in America, as well as bombings in Paris by Algeria's Armed Islamic Guard, have been exploited by strident voices of the right—politicians like France's Le Pen, neo-Nazi youth in Germany, and right-wing political commentators in the United States. One European expert warned:

While Europe has overcome the cold war ... it now risks creating new divisions and conflicts, such as a white, wealthy and Christian "Fortress Europe" pitted against a largely poor, Islamic world. That could lead to terrorism and another forty years of small, hot wars[.] [35]

The diversity of Muslim politics

The realities of Muslim politics and societies refute images of a monolithic, pan-Islamic threat. Despite a common "Islamic" orientation, governments reveal little unity of purpose in interstate and international relations due to conflicting national interests or priorities. Qaddafi was a bitter enemy of Anwar Sadat and Jafar al-Numayri at the very time that all were projecting their "Islamic images." Today he remains at odds with

---

[33] Bernard Lewis, "The Roots of Muslim Rage," p. 60.
[34] James P. Piscatori, *Islam in a World of Nation States* (Cambridge University Press, 1986), p. 38.
[35] Dominique Moisi in Judith Miller, "Strangers at the Gate: Europe's Immigration Crisis," *New York Times Magazine*, Sept. 15, 1991, p. 86.

Sudan's Hasan al-Turabi, portrayed in the press as the "Ayatollah of Africa," as well as with Egypt's Hosni Mubarak. Khomeini's Islamic Republic consistently called for the overthrow of the House of Saud and other Gulf states on Islamic grounds. In 1998, it reversed its policy and moved to mend its fences with Saudi Arabia while at the same time denouncing the excesses of the Islamic government of the Taliban in Afghanistan.

Islamically identified governments also reflect differing relationships with the West. Libya and Iran's relationship with the West, and the United States in particular, has often been confrontational. At the same time, the US has had strong allies in Saudi Arabia, Egypt, Kuwait, Pakistan, and Bahrain. National interest and regional politics rather than ideology or religion remain the major determinants in the formulation of foreign policy.

Civil society, democratization, and foreign policy

As we have seen, Islam has reemerged as a significant political and social force in civil society. Islamic candidates have been elected prime ministers and speakers of parliaments, cabinet ministers, and parliamentarians in Egypt, Algeria, Sudan, Kuwait, Pakistan, Jordan, Yemen, Malaysia, Turkey, and Lebanon. The performance of Islamist groups in national and municipal elections since the late 1980s has defied those who had insisted that Islamic movements were unrepresentative and would not attract voters. The FIS sweep of Algerian elections and the likelihood that they would come to power through the ballot box, as did the subsequent election of Necmettin Erbakan of the Refah Party as Prime Minister of Turkey, exacerbated the fears of many rulers in the Muslim and in the West. The Algerian military's intervention and repression of FIS, the Turkish military's role in forcing the resignation of the Erbakan government and the subsequent banning of Refah, North African and Egyptian governments' indiscriminate crackdown on their Islamic movements, as well as Western governments' concerns have been justified by the charge that Islamists were out to "hijack democracy." Ironically, participation within the system and relative success made movements more, rather than less, of a threat in the eyes of some. For leaders in the West, democracy raises the prospect of old and reliable friends or client states being transformed into more independent and less predictable nations. This prospect generated a fear that Islamic governments would undermine stability in the Middle East and broader Muslim world, make Western access to oil less secure, and threaten the security of Israel.

Lack of enthusiasm or support for political liberalization in the Middle East and broader Muslim world has been rationalized by the claim that both Arab culture and Islam are inherently anti-democratic (an issue never raised to a comparable degree with regard to the former Soviet Union,

Eastern Europe, or Africa).[36] The proof offered is the lack of a democratic tradition, more specifically, the paucity of democracies in the Muslim world. Why the glaring absence of democratic governments?

The political realities of the Muslim world have not been conducive to the development of democratic traditions and institutions. European colonial rule and post-independence national governments headed by military and ex-military rulers or monarchs have contributed to a legacy which has had little concern for political participation and the building of strong democratic institutions. National unity and stability as well as political legitimacy have been undermined by the artificial nature of modern states whose national boundaries were often determined or drawn by colonial powers and whose rulers were either placed on their thrones by Europe or simply seized power for themselves. Weak economies, illiteracy, and high unemployment, especially among the younger generation, exacerbate the situation, undermining confidence in governments and increasing the appeal of "Islamic fundamentalism."

Experts and policymakers who question whether Islamic movements will use electoral politics to "hijack democracy" ("One man, one vote, one time") often fail to show equal concern that few rulers in the region have been democratically elected and that many who speak of democracy only believe in "risk free democracy." They permit political participation and liberalization as long there is no risk of a strong opposition (secular or religious) or a potential loss of power. Failure to appreciate that the issue of the hijacking of democracy is a two way street was reflected in the responses (an awkward silence or support) of many Western governments and experts for the Algerian military's intervention, the cancellation of the results of the democratic electoral process and the Turkish military's suppression of the Refah party, and the growing authoritarianism of the Mubarak government.

Perception of a global "Islamic threat" contributes to support for, silence, or "strategic" acceptance by Western governments of repression of Islamists and their institutions (as well as any other significant opposition) by governments in the Middle East and the broader Muslim world and thus to the creation of a "self-fulfilling prophecy." The thwarting of a participatory political process by governments that cancel elections or repress populist Islamic movements fosters radicalization and extremism. Many Islamists who experience regime violence (harassment,

---

[36] For an analysis of this issue, see John L. Esposito and James P. Piscatori, "Democratization and Islam," *Middle East Journal* 45, Summer 1991; John L. Esposito, "Islam, Democracy, and U.S. Foreign Policy," in *Riding the Tiger: The Middle East Challenge After the Gulf War*, ed. Phebe Marr and William Lewis (Boulder, CO: Westview, 1993); *Islam and Democracy: Religion, Politics, and Power in the Middle East* (Washington, DC: The United States Institute of Peace, 1993), and John L. Esposito and John O. Voll, *Islam and Democracy* (New York: Oxford University Press, 1997).

imprisonment, torture) conclude that seeking "democracy" is a dead end and become convinced that force or violence is their only recourse against repressive regimes. Official silence or economic and political support for regimes is read as complicity and a sign of the West's "double standard" for the implementation of democracy. Regime repression and violation of human rights and a compliant US or Western policy towards such actions creates conditions that lead to political violence. It seemingly validates the prior contention and prophecy that Islamic movements are inherently violent, anti-democratic, and a threat to national and regional stability.

More constructive and democratic strategies are possible. The strength of Islamic organizations and parties is as much due to their constituting the only viable voice and vehicle for opposition in relatively closed political systems. The electoral strength of Tunisia's Renaissance Party, Algeria's FIS, Jordan's Muslim Brotherhood, or Turkey's Refah Party has come not only from a hard core of dedicated followers but also from the fact that they were the most credible and effective alternative "game in town." Thus, their electoral support included both those who voted for their Islamic agenda as well as those who simply wished to vote against the government. Opening up the political system and strengthening the institutions of civil society fosters the growth and strength of competing opposition parties, alternative choices, and thus weakens Islamic parties' monopoly of opposition voters. Promotion of the values and institutions of civil society is a hedge against the perpetuation of a culture of authoritarianism, secular or religious.

Finally, the realities of a more open marketplace—having to compete for votes or coming to power and having to rule amidst diverse interests—can force Islamic organizations (as they often do secular political parties) to adapt or broaden their ideology and programs in response to domestic realities, and diverse constituencies and interests. The history of many contemporary movements reflects this reality. Mawlana Mawdudi, founder of the Jamaat-i Islami, was an early critic of both nationalism and democracy. Subsequently, the Jamaat, as also the Muslim Brotherhood (in Egypt and Jordan for example), came to accept and "Islamize" democracy, participating in elections and using it as a yardstick to critique incumbent governments. Islamic movements like Tunisia's Ennahda, Turkey's Refah Party, Islamists in Egypt, Jordan, Kuwait, Yemen, Bangladesh, Malaysia, and Indonesia have also followed suit, changing and evolving ideologically. These changes have not always resulted in similar outcomes, as witnessed by the divergent views of the Muslim Brotherhood and Ennahda as compared to the Jamaat-i Islami regarding the role of women in public life.

All are challenged to recognize that democratization and the building of strong civil societies in the Muslim world are part of a process of experimentation, necessarily accompanied by failure as well as success. The transformation of the West from feudal monarchies to democratic nation states took time, trial and error. It was accompanied by political as well as intellectual revolutions that rocked both state and church in a long, drawn-out process, among contending voices and factions with competing visions and interests.

Islam and pluralism

A critical issue in Muslim politics today is that of pluralism. Historically, the monotheistic visions of both Islam and Christianity and the belief of each that it possessed the final and complete revelation of God and was charged to call all to salvation resulted in competing claims and missions and produced theological and political conflict. In the 19th and 20th centuries, much of mainstream Christianity grappled with and came to grips with the realities of pluralism in the modern world. The outcome was the result of a process of reform in which doctrines were reexamined and reinterpreted. For example, Roman Catholicism in the late 19th and first half of the 20th century resisted and condemned much of what was termed "modernism" (from popular sovereignty and elections to pluralism). However, at Vatican II the church for the first time officially recognized and accepted pluralism.

For Muslims today the issue of pluralism is directly related to the status of non-Muslims in Islamic law as *dhimmi*, protected minorities, as well as that of Muslim minority communities living under non-Muslim rule or non-Muslim governments. While historically Islam often proved more flexible in tolerating non-Muslim (People of the Book) as minorities whose protected (*dhimmi*) status enabled them to live and practice their faith under Muslim rule, that status amounts to second class citizenship in the modern world. In addition, the persecution and suppression of non-Muslims by some Muslim governments and by some Islamic movements underscores the need for reinterpretation (*ijtihad*) and reform (*islah*) if the rights of all citizens are to be guaranteed.

Today, due to an unprecedented number of Muslim immigrants and refugees, there are more Muslim minority communities in existence across the globe than at any previous time in history. While some Muslims wish some day to return, most face living in new non-Muslim homelands permanently. This reality raises many questions of citizenship: from loyalty and political participation to living in societies whose laws are not based upon Islamic law. Thus, for Muslims today and for Muslim reformers, pluralism is a critical concern both for Muslim majority countries and for Muslim minority communities. From Egypt to Indonesia, scholars debate and reinterpret Islamic doctrines and laws. As with other faiths, the lines of the debate are often drawn between traditionalists, who wish to simply follow the authority of the past, and modernists or reformers who argue the need and acceptability of a fresh interpretation of Islamic sources, a reformulation of Islam.

Related to a reexamination of the concept of pluralism is that of tolerance. Historically, religious tolerance has tended to be simply equated with non-persecution of others, allowing or suffering their existence. However, the realities of contemporary life in a global society require that tolerance be based more genuinely on mutual understanding and respect, the ability to agree to disagree. Reflecting on the true meaning and basis of tolerance, Singapore's Association of Muslim Professionals noted: "We need to emphasize that endeavours which merely promote 'tolerance' of cultural differences or merely impart disjointed 'quaint facts' about another ethnic group contribute little to—and perhaps in fact undermine—the achievement of multi-culturalism or inter-cultural understanding."[37] One need not deny essential religious, ideological, or political differences to be able to function as neighbors domestically and internationally. Differences of opinion and opposition need not be perceived as a threat.

A diverse group of Muslim intellectuals and activists (Rashid Ghannoushi, Muhammad Selim al-Awa, Yusuf Qardawi, Mahmud Ayoub, Anwar Ibrahim, Kamal Aboul Magd, Fahmy Howeidy, Abdurahman Wahid, Nurcholish Madjid, Abdulaziz Sachedina, Fathi Osman, Tariq Ramadan, and Azzam Tamimi) have produced a growing body of literature that reexamines Islamic traditions and addresses issues of pluralism both at the theoretical and practical levels. Recognizing the need to open up the one party or authoritarian political systems that prevail, as well as face the multi-religious and multicultural demographic realities of their societies, they have both reinterpreted Islamic principles to reconcile Islam with democratization and multi-party political systems and recast and expanded traditional doctrine regarding the status (*dhimmi*) of non-Muslim minorities. In addition to employing traditional concepts like consultation (*shura*) and consensus (*ijma*) to limit the authority of rulers, words like party (*hizb*) have been reinterpreted, acknowledging a positive connotation and applying it to political parties (Hizb Ennahda) and religious groups (Hizbollah) rather than that of difference and division which undermine rather than promote the good of society.[38]

Islamists and other Muslim intellectuals have marshaled scripture and history to argue that Islam supports the equality and pluralism of the human community. Quranic passages which affirm that God chose to create the world with different nations and tribes (Sura 5:48, 30:22, 48:13) are emphasized. They argue that Quranic pluralism was practiced by Muhammad and the early community in their recognition and extension of freedom of religion, worship, and protection (*dhimmi*) to non-Muslims. Some, like Professor Mahmoud Ayoub, assert that rather than implying a second-class

---

[37] *Tanahairhu: Singapore Malay/Muslims 1991–1996*, p. 48.

[38] Yvonne Yazbeck Haddad, "Islamists and the Challenge of Pluralism," Occasional Paper (Washington, DC: Center for Contemporary Arab Studies and Center for Muslim-Christian Understanding, 1995), 15ff.

citizenship, the word *dhimma* (which is not in the Quran but found in the Hadith) was intended to designate a special covenant of protection between Muslims on the one hand, and Christians and Jews on the other. Others note that the term *dhimma* refers to the form of a covenant not its content and that content can be redefined today in light of new realities.[39]

Increasingly, both the writings of Muslim intellectuals and the experience of Islam in Southeast Asia become more relevant to the broader Muslim world. The multi-religious and multi-ethnic societies of Malaysia and Indonesia in diverse ways provide a substantial example of pluralism—the issues, problems and possibilities for change, accommodation, and coexistence. While Malaysia did experience Malay-Chinese riots in 1969, Malaysians continue to construct a Muslim majority society in which non-Muslims have enjoyed a degree of political and religious equality as well as democracy unknown in many parts of the Muslim world. Indonesia's de-politicization of Islam has ironically engendered both a deeper Islamization of Indonesian society and a diverse group of voices (Muslim and Christian) committed to a pluralist society.[40] The conflicts and contradictions of this process were seen strikingly during the last days of Suharto in the scapegoating and attacks on Chinese. They have been equally visible in the Muslim-Christian conflicts in 1999 and 2000 under President Abdurahman Wahid, the liberal leader of the Nahdatul Ulama, a religious organization with more than 30 million members and a champion of religious and political pluralism.

Just as Muslim politics reveal the profound debate and conflict over issues of political liberalization, democratization, pluralism, the rights of women and minorities, so too a generation of Muslim intellectuals and leaders is attempting to reexamine and reinterpret its faith in light of modern realities, debating many of these critical questions. Whether this new current will prevail in the face of authoritarian regimes, conservative religious authorities, and secular forces remains to be seen.

The empowerment of Muslim women

Islamic activists and intellectuals have in recent years engaged in a reassessment of women's status and role in society. They represent a range of positions. If some advocate a restoration of past practices, others opt for a process of reformation, emphasizing not only greater gender equality in worship and piety but also in education and employment. As previously noted, Islamic movements like the Muslim Brotherhoods of Egypt and

---

[39] Mahmoud Ayoub, "Islam and Christianity: Between Tolerance and Acceptance," in *Religions of the Book: The Annual Publication of the College Theology Society*, ed. Gerard S. Sloyan (Lanham, MD: The College Theology Society, 1992), p. 28.

[40] Robert Heffner, "Modernity and the Challenge of Pluralism: Some Indonesian Lessons," *Studia Islamika*, 2:4, 1995, p. 25.

Jordan and Tunisia's Ennahda have emphasized increased access to education and employment. Women are becoming more visible in the councils of Islamic organizations. Islamist women are increasingly found in the professions (physicians, journalists, lawyers, engineers, social workers, university professors) and as administrators and staff in schools, clinics, and social welfare agencies.

Today, Muslim women, representing many ideological orientations, are increasingly writing and speaking out for themselves on women's issues. They seek to empower themselves not just as defenders of women's rights, but also as interpreters of the tradition. Many argue that patriarchy as much as religion, indeed patriarchy linked to religion, accounts for many customs affecting gender relations that became long-standing traditions. The primary interpreters of Islam (of the Quran, traditions of the Prophet, and law) were males functioning in and reflecting the values of patriarchal societies. Religion was linked to patriarchy both through its interpreter-scholars and their appeal to Islam to legitimate their interpretations or formulations of doctrine and law.

Women scholars and activists draw on the writings and thought not only of male scholars but also, and most importantly, a growing number of Muslim women scholars and activists who utilize an Islamic discourse to address issues ranging from dress and education to employment and political participation. In areas as diverse as the Arab world, Iran, South and Southeast Asia, women have formed their own women's organizations, created their own magazines, and contributed to newspapers in which they set forth new religious and social interpretations and visions of gender relations. Organizations like Women Living Under Muslim Laws (Geneva) and Sisters in Islam (Malaysia) have become visible and vocal representatives within their own countries and internationally, writing, publishing, speaking out, and participating in international conferences such as the Cairo conference on population and Beijing's conference on women. Though small in number, they may well, as has occurred in other religions, prove to be an effective vanguard in a long-term process of reassessment, reform and transformation.

Today, we are witnessing a new historical transformation in the Muslim world as many, seeking more autonomy and broader participation in public life, pursue greater political participation and/or develop institutions of civil society. Risks exist, for there can be no "risk free democracy." Those who fear the unknown, what specific Islamic movements in power will be like or how they will act, have a legitimate concern. However, if we fear their suppression of opposition, lack of pluralism and tolerance, and violation of human rights, then the same concern must apply equally to the plight of those Islamists who have shown a willingness to participate within the political process under current regimes in Tunisia, Egypt, Algeria, Turkey,

Jordan, and Yemen where the results of free parliamentary elections and the institutions of civil society (non-state political organization, professional associations, NGOs, financial institutions, the press and media) have been undermined or aborted. It is equally important to note that Islamist governments (the Taliban in Afghanistan, the NIF-backed government in Sudan, and Khomeini's Iran) are vivid reminders that religious authoritarianism is as dangerous as secular authoritarianism.

Governments in the Muslim world, who espouse political liberalization and democracy, are challenged to promote and strengthen the development of civil society—those institutions, values, and culture that are the foundation for true participatory government. They must be willing to allow alternative political voices to function freely in society and express their opinions and dissent through the formation of political parties, private associations, newspapers, and the media. Islamic activists and movements are challenged to move beyond slogans to programs. They must become more self-critical in speaking out not only against local government abuses, but also against those of Islamic regimes in Sudan, Afghanistan, and until recently Iran, as well as acts of terrorism committed in the name of Islam by extremists. They are challenged to provide an Islamic rationale and policy that would extend to their opposition and to minorities the very principles of pluralism and political participation that they demand for themselves.

The extent to which the growth of Islamic revivalism has been accompanied in some countries by attempts to restrict women's rights and their public roles, the recent record of discrimination against the Bahai in Iran, the Ahmadi in Pakistan, and Christians in Sudan, as well as sectarian conflict between Muslims and Christians in Egypt, Sudan, Pakistan, Indonesia, and Nigeria pose serious questions of religious pluralism, human rights, and tolerance.

The contemporary Islamic revival has challenged many of the presuppositions of Western liberal secularism and development theory that modernization means the inexorable or progressive secularization and Westernization of society. Too often analysis and policymaking have been shaped by a liberal secularism which fails to recognize that it too represents a worldview, not *the* worldview or paradigm, and can easily degenerate into a "secularist fundamentalism" that assumes its principles to be a self-evident and universal truth or norm. Thus alternative worldviews or ideologies are easily dismissed as abnormal, deviant, irrational, and a "fundamentalist" or extremist threat.

Several factors must be kept in mind when speaking of the compatibility or incompatibility of Islam and democracy. Those who argue *a priori* that Islam and democracy are incompatible must recall that the same could be said, and indeed was said, by a variety of secular and religious intellectuals and leaders in the past about Judaism and Christianity. Both these traditions, their beliefs and values, were formulated long before modern democracy and, indeed, were used in the past to support and legitimate non-democratic states and empires, from divine right monarchies to forms of dictatorship in which notions of modern pluralism and human rights were unknown. Yet, both Judaism and Christianity, like all of the world's religions, have historically proven to be open to reformulation and change as the sacred texts and beliefs of the religious tradition are adapted and applied in changing historical contexts. As a result, many Jews and Christians today, lacking an historical awareness of the development of their traditions, believe that Judaism and Christianity are not only not incompatible but even are the sources of western democratic traditions.

The Muslim world also knew pre-modern authoritarianism, followed by European colonialism which, despite its protestations of a "mission to civilize," was not motivated by a desire to promote civil society and democratization. Moreover, as noted above, the emergence of modern Muslim states saw authoritarian rulers often placed on their thrones of power by European colonial powers. Europe, along with America, despite its official commitment to the spread of democracy, continued to tolerate and support dictatorships and authoritarian rule in the Muslim world (as in many other parts of the developing world) during the post-independence and Cold War periods out of self-interest to block the spread of communism or to assure access to oil.

With regard to the compatibility of Islamic belief and values with democracy, some Muslims, as well as non-Muslims, assert their incompatibility. They range from the conservative monarchy of King Fahd in Saudi Arabia, who sees democracy as a Western concept incommensurate with Islamic traditions, to militant movements like Hizb al-Tahrir. Many others in the worldwide Muslim community believe that Islam is capable of reinterpretation (*ijtihad*) and that traditional concepts of consultation (*shura*), consensus (*ijma*), and legal principles such as the general welfare (*maslahah*) provide the bases for the development of modern Muslim notions or authentic, more indigenously-rooted, versions of democracy. Some reinterpret traditional beliefs to essentially legitimate Western-generated forms of democracy; others wish to develop their own more indigenously rooted forms of political participation and democracy appropriate to Islamic values and realities.

The history of Islam's generating and supporting new intellectual traditions as well as government and social institutions is a matter of record. Here it is important to remind those who speak of democracy as if it were a self-evident truth, univocal in meaning and expressed in a single model, that (1) the introduction of democracy was accompanied by much skepticism among many rulers, elites, and religious leaders alike, and (2) the western experience has known many forms of democracy from Athens to modern western interpretations and models operative in Europe and America. It would be more correct when speaking of democratization in global politics or, more specifically, of Islam and democracy to first ask "which democracy"? The existence of different meanings and understandings of democratization as well as the danger of exploitation of democracy by authoritarian governments and demagogues alike must be seen as neither foreign to the West nor to other societies.

In the final analysis, as is self-evident, it will remain for Muslims to determine the nature of their governments, to introduce or refine forms of political participation or democratization that seem appropriate. While there may be much room for differences and debate, the challenge today is for all parties or factions, despite political and ideological differences, to commit themselves to the creation and strengthening of the culture, values, and institutions of civil society.

Part II

RE-ISLAMIZATION IN
THE PUBLIC SPHERE

4

ISLAM AND THE COMMON MORTAL

Fariba Adelkhah

The election in May 1997 of Mohammad Khatami, a left-wing reformer and outsider, to the Presidency of the Iranian Republic, against the favorite candidate, the parliamentary speaker Nategh Nouri, appeared to confirm the erosion and the opening up of the Islamic regime instituted after the 1979 Revolution. For a number of observers, the hypothesis of Iran's entry, along with the Muslim world in general, into a "post-Islamic" era had been substantiated. However, one can wonder if it has not been, in fact, a renewal of the Islamic Republic.

Let us underline first of all that Mohammad Khatami is himself a man of the establishment. He is not a product of "civil society" (to give it its proper name) as was so often reiterated after his surprise victory. His political itinerary is very different to that of, say, Vaclav Havel in Czechoslovakia. Certainly he knew how to take responsibility, both through his speeches and his actions, for the demands made by large sections of the country concerning civil liberties and the setting up of a lawful state. However, nothing indicates that such aspirations conflicted with the revolutionary heritage of 1978–9, whatever part political coercion played in the power struggle.

More fundamentally, it would be difficult to define Islam properly, and to determine what is "pre" and what is "post"-Islam. As a political and social phenomenon, Islam was never rigid, at least not in the context of Iranian society. In particular, it inspired numerous ideological debates and has never held to a particular model, nor indeed to a specific economic policy, such as was the case with Soviet socialism. In other words, Islam has never been isolated from the dynamics of social change, nor from that of globalization. It is for this reason that Islam takes on different guises in different countries or historical context.

As far as Iran is concerned, the revolutionary break is not confined to an Islamic protest movement—the liberals, the Marxists, and the nationalists all played a significant part in mass mobilization—and it has not cancelled out the achievements of the old regime. Concerning the position of women, the militant Muslims even took upon themselves to defend certain clauses in the Civic Code that could have been questioned just as much by the conservative clergy as by the revolutionaries themselves.[1] Furthermore, the Republic has had to face developments which have had nothing particularly Muslim about them, and which the monarchy before them was equally confronted with, in particular the regional pressures of the Kurds, the Azaris, the Turkmenis, and the Arabs, as well as the military threat from Iraq. We often forget that Iran has had long-standing problems, stretching back far beyond twenty years.

Mohammad Khatami's election victory: Break or continuity?

It is proper from this point of view to distinguish between different phases. After the first euphoric months of post-revolutionary liberty, the exacerbation of independence groups, the terrorism of radical Muslim groups—such as Forghan and the People's Mojahedin—and above all the hostile war imposed by Saddam, all led to a state of "terror" and to a so-called "cultural revolution." Imam Khomeini's intervention in 1983 put an end to it, although not without having to impose the principle of *velayat-e faqih* (government by the jurisconsult) on the clergy and political classes.

The necessity of setting up a war economy, due to the conflicts with Iraq, meant that the regime became even more authoritarian and centralized. Nevertheless, the struggle between the different political factions, so virulent in 1985 that they provoked the self-dissolution of the Islamic Republican Party, foreshadowed the emergence of a real pluralist Islam. This consecrated Ali Khamenei's accession to power (as Supreme Leader) and that of Hashemi Rafsanjani (as President of the Republic) after the 1988 ceasefire and the death of Imam Khomeini in June 1989. The political and economical liberalization carried out by the new team in the decade that followed meant that one could talk about a "Thermidor in Iran."[2] Nonetheless, it should still be recalled that this historical metaphor refers much more to the professionalization of the revolutionary class than to its "moderation" or to the questioning of its revolutionary heritage. In France, from 1795 to 1815 the Directory and the Empire institutionalized revolutionary changes and gave them new political expression as well as assuring the transition from "revolutionary passion" to "revolutionary reason," precisely the same terms that have been used in contemporary Iran.

In these conditions, Mohammad Khatami's election to the Presidency of the Republic—which was not only preceded by an intense electoral campaign but also a hitherto unseen participation in the 1996 legislative

---

[1] Fariba Adelkah, *La Révolution sous le voile. Les femmes islamiques d'Iran* (Paris: Karthala, 1991).

[2] Fariba Adelkah, Jean-François Bayart and Olivier Roy, *Thermidor en Iran* (Brussels: Complexe, 1993); Anoushiravan Ehteshamiht, *After Khomeyni: The Iranian Second Republic* (London/New York: Routledge, 1995).

elections—signaled a restructuring of the regime rather than its end. This obviously did not exclude conflicts at the heart of the party. Immediately after the presidential elections the struggle between factions intensified even more and the outcome of these tensions still remains uncertain.[3]

In July 1998, one of Khatami's main supporters, the energetic mayor of Tehran, Gholam Hoseyn Karbastchi, was charged with the misappropriation of public funds and sentenced to five years in prison by a justice system still under the control of the conservative faction. In addition to this, and during the same year, the Minister of the Interior Abdollah Nouri was stripped of his post and several newspapers of a reformist tendency were closed. Worse still, several intellectuals were assassinated by people alleged to be working for the Intelligence Service. But the game was far from being over, for the simple reason that the Supreme Leader, known to have conservative sympathies, expressed his support for Mohammad Khatami's policies on several occasions, including the delicate subject of relations with the United States and the reestablishment of diplomatic relations with Great Britain after Imam Khomeini's death sentence against Salman Rushdie. Thus, in February 1999, the local elections seemed to turn in favour of the presidential majority. Of a profoundly collegial nature, the regime showed itself capable of keeping its leaders in the fold even if they were in disgrace. The Islamic left, ousted from Parliament between 1992 and 1996, continued to be represented in other important institutions and to influence a substantial number of publications. Hashemi Rafsanjani, who was unable to stand for President of the Republic in 1997, was nominated President of the Expediency Council and remains one of the central figures of the Republic today.

In reality, the sharing of power between the Supreme Leader, the President of the Republic, the Parliament, and the Council of Guardians has assured the stability of the different institutions, although it is true that this has been at the cost of a certain opposition to change involving inevitable compromises between the different political groups. This does not mean that the state has not undergone any changes. The faction struggles over the past few years prove the opposite, and the intensity of the current debate on *velayat-e faqih* and the reforms of the Constitution in 1989 suggest that the Islamic Republic is definitely an evolving structure. However, the "Thermidorian" political class knows how to face and defend its revolutionary heritage, as well as its privileges. Whilst waiting for the results of an appeal that he had lodged, and whilst expressing his criticism concerning the Council of Guardians over their methods in selecting candidates, the reformist Mayor of Tehran Gholam Hoseyn Karbastchi did not hesitate, during a press conference in October 1998, in asking voters to

---

[3] Jean-François Bayart, "Jeux de pouvoir à Téhéran," *Politique Internationale* 82, winter 1998–9, pp. 107–22.

participate "en masse" in the elections to the Assembly of Experts, and thus save "the honour of the system."

The question is not whether the Republic has become less Islamic or whether it is post-Islamic, but rather to distinguish the strong points which have given it a new lease of life. This new lease of life is due to its renewed legitimacy taken from the large voter turnout at the 1997 presidential elections, as well as the undeniable popularity of Mohammad Khatami. The evolution of the state seems to be particularly associated with a whole series of social dynamics which it has encouraged and to which it must adapt itself. Amongst these one must particularly mention the population's reaction to the war with Iraq; urbanization (61 percent of the population live in towns); literacy—notably amongst women; the increasing number of students; the growing youthfulness of the population due to the sharp demographic rise up till the beginning of the 1990s; the beginnings of a demographic transition due to a spectacular drop in fertility rates; the development of an informal economic sector which encouraged the entry of women to the labor force; and more generally the effects of the economic crisis.

Essentially this reconstitution of the Islamic Republic can be summarized in three ways. Firstly, the bureaucratization—and above all the rationalization of social life—has progressed considerably in the last twenty years. No sphere of society has escaped this trend, and notably not religion. The organization of the clergy, theological teaching, and the collecting of religious taxes have all been noticeably institutionalized. As a consequence, the relationship between the believer and his/her faith has changed even more, as has been extensively covered by the media. Therefore, religious practices such as pilgrimages or charitable acts have contributed to the emergence of a public space that is largely sectarian, but which also feeds simultaneously the new socio-political tendencies.[4] Abdolkarim Soroush's audience is no doubt the most well-known illustration. A key figure in the cultural domain of Islam at the beginning of the 1980s, he expressed at the time a personal reflection on the historicity of religious facts and on the role of the subject in them. On this point he became the master thinker of the Islamic left, which renounced its tendency towards direct action and opted for a critical and constitutional conception of the Islamic Republic and of *velayat-e faqih*, whilst remaining close to Ayatollah Montazeri's position. As the dethroned successor to Imam Khomeini, he has been kept under virtual house arrest at Qom, and is the declared opponent of the current Supreme Leader as well as being one of the most popular dignitaries in the country. Such interactions between the religious fields and the political ones are also to be found on the right-hand side of the chessboard. Due to the diversity of

---

[4] Fariba Adelkhah, *Being Modern in Iran* (London: Hurst), Chs. 3 and 5.

theological schools and publications, the debate is no less lively amongst the conservatives. This has led some of them if not to support Mohammad Khatami, then at least to initiate new approaches. These include the attempt by Ahmed Tavakkoli to launch the daily newspaper *Farda* in 1998, as well as the vacillations of the Association of Religious Teachings and Teachers at Qom during the presidential campaign, where the compromises between the right-wing majority in Parliament and President Khatami showed that this tendency is also in the process of reconstitution. The Islamic Republic, whatever its strict political expressions, and unlike the Soviet and Marxist regimes, seems to have assured the recognition of social facts by political groups—in this it has never been totalitarian—and they have contributed to its vitality. The private family sphere, the religious sphere, and the economic structures have continued to modernize and diversify, thus giving a certain consistency and appearance to the themes of civil society that Mohammad Khatami has put before the Republic since 1997. There also manifestly exists a clear convergence between his emphasis on the necessity of instituting a lawful state and the increasing tendency of social leaders to resort to enacted laws and to the judiciary for settling conflicts within families over property and economic issues.

The development of the faction struggle between the different currents of the political seraglio has become more and more dependent on feedback in the public space. In 1998, for example, the Karbastchi affair showed that judiciary decisions have now become the subject for debate in the media and in public life, and can therefore be contested. Thus, certain civil servants from Tehran Town Hall complained in the press about bad treatment that they had received in prison, and Parliament took up their case. Gholam Hoseyn Karbastchi's imprisonment in April set off demonstrations by his supporters, and in June and July the televising of his trial was watched by the same audiences that had watched the World Cup soccer matches. Added to this, in September and October, the system for selecting candidates to the Assembly of Experts opened a constitutional discussion on the role of that institution and, above all, on the very principle of screening of candidates by the Council of Guardians, as well as relaunching the polemic on the concept of *velayat-e faqih*. In a more tragic manner, the assassination of various intellectuals and of legal opponents such as the Forouhar couple received much criticism and questioning in the newspapers and, once again, through street demonstrations, which one after the other contributed to the telling of the truth and to the questioning of the security forces right up to high ranking officials in the Ministry for Information. We are far from speaking of a real democratization as the following dramatic examples show: Ansar-e Hezbollah's attacks on their political foes (including ministers), the circumstances surrounding the death sentence on the editor-in-chief of *Iran News* Morteza Fourzzi, or those of the banning of the *Tous* newspaper. However, the progress made in pluralism as well as the public use of reasoning are undeniable and even appear to be irreversible.

Secondly, and paradoxically, the political sphere has not ceased differentiating itself from the religious sphere ever since the institutionalization of the Islamic Republic. This rests on a legitimacy which is both religious and democratic. This duality has had repercussions right at the heart of the country's political structures. The twenty or so popular debates that have been held since the Revolution, such as the debate between constitutionalists and transcendentalists on *velayat-e faqih*, or the reservations held by a large part of the high-ranking clergy concerning excessive politicization in the religious sphere, have all favored the disassociation of the latter from its relationship with the state. Political developments in the last few years have given numerous illustrations of this evolution. In the winter of 1994–95, Ali Khamenei, the Supreme Leader, found that he was unable to make others accept his primacy as the "Guiding Light" in the same way that other great Ayatollahs had done before him, and as a consequence Ayatollah Montazeri kept his religious followers despite the degradation of his relations with the state. More recently, the Council of Guardians accepted only one candidate for the Assembly of Experts in the Qom province, which shows once again the distancing of the Holy City in relation to the religious ideology of the state. At the very pinnacle of the state structure, there is a complementarity between the roles of the Supreme Leader, the incarnation of religious legitimacy and of revolutionary state, and the President of the Republic (who is responsible for government affairs). This complementarity, which already characterized the relations between Ali Khamenei and Hashemi Rafsanjani, and appears to be repeating itself with Mohammad Khatami, shows the diversification of these two spheres very well.

Thirdly, the Islamic Republic has maintained the centralization of the state inherited from the Pahlavi regime. However, it simultaneously upholds an increasing differentiation between different national spaces. Large regional towns such as Mashhad, Shiraz, Isfahan, and Tabriz bear this out. Furthermore, the 1980–88 war, the opening of the northern border following the fall of the Soviet Union, the magnitude of Afghan and Iraqi immigration, and the intensification of commercial trading (whether legal or not) with the Gulf have all succeeded in reconstituting the human and economic geography of Iran. The regeneration of the Republic owes much to this provincial dynamism which is found in all social and cultural spheres. Likewise, the increasing power of certain places of pilgrimage and certain free zones in the Gulf have participated in the renewal of relations between the two regions, through an increase in mutual exchanges between them. This renewal also underlies the extraordinary mobilization of charity which runs through Iranian society and which is currently being translated into real investments in the infrastructural sector. All this indicates that the

Islamic Republic is still competent twenty years after its establishment. Its faculty for adaptation, in spite of itself and without its knowing, must not be underestimated, particularly because the Republic is endowed with genuine representational institutions that guarantee a minimum amount of interaction between state and society, whatever the part that coercion plays in all this. On the other hand, the exiled opposition appears to be out of touch with reality within the country and is far from representing a viable alternative.

The state's main challenge today is of an economic nature: the collapse of domestic crude oil prices as well as the global crisis means that a structural adjustment is needed and that the unyielding corporate power structure seems incapable of putting it into motion. The deterioration in the standard of living has already been the cause of numerous riots since 1992. However, until the contrary is proved, these protests would seem to be of a social nature rather than a political one. Twenty years on from the Revolution, the Islamic Republic is still following its original course.

Contrary to what has been said, this has not been an out-and-out struggle between conservatives, moderates, and radicals. Paradoxically, what is taken as Mohammad Khatami's strength can sometimes be considered his weakness or failure. This can be explained as follows. In a society as diverse as Iran today, the notion of a providential figurehead is no longer relevant and Mohammad Khatami will never be considered the savior of Iran as some would wish. On the contrary, he presides over the negotiations, deliberations, and stable compromises of not only the different factions within his majority party—mainly the Islamic left and the Servants of Reconstruction group—but also (and above all) with the Right, even if its *de facto* politics has marginalized the different participants intimately associated with the development of the Republic since the Revolution. This is shown, for example, in the numerous skilled workers who come from an ex-serviceman background. In doing this Mohammad Khatami has affirmed his autonomy in relation to the forces that brought him to power. This has been attested by the creation of the Islamic Iran Participation Front, and also in the way that Hashemi Rafsanjani cut his original links with the right-wing movement by creating the Servants of Reconstruction group. From this point of view Gholam Hoseyn Karbastchi's disgrace is not necessarily bad news for the President of the Republic. The essential truth, however, lies elsewhere—in the eventual consolidation of a system in which the main forces remain represented within the institutions, or at least within political and civic society, and which at the same time shows itself capable of adapting to social transformations. In other words, the success, or at any rate the impact, of the Khatamist experience relies not on routing the conservatives but on the compromises that the reformers make with them. If this hypothesis is correct, then the political transition in Iran will be comparable *mutatis mutandis* with the democratic pacts that have been made in Latin America.

In short, Iranian society remains profoundly marked by the Revolution and by the regime which followed it. In this sense it has remained Islamic and even, on the whole, Islamist, in that its ideology as well as the republican institutions have contributed to the building of the infrastructure in all spheres. It is therefore not a question of knowing if Iran is post-Islamist or not; the question is a doubtful one and, when all is said and done, not even a very interesting one. On the contrary, it would be better to understand the dynamics of this society, and more precisely, the interaction between the question of Islamic politics and the changes within family, economic, and religious spheres. Rather than tackling the crux of the problem and at the risk of becoming entwined in the intricacies of the debates on Islam, it would be better to analyze the social practices central to everyday life and people (independent of their sex, age, or other social grouping). These are the people who participate in religious life without being confined by it, and who are the object of political and economic investment, as in the case of the social customs and practices of death, which, as we will see below, is at the heart of the question of creating a public space.

Funeral practices and the forming of a public space

The process of forming a public space as a "public forum for reasoning" has been the result of tension between two closely linked phenomena, even if these phenomena sometimes appear contradictory. On the one hand, there is the rationalization and bureaucratization of social life, and on the other, the tendency to turn towards oneself—which Giddens calls *self-reflexivity*.[5] One of the main manifestations of this process of forming a public space has been the production of judicial laws that concern social life and that register the negotiations between each individual's personal work on self-reflexivity and the public policies of the people in power. However, if Islamic religious practices *stricto sensu* such as daily prayers or marriage customs—and even if marriage preparations are an important family affair—are of great significance, it is the customs surrounding death that dominate social life. They dictate the rhythm of calendar and daily life, as is seen in the rites concerning the first day after death, the third day, the seventh, the fortieth, the first anniversary of a death and then the second, and so on. Families do not cease commemorating the death of family members (nor of families-in-law, neighbors' families, or of friends). The weekly cycle is itself marked by the fact that Thursdays and Fridays are consecrated to those who have passed on (*raftegan*), and you only have to face the traffic jams on the motorway between Tehran and Behesht-e

---

[5] Anthony Giddens, *Modernity and Self-Identity* (Stanford University Press, 1991).

Zahra every weekend to realize the social significance of remembering the dead. It therefore goes without saying that the religious calendar itself is organized around the commemoration of martyred saints, such as Imam Ali, Imam Hoseyn, Imam Hassan, etc. Indeed, it need hardly be said that the Ashura processions, a fundamental part of the Shiite religion, are mourning ceremonies. Concerning death, the religious calendar also puts restraints on other spheres of social life: thus one does not marry during the months of Moharram, Safar, or Ramadan, periods which often coincide with a large number of Saint days. In the winter of 1995–96, Iranian television was obliged to repeat a number of episodes of the soap opera *Patriarch* several times over in order not to air a marriage scene at an inappropriate time. Finally, even the political calendar is dictated by the social and religious importance of death. In 1978, the revolutionary preparations followed the rhythm of commemoration dates concerning Saints, national heroes, and martyrs killed by the tyrants' bullets during demonstrations. In a matter of faith, no sooner had Imam Khomeini descended from the plane bringing him home from exile than he went to the Behesht-e Zahra cemetery. The terrorist acts of the Mojahedin movement, as well as the war with Iraq, inspired a cult of martyrs that has given rise to a veritable republican liturgy. This has scarcely lessened in intensity over the years, particularly because the bodily remains of active servicemen are still being repatriated as negotiations with Baghdad progress.

However, these funeral practices, rather than expressing a (non-religious) Shiite tradition, were in fact expressing social and cultural innovation. The relationship with death has been profoundly changed over the last few decades, and the media has greatly contributed to this change. During the war with Iraq, the remembrance of martyrs fallen on the battlefields was glorified in the newspapers and on television:[6] their biographies and photos were published and their near relatives were interviewed. In this context funeral ceremonies have been modified. Where they were organized by state or para-statal institutions, they tended to become bureaucratic, and they have dramatized the Ashura processions. Funerals started to be announced with black-bordered invitations and were accompanied by feasts. They were organized around a large pictorial representation of the deceased painted on a plastic canvas, a photograph of which was then reproduced in the obituary columns and consequently placed on the tomb along with personal effects. Through this new ritualizing, the deceased was no longer the absent one as he had been before, he was now considered as a hero amongst the living.

Most of these innovations continued after the war. Firstly, because the martyrs continued to be commemorated and their cult thus became an important source of benefit, even of social privilege, despite the

---

[6] Farhad Khosrokhavar, *L'Islamisme et la mort* (Paris: L'Harmattan, 1995).

continuing bitter feeling of useless death. Secondly, because the main part of funeral ceremonies today is based on the model inaugurated in the 80s. Thus, the portrait of the deceased is often carved on the tombstone, the custom of a procession has been continued, the last resting place is abundantly covered with flowers and greenery and is visited assiduously, and finally the dead person is made known through posters and obituary announcements in the press.

One interesting thing is that women have not been the last ones to benefit from this evolution. As recently as the 70s it was still not accepted practice to publicly call a woman by her first name, and when they died the eventual condolences (for the custom of condolences had not yet been really established) were addressed to the family without specifying the identity of the deceased. Here Imam Khomeini broke with tradition, as the first names of both his daughters, as well as that of his wife, were known. The latter, moreover, gave an interview after his death, not hesitating to recall certain details of their private life, such as his proposal of marriage and the criteria of her consent.[7] Nowadays she organizes religious services in memory of the Imam, in the *hosseynieh* (religious meeting place) at Jamaran, a place that has immortalized his memory through the use of television cameras. As his wife she has perpetuated his memory through imitating his way of greeting the crowds and of withdrawing from public life according to his particular customs. Even his son spoke in the press of the Imam's "*Fati azizam*"—his dear wife—as he had done in his will, preferring to use the intimate diminutive of her first name Fatima.[8] In contrast, Ali Khamenei's family stays very much in the background, and even Hashemi Rafsanjani, who travels willingly with his wife and whose daughters are very active on the public stage, prefers speaking of "our family" to designate his wife: "our family threw herself on me (to protect me)," he declared after the first attempt on his life in 1994. But this style of behavior, although maybe more acceptable in certain circles, is practiced less and less. In everyday life, the first names of women are known and used, including in politics. *A fortiori,* wives and daughters sign and co-sign mourning announcements by giving their respective first names in the same way as the men, just as in the West. They no longer conceal themselves behind such trite statements as "the family of such and such shares the grief of such and such a family."

Others address the messages of condolences when they are not the ones to take the initiative of announcing the death of their husbands or others close to them. Deceased women's photos can be similarly reproduced in the obituary columns or on tombstones; and these images have only been made possible through the wearing of the veil. The veil has not only

[7] *Ettela'ab*, Mar. 12, 1373/1994.
[8] *Keyhan*, Jan. 9, 1374/1995.

allowed religious boundaries to be shifted, but has allowed women modesty whilst adhering to religious norms. Hashemi Rafsanjani himself, although being traditionalist with regards to his wife, allowed photographs of his mother to be published when she passed away in 1995. While the funeral took place under a large poster of the old lady, the cameras showed the President of the Republic's every emotion. This was an important scene to the extent that publicity given to the private grief of a public figure thus contributed to the making of a public forum. For the first time in the contemporary history of Iran, an official funeral was given to an ordinary woman, something with which everyone could identify.[9] Only a few months before her death the press had published a report on a visit by Hashemi Rafsanjani to his mother in her village in the province of Kerman. The press titled the story: "Observations at an important meeting in a small house."[10] Thus the public learnt of the modest surroundings in which the old lady lived and through this simple episode the President's popularity increased.

In this way, albeit rather belatedly, death contributes not only to the individualization of the deceased, but also to the living. For example, at the moment of internment, a funeral oration is given in which the virtues of the deceased are voiced, as well as the individual grief of each of the living, named one after the other, often by their first names, and insisting, if need be, on the helplessness of the wife or husband and also invoking the functions or titles of close relatives. A discreet homage is paid to the qualities of the deceased and to the status of the family. For this reason death has become a more and more expensive affair and has established itself as a permanent preoccupation. It is a matter of accumulating enough money over the years to ensure that you receive a funeral service worthy of your status, and to acquire an appropriate plot for your grave—the prices of which have not ceased to rise. Through business speculation in cemeteries, the use of funeral caterers, the billing of funeral services, the publishing of obituaries in the press, and the printing of invitation cards, death has now become part of a middle class commercial world; and being middle class is something Iranians aspire to more and more.

Death is also, through this creation of individuality of social distinctions, a forum for rationalization and bureaucratization. The energetic mayor of Tehran wasted no time in taking over the control of the large cemetery at Behesht-e Zahra, the name of which means the heaven of Zahra (the Prophet's daughter). The cemetery, situated to the south of Tehran, measures 400 hectares[11] and adjoins Imam Khomeini's mausoleum; it is the same cemetery that Imam Khomeini came to immediately

---

[9] *Akhbar*, Oct. 2, 1374/1995.

[10] *Keyhan*, Jun. 1, 1374/1995.

[11] The cemetery only uses 200 hectares at the present time, the other 200 are being kept in reserve.

after his return from exile. It is also where many martyrs of the revolution and of the war are buried. The cemetery's mortuary aims to centralize all the deceased from the capital and to register each death. The mortuary also supplies families with a means of transport from the cemetery to the outlying countryside if necessary or if they so wish.[12] The emphasis is on hygiene, precision, and efficiency. The body is first taken by ambulance to the hospital, where it is bathed and cleaned by professional medical staff; the close relatives watch from behind a glass screen. The hospital authorities usually then prefer the body to be taken to the cemetery, where the wake is held. As to precision, the administrative office at the cemetery is computerized and can give quick decisions as to the siting of graves. It also keeps records as to the causes of death. As concerns efficiency, the cemetery aims to take no longer than twenty minutes to complete the necessary formalities, including the selling of a permanent plot, letting a plot for thirty years, receiving payment for various funeral accessories such as hiring a singer (a *maddah*) and setting up hi-fi equipment, the letting of a reception hall, supplying the catering, the flowers, mourning clothes, a headstone, the printing of notices, and even publishing the obituary in the daily press. The municipality's obsession with rationalization and hygiene goes to the point of contemplating the mechanization of the process of bathing and cleaning of bodies, a move which has met with theological opposition and which would need a *fatwa* to authorize it. However, a visit to Behesht-e Zahra leaves a strong impression, with its air of an ideal city, its straight lined avenues and mounds, its fountains and numbered plots, its clean empty graves, dug according to religious tradition and awaiting their occupants. However, the place also often has tragicomic scenes where the sheer number of funerals taking place at the same time means that sound systems can overlap, and that the hired singers wail themselves hoarse running from one funeral to another, followed by young assistants carrying their sound equipment to minimize delay. Sometimes in the confusion, families no longer know who they are mourning for, or get into the wrong bus when the funeral disperses.

Those who speak of rationalization often speak of innovation. Since 1983 tombs have been allowed to have two levels, shrouds are now stitched contrary to traditional customs, and believers are encouraged to be future organ donors in return for a discount in funeral expenses—in which case another form has to be filled in. The distance between graves has been reduced to fit in 1,200 plots in an area that would previously take only 1,000. The majority of these modifications were legalized through *fatwas*, due to the worry about purifying the faith of its unconventional practices, be it from a religious, rational, or scientific point of view.

---

[12] Following the example of all the other public services, these means of transport are expensive and have been hotly criticized by passengers.

However, those who speak of rationalization also frequently speak of inequality. The cemetery at Behesht-e Zahra can be seen to be socially differentiated between the more sheltered permanent graves and the rented burial places, which are usually much less well looked after. Family tombs, as in Europe, are a sign of wealth and again certain areas are reserved for martyrs or artists, thus making them politically or culturally distinct.[13] This partly explains why the process of bureaucratization and the individualization of death has not been without conflict. For example, the administration in Behesht-e Zahra, through its concern for efficiency and cost-efficiency, is always in favour of giving out contracts to private companies, but within the right-wing free market policies of the state was unable to privatize the bathing and cleaning of the deceased due to the outcry of the press, and this has caused many problems. Last but not least, the development of cemeteries has become a much disputed urban stake, thus prolonging the battle for land and property which has ripped through cities in modern day Iran right up to buying one's eternal resting place. At Isfahan for example, the university, anxious to buy an old Christian cemetery in order to enlarge its premises, met with opposition from not only the large Armenian community there who declared that Shah Abbas had donated the land to them in perpetuity and who wished to build houses on it, but also from a city council department who wished to build an amusement park there. The dispute has been temporarily put on hold while an application to class the site as of tourist and historical value to the town is considered. Again at Tabriz, the city council intends to buy up a Christian cemetery, despite opposition from the French government, who is the owner.[14]

In Tehran, the Imamzadeh Abdollah cemetery which lies on the road to Rey has been the object of sizeable conflicts. This burial ground has always been a favorite amongst the better off due to its location and charm. A law passed before the Revolution forbade the selling of new plots, with the result that wide-scale speculation and fraud ensued concerning the ownership of different plots. In order to break the ring of speculators—the famous *dallal* held in contempt by Gholam Hoseyn Karbastchi being an example—the city council stepped in and forbade any further interments. Gossip then amplified to the proportions of a project to build a park there, to the great worry of grave plot owners. The city council protested its innocence and restated its intentions to simply improve the site and to break the ring of land speculators. However, once again the city council's energetic methods went awry: 800 grave plot owners swore that, contrary to the

---

[13] In 1995 one could rent a burial place for 10,000 toman, or buy it for between 30,000 and 200,000 toman. Family tombs were valued at about 3 million toman.

[14] The cemetery contains the tombs of the first Europeans, some of them well known, who came to work under the Safavids. Interview with Ali Mazaheri in November 1996 in Isfahan.

administration's assertions, they had never given their permission for any-thing to be demolished, and demanded henceforth to be party to the negoti-ations for the improvement of the Emamzadeh Abdollah site. The death business thus became a way for citizens to express their desire to partici-pate in land speculation.[15] In a similar way, the speculation over eternal resting places in Behesht-e Zahra prompted the authorities to severely restrict the ownership of plots as well as their use. Only those holding the title of ownership and their immediate family could be buried there. All future transfers were stopped, in order to prevent intermediaries buying the family plot and reselling individual graves at higher prices; in other time-honored words "their hands were cut off."

What needs to be understood from all this is that the process of individu-alization, of bureaucratization, and of rationalization in the most universal act of all—that of dying, which is in Iran almost without exception lived out in religious terms—forms an essential part of creating a public forum. We have already seen many indications of it here. But this point needs to be clar-ified one more time. Above all, one must underline the emotional, social, and economic investment that death involves for nearly all Iranians. Every Thursday afternoon, time is devoted to commemorating the dead, and on Fridays, the day of rest, families hurry to visit their dear ones' tombs. The ritual is prepared at home and in the neighborhood, in particular through the making or buying of dishes and fruit which are then distributed to neighbors and passers-by in memory of the dead. This form of religious sociableness is a definite part of the public forum. One of the consequences is, as has already been shown, the resulting traffic jams on the motorway between Tehran and Qom. To this one must add the specific commemorations of the third, seventh, and fortieth day, the first anniversary of death, as well as the different commemorations that follow, including that of Noruz. Each of these occasions is a pretext for distributing food, and certain reception rooms at Behesht-e Zahra are large enough for 5,000 guests. Yet this funeral sociability is not in any way isolated from other spheres of life, in the same way that *jaleseh* (women's religious gatherings) are not exclusively religious meetings. Young people exchange looks and future mother-in-laws often size up suitable suitors at these gatherings. The same singers (*maddah*) who sang the praises of the dead and whose talent is measured by the quantity of tears shed by the audience, also enliven wedding parties; to this end they will often go from a funeral to a wedding. One may perhaps catch the situation by quoting Peter Brown's description of the situation in late antiquity: "The rise of the cult of saints is without a doubt seen by contemporaries as a breaking down of imaginary boundaries that the elders had established between Heaven and Earth, divine and

---

[15] *Akhbar*, Jan. 15, 1375/1995.

human, the living and the dead and space both civic and non-civic."[16]

In their intensity these various funeral practices have inspired an increasing involvement on the part of the authorities. The management at Behesht-e Zahra distributes booklets, either freely or at very little cost, describing funeral procedures step by step, not only to comfort the bereaved families, but also to reconcile them to the idea of death, and forestall any eventual differences with future interlocutors. It even wishes to encourage academic research on the subject. The act of dying involves the written word more and more, not only as concerns registering a death and collecting statistics, but also in the realm of scientific knowledge. It must now join harmoniously with the exigency for self-reflexivity that is inherent to globalization.[17] Besides the written word, images too play an important role, as an increasing number of funerals are photographed and filmed, in the same way that weddings and feasts of homage are. Besides, this creation of a public forum through the formalities of death also involves the business world (*sherkat*). As we have seen earlier, private companies are becoming more and more involved in funeral activities in accordance with the general evolution of society, as well as sponsoring the funeral expenses of employees, martyrs, and even the needy. Finally, public management of death obviously brings together two fundamental processes in the creation of a public forum, that is, the creation of municipal parks and sporting events. The administration at Behesht-e Zahra manages the largest green space in the city. It is a far cry from the dangerous, arid area full of lizards, snakes, rats, and anthills that it used to be. It is now a fertile area cared for by armies of gardeners as well as by the families themselves, who contribute to the growing of plants on individual graves. As in the public gardens of the capital, the cemetery has refreshment rooms and play areas. In short, the zealous state administration has endeavored to produce a paradise on earth. In the same way, the cult of martyrs tends to lend itself, in rather a confused way, to a sportive imagery, no doubt because one can speak simultaneously of youth and heroes. Thus, the *Keyhan* newspaper publishes daily items in its sports columns on young martyrs who have died on the battlefields, and the commemorations of Imam Khomeini's death are accompanied by cycling, athletics, and even soccer competitions. One can see that a dying person is becoming more and more an *adam-e ejtemai*, a being-in-society. It is revealing moreover that messages of condolence published in the press are frequently published by companies. Belonging to the world of *sherkat* and no longer to that of the guilds is now the sign of social recognition. In the same way, offerings to a deceased one's family now often take the form of calculated donations. Rather than offer a meal to close relatives on the commemoration date of the deceased's death, it

---

[16] Peter Brown, *Le Culte des saints. Son essor et sa fonction dans la chrétienté latine* (Paris: Cerf, 1996), p. 34.

[17] Giddens, *Modernity and Self-Identity*.

is now preferable to make a donation to charity—to a mosque, to a family in need, to pay for a child's medical care, or even to pay for a dowry for a poor family—and this is announced in the national press.

Funeral practices and the creation of a political forum

Adding to the eloquence of Behesht-e Zahra, the surrounding area houses not only Imam Khomeini's mausoleum and his theological college, but also new fruit and vegetable halls, the future airport and its hotels, and the first underground railway line. The grand cemetery of Tehran is no longer the antithesis of the living city, but is instead becoming the center of gravity for the capital in the century to come.

We can pinpoint this contribution of funeral practices to the emergence of a civil society and a public forum by emphasizing two things. On the one hand, they are an essential element in the charity movement, representing the main form of social mobility; on the other, the funeral practices have directly contributed to the building of political society and to political mobility. Thus, funerals of a certain number of well-known people have been the scene of several more or less radical political demonstrations. Public memorial services have been held for Mohammad Mossadegh and Ali Shariati. Medhi Bazargan's funeral in January 1995 was followed by a sizeable crowd and was dotted with slogans acclaiming liberty. In an even more explicit manner, the funerals of various intellectuals assassinated by the state secret service in autumn 1998 were the scene of several impressively large manifestations of respect, of solidarity, and the rejection of violence—something which may have encouraged President Khatami to radicalize his speeches and to gain an advantage over his opponents. The fact that these funeral demonstrations benefit from being perfectly legal makes their repression or political disqualification a *de facto* impossibility.

In a more subtle way, one can without a doubt find numerous religious processes in Iran that historians have shown to have contributed to the development of the city. In the 5th century, according to Peter Brown, Christian bishops in Western Europe "founded cities in the cemeteries."

[They] ended up orchestrating the cult of saints in such a way as to establish their own power within the old Roman towns rather than in the new towns outside the city walls. The bishop's residence and his principal church were always to be found within the walls. Nonetheless, it was through carefully arranged relations with the grand sanctuaries built at some distance from the city—St. Peter's on the Vatican hill outside Rome, St. Martin's a little apart from Tours—that the bishops of the old Roman cities retained their superiority in the Europe of the Middle Ages.[18]

The analogy is obvious. There is a further clear analogy with the Marqad-e Imam/Behesht-e Zahra complex, managed respectively by the Khomeini

---

[18] Brown, *Le Culte des saints.*

family concerning the Imam's mausoleum and by Tehran city council for the large cemetery. Ever since the Imam visited the cemetery after descending from the plane bringing him home from France, Behesht-e Zahra has been one of the great pillars of the Iranian Republic, and the mausoleum is an obligatory visit for state guests. Every Friday morning a ritual is performed at Behesht-e Zahra. *Salavati* (free) buses convey the faithful there, the *do'aye nodbeh* (a special prayer) is read, and families pay their private respects to their dead. The country's leaders do not miss an opportunity to speak there at regular intervals, and one remembers, for example, that the second assassination attempt on Ali-Akbar Hashemi Rafsanjani took place within its walls in 1994. In short, the sanctuary and the cemetery dominate the center of power from the edge of the city.

At first sight, the other great sanctuaries in Iran do not correspond to this model as they were built in the very center of the towns, or at least that is where they are to be found today. This is particularly the case with Imam Reza's mausoleum at Mashhad, that of Hazrat-e Ma'sumeh at Qom, and of Shahzadeh Abdolazim at Rey. In fact, one can also observe in these situations an exterior relationship both towards the center of the political system and towards the mass of believers who go there —an exterior relationship which goes hand in hand with the force of its symbolic influence. Situated 120 kilometers south of Tehran, Qom equally exercises its power over the Republic's institutions, and notably over the magistrate of the Society of Teachers at the Religious School, who has shown his political bias through his intervening in the process of selecting candidates for elections. The Holy City is the twin or the godmother of the capital, towards whom everyone turns for assent. In the same way, Astan-e Qods of Mashhad, as autonomous as it is, represents a fundamental resource in the national political game; the Supreme Leader is nearby and regularly dusts the offerings left by pilgrims in the sanctuary. As long ago as the 19th century and right up to the 1970s, Shiism was recognized as Iran's national religion, through the influence of Karbala and Najaf, and it was from the latter that Imam Khomeini carried out his preaching against the Shah.

It is clear that in this way the sanctuaries conceal a crude fact: "the accumulation of wealth and patronage," to quote Peter Brown.[19] The economic function of holy places with their various bazaars is obvious. However, this should not be separated from the accumulation of influence or of political visibility that the economic function allows or that it accompanies. The running of a sanctuary is not only a question of good management. It has become a key tool in the political power struggle, and even a means of admission to political circles. This has been largely due to Imam Khomeini's mausoleum, which his son Hassan has continued to manage very efficiently, and that he has also used to his

---

[19] Ibid., p. 58.

political advantage. Similarly, Hojjatoleslam Mohammad Rey Shahri, the leader of Iranian believers' pilgrimages to Mecca, has built his political career around Shahzadeh Abdolazim sanctuary, of which he was made chief administrator by the Supreme Leader in 1990. He now publishes a daily newspaper called *Rey*, and was a presidential candidate for the center left in the 1997 elections.

These examples illustrate the importance of holy places in the political forum very well. Each of the main presidential candidates identified with and used the prestige of a particular sanctuary: Ali Akbar Nategh Nouri with that of Astan-e Qods, Mohammad Khatami with the Marqad-e Imam, and of course Mohammad Rey Shahri with that of the Shahzadeh Abdolazim. In this way, religious ceremonies, repeatedly and willingly shown on television, have become crucial moments in political expression. As far back as 1996, prospective candidates for the legislative elections used *eftar*, the time after sunset during Ramadan, to publicize their manifestos and to discreetly campaign, even though the official presidential campaign had not yet started. The weekly satirical magazine *Golagha* published an article entitled: "Vote for me, I am an orphan."[20]

It is therefore plain to see that the state is committed to systematically listing holy places, renovating and improving them, and consequently trying to control them by giving the management of these places to the clergy. The local populations too can aspire to esteemed recognition through the reputation of their sanctuaries. They are also a source of finance and wealth, even if conflicts inevitably arise between the sanctuary's desire for autonomy and the administrative clergy's involvement. Just as with Latin Christianity, there has been a significant development in the cult of saints, due largely to the people themselves. There has been a large movement nationwide towards institutionalizing the sanctuaries, a fact which presents an insurmountable obstacle for politicians, for governmental plans, and even for local notables. The movement concerns the majority of believers who, in a rather confused way, negotiate the outlines and orientation of the religious aspect of the public forum. Thus they can, as good citizens, revive the memory of such and such a saint unjustly forgotten, or decide, as was the case during the war with Iraq, to pay homage to Imam Hassan the pacifist rather than the intransigence of Imam Hoseyn, as exalted by the official state speeches. Or again, they can decide to piece together a saint from amongst the living or the dead of their close relatives, through a revelation or some extraordinary combination of circumstances. This process of producing saints from amongst the masses means that total centralization of the religious sphere is rendered impossible. Rather, there is an interaction between different religious bodies, and from this specifically a public forum has been formed. At the very

[20] *Golagha*, 46, 1374/1996.

least, this is a hypothesis that we can consider. It is also necessary to widen the group of entrepreneurs who are at the center of this social mobility in favour of saints. Speaking of Latin Christianity, Peter Brown writes:

Far from describing a reluctant political concession to the blind forces of habit formed by the "common herd," one met with a serious-minded managerial group, who took initiatives, made choices and through doing all this, created an official language which persisted throughout western Europe right into the heart of the Middle Ages.[21]

In Iran, the creators of saints find recruits amongst "good citizens." These creators are always ready to hold aloft the banner of honor of some saint that they care about. The creation of this sectarian public space brings us back to the problem of "pilgrimage" as formulated by Victor Turner, and brought up again by Benedict Anderson,[22] concerning a national "imagined community." All the more so since the pilgrimages in Iran to the resting places of saints that involve millions of believers every year are not only of a religious nature. They equally furnish an occasion to visit family, to do a little traveling, to over-indulge a little, and even to do business.

One often speaks about "pilgrimage and relaxing"[23] (*ziyarat-o siyahat*) or of "pilgrimage and trade" (*ziyarat-o tejarat*). In other words, the ongoing process of creating a sectarian public forum is intertwined with that of creating a civic bourgeois society, a consumer society, and a political one. It is difficult for the analyst to isolate the institutionalization of a multi-layered religious sphere, where the rationalization of different practices and their place in the imagination both vie for the individualization of believers, from the rise of *sherkat* and the commercialization of daily life to the spread of political and electoral activities. The social specificity of religion thus becomes relative.

For example, pilgrimages to saints' resting places provide women with an opportunity of "being-in-society," in particular amongst the middle classes. They can now visit places such as Mashhad, Damascus, or Mecca whilst among parents or friends, or even to go on organized trips with people from the same religious group, school, business group, or workplace. They use the occasion not only to pay their respects to a particular saint, or to the Prophet, but also to stay in a hotel, to go out to restaurants, to visit places, and to shop. They can now, like their menfolk, be missed at home, be welcomed warmly upon their return, and have stories and adventures to tell. To paraphrase Peter Brown once again, the Islamic Republic has created a new class of benefactors within the religious sphere, that of

---

[21] Brown, *Le Culte des saints*, p. 69.

[22] Victor and Edith Turner, *Image and Pilgrimage in Christian Culture: Anthropological Perspectives* (Oxford: Blackwell, 1978); Benedict Anderson, *Imagined Communities*, expanded edn. (New York: Verso, 1991).

[23] One must consider that the development of tourism in Iran owes a lot to the organization of so-called tourist pilgrimage institutions in the country.

women—women whose charitable and social work is tireless and is even carried over, if need be, to political circles. Many of them made charitable donations to soldiers at the front during the war with Iraq, and to the Palestinian cause during Yasser Arafat's visit in 1979. An unkind cartoon at the time showed the Fatah leader smiling triumphantly and leaning towards his female audience to thank them for the pile of gold jewelry they had offered him. The massive presence of women in the sanctuaries proves their integration into society, for the sanctuaries are not only places of worship, but also of managerial innovation, economic rationalization, and political participation.

In summarizing the possible relationship between funeral practices on the one hand and the process of forming a public and political space on the other, there are a certain number of obvious and trivial facts that one must nevertheless mention. Death is universal and sacred. On this account it transcends political, social, and ethnic differences, and constitutes a virtual privileged meeting between the different members of society, including the holders of political or religious power and ordinary believers. On this point, death is also a time of choosing between different transactions, even of making claims and of making them legitimate. In the same way, death renders social affirmation in the public forum respectable: the cult of martyrs, or to be more mundane, the funeral ceremonies have made not only young people, but also women, both socially and politically more visible in daily life, as well as at the very heart of government bodies. Thus death has opened a permanent renegotiation of the borderlines between private and public life. Intimate and of the family as it is, death has given the "being-in-society" an opportunity to define itself through funeral rites. In other words, death cannot be reduced to the suffering and mortifying feelings so often associated with revolutionary zeal or its betrayal.

We can thus see how the debate around political Islam and alleged post-Islam is very often too limited. To confine it to a strictly political argument, if not to a single political discourse, leaves the essential social dynamics that participate in the forming of society out in the dark, whether they are politically orientated or not. For it is not only the funeral practices but all social practices which sketch the contours of the Islamic experience in the precise context of different societies, and which make Islam a shared adventure rather than an intriguing plot by a few agitators or a regime imposed by coercion alone. Whatever its political dimensions, Islam does not overshadow the social part of society. In that aspect it is not strictly speaking totalitarian, as is the case with Soviet or Maoist communism. Quite the contrary, Islam leaves a certain space, at least in Iran, to real interactions between public institutions and the spheres of family, religious matters, and even economic practices, to the extent where the illusion of an "Islamic economy" has fast disappeared. One way of reflecting on the matter would be to work on the "lifestyle" (Max Weber) that is nourished and fed, particularly in the social categories where it has had most support, and which cannot be reduced to merely mean the disinherited and disappointed, or the misfits of social change.

5

A RETURN TO THE SHARIAH?

EGYPTIAN JUDGES AND REFERRING TO ISLAM

Baudouin Dupret

This chapter seeks primarily to explain how in contemporary Egypt reference is made to the Shariah Islamiyyah, the Islamic law, taken here in a wider sense than its strictly legal one. Indeed, the Shariah is often referred to as the principle explaining the Islamic project. However, few attempts have been made to analyze the content of this reference and its methods. Does it refer to a clearly identified legal model that would thus only need to be reinstated, or are we dealing with a purely ideological discourse that uses the Islamic idiom for strictly political ends? The situation is not clear-cut, and I will seek to show the complexity of the use of references to Islam in Egyptian legal practice.

I will do so in three steps. Firstly, I will briefly survey the fields of Egyptian law where reference to religion is explicitly made. This will provide us with the main elements of the issue at hand and will put an end to speculation on the radically Islamic nature of Egyptian law. While doing so, I will also draw a basic typology of the judicial rulings referring to Islam. This will give us an initial insight into the ways that legal practicians interpret texts, some of which refer to Islam. This first section will thereby allow us to gauge the scope of the legal provisions on which the Islamic discourse focuses and the ways by which the judges use or get round the breaches that are thus left open.

Secondly, I will sketch a typology of the perceptions of the Shariah that the practicians of Egyptian law may hold. The aim is to look at how legal practicians use their readings to serve their ends. In examining what the legal actors think is or ought to be, I seek not to substantiate their discourse but rather to locate them in a power structure of which their discourse is both a reflection and a determining factor. A series of interviews with lawyers, judges, and professors of law, Shariah, and *fiqh* provides us with a body of perceptions of law and of the various legal repertoires that jurists use professionally and claim ideologically.

Finally, to conclude my overview, I will examine three recent cases in order to lay the foundations for my non-substantialist approach to Islam and to the normative discourse that claims to draw from it. There is the Abu Zayd case, in which a divorce was enforced on grounds of apostasy, a litigation on the wearing of the veil at school, and a case of trans-sexuality. In my view, these three cases reflect well the malleability of the reference to the Shariah in Egypt, that is, at least within the realm of law. The Shariah stands out as a legal repertoire, a resource that practicians have at their disposal and that they use simultaneously or in conjunction with others, in a game whose nature seems primarily rhetorical or discursive. These available means of discourse and legal action are used to a greater or lesser degree, according to the circumstances of time and place. It is this use that gives them a meaning, a content, and not their inscription on tables of the Law that are set for eternity. In this sense, the so-called return to the Shariah should be viewed as the invention of a new Shariah in the contemporary political, legal, and judicial setting.

The reference to Islam in law and in judicial practice

Whatever the importance given to Islamic law and to its norms in the construction of contemporary Egyptian statute law, the focus here will only be on what remains today as explicit reference to Islam. Indeed, my goal is not to trace the Islamic roots of the rules of Egyptian law, but only to locate the realms of this law where Islamic arguments still seem relevant. Three areas can be identified: criminal law, civil law, and constitutional law.

Islam in Egypt is the religion of the state (Const. art. 2) and its public management is the duty of the Shaykh al-Azhar, of the Mufti of the Republic, and of the Minister of Waqf, under the direct authority of the President of the Republic.[1] Regarding criminal matters, the sole explicit reference to Islam is the mandatory consulting of the Mufti of the Republic in cases where a death penalty is handed down by the Criminal Court.[2]

The realm of civil law contains a number of more substantial references to Islam. First, as regards procedure, the question was recently raised as to whether the *hisbah,* that is, the lawsuit to protect Islam that can be initiated by any Muslim, without his own interests having to be directly at stake, was still admissible in Egyptian law. Law number 3 of 1996 has confirmed the existence of this procedure while setting strict conditions for its use.

---

[1] P.-J. Luizard, "Al-Azhar, institution sunnite réformée," in *La Réforme sociale en Égypte*, ed. A. Roussillon (Cairo: Dossiers du CEDEJ, 1995); M. Paradelle. "Entre juge et mufti: la place du religieux dans l'organisation judiciaire égyptienne (A partir d'une lecture de l'article 381 du code de procédure pénale)," *Droit et cultures* 30, 1995, pp. 77–89; M. Zeghal, *Gardiens de l'islam. Les oulémas d'Al-Azhar dans l'Égypte contemporaine* (Paris: Presses de la FNSP, 1996).

[2] Paradelle, "Entre juge et mufti," p. 77.

Furthermore, in civil law there are also a number of explicit provisions, the most important of which is found in the first article of the Civil Code of 1948. This stipulates the principle of the sole competence of the law for all the matters it regulates and, "in the absence of an applicable legal provision," the competence of the judge to give a ruling "according to custom and, in its absence, according to the principles of the Shariah" (art. 1). Islamic law is thus ranked as the second subsidiary source to the law. Also, a realm is explicitly acknowledged for Islamic law and its principles in various sections of the Civil Code, particularly as regards successions (art. 875) and wills (art. 915). As for personal status (marriage, divorce, separation, alimony, child custody, inheritance, etc.), it is totally referred to the individual's denomination, each of those acknowledged in Egypt having its own specific legal texts and competent judicial chambers for the various levels of jurisdiction. As regards Muslims, a series of texts have codified the Hanafi legal tradition.[3] Regarding family matters, these are chiefly law 25–1920 and decree 25–1929, both amended by law 100–1985.[4] In the same way, laws 77–1943, 71–1946, and 25–1944 came to regulate in detail the realm of succession. Let us note that, understandably, no reference to Islam is made within these texts which already only apply to Muslims, except for cases of inter-communal marriage where it is forbidden to a Muslim woman to marry a non-Muslim.

Certainly the Constitution takes up central stage with regard to the reference to Islam in Egypt. This is mainly due to its article 2, which states that "Islam is the religion of the state, Arabic is its official language, and the principles of the Shariah are the main source of legislation." This article was amended in 1980 so that the principles of the Shariah have moved from the status of being *a* main source of legislation to that of *the* main source of legislation. Furthermore, this provision was used as grounds for claims of unconstitutionality brought before the Supreme Constitutional Court of Egypt (*al-Mahkamah al-Dusturiyyah al-'Ulya*).

As Bernard Botiveau says, "today the judicial system, in its general principles and in its outline holds many of the basic characteristics usually found when describing the judicial structure of a modern state."[5] These include separation of judiciary and administrative jurisdictional orders, of civil and criminal jurisdictions, independence of the judiciary, etc. The present system is unified and similar to the judicial structure of the countries with a French legal tradition. There is no longer any specifically Islamic jurisdiction, since the denominational courts were abolished and

---

[3] For Orthodox Copts, personal status regarding marriage and divorce is regulated by a decree of 1938.

[4] El Alami, 1994, "Law N°100 of 1985 Amending Certain Provisions of Egypt's Personal Status Law," *Islamic Law and Society*, 1:1, 1994, pp. 116–36.

[5] B. Botiveau, "L'exception et la règle. La justice vue par les magistrats (Annexe: L'organisation judiciaire de l'Égypte)," *Bulletin du CEDEJ*, 20, 1986, pp. 81–113.

replaced in 1955 by specialized sections of state courts. Civil law is divided into summary courts (for minor issues) and plenary courts at the first instance level, courts of appeal, and the Court of Cassation. Administrative law is handled by the Council of State, an institution made up of three sections (judiciary, consultative, and legislative), the highest of which is the High Administrative Court.[6] Egypt also has a Supreme Constitutional Court that has been carrying out its duties since the promulgation of its organic law (law 48–1979) and the adoption of its internal regulation code.[7] The Supreme Constitutional Court is competent regarding the interpretation of laws, controlling constitutionality, and conflict resolution concerning competence between jurisdictions. It can be referred to by any judge if the constitutionality of a law or of a statutory text is challenged.

Following this brief review of the sources of the law, of the role of the Islamic principle within it, and of judiciary competence, I will now focus on the Egyptian judges' attitude towards issues involving a reference to Islam. To this end, I will sketch a typology of the decisions referring to the Islamic legal repertoire.

The need to establish such a typology may take as its point of departure the decision by an Egyptian judge to sentence the enforcement of the Shariah punishment against an individual apprehended in a state of intoxication in a public place:

"Whereas the court refers to the preceding rules (rules contained in the doctrines) to judge on the nullity of any law contrary to the regulations of Divine Law, at the head of which are the repressive provisions concerning the present case. They are all invalid by absolute nullity. They are deprived of the reference to legality (shar'iyya). Thus the Shariía and its rules must be implemented, as a result of obedience to God and to His Envoy and by making possible the institution of His rules in the state."[8]

District court of 'Abidin, March 8, 1982

Beyond its declamatory nature, this type of ruling challenging statute law is only one among several types of reference to the Islamic legal repertoire. The rulings can be divided into four categories. The first is made up of rulings defining the content of Islam as a recognized and eventually privileged religion, or of the Shariah as a legislative reference. In the second category are found arguments utilizing Islam as a source of legitimation for rulings related first and foremost to the institutional form of the state or to a

[6] Kosheri, Rashed, and Riad, "Egypt," *Yearbook of Islamic and Middle Eastern Law* 1, 1994, pp. 125–41.

[7] R. Jacquemond, "Égypte: la Haute Cour Constitutionnelle et le contrôle de constitutionnalité des lois (1979–1987)," *Annuaire international de justice constitutionnelle* 4, 1988, pp. 271–95, and R. Jacquemond, "Dix ans de justice constitutionnelle en Égypte (1979–1990)," in *Politiques législatives: Égypte, Tunisie, Algérie, Maroc* (Cairo: Dossiers du CEDEJ, 1994).

[8] District court of 'Abidin, March 8, 1982. In M. 'A. H. Ghurab, *Jugements islamiques contredisant les lois positives* (in Arabic) (Cairo: Dar al-Itisam, 1986).

specific conception of public order. The third concerns the positive ratifying of rules of statute law whose wording is self-sufficient in itself and so does not explicitly justify the same kind of reference. Finally, in the fourth category, there are certain judiciary rulings that go as far as invalidating statute law in the name of the Shariah. Statute law, then, does not seem overly disturbed by references made to Islam and to its normative provisions, as long as these references are not made in order to challenge its validity and/or to require its subordination to an order external to it.

The first category, that of "objectivization," deals with situations where reference is made to Islam as a religion of which free worship is claimed. Such is the case for the question of wearing the veil at school. In this case, it is the definition of the Islamic norm itself that is the object of the dispute brought before the courts, where reference is made to the provisions dealing with religion, freedom of conscience, and public worship in statute law. The judgments of the Supreme Constitutional Court, when it gives a decision on the nature of the Shariah as a legislative reference, are also included in this category. In a judgment of May 15, 1993, the Court came to explicitly position itself in the realm of the Shariah and of its interpretation. Differentiating between the absolute and the relative principles of the Shariah, the Court stated that its control only extended to the absolute principles, without these being clearly identified.[9]

The second category, that of "instrumentalization," covers instances where reference to Islam is made in order to ground a ruling pertaining to a specific view of public order. In this case, the harm to Islam is instrumentalized by the judge or by the parties who, under this guise, seek a different objective. Here many reasons may be put forward. It can be argued that harm is made to Islam as the religion of the state and as a pillar of the institutions. For example, it is on this basis that, in another context, the Communist Party of Morocco (PCM) was banned:

Whereas the request of the Prosecution ... stems from the incompatibility of the principles of the PCM with Islam and the Islamic institutions;
Whereas it was wrongful for the first judges to consider that it was an accusation of heresy reaching beyond the competence of the regular courts ...;
Whereas HM King Mohammed V stated many times that any materialist ideology was contrary to the religious precepts of which he is the spiritual guardian ...;
Whereas the sovereign has thus directly and unambiguously identified the doctrines inspired from Marxism-Leninism ...;
For these reasons, the Court ... declares the dissolution of the association, with all the legal consequences.[10]

---

[9] On the evolution of the High Constitutional Court's jurisprudence regarding article 2, see B. Dupret, "A propos de la constitutionnalité de la shari'a: Présentation et traduction de l'arrêt du 26 mars 1994 (14 Shawwal 1414) de la Haute Cour Constitutionnelle [*al-mahkama al-dustûriyya al-'ulyâ*] égyptienne," *Islamic Law and Society* 4:1, 1997, pp. 91–113.

[10] The Court of Appeal of Rabat, 3 February 1960, the Supreme Court, May 28, 1964.

In other words, it can be argued that harm to Islam as the religion of the majority also affects public order. It is following such logic that in Morocco as well as in Egypt the Baha'i sect was considered heretical. In the former country, during the Nador trial, the accusation of heresy led to the sentencing to death and the execution on December 10, 1962, of three members of this faith rooted in Islam.[11]

The third category, that of "overvalidation," involves cases where reference is made to motivations which, in and of themselves, lie beyond the scope of the judiciary dispute. The judge grounds his ruling in general principles, such as that of religion and of the principles of law that stems from it in a state that makes Islam its religion. This in itself does not seem to be a particular problem. Resort to such principles serves to reinforce statute law. It is thus simply considered as a quasi-stylistic formula which faces no opposition. Bernard Botiveau refers to the resort to the Shariah as a measure of ratification.

The judge normally grounds his decisions in the 1985 law and in the provisions maintained from the 1929 law, more rarely in the 1920 law; equally, when in existence, in the running jurisprudence of the Court of Cassation. However, it happens frequently that he (the judge) also justifies his judgment either by a provision accepted by one of the Sunni schools of Islamic law, or by a ranking of the sources that is not always perceivable in the current debates on Islamization of law. In the former case, it confirms the current application of a rule justified by a number of precedents cumulated by an age-old tradition; by way of example, he quotes "the dominant view" ascribed to the Hanafite fiqh or an "established principle of fiqh" enjoying the consensus of all four Sunni schools, such as the mandatory providing for the wife. In the second case, the direct references to the Shari'a tend to legitimate the ruling by a very powerful principle: for instance the necessity of a harmonious life must lead to the acceptance of separation; the importance of the *nafaqat al-mut'a* (Koran II, 236), a special pension paid after a repudiation; or the *hadîth* legitimising in a general fashion divorce on the basis of injustice suffered subi (*Lâ darar wa lâ dirâr*, neither damage nor retaliation disproportionate to the damage. In a few cases, the judge will combine in a same judgment practically all the available sources, Shari'a, sunna, consensus of the Ulema, jurisprudence of the old Islamic courts, and statute law; for instance in order to establish that the alimony should be calculated based on the income of the husband.[12]

Finally, in the case of the "invalidation" category, the question is very different since the situation comes down to using the Shariah and the details of its normative formulation to invalidate statute law. Such is the case for a number of judgments passed by Judge Ghurab, in which he hands down a decision that he calls Islamic, in opposition to statute law,

---

[11] M. Tozy, "Islam et état au Maghreb," *Maghreb-Machrek, Monde arabe* 126, 1989, p. 27.

[12] B. Botiveau, *Loi islamique et droit dans les sociétés arabes. Mutations des systèmes juridiques du Moyen-Orient* (Paris: Karthala, 1993), p. 225.

which by the same token he declares illegitimate. Here is another excerpt from a ruling made by this judge:

"Thus, the existence of laws that are contradictory (with the Shariah) has become impossible, with the implication that to apply the laws of the Shariah is to implement the textual content of the Constitution itself and to purify the legislator from any form of profanation."[13]

The established legal and judiciary system thus finds itself faced with an obviously unacceptable assertion, a situation which leads it to react accordingly (judicial admonition and administrative measure attaching the judge to a non-contentious administration). But let us note the fact that what sets Judge Ghurab's stance apart is his explicit invalidation of statute law while the fact of using Islamic principles to ground a legal ruling is not uncommon.

Perspectives on Islam in law

In this section, I will examine the perceptions that various types of legal practicians hold of Islam and of its role in Egyptian law. Let us begin by underscoring the duality, indeed the plurality of repertoires to which these various actors refer explicitly (Islamic and statute law repertoires), even if it is only so as to challenge the relevance and/or the legitimacy of one of the two:

In Egypt, we have a mixed legal system: statute law is applied and Shariah is applied. The Shariah is the basis on which statute law rests.
(Interview with MD, lawyer, October 1994)

This acknowledgment of a plurality of repertoires may seem trivial, but overvaluing the Shariah may lead to a refusal to grant it a legal status that in a way it transcends:

There is a huge difference between a legislative document and the Shariah. The Shariah is not a legislative document but a life program.
(Interview with NH, lawyer, January 1994)

The simultaneous presence of various legal realms each reflecting a certain level of internal coherence brings forth the question of the transfers and adaptations that can be made between them. In other words, to what extent can the perceptions of the different legal repertoires be used outside their own original setting? In the Egyptian legal context, it seems that the actors operate through a displayed command of the various repertoires whose numerous provisions would be easily transferable, as long as the predominance of the religious reference is expressly acknowledged:

---

[13] District court of 'Abidin, 8 March 1982 in Ghurab, *Jugements islamiques.*

"Positive laws do not run against Islam, no more than they are in line with it. They are the laws proper to a state that is called the Arab Republic of Egypt. That is what I want you to understand. They are neither against nor in favor of Islam. They are not related to Islam. ... And so, in my work I deal with Egyptian law, I do not deal with a law that is against or in favor of Islam. I do not deal with this issue. For me, Islam doesn't and never will come down to laws."[14]

It is only the question of the referent that creates a problem, and not the content of provisions of which the actors acknowledge the very wide compatibility:

"The interpretation of texts and their application should refer to Islam. If this referential framework were found today, 90% of our problems would be solved."[15]

This notion of referent reflects the perception of a cultural normality, that of the authentic tradition that society supposedly considers as the sole legitimate one:

"Until the present, the Shariah is better suited for our societies. Why? Because people easily understand it. Why? Because it is related to the Koran which hundreds of thousands of people have memorized in each country. ... If I transform the humanly acceptable legal values into culturally acceptable ones, I guarantee them a better understanding, a better application, and that they will be considered as binding by the people. If people feel that it is their law and their religion, they will comply to it."[16]

Following the same logic, we find the construction of a cultural identity that can only come about through the construction of a cultural otherness. Law plays a major role here. It is in this sense that in any case I understand the discourses on the cultural integration of the legal heritage:

"We think that the Shariah is one of the visible signs of the expression of our independence towards the Western project. ... Such is the conflict today. It lies in the fact that it is our right, as a community that has a history and a heritage, to be governed and educated according to our history and our heritage."[17]

The idea of a social "normality" of Islamic law leaves the question of the content of this "normality" shelved. We can quite easily talk of a standard with regard to the discourse of legal practicians on the Shariah. The position of these actors is indeed located at the junction between technical knowledge and the common sense of the Shariah. This is due as much to a "latent legal knowledge" and to a "loss of legal knowledge accurate

[14] Interview with NH, lawyer, January 1994.
[15] Interview with AW, lawyer and former magistrate, June 1994.
[16] Ibid.
[17] Ibid.

enough to be explicitly argued"[18] as to a manifest will to subsume the legal dimension of the Shariah to its ethical and globalizing dimension.

"The rule on which there is general agreement is the right of the Creator to govern. As long as He is the One who creates, it is Him who knows all, whether it be past, present, or future. This right (*haqq*) is for the good of the governed (*mahkum*), since the one who creates doesn't need anything from the creation, from His creation. As long as He governs ... , there will be impartiality and equity. It is a basic condition of equity. It is a basic rule on which the sacredness of the judge stands. Consequently, the judge must meet various well-known requirements, by virtue of the Constitution : he must be virtuous (*muhsin*) and, when examining a petition, he must not seek anything other than signs of truth (*haqq*). The law says that if the judge has a stake in a petition, he must put off the case and part with it."[19]

I could never emphasize enough all that this type of discourse conveys on the transformation of the Islamic legal repertoire, well beyond any idea of reproduction. We are dealing here with the notion of legal memory, with the cognitive process of the construction of tradition. In this matter as well as in others, the need is not so much to oppose a "true history" to a "biased history" as to measure the extent to which history, especially in the legal and political realm, is primarily a historiography. Creating a classical model does not provide meaning as a standard of the deviations and/or conformities of the present. However, it allows the gauging of the actors' perceptions of such-or-such object at a certain point in time. In this sense, the classic referent, the reference to tradition, can only be analyzed within the framework of a process of (re)construction. Any tradition is a construct, even if this seems unacceptable to its supporter who acts "as if" that was not the case.

Thus, what we have before us is a staging of the self, whether collective or individual. The actors carry anticipations regarding what they believe to be socially acceptable and desirable. Their self-perception, which narrowly determines their behavior and the content of their actions, itself stems from perceptions and anticipated assessments of the social realm. As the staging of oneself, but also as the staging of the society to which the jurist attributes a compound of idealized norms, the process is not so much a reflection of social expectations as the result of what he perceives as social expectations and, above all, of the position he is seeking within that setting. This is one of the angles from which to analyze the discourse on the lawyer's role in today's Egypt as well as in the Islamic state to come:

"From my point of view, the role of the lawyer in the old Islamic legal system was of course different. He was only the representative of the party, only the spokesman of the expressions and perspectives that he served to represent. Today

---

[18] M. C. Foblets, *Les familles maghrébines et la justice en Belgique. Anthropologie juridique et immigration* (Paris: Karthala, 1994), pp. 109–10.

[19] Interview with MN, lawyer, January 199.4

the lawyer has become an expert to whom one refers for consulting on legal and particularly procedural matters, and then to express the interests of the individual he is representing and not his own point of view. ... I think that, if there were a legal and judicial system based on Islam, the system of legal, commercial, and criminal procedures would not be eliminated. Thus, by their very nature, these systems require the presence of lawyers who can fill the function they are now filling. The other part of the question is to know what the lawyer must do in the context of the present political system. He must comply to professional honesty and not defend injustice. ... Second, it is imperative that the lawyers who live in a society like ours acquire a deep knowledge of the Shariah. ... Third, we must underscore the similarity of the function of lawyer and judge in bringing together the prevailing texts and the foundations of the Shariah."[20]

However, it is above all the issue of crossing into the political realm that remains essential for assessing the attitudes of the professionals of law we interviewed. The idea of solidarity without consensus[21] can surely be used in the case at hand here. It remains to be examined what, beyond the solidarity with regard to referring to the Islamic legal repertoire, explains the disagreement as to the implications of this reference, indeed as to its content (at least, when this is a disputed matter). Up until now, the only explanation that to me seemed to shed light on the question is of a political nature, such as the stakes involved in holding power and the use of the Shariah in this context:

"If (the constitutional text says that) the Shariah is the main source, we thereby eliminate all of the laws contradicting the Shariah. Such a step requires the introduction of many judicial *petitions* in numerous cases. I am personally convinced that this type of legal conflict means the downfall of the state, a downfall that the Supreme Constitutional Court cannot allow, no more than any individual with common sense. That is why we settled for the general orientation of the text, just as the judges did."[22]

"The criticism made to the Islamists is that they want to apply the Shariah without consulting the people. We say that if we sought the people's opinion freely and democratically, they would choose the power of God rather than that of the people. That happened in the past in Algeria and in Sudan. This success in Algeria and in Sudan comforted the perspective of those who call for elections as a means to change the leadership. ... If in Egypt the people were given the opportunity to choose their leaders, they would certainly choose the Shariah."[23]

Some people think that everything is constraining, even some customs. I don't think this movement, called "Salafite", can serve as a basis for modern society. But a trend taking the Shariah as a referential framework for the laws may favor the renewal of

[20] Interview with lawyer AW, June 1994.
[21] D. I. Kertzer, *Rituals, Politics and Power* (New Haven: Yale University Press, 1988), and the use that J.-N. Ferrie makes of it in "Prier pour disposer de soi. Le sens et la fonction de la prière de demande dans l'Islam marocain actuel," *Annuaire de l'Afrique du Nord* 33, 1994, pp. 113–27.
[22] Interview with NH, lawyer, January 1994.
[23] Interview with MN, lawyer, January 1994.

the rules pertaining to daily transactions. This is one type of opposition. Another type, this one political, sets the organizations involved in violent activities against those calling for moderation. The question here is if it is possible to apply the Shariah simply through spreading the word. Some think that society needs a violent movement. Of course, the moderates hold that renewal is possible, while the proponents of violence refuse it. It is the social conditions that are accountable for this.[24]

In Egypt, the Shariah can be applied within a day or overnight. ... We promulgate the decrees for its implementation, the government agrees and the Shariah is immediately applied, without any problem.[25]

The claim of the Islamic trend is the implementation of the Shariah. ... But it is possible that many people are calling for the application of the Shariah. Any society has a particular ideology that reflects the whole of the beliefs (that prevail in it). We are an Islamic country and any leadership that would stray from this truth would be at fault. With regard to the Shariah, I can tell you that a great number of rules are implemented, and at the same time others are suspended.[26]

It is possible that one of the core elements of the issue lies here. Calling for the implementation of the Shariah may indeed well reflect the wish to change what is socially accepted and desirable (or at least supposed as such) into a set of prescriptive and proscriptive rules. It is as if somehow there were a structural inversion: from a "cultural order" conveyed and manipulated by the norm, we would move to a "legal order" influencing culture and setting its legitimate norms. This transition probably takes place through a process that gives strength to the norm. However, this is possible only if the initial normative repertoire can be given a regulatory nature, and this depends on whether historically and ideologically it has already actually functioned in such a way and/or has been considered as such. This is most certainly the case with the Shariah. But this condition alone does not suffice. It must be combined with conditions of a more political nature driving some actors to wish to include these regulatory features into the normative repertoire.

We may also observe that, as it functions on the basis of social and cultural models, law operates through categorization, a fact that has an impact on the reality that a social group builds for itself as well as on its self-definition. This categorization comes about by establishing limits, borders, by what we may call a "liminarization process." In this sense, law plays a role in the assertion of identity, but this doesn't necessarily mean that this assertion cannot be conceived in terms other than interactionist and non-substantial ones. In the Egyptian setting, and for the people we interviewed, this is reflected in the statement that Islam is radically different

---

24 Interview with BI, magistrate, November 1993.
25 Interview with MZ, *'alim* (scholar), January 1994.
26 Interview with MB, lawyer, November 1993 and January 199.4

from other legal cultures, or at least that Islam is distinguishable owing to
the fact that it has a legal culture with particular basic principles:

> It is not possible that the Islamic community, which is made up of many hundreds
> of millions of members, suggest a civilizational project disconnected from Islamic
> law. It wouldn't be its project. [27]

The analysis of law, of its repertoires, and of the perceptions that the
various actors hold of it allows us to underscore the extent to which the
(particularly legal) norm makes up a central component of the assertion of
collective identity:

> As a matter of principle, Islamic law constitutes one of the aspects of our faith and
> we feel towards it a need similar to thirst for water or hunger for food. It is the
> backbone of the Islamic civilizational system. If the backbone of this system snaps,
> it is the Islamic civilization that disappears and becomes an altered reflection of the
> Western, Buddhist, or other civilizations. [28]

In its process towards the coalescing of identity, law operates on the basis
of the assertion of both historical continuities by means of reinterpretation
of the existing rules, and cultural discontinuities through the creation of
boundaries defining the common tie underlying identity. The legal discourse
and the emphasis put on either of the legal repertoires reflect the typifying
role of the legal norm. Law thus serves to build a unity based "on a process
of division and a practice of exclusion."[29] As for the behavior of the actors,
its aim is above all to create the impression of conformity to the rules of the
group, "while in fact their action is contradictory to the rule or is not based
on the principle of total obedience to the rule."[30] Thus is revealed that what
counts above all is the public assertion of group belonging and not the adoption of practices that substantially speaking are proper to it.

The judge, the state, and the Shariah

In this third section, I will expose briefly three cases where an Egyptian
magistrate was led to refer to the Shariah and to claim to base his judgment on
its provisions. These examples of reference to the Islamic legal repertoire will
allow me to put forward my general approach to the reference to Islam in law.

The first case deals with the wearing of the veil at public school. As the
natural tutor of his two daughters, a father petitioned the administrative
court of Alexandria against the Minister of Education, requesting that the

---

[27]   Interview with AW, lawyer and former magistrate, June 1994.

[28]   Ibid.

[29]   F. Ost, "Essai de définition et de caractérisation de la validité juridique," in *Droit et
pouvoir*. Vol. I. *La validité*, eds. F. Rigaux and G. Haarscher (Brussels: Story-Scientia,
1987), pp. 97–132.

[30]   P. Bourdieu, *Raisons pratiques. Sur la théorie de l'action* (Paris: Seuil, 1994), p. 239.

ruling be suspended and declared void that forbade his two girls' entrance to secondary school. Indeed, when the time came to enroll his two girls in school, he was informed of their expulsion based on a departmental order that forbade access to school to pupils wearing the full veil (*niqab*); this decree orders the compulsory wearing by pupils of a standard uniform complying with the features it defines. For the plaintiff, this was seen to contradict articles 2 (see above) and 41 (individual freedom is protected and it is forbidden to undermine it) of the Egyptian Constitution. The administrative court then referred the case to the Supreme Constitutional Court. In its judgment of May 18, 1996, the Court recalled its interpretation of article 2. For the Court, the logic behind wearing the uniform is to protect the sense of decency of the girl and the ways and customs of society. The legislator can legitimately impose limits to the dressing mode without it running against the principle of protection of individual freedom, as long as he does so for the sake of preserving identity. Islam improved the condition of women, and this explains that it prompted her to secure her sense of decency. It ordered her to veil since this protects her against vulgarity. And so in matters of dress and according to the Law (of God), the woman cannot use her free will. On the contrary, her dressing style must reflect the responsibility that she takes upon herself in the world. But since the style of female dress is not discussed in absolute in Quranic texts, there is room for interpretation and the intervention of the legislator, who must respect the mores as well as the requirements of life in modern society. According to the Court, by authorizing the veil as long as it is not imposed and as long as it does not limit the young girl's capacities to integrate, the departmental order does not run against article 2 of the Constitution. Furthermore, in distinguishing between freedom of thought and freedom of worship, the Court underlined that while the first cannot be restricted, the second can for the sake of higher interests, such as public order and morality. And education is part of those higher interests that the state must protect and that authorize regulating school dress. Thus the Court decided to turn down the petition, which meant that the young girls could not return to school wearing the full veil.

The second case aroused quite a bit of interest. It is the trial of Nasr Hamid Abu Zayd, assistant professor of Islamic studies and literature at the University of Cairo, author of works of exegesis. In May 1992, Abu Zayd was refused the title of professor on the grounds that he had attacked Islam and apparently had said heretical things. On May 16, 1993, the case took a new twist as a group of lawyers petitioned the court of first instance requesting that a judgment be passed to separate him from his Muslim wife on the grounds that his publications apparently "included blasphemous elements that place him outside Islam" and since "among the

consequences of apostasy which is unanimously admitted in jurisprudence, there is the decision to separate the spouses."[31] While Abu Zayd's
defense was structured, among other things, on the absence of a personal
interest for the plaintiffs, on the contrary the Court of Appeal of Cairo
confirmed the validity of the *hisbah* procedure (see above). Having
founded the legality of the *hisbah* procedure in Egyptian law, the Court
then based its argument for Abu Zayd's alleged apostasy on showing that he
had "refuted the Koranic verses that hold that the Holy Koran is the word
of God [... and said] that it is a human writing and a human understanding
of the revelation." For the Court, all of these claims make the one who
holds them an apostate, and that is supported by the unanimous agreement
among the ulama and imams. Consequently, the judge drew the conclusion that Abu Zayd must be separated from his wife. This judgment was
confirmed by the Court of Cassation, but its enforcement was eventually
suspended by the judge in charge of applying sentences.

The third case, dealing with the authorization for sex change operations, did not have significant legal repercussions, even though it was
much covered by the media. Also, it does not explicitly concern the realm
of Islamic law, even though what underlies the core of the dispute are
diverging views on morals based on Islam. In 1982, a student in medicine
from al-Azhar University, Sayyid 'Abd Allah, consulted a psychologist
claiming to suffer from deep depression. The psychologist examined him
and concluded that the sexual identity of the young man was disturbed.
After three years of treatment, she decided to refer him to a surgeon so that
he could undergo a sex change operation that eventually took place on January 29, 1988. This type of operation involved many consequences of an
administrative and legal order. The first was the refusal of the dean of al-
Azhar University's Faculty of medicine to allow Sayyid to write his examinations, while also refusing to transfer her to the Faculty of Medicine for
Women. To obtain this transfer, Sayyid made a request for a name change
at the Administration Office for civil status. The University of al-Azhar
maintained that Sayyid, who in the meantime had changed his name to
Sally, had committed a crime. Indeed, according to the University, the
doctor who made the operation had not changed his sex but had mutilated
him, and this simply to allow Sally to have legitimate homosexual relations. Meanwhile, the representative of the Doctors' Syndicate of Giza

---

[31] Court of first instance of Cairo, January 27, 1994. See also B. Dupret, "A propos de
l'affaire Abu Zayd, universitaire poursuivi pour apostasie; le procès: l'argumentation
des tribunaux," *Maghreb-Machrek* 151, 1996, pp. 18–22; B. Dupret and J.-N. Ferrie,
"For intérieur et ordre public, ou comment la problématique de l'Aufklärung permet de
décrire un débat égyptien," in *Droits et sociétés dans le monde arabe. Perspectives
socio-anthropologiques,* eds. G. Boëtsch, B. Dupret, and J.-N. Ferrié (Aix-en-Provence:
Presses Universitaires d'Aix-Marseille, 1987); K. Balz, "Submitting Faith to Judicial
Scrutiny Through the Family Trial: the 'Abu Zayd Case,'" *Die Welt des Islams* 37, 1997,
pp. 135–55.

summoned the two doctors who had performed the operation before a medical board that ruled that they had made a serious professional error by failing to prove the existence of a pathological problem before operating. On May 14, 1988, the Doctors' Syndicate sent a letter to the Mufti of the Republic, Sayyid Tantawi, asking him to issue a *fatwa* on the matter. This one came on June 8, 1988, concluding that if the doctor showed that it was the only cure for the patient, this treatment was authorized. However, this treatment cannot result solely from the individual desire to change sex, but must be the therapeutic result of a pathological diagnosis decided by the proper authorities.[32] This *fatwa* is not clear on whether the "psychological hermaphroditism" from which Sayyid suffered was an admissible medical reason or not. Thus everyone claimed that the text supported his own view. On June 12, 1988, al-Azhar brought the matter before the courts, holding that the surgeon had to be condemned in compliance with article 240 of the Penal code for having inflicted permanent injury to his patient. The Attorney General and his deputy public prosecutor then decided to examine the case. They referred it to a medical expert, who concluded that while from a strictly physical point of view Sayyid was a man, psychologically he was not so. The diagnosis of psychological hermaphroditism was therefore relevant and surgery was the proper treatment. According to the report, the surgeon had only followed the rules of his profession, since he had consulted the competent specialists, had carried out the operation correctly, and had not inflicted permanent physical disability to the patient.[33] The latter could thus be considered a woman. On December 29, 1988, the Attorney General decided not to follow up the charge. The final report confirms that the operation was carried out according to the rules.

One year later, the file was closed and, in November 1989, Sally received a certificate establishing her status as a female. In view of the continuing refusal of al-Azhar to admit her into the Faculty of Medicine for Women, she submitted another claim to the Council of State, which, one year later, nullified al-Azhar's decision and authorized Sally to register at whatever university she wished in order to complete her final exams. The case did not end with this ruling. In September 1999, the Cairo Administrative Court issued another ruling which recognized that Sally had taken all the necessary legal measures to register at al-Azhar University. The court therefore ordered the university to admit her to the Faculty of Medicine for Women.[34] On November 14, 1999, al-Azhar filed an

---

[32] For the details of this case and the text of the *fatwa*, see J. Skovgaard-Petersen, *Defining Islam for the Egyptian State. Muftis and Fatwas of the Dar al-Ifta* (Leiden: E.J. Brill, 1997), pp. 319–34.

[33] Niyaba, "Mémoire du Parquet général dans l'affaire n°21, année 1988," (in Arabic) *Majalla hay'a qadaya al-dawla* 35:4, 1991, pp. 159–69.

[34] al-Hayat, 30 September 1999; Court of Administrative Justice, case no 4019/50, 1st circuit, 28 September 1999.

appeal against the administrative court decision, charging that Sally did not meet its moral and ethical standards[35] in view of the fact that "she performs as a belly dancer in night clubs and has been arrested several times on vice charges".[36] The same Administrative Court issued a ruling, on June 20, 2000, suspending the implementation of the September 1999 ruling, on the ground that new evidence had been produced (interviews with newspapers, including photographs of Sally dressed as a belly dancer) which contradicted the conduct required of a woman belonging to this Faculty. Accordingly, the Court transferred the case to the State Litigation Office for further inquiry.[37]

These three cases allow me to conclude this chapter by putting forward a model to interpret the recourse to the Shariah within the Egyptian legal and judicial realm. Because it deals with the idea of normality, law claims to be the technical transposition of a social and historical reality that is clearly perceivable. The term "norm" indeed has two meanings, one rather legal and the other statistical. Far from simply coexisting, they tend to become confused. If we say of one thing that it is normal because it is consistent with the most common type, there still remains, either implicitly or explicitly, a reference to values, to an idea of what must be. "If the notion of normality is ambiguous, it is because it constantly adds normative content to description."[38] Theoretically speaking, normality is not part of the conceptual realm of law. This being the case, we cannot ignore the surreptitious reintroduction of the concept in jurisprudence. The normal then becomes a legal category, under the guise, among others, of the notion of "standard" (an explicit reference to an implicit idea of normality). And thus law "ratifies and spreads a certain idea of normality and partakes in the effective normalization of behavior."[39] On the descriptive plane, law claims to account for the prevailing social norms and to make them legally binding, while on the normative plane, law prescribes the social norms it intends to approve. This inevitably creates a feedback effect, the norms considered normal in law, and so thereby guaranteed, tending to determine in return social normality. We thus notice on the part of the legal practitioners the systematic tendency towards "conforming" the normal to the legal, and conversely towards "making coincide" social normativity with legal normativity.

---

[35] According to the court, al-Azhar held that belly dancing "is contrary to the provisions of Islamic *sharî`a*" and "contradicts the conduct which must be adopted by someone who belongs to one of the faculties for women depending on al-Azhar University, which is singular in that it strictly imposes a specific conduct which may not be trespassed." (Court of Administrative Justice, case no 1487/54, 20 June 2000.)

[36] *Middle East Times*, 18–24 November 1999.

[37] Court of Administrative Justice, case no 1487/54, 20 June 2000.

[38] D. Lochak, "Normalité," in *Dictionnaire encyclopédique de théorie et de sociologie du droit, 2e édition corrigée et augmentée*, ed. A. J. Arnaud *et al*. (Paris: LGDJ, 1993), p. 393.

[39] Ibid.

The task of conforming the normal to the legal and of the conjunction of social and legal normativity raises the question of the status of the legal norm claiming to reflect normality, that of nature as well as that of common sense. The rule imposing the veil is one of these. The court presents it as ethically, socially, and historically based. A rule does not exist on its own, and it is not followed simply because it is there. A rule exists as the inclusion of an understanding that we feel in harmony with others. Legal formalization does not in itself determine the existence of the rule, no more than a map would determine the spatial layout that it sketches more or less accurately. A rule exists as a set of practices forming a background that is possibly, but not necessarily, represented and representable, and the regularity of which is the object of an incorporation: it is reproduced with no other justification than the simple feeling of doing so by conformity. The legal practicians claim to be acting according to rules that exist, but these do so first and foremost as available resources, as parts of normative repertoires, and as traces of previous formalized practices. According to Bernard Lepetit, a rule is a form that exists due to previous practices, but that can serve for different practices.[40]

The three cases that I have briefly presented clearly show the existence of normative forms to which magistrates give a content when they give a ruling. The relationship between the forms and their "substantialization" may be compared to the shared images serving as a kind of paradigm.[41] These images, at once both descriptions of typical actions and tacit social judgments, are temporally and culturally contingent. Like the process of narrative typification, the process of substantialization, dealing with the use of normative forms available according to the needs and constraints of interaction, is a judgment of relative similarity. The normative form works like a shared image, or better yet, like a paradigmatic narrative typification. Through a judgment of relative similarity, the normative form serves as a criterion for the legal definition of events which, because of their context, the actors are compelled to evaluate analytically and normatively. It is the result of the legal definition of these events that makes up the content as such.

It appears then that the process of typification must above all be linked to the structure of judicial action. We thus come to inquire now about an "economy of typifications" determined for a large part by the realms of interaction, realms that work according to a functionally identifiable mode and in a way specific to their use by the actors. Symbols and rhetoric thus

---

[40] B. Lepetit, "Histoire des pratiques, pratique de l'histoire" and "Le présent de l'histoire." in *Les Formes de l'expérience. Une autre histoire sociale*, ed. B. Lepetit (Paris: Albin Michel, 1995).

[41] B. S. Jackson, *Making Sense in Law. Linguistic, Psychological and Semiotic Perspectives* (Liverpool: Deborah Charles Publications, 1995), p. 152.

become resources rather than sources,[42] forms rather than contents, which the systematic study of identificatory mechanisms compels us to distinguish from the occurrences that actors seek to define.[43]

Furthermore, what about the relations of law with history, a discipline of which law is presented as the heir? It does not suffice to recall the notoriously known fact that very often the content of the law outlives its spirit; the analysis of the type of relations that bind them still remains to be undertaken. A number of hypotheses regarding substantialization can be put forward[44] that shed an initial light on these forms of law which are available to the legal practician in a particular social setting. As I previously mentioned, these means available for normative action appear as the traces and resources that historical and biographical memory make available to the actor.

The norm is created by way of sedimentation, but that of its form and not of its content. Sedimentation, that is, in the sense that the process, central to the idea of "memory," consists in the subjective intervention aiming to (re)construct the original reference and the milestones linking to it. The norms, tied to a founding past, are constructed, deconstructed, and reconstructed. Any particular moment in time is "a layer of a constantly changing diachronical accumulation of sediments brought by generations of different people."[45] However, these layers only significantly affect the present if they interact and, rather than reproducing separate structures evolving concurrently, they partake in the formation of the "top layer" of the new normative sediment that is coming into being. Due to its compound nature, this top layer is both the result of a number of normative "possibilities" and the closing of the normative repertoires available at that given moment. Furthermore, this sedimentation is formal insofar as it is true that it is not the thing *per se* that is socially relevant, but rather the perspectives used to assess this thing, these perspectives being closely determined by the setting of interaction. In this regard, the notion of traditionizing context seems particularly relevant.[46] The claim is that the authority of a norm declared constraining by a judge stems more from the setting of its statement, which in some way would make the conjunctural conditions transcendental, than from its part in a transfer process. The "traditionizing" of a claim and, consequently, its normativity come about

[42] Ferrie, "Prier pour disposer de soi."

[43] B. Dupret, "La définition juridique des appartenances. La typification narrative de l'action identitaire devant les juridictions suprêmes d'Egypte et d'Israël," *International Journal for the Semiotics of Law/Revue internationale de sémiotique juridique* 10:30, 1997, pp. 261–91.

[44] Ibid.

[45] M. Krygier, "Law as Tradition," *Law and Philosophy* 5, 1986, p. 242.

[46] J. Bouju, "Tradition et identité. La tradition dogon entre traditionalisme rural et néo-traditionalisme urbain," *Enquête* 2, 1985, p. 106.

from the fact of having been made by the authorized person, at the proper time and place. We can say that the trial is the ritual moment *par excellence* where a referent is given a traditional symbolic value, thereby concealing from the actors the contingent nature of the process, and reasserting a view of the world, of its norms, and of its history "as they are."[47] Therefore, normative sedimentation is not an act of heritage but rather a complex process of appropriation and reinterpretation establishing new truths. Thus the norm has no existence in itself except when it is being used. It explicitly becomes a repertoire, that is, a (rhetorical) resource available to the actors and shaped and modified through practice.[48]

In the interpretations of the legal rules that the magistrate makes with regard to the Shariah, the judge authoritatively gives a formal rule an exact and constraining meaning by conferring on it the status of a historically based and socially sanctioned religious requirement. And the judge would supposedly be the only individual able to conceive of this rule simultaneously as a norm to be imposed upon society and as a social normality to be given legal status. Various obligations whose normality are displayed are morally and legally sanctioned by a judge presenting his interpretative mode as the current and cultural reflection of a timeless will. In its quest for a morality in compliance with its perception of religious and social normality, law gives strength to purely formal prescriptions inherited from history. While claiming to reflect natural normativity, it actually created it. While claiming to return to the Shariah, it actually reinvented it.

[47] D. Carzo, "Le droit comme fait social total," in *Legal Semiotics and the Sociology of Law*, ed. B. S. Jackson (Oñati: International Institute for the Sociology of Law, 1994), p. 37, and Kertzer, *Rituals, Politics and Power*.
[48] Lepetit, *Les Formes de l'expérience*, p. 297.

6

WOMEN'S ISLAMIC ACTIVISM

BETWEEN SELF-PRACTICES AND SOCIAL REFORM EFFORTS

Connie Carøe Christiansen

In Morocco, young Muslim women are increasingly engaged in activities such as daily readings of the Quran, and daily prayers in extension of the obligatory five "pillars of Islam." Young women have become the kind of Muslims who attend meetings and take part in discussions of issues related to their religion and society. They teach Islam to others less learned in the religion and go to the mosque every Friday to hear the *khutbah* (sermon) of the imam and to meet best friends there. They have become attentive to their own style of conduct and dress, and now prefer the *jellaba* or other loose and long garment and have started to wear the *hijab* (headscarf) and to articulate their own faith in terms of wearing this *hijab*. They tend to frame their arguments for their religion in critical and political terms, substantiated as a systematic neglect of the Muslim point of view, even in so-called Muslim societies, just as they generally challenge the validity and authenticity of their compatriots' religious practice. They go on camps for as long as a whole week where all they do is pray, read, and discuss issues related to Islam and its proper practice with other women who share the same commitment. They form part of an intense network of friendship united by their shared commitment to implement Islam, and they join the openly declared competition among them to further improve the religious practice and general conduct.

In this chapter I propose a framework for analyzing these practices. Although I have found "Islamic activism" more accurate as an analytic term, I consider the activities described above as part of a more encompassing phenomenon, "Islamism," thus emphasizing the activists' self-designation. I have privileged three angles for this endeavor: education, mobilization, and "emerging selves," which will be elaborated upon below. Judging from the activism of, primarily, university students in the town of Fes, Islamism signifies an emphasis on bodily self-control and an attitude to life that highly values accomplishments of the believer in the form of work, studies, and the promulgation of the Islamist vision, all of which promote certain capabilities of the individual Islamist. For a closer study of the social practices of women's Islamic activism I have found the concept "technologies of self," developed by Michel Foucault in his latest works, especially fruitful.[1]

Among Islamist women, a focus on individual conduct and self-development is thus sometimes outspoken, in contrast to declared intentions of promoting social reform among other Muslims. Is this preoccupation in fact overshadowing Islamism in Morocco, rendering it difficult to regard it as a social reform movement? Along these lines, I want to question the extent to which women's Islamic activism is concerned with promting social reform in other people's lives—or in the general society—and to which extent the active women are more concerned with improving their own individual conduct as Muslim women. Ultimately, I ask if this schism is a real dilemma or rather a dynamic between activities of individual reform and activities of social reform.

Angles of approach

The setting for this discussion consists of a generally de-politicized and marginal, to some extent even disintegrated, Moroccan youth in the city of Fes, one of the major cities in Morocco and an ancient university town. It is popularly known as an important cultural patrimony, and as formerly hosting the Moroccan elite under European influence, while today it is dominated by trade, tourism, and textile industries. I conducted fieldwork during two terms, from July to December 1994 and again from February to March 1997, contacting, primarily, Islamist women in Fes. I contacted Islamists at different points in town, but preponderantly at the university campus. Altogether 48 women and 9 men who are Islamist in some way or another were approached and interviewed for different lengths of time. Of the 48 women, just above 25 percent were either unemployed or housewives and just below 75 percent were students at institutions of higher education (two were still at grammar school). Ages ranged from 17 to 43 years, but most were in their 20s. With a couple of exceptions, the university students were not married, but 12 were married women. The husbands tended also to be of Islamist persuasion. I encountered women from two Islamist organizations and one Sufi-Islamist organization. Around 20 of the women were organized, most of them in *Al-adl wa al-Ihsan* ("Justice and Benevolence") which appeared to be in a strong position among the female students at the university dormitory.

---

[1] Michel Foucault, *Technologies of Self. A seminar with Foucault,* ed. H. Martin *et al.* (London: Tavistock, 1988), and *The care for the self: The History of Sexuality: 3* (London: Penguin, 1990).

In Morocco, the position hitherto occupied by certain urban families of predominantly Western and secular orientation as the cultural and political elite, the model for others to follow, is currently under attack. Islamism thus marks a shift; a moment of declared intention to turn towards more "indigenous" or "authentic" ways among a rising middle class. Here dissatisfaction with the result of decolonization reigns and, in light of dependency on World Bank decrees[2] and generally heavy Western influence, has lead to demands of what Zeleza calls "a second independence."[3] This demand is raised at a point in time where broad masses have become sufficiently educated to assume a confident collective attitude.

Mass higher education. From a historical and general viewpoint, the world of Moroccan women has been enlarged in the sense that the horizons of Moroccan women have been widened. Since independence from French colonial rule in 1956, the national school system has evolved into a mass education system for children of both sexes, although for girls to a lesser extent. In 1992–93, 43 percent of the pupils in Moroccan secondary education were girls.[4] The general widening of horizons is not only due to increasing levels in schooling and education, but should also be related to the development of a consumer society in Morocco, which includes the consumption of media: satellite television, newspapers, magazines, videos, radio broadcasting. This is significant since adoption of the principle of mass education in Morocco has not rooted out widespread illiteracy,[5] not

---

[2] Morocco has been submitted to IMF-decrees and other measures of "structural adjustment," in fact invalidating the sovereignty and possibility for democratic influence in Morocco.

[3] Paul Tiyambe Zeleza, "Imagining and Inventing the Postcolonial State in Africa" (Paper for conference, "States of imagination," Centre for Development Research, Copenhagen, Denmark, Feb. 13–15, 1998).

[4] *Femmes et condition féminine au Maroc* (Morocco: CERED, Direction de la Statistique, 1994).

[5] However, this is slowly decreasing. In 1994, the total percentage of illiterates was 54.9, whereas in 1960 it was 87.0. For women alone the numbers are 67.5 and 96.0 respectively. Youssef Courbage, "Le Maroc de 1962 à 1994: Fin de l'explosion démografique?" *Monde Arabe, Maghreb-Machrek* 153, 1996. As Jansen has noted, a paradoxical situation has emerged: a relatively large group of well-educated women and at the same time a high frequency of illiterate women. Jansen has tried to explain this paradox in the case of Jordan by looking at the activities of Christian missionary schools from around 1900 onwards. She found that the missionaries in general demonstrated special interest for the education of girls and sometimes assured that individual women were sent to Europe for further education. Willy Jansen, **"Christian Teaching in an Islamic context. The rise of women's education in Jordan"** (paper for conference, "Worlds and Visions. Perspectives on the Middle East Today," Network for Middle Eastern Studies in Denmark, Dec. 5–7, 1997, Aarhus University). This practice has been confirmed by Julia Clancy-Smith as taking place in Tunisia around the same time period. Julia Clancy-Smith, "Visions of knowledge: Muslim women and education in North Africa 1880–1930," in ibid.

least in areas with a population of low density.[6] It has, however, resulted in a considerable widened access for women to institutions of higher education. In 1995–96, the total number of university students was 245,950 in a population of 26.5 million.[7] Of these, 41 percent, or 103,160, were women,[8] a number which has been steadily increasing in recent decades (in 1991–92, just four years further back, it was 37.5 percent).

Women's access to higher education seems currently to go hand in hand with the growth of Islamism, involving the type of activities outlined initially in this chapter. The women committed to Islam in the way described above, whom I approached in different places in Fes, were generally undergoing some kind of higher education or had already terminated one. This may support a consideration of Islamism in terms of education, in itself, and in correspondence with national educational possibilities, whereas a focus on more conventional politics may obscure this aspect.

Mobilization. Islamism has, to an unprecedented extent, mobilized Moroccan women to take a stand in the world of modern politics, in a situation where Moroccan elites in alliance with the late King Hassan II have practically excluded Moroccan youth from any formal participation in politics.[9] The ability of Islamism to mobilize young women on a broad scale is one of its most significant features, which has not yet been fully accounted for, and this effect is practically unique for Islamism in Morocco.[10] In Burgat, Eickelman, Taarji, Kofoed Rasmussen, and Sadiki, encounters with more visible or even public figures—such as Islamist leaders and ideologues—are the bases for analysis.[11] The Islamic activities of well-known, public Islamist

---

[6] The differentiation between urban and rural population is significant; for women in urban millieus aged 25–30 the number of literates is 36% (in 1991) and in rural milieux it is 5%. *Femmes et condition féminine au Maroc.*

[7] Ibid.

[8] Ibid.

[9] Mounia Bennani-Chraïbi, *Soumis et rebelles: les jeunes au Maroc* (Paris: CNRS Editions, 1994), p. 175ff.

[10] Some women are, however, organized in feminist organizations and in the political parties' women's associations which are to a large extent one and the same thing. According to Dialmy, there are no totally independent feminist organizations in Morocco. Abdessamed Dialmy, "La femme arabe: entre féminisme et islamisme. Le cas du Maroc" (unpublished paper for conference, "Worlds and Visions: Perspectives on the Middle East Today"). Here he also points to the fact that the social base of these women's/feminist organisations is limited to primarily the middle class.

[11] François Burgat, *L'Islamisme au Maghreb. La voix du sud* (Paris, Karthala, 1988), and *L'Islamisme en face* (Paris: La Découverte, 1996); Dale F. Eickelman, "An Islamic Reformation?" (lecture at conference, "Worlds and Visions. Perspectives on the Middle East Today"); Hinde Taarji, *Les Voilées de l'islam* (Casablanca: Editions Eddif, 1991); Lene Kofoed Rasmussen, "Den muslimske kvinde genfortalt. Islamiseringen af kvindespørgsmålet i Egypten" (Ph.D. thesis, Carsten Niebuhr Institute of Middle Eastern Studies, University of Copenhagen, 1999); and Larbi Sadiki, "Islamisation,

figures are, of course, also local, or rather localized, as they take place in a specific setting. But what is the effect of Islamism in the daily practices of lay members and supporters, so to speak, the next step in the dispersal of Islamist practices and ideas? At this level people relate to public figures, considered relevant models or not, rather than setting themselves up as models, at least not for people beyond face-to-face reach. In this way it makes sense to distinguish between core intellectuals and lay intellectuals. This does not preclude lay Islamists from becoming models of Islamic conduct in face-to-face relations, or at least in a physical co-presence.

So far the promotion of a woman's cause in Morocco has been the preoccupation of elite women, inspired by Western feminism. Islamism may signify a moment of dissemination of women's awareness, which in its less radical version is more in accordance with larger segments of the population. Islamist women have not obtained leading positions in Islamist associations in Morocco so far, but neither have women in officially recognized parties.[12] Nonetheless, women's Islamic activism demonstrates investments and strategies of the participating women, indicating the amount of effort it takes to purport an identity as a practicing Muslim *and* an intellectual, modern woman.

Bennani-Chraïbi argues that, in the case of Morocco, youths are only voicing their dissatisfaction to the extent that an oppressive political system lets them.[13] As unemployment rates for university graduates are increasing, the aforementioned widening of horizons may have as its most significant consequence that Moroccan youths, male and female, are becoming acutely aware of their own situation as excluded from the material prosperity that they partly observe and partly imagine, from social welfare, and from political influence in their own society.

This study therefore concerns emerging political subjects at the point of mobilization, that is, at the point where people—here more specifically, women—become convinced that it matters what they do and what they say about how societies should be organized. The fact that they are mobilized may turn out to be much more important than whether it happens on socialist, secularist, liberal, Islamist, or for that matter, feminist grounds.

Emerging self. Approaching Islamism and Islamist circles provokes some transformation in the way the individual woman perceives her life, its trajectory and goals. The "Islamist veil"[14] is in this perspective a mediator

---

Globalisation" (paper for the conference "The Middle East in a Globalizing World," Nordic Society for Middle Eastern Studies, Oslo, Aug. 13–16, 1998).

12 Dialmy, "La femme arabe," 1996.
13 Bennani-Chraïbi, *Soumis et rebelles.*
14 Nilüfer Göle, "Secularism and Islamism in Turkey: The making of elites and counter-elites," *Middle East Journal* 51:1, 1997.

of Islamic activism as a personal, individual, perhaps even self-centered project, although it may be paired with a concern for the community beyond Islamist circles. Women become attracted to Islamism, not so much because Islam is the "lowest common denominator of identity,"[15] although this may be true, but because Islamic activism in addition enhances skills, knowledge, competencies, and, in the last instance, the kind of self which is integral to a modern lifestyle. Such skills, moreover, are a precondition for the possibility to influence a modern nation state. Islamism offers a vision of a meaningful life in an orderly, dignified society, with basic needs such as food, clothes, housing, education, and work fulfilled, as well as available consumption possibilities. Islamism is, in other words, the locus for hopeful aspirations to the Moroccan society for some of its inhabitants and it signifies an activist approach to make them come true. The skills and competencies promoted by Islamism as a consequence of this vision are steps towards social prestige and upward social mobility. They, in brief, at once presuppose and generate a strongly felt self. The development of this self is a third element in the framing of Islamic activism that I am presenting.

Edifying Islamism

All three angles of approach—mass higher education, mobilization of women, and emerging selves—are thus interconnected. The term "education" covers a wide-ranging spectrum of activities, experiences, and bodily practices, but it all comes down to social processes having a profound influence on what kind of person you are. Education may be approached as "implying certain modes of training and modification of individuals, not only in the obvious sense of acquiring certain skills but also in the sense of acquiring certain attitudes."[16] However, in order to discuss educating processes and their consequences specification is clearly needed. I have thus selected some activities and processes, which count only as examples of how education occurs in Islamic activism. As already indicated, these activities include reflections, for example, on the relation between self and society, bodily disciplining, studies, and interpretations tested in group discussions. These and similar practices have led me to assume that there are certain consequences of Islamism, such as accumulation of skills and knowledge, that have been largely ignored.

---

[15] Rémy Leveau, "Youth Culture and Islamism in the Middle East," in *The Islamist Dilemma*, ed. L. Guazzone (Reading: Ithaca Press, 1995).
[16] Foucault, *Technologies of Self*, p. 18.

The dynamics of education

Among Islamists, it is a declared religious obligation of any Muslim, male or female, to become educated and learned. Islamist women, in tune with Islamist ideas in general, tend to emphasize education, of the mind and the body, as a religious obligation of every human being. It is therefore in line with this explicit appreciation of education that I suggest educational practices as integral to Islamist practices. As with any other educational setting, Islamic activism concerns a transformation of the human being, which implies a submission to certain standards. Women's Islamic activism should similarly be regarded as a transformation—a reshaping of the body and the mind—or, as has been suggested by Comaroff and Comaroff in quite a different context, a bodily reform.[17]

Accordingly, one result of successful education is a complying body. Paradoxically, it could be argued that the other side of this compliance is a process of empowerment: the acquisition of tools and skills with which to confront and influence the world. Competencies such as assertiveness, the construction of a coherent argument, and experiences with practical organization are outcomes of Islamic activism which, although not unwelcome, are not necessarily directly intended. Nonetheless, they are indispensable aspects of the skills and attitudes demanded of an influential group of people, an avant-garde, pushing other groups towards changing social practices and promoting new visions of society; in other words, a reform movement. This tension between a certain formation and shaping of the individual and an accumulation of, to some extent, embodied tools is one of the core dynamics investigated by the present study.

According to Bourdieu, social processes in general should be seen as a dialectic movement of objectification and incorporation or "the internalization of externality and the externalization of internality."[18] I propose that this dialectic is intensified in educational practices and in situations of rapid social change, demanding new approaches and competencies from people. These processes imply that the individual person increasingly sees him or herself from an external point of view, inherently leading to a distanced and relativized view of the self as well as of the surroundings and the people inhabiting the surrounding space. This kind of objectification thus concerns social positioning articulated through bodily practices, producing distinction among groups of people.[19]

---

[17]   John Comaroff and Jean Comaroff, *Ethnography and the Historical Imagination* (CO: Westview Press, 1992).

[18]   To Bourdieu these processes therefore form part of the processes in which the *habitus* is developed: "The appropriating by the world of a body thus enabled to appropriate the world." Pierre Bourdieu, *Outline of a theory of practice* (Cambridge University Press, 1977), p. 89. In this sense the dynamics of education should be seen as a condensed version of social processes *in general*. Ibid., p. 72.

[19]   Connie Carøe Christiansen, "Self and Social Process in Women's Islamic Activism. Claims for Recognition" (Ph.D. dissertation, Institute of Anthropology, University of

Technologies of self

The declared intention of Islamist women is to strip everyday life of elements which are disturbing to essential obligations of a Muslim. Consequently, the individual woman structures her everyday life in order to make the most of it; so as not to waste any time that could have been spent deploying the teachings of Islam in her own or other people's lives. This effort results in a program, or time schedule, weekly or daily, in which the different obligations and activities are specified to take place at certain times.

A specific perspective on the self, emanating from educational practices, results from placing as a core term technologies of self, i.e. the various techniques which, when put in use, result in a forging, or building up, of the self. These technologies permit "individuals to effect by their own means or with the help of others a certain number of operations on their own bodies and souls, thoughts, conduct, and way of being, so as to transform themselves in order to attain a certain state of happiness, purity, wisdom, perfection, or immortality."[20]

Technologies of self are applied by the individual as means to reach an end. Just like other types of technologies (technology of production, technology of sign systems, technology of power) they imply the double inscription of education: a shaping of the subject along with an acquisition of skills, both of which involve bodily practices. Thus technologies of self are relevant for Islamist women aiming at practicing Islam as correctly as possible, as they attempt to approach the ideal Muslim woman. This perspective, moreover, allows some insight as to the question of what kind of self is developed in Islamic activism—and appears to be coherent and strongly felt, rather than composite or fluid.[21]

To sum up, I argue that Islamism, by deploying a specific set of social practices—technologies of self—provides a setting for education. I focus on Islamic activism as a distinctive religious practice, connected to a body of distinctive, yet interrelated representations of Islam, characterized by a completely modern preoccupation: the search for authenticity. I ask what women find attractive in Islamic activism—rather than what pushes them to take part in Islamic activism. Restoration of some Islamic authenticity is central for the Islamist vision. Consequently, the search for "authentic knowledge" is a main issue in Islamism, and much Islamist activity is devoted to its exploration. Thus educational practices are core activities in women's Islamic activism in the material for discussion here. But the features of women's religious activism which signify a preoccupation

---

Copenhagen, 1999), pp. 39–42.

[20] Foucault, *Technologies of Self*, p. 18.

[21] Carøe Christiansen, "Self and Social Process," p. 180.

with education are shared with Islamist movements outside of Morocco.[22]

In the following section I discuss a number of activities among Islamist women as implying techniques, which align with the techniques discussed by Foucault. Therefore, I proceed with specifying the educational implications of women's Islamic activism, and I propose that development of the self is an inseparable part of the education going on within Islamist circles. Thus Islamic activism is theorized collective action in which the body is regarded as an instrument for social reform.

Self-practices and social reform

"I have improved." (Hakima)

"To be Islamist is to wish for development, and even the wish is not enough, to be Islamist is to begin to reform, to plan to be, with all our capacities and all possible means." (Yazmine)

The above two statements from two different female Islamist university students make evident the centrality of activism in the universe of Islamism. Moreover, the statements cover two areas of Islamic activity: the efforts to improve personal conduct and religious practice as an individual believer and the involvement with the surrounding society as part of a reform movement. What are the connections between these two sides of activity? Are they connected at all?

Posing this question, I also ask if the preoccupation with individual religious practices and their perfection among Islamists results in an inwardly directed orientation, towards the self—rather than a wish and will to reform society. I argue that the most significant division is not between individual and collective activities, but between activities of cultivating the self versus activities of reforming society. Both sorts of activities are carried out collectively and individually. I contend that assumption or "theory" prevailing among Islamist women, claiming that an investment of mind and body is a precondition of social reform, is of relevance for this discussion. Theorizing along these lines forms the base on which the Islamist body is inscribed in a program with the intention to instigate social reform. This programming ensures that religious practices are carried out as prescribed. Further, I claim, this program is a technique of self, managing processes of externalization and internalization among Islamist women, balancing processes of self-enhancement and engagement with the welfare, organization, or morality of the collective.

---

[22] For Egypt, see Kofoed Rasmussen, "Den muslimske kvinde genfortalt." For Jordan and Malaysia, see Anne Sofie Roald, *Tarbiya: education and politics in Islamic movements in Jordan and Malaysia* (Lunds Universitet: Religionshistoriska avdelningen, 1994).

The relevance of the body. The body seems to be in the forefront of assessments of religious belief by Islamist women, whether referred to directly or indirectly in the reference to religious practices:

"The body is not transcended as in Christianity, but the body is programmed in Islam." (Meryem)

This comparative statement by Meryem reveals her awareness of the body as programmable. The programmed body is regarded as a first step in a more general transformation of society, as further statements here below will reveal. Thus, practicing or applying Islam is meant to be an all-encompassing activity, relevant for all spheres of life.

"I practise the religion in the mosque, on the street, in the house, on the bus, in every movement I practice the religion. The real Muslim is the person who abstains from certain practices because the religion is in existence. The religion has no spatial and no temporal limits." (Yazmine)

The religion is supposed to be present in all your movements, all the time. Furthermore:

"Belief or faith exists in the heart but manifests itself in the exterior through the body and conduct, because the conduct of the believer is not the conduct of the atheist or the non-believer. And the relation between the heart and the body, between the interior and the exterior is mutual, psychic, it is even a sort of dialectic. The psyche and the body influence each other[...]" (Yazmine)

Yazmine asserts a dialectical relationship between the body and the internal (heart, psyche, feelings). If the internal does not correspond to the external there is disharmony, causing unhappiness.

"Islam is the life. When one is talking, walking and asleep, one has to apply Islam, in living one is applying Islam. Everything is explained in Islam." (Nabila)

Nabila emphasizes the salience of applying Islam by equating it with life. The pervasive character of her religious commitment is also the message of Hakima, expressed in this way:

"I organise my time well. I go to the mosque, and I am always present at the religious meetings with my mates from the dormitory, and I am present at the House of the Quran[.]"

The evidence of her religious commitment is the activism. What is interesting here is not whether she in fact takes part in all the mentioned activities or not, but the fact that she conceives of her commitment, even her faith in terms of activism, religious practice. This is in accordance with the fact that all the women have affirmed the intimate relation between faith and religious practice. Without exception it has been referred to as a *sine qua non*.

In the cases of Rachida as well as of Hind below, this amounts to a sheer equation: Faith in Islam *is* its practice, or: To be convinced is to practice the religion. If faith in God is manifested only in the heart, according to Rachida, it is not part of reality. Faith enters *after* practicing Islam, as a result of this practice, rendering the religious practice quintessential.

An instrument of reform. Comaroff and Comaroff find that the link between bodily reform[23] and processes of social transformation is strong evidence that the human frame mediates between self and society, something originally proposed by Merleau-Ponty.[24] As they put it there are " ... implications of actual bodily experience for imagining and acting upon the forces of history."[25] Comaroff and Comaroff refer to Zionist ritual as "untheorised collective action" which they explain as action not accompanied by explications and conceptual categories. Its logic remains in the corporal signs.

In contrast, Islamist women's actions are highly theorized. At least the above statements testify to their verbalized and articulated character, including the relation between individual bodily conduct and society. The female activists directly refer to the centrality of the regulated body for the fulfillment of the task they have set for themselves. The Islamist body, again in contrast to the case analyzed by the Comaroffs, does not mediate social transformation as a way to cope with it, or *cure* it. The Islamist body appears to be an instrument of deliberate social reform, rather than a site for elaborating social transformation. The ability of the body to become a means of social transformation is recognized and utilized among Islamists. Thus they have strongly objectified their own bodies and the working out of a program for one's own activities seems to be part of this objectification.

Let us look closer at some selected aspects of bodily reform in women's Islamic activism. I suggest that the activism amounts to a reordering of the body linked to hermeneutic practices, based on questions such as "Who am I?" and "What is Islam?", thus projecting the connections between self and society. The outcome of the reordered, regulated or reformed body, I argue, is education—or more precisely, is one of the elements constitutive of an educated person. The body is invested in the processes making a person educated, and this is a significant element of women's Islamic activism. The activities should be read as an extension of how the relation between body and society is theorized. They are the women's illustration of how they apply Islam—and thereby apply the theory on the relations between body and society. A change of bodily practices is regarded as

---

[23] It should be understood as changed bodily practices, and not as could be assumed, actual changes of body parts. The case of the girl at the dormitory who gets an abortion is an exception to this rule. See below in this chapter.

[24] Comaroff and Comaroff, *Ethnography and the Historical Imagination*, p. 70.

[25] Ibid., p. 72.

integral to the processes put in motion when women engage in Islamic activism. This view is mirrored in Malika's statement that:

"Islam is a development of my personality, and of everybody's personality when submitted to the same conditions." (Malika)

A change of general conduct

Islamist women's activities were reported as involving a change of general conduct. These changes include a revision of the way she prays; her prayers have become punctual, correctly conducted, and supplemented with extra prayers, compared to the way she prayed before her new and intensified engagement with Islam. The changes also include Quranic studies, and memorization of the Quran, as well as activities having an expansion of religious knowledge as—sometimes—the explicit purpose. These include attending meetings where Islamic issues are discussed; consumption of Islamist media (books and pamphlets, cassettes and videos); attending the mosque to listen to the *khutbah* (sermon); and finally, going on camps with other Islamist women, consecrated to improving conduct and knowledge as a Muslim. Here, however, due to limits of space, I go into further detail only with the issue of a change of general conduct. This "general change," as it was referred to by some of the women I encountered, can be detected in a new approach to everyday routine activities. The women pointed to organizing one's time, working diligently, and a heightened attention to conduct and clothing, as well as fasting in surplus of obligatory fasting and abstaining from extra-marital sex as indicators of this change of general conduct. I specify each of these points as they came up in the interviews.

Organizing one's time. Along with Hakima, cited above, Rachida pointed to organization of her time as a significant element of her activities:

"I organise my time and I do my prayers on time, I behave well with my friends, with anybody... ."

Nora has chosen almost the same words:

"I organise my time, my conduct, it is my confidence in Islam which allows me this effort and the relief it brings along."

Essential here is the close connection between organizing one's time and regulating one's actions. Time management and body management appear as inseparable operations. As Meryem has already announced, the body of a Muslim is a programmed body. According to the women's presentations of Islamist practices, this should be understood quite literally.

Working diligently. By putting forward the obligation to be hard working and diligent the activist ethos of Islamism is underscored:

"Before I passed my time in emptiness. Now I cannot—I have to do something: read, search, work." (Hind)

"I am directed by my conscience, the desire to be the best in all cases, also the case of the last day (the other life), because the believer wants a good life materially, as well as spiritually. The styles between the two life-sections differ but they are complementary. This means that I search for a balance with a pure consciousness, an initiative for God, very loveable, very just." (Rahma)

Both statements signify an approach to religion and life as a constant effort to improve. Nora and Hind (who are roommates at the dormitory but were interviewed separately) continued to describe this state of constant activity, first by declaring that they can do better. Hind expressed it as a feeling that her "conviction is not yet complete." Conviction and practice are here synonymous. Nora equally estimated that she has not yet "reached the limits" of her faith.

Furthermore, to Nora, faith emerges as a consequence of reading the Quran, of a more general reading, and of competing with the sisters in the perfection of religious practice, echoed in Rahma's desire to "be the best in all cases." To Nora it is *jihad* (great efforts to please God) to disseminate Islam. She continues:

"The essential is to practice Islam well and to realise the personality capable of reworking the society. I must not be a passive person."

The Islamist woman is presented as preoccupied, active and engaged in what she is doing.

Heightened attention to conduct and clothing.

"I have revised all my conduct, meaning I have separated what is permitted from what is not permitted."[26] (Nora)

In accordance with Nora, Islamist women claim to have "revised" their conduct and as a consequence, have started veiling. Veiling, i.e. wearing the *hijab*, applies to all the women here, but some of them specifically relate it to an attention to general conduct and clothing.

Fatima told me about another, very concrete, case of bodily reform. She was deliberately trying to correct her own behavior towards her four children. She wanted to stop hitting them, since she found that wrong. Her temper now and then got away with her, and she would hit them still, but it was her goal to stop it, and she was working to accomplish it. "If I shall not enter paradise," she claimed, "it is because I hit my children."

---

[26] Hafida, Samira, Nouzha, Mounira, and Sohour all informed me that an angel is sitting on each of one's shoulders: One writes down your good deeds, the other the sinful ones.

Fasting in surplus of obligatory fasting. Fasting every Monday and Thursday in accordance with the Sunnah of the prophet is another way of underlining your commitment. This practice was mentioned by a couple of women as part of their own practices. Fasting six days in the month following the Ramadan, *Shawal*, may similarly signify your devotion to improve your religious practice; other women stated that this form of fasting was part of their own religious practice. Fasting implies bodily control or mastery over an immediate bodily need. Fasting in surplus of what is strictly necessary to fulfill religious obligations is a practice which evidences a commitment to supererogation—to do better than what is simply acceptable; a wish to behave even more correct as a believing Muslim. This aim also guides the field of sexuality.

Controlling sexuality. Samia declared that a Muslim woman is a woman who does not just follow her desires. She must be able to control herself. Halima seems to agree with her in this matter:

"As a Muslim woman one does not accept the control of men, because the woman has to control herself."

Abstaining from sexual relations before marriage may similarly lead to a feeling of a controlled self, especially as many of the female university students marry relatively late. One woman was still not married at the age of 41. After seeking advice from a local man learned in Islam, she had rejected marriage proposals from a couple of men, because they were not of a proper Muslim character, but she was still hoping to find a man who suited her.

The obligation to refrain from illegitimate sex was apprehended as indispensable by all, including the male students I spoke to. None of the women indicated sexual relations after they had taken up Islamist practices,[27] but some referred to such relations as having taken place *before* their new commitment to Islam, and presented them as an indication of how they now lead a completely different lifestyle. In so doing, they follow the narrative pattern of novel characters, Egyptian media stars, and others who likewise claim to have started their lives over again when they discovered Islam.[28]

---

[27] In a poor quarter of Fes I spoke to a doctor who had his own clinic there. He informed me that a veiled woman who was unmarried came to him to get an abortion. To him this was proof of Islamist women's hypocrisy, and stories akin to this one necessitate much effort to obtain credibility as an Islamist woman.

[28] Lila Abu-Lughod, "Movie Stars and Islamic Moralism in Egypt," in *The Gender/Sexuality Reader: Culture, History, Political Economy*, eds. Robert N. Lancaster and Micaela di Leonardo (New York and London: Routledge, 1997), pp. 502–12. Fedwa Malti-Douglas, *A woman and her sufis* (CCAS Occasional Paper, Georgetown University, Center for Contemporary Arab Studies, 1995).

Two categories of activism

Islamic activism may be divided into two categories. One is constituted by activities performed individually or exclusively with fellow Islamists. This category is constituted by inwardly directed activities, within the supportive group, and the activities here may be regarded as an internal build-up of resources, which are in other instances directed outwards at the surrounding society. Self-practices involving bodily reform are a pervasive trait of these activities. They are primarily individual activities; praying, fasting, reading the Quran—often done in solitude but sometimes in a group—along with discussions, lectures, and advice. Certain bodily practices must, according to circumstances, be observed on the Muslim woman's own initiative: the ritual washing before prayer and after sexual intercourse, for instance, as well as making sure that she conducts her prayers on time.

The activities aiming at a change of general conduct belong to this category. Below the discussion will shift to the other category where activities are either directed at or involve people placed outside Islamist circles. For discussion I extract different kinds of social work. This work includes charity activities such as visiting the hospitalized or ill and raising money for orphans or others who are dispossessed. However, teaching seems to be a much more frequent activity, along with counseling (*nasihah*) and efforts to convince others of the "Islamic solution." This category of activism moreover includes such activities as student politics, different kinds of performances (*tajwid*—recitals of the Quran, *anashid*—singing Islamic songs, and the performance of sketches, presenting an audience with a lesson in Islam), and the organization of "Islamic celebrations." According to the character of the event, the latter are referred to as *umsiyyah diniyyah* (religious evening) or *haflah islamiyyah* (Islamic party), featuring the sort of performances just mentioned. Here emphasis is less on bodily reform and self-cultivation. Rather, in this context the cultivated self becomes an asset, activated in the effort to implement social reform, illuminated by the various types of performances that some Islamist women train themselves to master.

Participating in these activities may be a way of socializing and getting together with fellow Islamists, but activities are organized, so that an insider's knowledge is not necessary. Other activities are exclusively directed at outsiders. Assia described the relevance of society for the activism in this way:

"I must work for society, which is in need of me. I must not go separate. I must integrate myself to society and I must resist in order to reach my goal, which is to participate in attracting people to the religion."

Her statement, reminiscent of Yazmine's remarks, quoted earlier, testifies to a theory of social reform, clarifying that improving your own personal

practice, disregarding the non-practitioners surrounding you, is insuffi-
cient. The goal of your own practice, in other words, should also be placed
outside of it.

This theory is exemplified by the following presentation of actions.
The women claim to take part in activities aiming at social reform—or at
least social amendments—and thereby they sustain the message that the
social relevance of bodily reform should be taken seriously.

Teaching. Teaching the Quran and Islamic practices to illiterate women or
children is the activity most frequently mentioned as the kind of voluntary
social work carried out by the women. As soon as you have acquired a
certain amount of knowledge on Islam, it appears to be a common practice
to start teaching your peers at university, friends, and neighbors, perhaps
at the local *Dar al-Qur'an* (a house or an apartment that has been donated
as charity for the purpose of Islamic teaching—such a house is to be found
in practically every quarter of Fes).

Thus Nabila is one of the women who teaches illiterate women correct
religious practice, as she explained to me when I joined her class for a
couple of lessons. Also Safia and Amal lecture the Quran to poorly educated women at an "Islamic center." At the same place Fatiha teaches children to read the Quran, whereas Sohour teaches a group of women in her
own house. Malika too has worked voluntarily for children:

"I was even a member of a youth club, I was leading the children as a step for the
veiled women to take a social responsibility, to finally programme well in the
Muslim sense, making a programme for the children's activities so that they learn
what is Islamic. ... This was a very rich experience, for my patience, and for
improving dialogue. The aim is to participate in others' lives with patience, not to
isolate oneself, so that one does not become isolated, or build up isolation."

Malika explicitly enlightens us about the motivation for her social work as
one of being responsible and engaging with the society. Aside from that,
she estimates that this work had an improving effect on her character. She
refers to a double purpose: improvement of children's perception of Islam
and improvement of her own religious practice.

Fatima stands out. She has opened a kindergarten as a private enterprise
and here she instructs the children in Islam. Aïsha also stands out, as she is
yet another woman who teaches the Quran, although not on a voluntary
basis. She teaches children in a *Dar al-Quran*, which is recognized by the
state, also providing her salary. Nabila, who is employed as a teacher in
secondary schooling, on the other hand, emphasized that she did not want
any salary for her teaching at the local (private) *Dar al-Quran*, nor would
she accept a small amount for helping me in my work.

Counseling. To Nora *jihad* means the dissemination of Islam by
attempting to convince others. She and Lubna referred to the brotherhood

(or sisterhood) they found when they got involved in Islamist circles. Rachida (residing at the dormitory) likewise told at length about the attraction that the group of Islamist women at the dormitory had presented to her by their manners, their kindness, and willingness to help others in need. Fouzia, also residing at the university dormitory, specified that counseling or advice on conduct by reference to Islam is practiced among groups of Islamist women as well as *vis-à-vis* friends and neighbors.[29]

Two sisters, Hala and Badiya, recounted the way counseling occurs among female Islamist students at the university mosque. A letterbox is placed in the mosque and any student may anonymously write down a question or an issue on a piece of paper, and put it into the box. The issues may also be of a personal character. The box is emptied in the presence of the group of female students who frequent the mosque and the issue is discussed among them, in an attempt to find a solution to the problem. This forum may also act as a mediator for coupling a girl with a certain male student that she would like to marry. The one who put the letter in the box may step forward and say, "I wrote it!" But the inquirer may also remain anonymous.

The female Islamist students staying at the dormitory told me that similar proceedings take place in the Islamist cells there, with the reservation that the enquirer is not anonymous. Advice sometimes becomes tantamount to "helping each other out". Thus Hakima told of an incident where an unmarried girl staying at the dormitory had got pregnant. Her boyfriend would not have anything to do with her any longer and the girl was very upset. Then the sisters decided to help her obtain an abortion and they collected the money required for it among them.[30] Afterwards the girl started to attend their meetings, mentally in a bad shape, but slowly gaining hold of her self again until she finally decided to start veiling.

An engagement with your surroundings, including your roommates at the dormitory, is presented as a religious obligation. A Muslim woman should not be like a snail, as Samia pointed out. Motivations for social work may be intertwined with the religious obligation to convince others and guide them in the direction of Islam. In the eyes of the Islamist women I encountered, these motivations are not contradictory.

---

[29] The women who referred to this did not directly refer to the religious activity of *nasihah*, explicated by Talal Asad as an Islamic tradition of giving advice for someone's good, honestly and faithfully. It also has the meaning of sincerity, integrity, and doing justice to a situation. It is at once an obligation to be fulfilled and a virtue to be cultivated by all Muslims. Talal Asad, *Genealogies of Religion: Discipline and Reasons of Power in Christianity and Islam* (Baltimore and London: Johns Hopkins University Press, 1993), p. 214. *Nasihah* is also extended to political criticism. Ibid., and Henry Munson, Jr., *Religion and Power in Morocco* (New Haven and London: Yale University Press, 1993).

[30] It is a widespread assumption that Islamists, women and men, are against abortion. Still, Hakima and Faiza, both organized in Islamist organizations, recommended abortion within the first 40 days if an unmarried woman gets pregnant.

Everyday life programmed

Islamist women point to their everyday lives as organized and structured with significant implications for bodily conduct, not only in collective action but also in the individual woman's approach to religion and her own life. In other words they point to the program—or time schedule—structuring activities with consequences pertaining to regulation, control, and surveillance of the body. The material at hand, in other words, demonstrates a theory of bodily reform. According to this theory, bodily reform implies a reform of the person as a whole, suggesting that this form of theorizing affects programming among Islamist women. This program signifies the everyday life of Islamist women as planned and fully occupied, implying that time-management is one of the competencies that Islamic activism actually procures. The program is explicit in the case of some Islamist women who have pronounced it on a weekly or daily basis in the course of an interview-session while others claim to apply it just to parts of their activism, such as to their Quranic readings.

Meryem informed me of her weekly program of activities with the sisters in *Islah wa Tawhid* ("Reform and Unity"—the second of the two Islamist organizations in Morocco, currently in the strongest position):

Monday:	Day of fasting
Tuesday:	After the last punctual prayer, *Ishaa*, a session of *dhikr*: 1,000 times "God is tenderness", 1,000 times "no god but God", 1,000 times "no power but the power of God", and finally 1,000 times "God is glory."[31]
Wednesday:	Readings of the Quran and an interpretation, already prepared by one of the sisters who is presenting a summary of Ibn Kathir and Sayyid Qutb's: "In the shadow of the Quran."
Thursday:	Fasting and 112 prayers after *ishaa*.
Friday:	Presence at the collective prayer (around noon) and after the evening prayer (*al-asr*) visits to the poor and the sick in the community,
Saturday:	After *al-asr*, a session of *anashid* and an evaluation of the week's work, besides information from "brothers" and "sisters" in other regions.

According to this schedule she meets with the sisters four times a week. Allegedly, on her own she follows a similar schedule. Sunday is Meryem's only day of leisure where she sees her family and her other, as she says "laic [secular] friends." This schedule does not cover all her daily

---

[31] *Dhikr* is a ritual pronouncement of praises to God, known as a Sufi ritual. *Dhikr* was also mentioned by two other Islamist women as part of their religious activities. *Dhikr*, dubious as part of more general Islamist practice, was however not theorized or commented by any of the three.

activities, nor all her religious practices. Instead it may be regarded as Meryem's way of pointing to the elements of her daily life conceived of as Islamist activity. It is also a demonstration of all her efforts to apply Islam. In other words, this program is presented as a consequence of her commitment. Meryem is also busy as a student of International Law, so the information about this schedule serves to give an idea of the extent to which her everyday life is not only structured but also fully occupied.

While the extent to which the program is followed in practice is not documented by the mere existence of it, the program itself is a fact. It is a specification of religious practices, constituting the individual as "Islamist." But in the framework of a group the program becomes explicit in the need for coordinating activities with the rest of the group. It specifies what to do on a daily basis, intended to regulate individual as well as collective activities; it serves to regulate activities which build up the Islamist person as well as the activities aimed at reforming society.

In contrast, Nouzha claimed not to have a program, but still took part in activities such as collective readings of the Quran, *anashid*, *dhikr*, and prayers. As can be deduced from her need to point out that she does not have one, a program formulated by each woman on her own or with the group is a common Islamist practice, although it may be only the most devoted who establish a literal one. In fact, I was acquainted with a program in five instances: (1) as part of the activities taking place on campus, whether in the dormitory, in a private house, or elsewhere; (2) as a schedule of the Quranic readings that the individual woman performs on a daily or a monthly basis; (3) as a schedule of weekly duties and obligations; (4) as a certain order of events at the Islamic celebrations; and (5) as a way to regulate and ensure children's Islamic education. Even the women who do not refer to a program seem to follow one, structured by the daily punctual prayers, the regular fasting, the regular Quran readings, the weekly meetings with fellow Islamists, courses on Islam, and teaching. All this programming exists in parallel to their studies at university, which are, by the way, also scheduled. As has been made clear, time should not be left open for unimportant leisure activities—or for emptiness as some women put it—and pointing to the phenomenon of program in this case serves to both ensure and convey this.

Objectified bodies

The body is a constitutive part of most social practices. Nonetheless, it is striking that the body, bodily postures, and bodily movement are presented by activists as central to their practices. The body is already prescribed as part of Muslim practice in its most elementary form such as the prayer, but it seems that the body has to be further involved before an Islamist religious commitment becomes part of reality. The reasoning, or theorizing, accompanying the religious practices goes that if Islam is to be reinforced, reinvigorated, so must bodily practices. When belief and its practice are perceived as closely interconnected, a reformed and regulated body is a precondition for belief to become reality. A program serves as a technique to realize the self as a Muslim subject. In light of such reasoning, the installing of a program as an element in women's Islamic activism is rendered likely, even logical.

Consequently, reinforced bodily discipline, in condensed form, programming, appears as an inextricable part of Islamic activism—signifying bodily reform. Female, Islamist university students practice a transformation of Moroccan society through a transformation of each believer. However, the extent to which we are relying on reports of practices must not slip our attention. But social practice does not necessarily represent a sphere from which a more true version of social reality can be discerned (contrary to recorded speech or text), neither does it seem to represent a separate sphere of meaning production.[32] To the contrary, in the effort to develop self-knowledge, discourse and social practice are inseparable. It follows that discursive statements on the nature of Islam should be connected to social practices, rather than separated from it.

The body may be tuned to "systems of meanings lying silently within the conventions of a given world"[33] but those "systems" or rather, practices do not always remain "lying silently." It is noteworthy that by applying the technique of programming, Muslim subjects have explicitly set out to tune the body differently. Islamist women objectify bodily practices as they are revealed, become explicit, and are critically reviewed. And this objectification is a social practice. Consequently, it is in order to reveal hitherto non-verbalized, unnoticed, and unwanted social practices that a program is developed. It is a tool for the individual Islamist woman and as a technique it has the potential of mediating between inward, edifying practices and outward practices of reforming society. In other words, the angle of technology enables us to be specific in explaining how a new approach to self is generated. The point is that by the intervention of techniques of self, objectifying processes are put to effect, revealing a more strongly felt self.

The theory on the strong interdependence of a transformation of the person and a transformation of society is mirrored in the Islamist programming. Thus Malika explicitly linked her activities with children to the social responsibility that *hijab*-women are supposed to assume. In conclusion,

---

[32] Stuart Hall, "The West and the Rest", in *Formations of Modernity*, ed. Stuart Hall and Bram Gieben (Cambridge: Polity Press, 1991) p. 291.

[33] Comaroff and Comaroff, *Ethnography and the Historical Imagination*, p. 71.

women's Islamic activism consists of practices which are at once constitutive of a self, suitable for implementing social reform, and of practices intent on social reform.

Establishing a program is a technique of self with which Islamic activists are able to administer their own interrelated activities, self-practices directed at bodily reform and intellectual stimulation on the one hand, and activities directed at reform of the surrounding society on the other. Education, in this light, is an intensification of internalizing and externalizing processes. Accordingly, one specific way in which Islamic activism amounts to education is when Islamist women apply techniques of self.

Even though government executives in Morocco, along with their colleagues in Europe, tend to regard the Islamic opposition as a problem, this study is an attempt to avoid approaching women's compliance with "Islamic fundamentalism" as *a priori* a problem. On the other hand, Islamist women point to recognition as one of their core problems. They demand recognition from their compatriots and from government authorities, as well as from foreign observers and powers. Recognition is a social matter. It concerns the strategies with which women pave their way to the spheres of formal influence in Moroccan society, as well as the techniques they apply to become competent in those spheres, even though this may not be their explicit goal.

In such a wide perspective Islamism should be considered a social reform movement, supporting the rise and consolidation of new Moroccan middle classes in opposition to the former elite. There seem to be intimate links between self-practices and social reform efforts, rather than opposition. Islamic activism—and the techniques purported by it—is creating new spaces and new terms for wrestling with the core issues of identity, history, and culture, providing new possible ways of social and political integration for women in Morocco.

7

ISLAMIZATION AND EDUCATION IN EGYPT

BETWEEN POLITICS, CULTURE AND THE MARKET

Linda Herrera

In the view of Dr. Husayn Kamal Baha Eddin who began his tenure as Minister of Education by presidential appointment in 1991, something had gone terribly wrong with the nation's educational apparatus. Despite the centralized and heavily monitored formal education sector, schools were slipping dangerously out of the state's control and into the hands of "extremists" thereby posing a serious threat to the country's national security.

In this chapter we will attempt to trace changes in Egypt's formal education sector with a focus on the unofficial Islamization of schools at the pre-university levels. While a vast literature exists on Islamic resurgence and the Islamization of society in Egypt and the region since the 1970s, education has been largely neglected or misunderstood in the debates. By highlighting the interplay between the state, non-state actors, youth, and the market (rather than analyzing texts or school curricula), this study examines the role of formal education in wider social transformations relating to Islamization, civil society/state relations, and the cultural politics of contemporary Egyptian society. Furthermore, through ethnographic inquiries into private-sector "Islamic" schools that cater to the urban middle and upper classes, this study attempts to illustrate the new and diverse ways Islam is adapted to, and at the same time is transformed by, modern institutions.

Liberalization, Islamization, and education

A combination of social, political, and economic factors account for the gradual Islamization of both society and formal education over the past three decades. The relative opening of civil society and subsequent spread of organizations under the umbrella of "civil Islam"; the escalation of a spectrum of Islamist political movements—from militant to moderate; the substantial influx of money and piety from returnees from Arab Gulf countries; and, in more recent years, increased economic and political liberalization, all contribute in some way to the transformation of the social and educational terrain. While space does not allow us to treat each topic in turn, we will briefly review the debates on civil society as an example of how formal education gets marginalized or overlooked in the literature.

For the most part, formal schooling is absent in the considerable scholarly literature on the growth of civil society in Arab/Islamic states. When there is attention to education, it tends to concern programs sponsored by Islamically oriented associations in the realm of non-formal education such as literacy classes for adults, Quran reading classes at mosques, and Islamic nursery schools.[1] Islamic associations whose activities include establishing fee-paying private schools that serve the middle classes or even the elite have not been sufficiently treated. This oversight is probably due to two factors. Islamic associations are usually perceived as primarily serving the poor, or "the neglected segments of the population";[2] and, in the case of Egypt, civil society is largely understood to encompass organizations that fall administratively under the umbrella of the Ministry of Social Affairs, not the Ministry of Education where general private schools are located.[3]

It is likely that formal schooling as a field of inquiry is often neglected because of the assumption that schools under centralized and heavily bureaucratized management structures are implausible sites of non-state initiated change.[4] Indeed, the bulk of literature that specifically deals with formal education in Egypt and the Arab world adds little to advancing notions about the complex dynamics between educational and social change. For the most part, education studies are driven by outmoded human capital, modernization, and functionalist approaches that assume that omnipotent states orchestrate all significant educational activity and

---

[1] D. Sullivan, *Voluntary Associations in Egypt* (Gainesville, University Press of Florida, 1994); A. R. Norton, ed., *Civil Society in the Middle East*, vols. 1 and 2 (Leiden: E. J. Brill, 1995 and 1996); A. Kandil, "The Nonprofit Sector in Egypt," in *The Nonprofit Sector in the Developing World*, ed. H. K. and L. M. S. Anheier (Manchester University Press, 1998).

[2] Kandil, "The Nonprofit Sector in Egypt," p. 146.

[3] NGOs are heavily restricted and subject to laws that give the government the right to dissolve their boards, jail their leadership, restrict their funding and curtail their activities. Saad Eddin Ibrahim, *Egyptian Law 32 On Egypt's Private Sector Organizations: A Critical Assessment* (Cairo: Ibn Khaldoun Center, 1996). NGOS had been under the NGO Law 32 of 1964. On 28 Nov. 28, 1999 Dr. Amina El Guindi, Minister of Insurance and Social Affairs (MISA), issued the new and similarly restrictive NGO Law 153 of 1999 concerning voluntary associations and foundations.

[4] Although education is centrally planned, it is implemented and monitored at the level of the local educational governorate.

change.[5] Yet the process and outcome of schooling, even under centralized states, is vastly differentiated. The social institution of the school, far from functioning as a static social institution under the domination of an autocratic hegemonic state, represents a potentially dynamic site of political and cultural struggle and social change.

In a recent book, *Putting Islam to Work: Education, Politics and Religious Transformation in Egypt*, Gregory Starrett calls attention to the inadequacy of modernization approaches for understanding educational and social change in Egypt. He demonstrates, with theoretical nuance, that state policy is not passively accepted by its recipients, but is mediated, contested, and can result in unintended consequences. While a highly valuable contribution to the field of education, Islam, and social and political change, the central focus of Starrett's study is still the omnipotent, top-heavy state—its policies, reforms, and formal curriculum. He focuses, for example, on how Islamic discourse, which implicitly includes values and practices, is transmitted to children through state school textbooks rather than through actual human agents located in schools and elsewhere.[6] In other words, the state and the text receive far more weight in informing his analysis than local actors situated in schools. I do not mean to imply here that the state does not play an imperative role in determining and controlling multiple aspects of the educational process. Indeed, as educationist Martin Carnoy has argued, "Understanding the state's role is part and parcel of conceptualizing schools."[7] However, the organization and practice of schooling cannot be reduced to issues of state policy alone.[8]

In Egypt, as in other states of the region, mass formal education is highly regulated by the state. All Egyptian children from age six are legally obliged to attend the "Basic Education" phase of schooling which

---

[5] A. E. Mazawi, "The Contested Terrains of Education in the Arab States: An Appraisal of Major Research Trends," *Comparative Education Review* 43:3, 1999, pp. 332–52.

[6] Starrett's study does contain a cursory description of a religion class in a private language school, however, it adds little to his overall argument and therefore fails to shed light on the question of how schooling, as a practice and process, gets negotiated. G. Starrett, *Putting Islam to Work* (Berkeley: University of California Press, 1998), pp. 106–13.

[7] M. Carnoy, "Education and the State: From Adam Smith to Perestroika," in *Emergent Issues in Education: Comparative Perspectives,* ed. Arnove *et al.* (Albany: State University of New York Press, 1992), p. 143.

[8] B. Levinson, D. Foley and D. Holland, eds., *The Cultural Production of the Educated Person: Critical Ethnographies of Schooling and Local Practice* (Albany: State University of New York Press, 1996). Starrett is not alone in neglecting schools as vital sites of ethnographic inquiry. Anthropologists tend to avoid in-depth field studies of formal institutions of schooling, perhaps because, as one educational anthropologist conjectures, they "assume, rather unanthropologically, that Western-style schooling has the same effects everywhere," not to mention that "methodologically and ethically, ... schools are difficult places to study." B. Levinson, "Resituating the Place of Educational Discourse in Anthropology," *American Anthropologist* 101:3, 1999, pp. 598–9.

consists of the primary (grades 1–5) and middle school (grades 6–8) stages. There exist two parallel systems of education from which Egyptians can choose: "General Education" which is under the direct administration of the Ministry of Education (MOE), and the more Islamically oriented "Al-Azhar" education system under the administration of the governmental Al-Azhar Institutes Department of Al-Azhar University.[9] Our concern here is with Basic Education schools which represent a tacitly "secular" education.[10]

The MOE determines the curriculum, system of examinations, and overall organization of public and private sector general schools.[11] All schools are obliged to use standardized government textbooks and can only offer extra-curricular activities and classes with permission from the district education office.[12] To ensure that schools abide by correct procedures and practices, district educational inspectors make regular visits to individual schools. Despite the mechanisms of surveillance, control and monitoring, a veritable political crisis surfaced in the early 1990s: education, the Minister asserted, was slipping dangerously out of the hands of the government and falling into the hands of extremists. How could the nation's schools have deviated so far from the interests and objectives of

---

[9] NCER, *Development of Education in the Arab Republic of Egypt: 1986–1988* (Cairo: National Centre for Educational Research, 1989), p. 25. Since the reform of Al-Azhar with the Law of Al-Azhar of 1961, all Azharite schools follow the same curricula as general education schools with the addition of an intensive program in religious studies in subjects such as Quranic recitation, Quranic exegesis (*tafsir*), and Islamic jurisprudence (*fiqh*). Apart from the extra year in primary stage and the different administrative bodies that oversee the running of these schools, an essential difference between Azharite and general schools is that for the most part the two systems, via their secondary schools, track their students to different paths of higher education. The former prepares its students for Al-Azhar University the oldest Islamic university, established in 972 AD, and the later to the national state universities. Under certain conditions graduates of Azharite secondary schools can join national universities, and vice versa.

[10] "Secular" general schools contain a degree of religious instruction. All students are required to take a mandatory religion class—either Islam or Christianity depending on the student's religion. However, religion is not included in the student's overall grade point average (*majmu'a*). In terms of the ratio of Azharite schools to general schools in the Basic Education phase, in 1997/98 Azharite institutes constituted roughly 16% (2,480) of the total number of primary and 22% (1,546) of middle schools in the country. The general primary schools numbered 15,617 with general middle schools totaling 7,129. CAPMAS (Central Agency for Public Mobilization and Statistics), *Statistical Year Book: Arab Republic of Egypt* (Cairo: CAPMAS, 1999), pp. 186–90.

[11] The only schools that can operate in Egypt independent of MOE guidelines are international schools. These schools are open primarily to the holders of non-Egyptian passports. Egyptian passport holders have to obtain special permission from the Minister of Education to attend an international school.

[12] The Book Sector of the Ministry of Education prints and provides textbooks for all schools—public and private—at the pre-university levels. NCERD, *Development of Education in Arab Republic of Egypt: 1994/5–1995/6* (Cairo: National Center for Educational Research and Development), 1996, p. 62.

the regime? What's more, how did the process of educational Islamization, initially sanctioned to some extent by the state, spiral out of control to the extent that the Minister went so far as to characterize schools as "factories of terrorism" (*tafrikh al-irhab*)?[13]

The battle over national education

For the most part the nature of educational Islamization has been unofficial, or unsanctioned by the state. However the state has also played some role in promoting greater religiosity in the education system, particularly in the years 1987–91 when Ahmed Fathy Sorour was Minister of Education. Under his leadership the curriculum was revised and more religious/ Islamic content was added to it. Arabic language books, for example, contained more Quranic passages and the Social Studies curriculum placed greater emphasis on Islamic history.[14] Minister Sorour was also a public advocate of the return to conservative religious values. He repeatedly lamented the decline of ethics and religious morals in contemporary Egyptian society and stated the neccssity of them to be formally reintegrated into education.[15]

Before being able to formally implement a program of ethics into schools, Minister Sorour was abruptly transferred out of the office of Minister of Education and into the position of Speaker of the People's Assembly in 1991 to replace Rifaat al-Mahgoub who was slain in Cairo by members of a militant Islamic group. Under politically volatile circumstances, Dr. Husayn Kamal Baha Eddin, a paediatrician and previous Secretary General of the Nasser era Youth Organization (*Munazamat al-Shabab*), became the new Minister of Education by presidential appointment. He immediately reoriented education policy away from religion and any form of Islamization and introduced an entirely new discourse on education which linked schooling to the state's national security apparatus. Contrary to the decades-old rhetoric of education being a *service* of the state, like health care or infrastructure development, Baha Eddin introduced the concept of education as a cardinal component of its *national*

---

[13] In his book entitled *Education and the Future*, Baha Eddin writes: "Terrorism starts in the minds of people before it reaches the street. Before it uses bombs or guns it influences and misleads the minds of children and young people in factories of terrorism (*tafrikh al-irhab*). Education must face this phenomenon with all its energy." Husayn Kamal Baha Eddin, *Ta 'lim wa al 'mustaqbal* (Cairo: Dar al-Ma'arif, 1997), p. 55. Unless otherwise indicated, all translations from Arabic sources are my own.

[14] Ahmad Yusuf Saad, "Tahlil manhaj al-ta'lim al-asasi" (paper presented at Jam'iyyat al-tatwir al-dimuqrati al-'unf al-siyasi wa al-dini fi Misr: Hawafiz wa ufuq, Cairo, May 19–20, 1998).

[15] James Toronto, "The Dynamics of Educational Reform in Contemporary Egypt" (Ph.D. dissertation, Middle Eastern Studies and Educational Development, Mass.: Harvard University, 1992), pp. 151–2.

security on a par with the military. In a book written by the Minister in 1997 under the title *Education and the Future* he explains:

The first aspect of a new educational policy is that education is an issue of national security ... The use of the term 'national security' [referred] for a long time to military power, the shield that protects the nation from all dangers that threaten it. This term changed in the period after WWI and before the end of the Cold War because specialists, politicians and high-ranking military officers realized that national security [relates to] more than mere military power.[16]

Schools became entrusted with the new mandate of protecting the nation's youth from dangerous, or "extremist" elements within society.[17]

While Baha Eddin may have been among the first government officials to publicly locate schools in the national security apparatus, the Ministry of Interior had been treating education as a security liability for a decade. Since the assassination of Egyptian President Anwar Sadat in 1981 by Islamic militants, the Ministry of Interior had handled numerous criminal cases involving teachers and students from universities, schools, institutes and teacher training colleges suspected of involvement in illegal Islamist political groups. The Ministries of Education and Interior were in agreement that Islamic militants were using the nation's schools to carry out their political and social agendas that directly jeopardized the stability of the regime.[18]

To assess the extent to which schools were actually threatening national security, the Chancellor to the Minister of Education, Dr. Abd al-Fattah Galal, prepared a report for the education committee of the People's Assembly (the Egyptian parliament) in May 1993. He discovered that 90 schools and 300 teachers (listed by name) had links to illegal Islamist political groups, *al-Jama'a al-Islamiyyah* (*Jama'a*), the largest Islamic militant group in Egypt, *al- Jihad*, the militant Islamist group believed to have masterminded the assassination of President Sadat and al-Mahgoub, and *Ikhwan al Muslimin* (The Muslim Brotherhood), the reformist—and by that time nonviolent—Islamist group which was founded in 1928. Most of the schools involved in militant political groups were concentrated in Upper Egypt, specifically the southern cities of Qena and Asyout.[19] Baha Eddin stated in an interview, however, that his own investigations revealed that extremism was not limited to specific geographic regions of the country but was a nationwide phenomenon.[20]

---

16 Baha Eddin, *Education and the Future*, p. 84.
17 Starrett touches on this with his discussion of the state's violent response to private youth camps, but he doesn't put it in a context of overall educational policy or the political struggles in Egypt between the regime and Islamist political groups.
18 "Dancing on the Tunes of Extremists," *Al-Ahram*, April 22, 1993, p. 3. This and all other articles cited from Arabic newspapers are in Arabic.
19 "Teachers Wanted for Capital Punishment," *Roz al Yousif*, May 10, 1993, pp. 26–28.
20 "Militants Expelled from Schools," *Middle East Times*, Cairo, 1995, pp. 1 and 16.

The weekly semi-official magazine *Roz al Yousef* conducted its own investigation into religious extremism in schools in 1993. It reported that the Muslim Brotherhood was buying up pre-schools and elementary schools and that *Jihad* exerted control over teacher training institutes. For example Al-Mushir Secondary School in Asyout is described as a *Jama'a* recruiting ground and hideout. Teachers purportedly preached to students about the apostate Egyptian government, played recorded sermons of the dissident Shaykh Omar Abdul Rahman,[21] distributed the illegal Jama'a magazine *Murabitun* to students, and discriminated against Christian students by expelling them from classes and forbidding them from running for class elections. At Al-Qusiya religious institute, also located in Asyout, an English teacher and spokesman for the Jama'a instructed his students to write English from right to left since Arabic, the sacred language of the Quran, is thus written. The report cites other cases of how teachers in Upper Egypt lured students to their organizations by offering attractive extra-curricular activities such as soccer camps, book fairs, cultural events, and free private tutoring sessions at mosques. Along the same lines, a different study revealed how militant Islamic groups were using schools in a small village in Upper Egypt to store illegal arms.[22] Stories abounded in the press about how teachers were either forcing or scaring young girls into wearing the *hijab* (Islamic headscarf).

Baha Eddin enacted harsh measures to recapture the nation's schools. He pursued a strategy that included purging Islamist teachers, administrators, and materials from schools, and changing the school uniform regulation to restrict the Islamic uniform (*al-ziyy al Islami*).

Purging extremist teachers and thought from schools

In 1992, Baha Eddin initiated a policy of expelling teachers and administrators who "tampered" (*'abitha*) with the educational process.[23] Between the summer of 1993 and March 1995, roughly 1,000 educators were transferred out of schools and into other government posts. The Minister stated in an interview in 1995 that he was prepared to eliminate 10,000 teachers if necessary.[24]

---

[21] Omar Abdul Rahman is currently serving a life-sentence in prison in the United States for inciting terrorism. He was accused of instigating the 1993 World Trade Tower bombing in New York, among other acts.

[22] K. Maurith, "Al-ta'alim al-dini: bayna al-tasamuh wa al-'unf" (paper presented at Jam'iyyat al-tatwir al-dimuqrati al-'unf al-siyasi wa al-dini fi Misr: Hawafiz wa ufuq, Cairo, May 19–20, 1998), pp. 2–3.

[23] See *Ministerial Decision Number 162 for 1992*, Arab Republic of Egypt, 1992. For a discussion by Baha Eddin justifying his policy of purging teachers, see Baha Eddin, *Education and the Future*, p. 55.

[24] Husayn Kamal Baha Eddin, "Eliminating Extremist Teachers is an Urgent Measure: The Real Solution is to Develop the Curriculum (in Arabic)," *Al-Hayat*, Mar. 5, 1995, 17.

Information regarding extremist teachers reached—and continues to reach—the Ministry through three basic venues: parents, who convey their grievances through letters or personal visits to educational authorities; the press, which summarily reports pedagogical and curricular breaches at schools; and district educational inspectors who make regular supervisory visits to schools.[25] Numerous complaints in the early 1990s concerned teachers who attempted to influence children—often through tactics of fear—towards greater religiosity. Numerous schoolgirls were subjected to teachers who tried to persuade or compel them to wear an Islamic uniform of some sort. Other complaints dealt with the use of non-approved extra-curricular religious materials in the classroom. Cassette-recorded sermons of the *Torture of the Grave* (*Azab al Qabr*) were especially widespread.[26] Children were often forced to listen to sermons which described in terrifying detail how hideous snakes, agonizing beatings, and a fiery underworld awaited them in the afterlife if they failed to strictly abide by the tenets of their religion. The Minister recounted in a meeting how disturbed he was to receive a mother's complaint that her (unveiled) daughter could not sleep after listening to such a sermon in class for fear that a snake would creep up on her while she slept.[27]

District education inspectors were instructed to scour school libraries, teachers' rooms and classrooms for any unauthorized and potentially extremist or politically subversive materials. They confiscated religious books, magazines, political pamphlets, and religious tapes. Critics from among the secular liberal and religious camps argued that book censoring contradicted Baha Eddin's stated policy of religious tolerance and liberalism.[28] He stood firmly by his censorship campaign and invoked the role of the state as paternal protector of its children to explain why it was his duty to ensure that schools were cleansed of extremism:

We [censor] books that support extremist ideas that are against the valid teachings of Islam. Psychologically speaking a child is a person who does not have a formed character. ... He cannot fight ... so it is the state's responsibility to take care of the child and not leave him to face unhealthy situations ... I don't approve of censorship, but I have the duty to protect the child physically, psychologically, and mentally. Until he is formed he has to be under the protection of the family and state.[29]

Purging materials from schools proved less problematic than purging public sector schoolteachers and administrators who, as permanent

---

[25] Between 1995–98, I attended a number of press conferences held by Minister Baha Eddin where I gathered information on how the Ministry identifies extremist teachers.

[26] "The Complete Plan for Confronting the Network of Extremists in the Education Sector," *Akhbar al Hawadith*, May 13, 1993.

[27] "Dancing on the Tunes of Extremists," p. 3.

[28] "Supreme Court rules out veil," *Al-Ahram Weekly*, May 22–29, 1996.

[29] Baha Eddin in "The Complete Plan."

government employees, are protected by socialist-era labor laws. Instead of outright dismissals, educators were transferred—or more accurately banished—to other government positions sometimes hundreds of kilometers away where they would not have direct contact with children.[30] In a highly publicized case in 1993, a female teacher was transferred from her teaching post just outside Cairo to an administrative job across the country in Upper Egypt for playing the *Torture of the Grave* tape in her Arabic class.[31] The Minister pointed out that the Arabic class consisted of both Christian and Muslim students and the teacher was supposed to be providing instruction in language and grammar, not religion. To subdue some of the furor over her case, supervisors from the educational district intervened on her behalf and she was given a "long vacation" instead of the cross-country transfer.[32]

Some educators contested their transfers with litigation. In 1992, for example, Fayza Ziyadi, the principal of The Mother of the Believers Secondary School for Girls (*Um al-Mu'minin al-Thanawiyya li-al-Banat*) was transferred to an administrative office for purportedly forcing a girl to wear the *hijab*. She filed a lawsuit against the MOE and on February 18, 1993, the administrative court judge overturned the Ministry's decision on the grounds that "inviting students to be conservative, respectable and wearing *hijab* is not in opposition to the constitution which draws on the Shariah as the source of legislation."[33]

The Ministry's actions were not merely reactive, but also proactive. In efforts to challenge the religious extremist wave, the MOE sent teachers on training missions abroad, invited foreign educational experts to Egypt, built more schools, placed more emphasis on extra curricular activities, and invested in student social services and holiday camps. Schools also began organizing "counter-extremist" activities by holding religious seminars and debates.[34] Curriculum reform also figured into the overall counter extremist campaign. In one of his more controversial moves, Baha

---

[30] Ministerial Decision 355 for 1994, for example, orders that teacher Mr. Lutfi Ibrahim be transferred to a post "far away from schools." Newspapers often reported how teachers in Greater Cairo were transferred to offices in far away districts of Suhag, Qena, the Red Sea and Aswan. See, for example, "Minister of Education: The Terrorist in Our School," *Al Usra al Arabiyyah*, May 2, 1993.

[31] The teacher in fact worked in the district of Qalubeyya and was transferred to the Upper Egyptian city of Qena.

[32] "Dancing on the Tunes," p. 3.

[33] "Disputing the Minister of Education's Decision Forbidding the *Hijab* as an Obligatory Duty," *Al-Shaab*, Cairo, Jul. 19, 1994. The Teacher's Syndicate, which is supposed to provide protection and security for teachers, remained silent throughout this period of purgings. One critic pointed out that in its present form the Syndicate represented "just a dead body with no use ... either for the teachers or for education." "Minister of Education."

[34] "How Do We Fight the Extremism of Thought in Schools?," *Al-Siyasi al Misri*, Cairo, July 4, 1993.

Eddin invited the American Center for Curriculum Development to advise the MOE on how to make the curriculum more conducive to a tolerant, liberal, and technologically adept citizenry. Critics from all political spectra balked at American involvement in their curriculum, especially in religious studies. Baha Eddin reassured the public that he would continue to consult the *ulama*, the religious scholarly class, for advice on any changes pertaining to the religious curriculum. The Minister tampered with the idea of having one general religion class for all students instead of splitting Muslims and Christians into separate classes. He argued that separating out Muslims and Christians represented a form of discrimination, akin to separating children according to their color or sex. He argued that religion class should be a place where children "learn about moral conduct like developing a sense of cleanliness, which is a part of faith and also serves to protect the environment" and not a place where they become more aware of their differences (October 1993). The public opposition to a unified religion class was so overwhelming that the idea was eventually abandoned.

Issues of curriculum and classroom practice were eclipsed by concerns over schoolgirl veiling. As it became increasingly evident that large numbers of educators were pressuring or obliging schoolgirls to veil in some form or other, the Minister turned his attention to restricting veiling by revising the regulation on school uniforms. The *hijab* and other forms of veiling emerged as a highly controversial and litigious educational and political issue.

Beyond militancy: school uniforms and the cultural politics of education

From a legal perspective, educators, by requiring schoolgirls to wear Islamic uniforms, were not formally breaching any ministerial regulations. The Ministry set out to redefine the regulations governing school uniforms by implementing Ministerial Order 113 of 1994 on the Unification of School Uniforms.[35] Since much of the debate around uniforms concerns degrees of veiling, it is necessary to distinguish between different types of Islamic uniforms.

The new veiling which penetrated the education system and other sectors of society consists of three basic gradations: the *hijab*, a scarf of any color or pattern that covers the hair and is tied in a variety of ways; the *khimar*, a substantially longer solid colored nylon cloak that drapes over the torso and arms and is usually worn with a long skirt; and the *niqab*, a full face veil, ordinarily black, and worn with an ankle-length dress and gloves. Ministerial Order 113 of 1994 restricted veiling by outright

---

[35] Prior to Ministerial Order 113 of 1994, the Educational Decisions pertaining to school uniforms were numbers 139 of 1981 and 70 of 1962.

forbidding girls in grades 1–5 from wearing the *hijab* and required that girls in middle school (grades 6–8) obtain written permission from a guardian if they wear the *hijab*, thereby giving parents rather than teachers authority over the schoolgirl's attire. The Order prohibits girls from wearing the *niqab* at all educational levels. Any student in violation of the Order was forbidden from entering her school (Arab Republic of Egypt 1994).[36]

To ensure compliance with the decree, MOE inspectors and state security units were dispatched to schools throughout the country on the start of the 1994 school year. Guards blocked students dressed in defiance of the regulation—mainly primary school girls who donned the *hijab* and anyone who wore the *niqab*—from entering their schools. Many school communities reacted to the government's actions with outrage and protest. In a private "Islamic" school located in an upscale neighborhood in Cairo, tensions rose as students witnessed their young schoolmates being harassed at the school gate. A student in eighth grade at that time recollects the explosive mood at her school:

"Officials from the government came to the school and stood at the door saying that any primary school students wearing the scarf wouldn't be allowed to enter. They were asking girls to take off their scarves at the gate. The rest of us were standing in line for the morning assembly [*tabour*] and were aware of girls being kept out of the school. We all went to the corridor and sat down blocking the way and said we wouldn't move until the girls were allowed in. We started shouting out in unison, *La Allah ila Allah* [there is no God but God] until they agreed to let them in. We sat on the floor and another class joined us, and so on.

We were all very upset. The next day we made signs saying 'You cannot force anyone to disobey God.' If God tells you to do something, no one can convince you otherwise, not even your mother and father. All of us students were involved in this and we encouraged each other. The teachers also got involved. Even the girls who didn't used to wear the *hijab* came to school wearing it. We wrote slogans on the walls and encouraged each other to wear the *hijab*."[37]

The new uniform regulation caused a mix of outrage, confusion, and conflict among not only students and state officials, but also parents and school administrations. One father, on being told by the school principal that his primary school daughters would not be allowed to attend classes until they removed their headscarves, replied:

"How can I ask my daughters, whom I want to raise in accordance with God's satisfaction, to take off the *hijab*, even if they are young and not yet ordered to wear it? Isn't it our duty to make them get used to this in childhood? I am a simple

---

[36] Article 3 of Ministerial Order 113 of 1994 reads: "No student is allowed to wear a different uniform other than that mentioned in Article 1 of this decision. [If they do] they will not be allowed to enter the school or the classes. The uniform has to be proper and always kept clean."

[37] Interview with student in 1997.

Muslim and don't belong to any extremist organizations or even a [political] party. I just try to follow the instructions of our religion, the first of which is to raise my children in a proper Islamic way."[38]

The Minister encountered an onslaught of criticism from different ideological camps for interfering in the religious practices of individuals and the religiously oriented policies of schools. In a campaign to gain public support for his highly contentious uniform policy, Baha Eddin pursued a strategy which combined elements of Islamic orthodoxy with modern scientific reasoning.[39] He capitalized on his position as a Muslim by frequently quoting the Quran and making references to the Sunnah and Hadith (examples and sayings of the Prophet Muhammad), and also drew on his authority as a medical doctor by citing evidence from psychology, education science, and medicine. In an interview with the independent Islamically oriented *Al-Ahrar* newspaper for example, Baha Eddin argued, quoting the Quran as supportive evidence, that it is a violation of Shariah (Islamic law) to impose the *hijab* on the child, for religion is based on choice.[40] Similarly, in meetings with shaykhs of Al-Azhar, the guardians of orthodox Islam, he stressed his commitment to religious education, also with a verse from the Quran.[41]

Baha Eddin garnered the support of strategic religious figures including the Grand Mufti and Shaykh of al Azhar Muhammad Sayed Tantawi who issued a *fatwa* stating that "the *niqab* is not a requirement in Islam."[42] Tantawi also gave an interview with the semi-official daily *Al-Ahram* in which he supported the Minister, stating that he "is a strong Muslim, has organized thinking, and, I believe, would not issue a decision which violates the Islamic Shariah." He goes on to say that the Minister is not forbidding the *hijab*, he is simply making sure that the girl is not wearing it due to "external factors."[43]

---

[38] "New Instructions By Minister of Education Forbidding the *Hijab*," *Al-Shaab*, Oct. 31, 1994.

[39] I do not mean to imply here that Islam is somehow incompatible with modern scientific reasoning, for it is not. My interest is in showing how Baha Eddin invoked two quite distinct discourses, one based on religious doctrine, and the other on modern science, to support his position regarding a religious practice.

[40] "The Minister of Education Answers Questions from the Street," *Al-Ahrar*, Nov. 28, 1994.

[41] The exact quote by the Minister was "If a corrupt person came with a piece of news, you have to investigate it until you are right; otherwise you will be harming others and you will regret it" (*ya ayyuha al-ladhina amanu in ja'akum fasiqun bi-naba'in fa-tabayyanu an tusibu qawman bi-jahalatin fa-tusbihu 'ala ma fa'altum nadiin*). "Ending disputes over *hijab* in schools: Meeting between Minister of Education and Shaykhs of Al-Azhar University," *Al-Ahram*, Aug. 2, 1994, p. 7.

[42] "The *Niqab* penetrates Girls' Schools," *Sabah al Kheir*, Jul. 10, 1994.

[43] Tantawi in "The Decision of the *Hijab*: The Mufti of Al-Azhar supports it," *Al-Ahram*, Aug. 2, 1994, p. 1.

Changing into his scientific hat, Baha Eddin invoked modern psychology to defend his ban on child veiling and the *niqab*. He asserted that it was psychologically harmful for the female child to prematurely take on the responsibilities of adults by wearing the *hijab*. The child, he reasoned, should be allowed to play freely and enjoy her childhood, and the *hijab* can "stop the girl's psychological growth and limit her movement. All psychologists are against this."[44] Regarding the *niqab*, he argued that it was not only psychologically damaging to the wearer, but inhibited the educational process since teachers and students need to see each other's faces and make eye contact.[45]

Apart from being strongly contested in the press and among circles of students and parents, the uniform legislation also triggered a spate of lawsuits. Some parents sued for the right of their primary school daughters to wear the *hijab* to school, while others disputed the *niqab* ban.[46] The well-known Islamist lawyer Montasser al-Zayyat alone tried and won over 25 *niqab*-related cases in the lower courts. In a 1996 appeal that reached the Supreme Constitutional Court—Egypt's highest court—Ministerial Order 113 of 1994 was eventually ruled constitutional.[47] However, Islamic dress remains a highly divisive issue and new cases relating to the Islamic uniform continuously appear before the Egyptian courts.[48]

The battles over the school uniform, more than any other single issue, revealed the extent to which the Islamization of education constituted a far more complex phenomenon than had previously been understood. In the early 1990s, the Egyptian regime perceived the Islamization of education as posing a straightforward political, or security threat; members or sympathizers of Islamic militant groups were penetrating schools and the Ministry undertook measures to stop their influence. However, Islamist political militancy, even in its height, constituted only one—and arguably not the most powerful—force of the Islamization of education. By the mid-1990s, Islamist militancy began to wane considerably due in large

---

[44] "Ending disputes over *hijab* in schools," p. 7

[45] "Supreme Court rules out veil."

[46] "Disputing the Minister of Education's Decision," and "Court throws out veil ban," *Middle East Times*, Aug. 29–Sept. 4, 1994, p. 1.

[47] See Dupret in this collection on the *niqab* case that reached the Supreme Constitutional Court.

[48] The following represent three examples of recent cases involving Islamic dress. A *niqab*-wearing woman (*munaqiba*) from al-Azhar University sued the American University in Cairo (AUC) in 2002 for being denied entry into the library as an external student. AUC banned the *niqab* in 1999 when it was confronted with its first *munaqiba* student. The case is pending. In March 2002 an Egypt Air pilot was fired after she took the *hijab*. She is suing Egypt Air and her case is currently pending. In the fall of 2000, a 12-year-old girl and her three younger brothers (aged eleven, nine, and four) were expelled from Champollion School in Alexandria, a private school attached to the French Ministry of Education, because the girl wore the *hijab* to school in contravention of the school's secular policy. The parents won the case and are waiting to be awarded damages.

part to aggressive state action, yet the cultural and social facets of Islamization have remained a powerful, if fragmented, social force.

As the debates over the school uniform have unfolded, it has become increasingly evident that large numbers of Muslim parents and students approve of the Islamization of education—not for political, but for cultural reasons.[49] They consider it appropriate for educators to socialize Egyptian youth as pious and culturally conservative Muslims. Many parents with the means to do so even specifically seek out private schools with an "Islamic personality" to ensure that their children receive what they consider a proper moral/religious and scientific education. However, the nature of religious socialization varies from school to school, and shifts over time.

To assess the extent to which educators, school owners, parents, the state, and students negotiate issues of religious/moral socialization, we will turn attention from the policies of the MOE to actual school cultures. In this context a category of private sector schools known as Private Islamic Schools is particularly crucial.

Private Islamic schools: Between the state, non-state actors and the market

Islamically oriented general private schools, or "Private Islamic Schools" (PIS) first began appearing in Egypt in the 1970s contemporaneous with the Islamic resurgence movement. Like the burgeoning Islamist projects and non-governmental associations which included health clinics, orphanages, banks and investment companies, publishing houses, youth organizations, and political groups, Islamic schools emerged onto the civic landscape in response to a shifting cultural, socio-political, and economic terrain. Private Islamic schools (PIS) which have multiplied since the late 1970s, can be conceptually located in the increasingly Islamized civil society. At the same time, as profit making fee-paying schools, they also constitute a form of Islamically oriented business.[50]

Administratively, PIS are general schools under the authority of the MOE. They differ from public sector and other private sector schools insofar as they integrate extra-curricular religious classes into their programs of study and attempt to render the daily life of the school "Islamic." Like other private schools they charge tuition fees, have more leeway than public schools in the hiring and selection of staff, and have an independent owner and board of directors. In 1989, the Ministry officially acknowledged PIS as

---

[49] The Egyptian Christian community has clearly not been in favor of the Islamization of education. Although it is important to understand and address their response to the situation, a discussion of their grievances is beyond the scope of the present chapter.

[50] I. Farag, "L'enseignement en question. Enjeux d'un débat," *Egypte/ Monde Arabe* 18–19(2 & 3), 1994, pp. 241–329.

a distinct category of private school and provided guidelines regulating extra-curricular religion classes and additional religion exams.[51] However, after the MOE crackdown on the Islamization of schooling in the early 1990s, a number of schools that would have registered as PIS refrained from doing so for fear of excessive government surveillance and possible harassment. Islamically oriented private schools continued to be established in the post 1991 period, however, as general private schools.

While only a handful of PIS existed in 1978, their numbers steadily increased and by 1996 they numbered roughly two hundred. PIS represent an overwhelmingly urban and northern phenomenon with a total of 56 percent of them located in Greater Cairo and 28 percent in Alexandria.[52] The urban professional classes, many of whom worked for a period of time in an Arab Gulf country where their children might have attended schools where Islam formally plays a more significant role in the curriculum and school culture than in Egyptian schools, provided an eager market for PIS.

PIS do not represent a consolidated or monolithic education movement. Rather, individual schools, which cater to a broad socio-economic cross-section of the urban population, are founded and operate independently of each other. Although they call themselves "Islamic" they are not linked with Azharite institutes, nor do they necessarily depend on the *ulama* (Muslim scholarly class) for religious supervision. Rather, individual school directors and senior administrators, many of whom have not had formal religious training, determine their school's religious policies.

To illustrate the diversity within PIS, we will turn to two case studies. The first school is linked to an Islamic NGO and represents a more culturally conservative PIS intended for middle to lower middle-class children. The second school is registered with the MOE as a private English language school and caters primarily to the urban upper classes. By profiling the two schools we will assess how education and Islam are mediated by different cultural, gender and market considerations.

Negotiating gender: The school of an Islamic charitable association

In 1981, Al-Fath Private Islamic School opened as part of an Islamic NGO, Al-Fath Islamic Charitable Association.[53] Attached to Al-Fath

---

51 Arab Republic of Egypt, *A Decree Draft for the Private Islamic Schools: Decree 1 for the year 1989 Concerning the Private Islamic Schools* (Cairo: Ministry of Education, 1989).

52 Linda Herrera, "The Sanctity of the School: New Islamic Education and Modern Egypt" (Ph.D. dissertation, Graduate School of Arts and Science (Program of Comparative Education), New York: Columbia University, 2000, pp. 103–8).

53 The author spent the 1998/99 scholastic year as a researcher in Al-Fath Islamic Private school.

mosque in a suburb in southern Cairo, the association was founded in 1976 by Shaykh Mohammad Abd Al Salam Mutawali, a previous functionary at the Ministry of Religious Endowments (*Wazarat Awqaf*). He had been educated at Azharite institutes through the secondary level (Grades 10–12), at which point his formal education ceased. Al-Fath Islamic Charitable Association was initially established for the purpose of providing low-cost health services to the poor. It branched out to include a range of medical, educational, and social services. Its medical services consist of two hospitals and a center specializing in heart diseases; its educational services include a nursery school, Al-Azhar Institute for Boys, a Quran reading center, and the Al-Fath Private Islamic School; and its social services are comprised of an orphanage with 140 children and a fund to aid poor families and widows. Shaykh Mohammad is currently planning to establish a center for the mentally disabled, a home for the aged, a general library, and a lecture hall.

The association expands when it generates enough income to do so. Donations make up a major part of its funding. However, Al-Fath Islamic Private School, with a total of 1,600 students, also constitutes a substantial and steady source of income. The co-educational school, although linked to a charitable association, is not a charity school, but a profit-generating enterprise. All students must pay the one-time registration fee of LE1,000 and annual tuition fees of LE400 per year for primary school and LE475 for middle school. The school's annual net profit is roughly half a million LE, most of which is reinvested in the activities of the mother association.[54]

Unlike other private schools in the vicinity, the tuition at Al-Fath is extremely modest, but the school also offers far less by way of extracurricular activities and equipment. For example, Shaykh Mohammad has persistently refused to equip the school with computers despite numerous requests from parents. He reasons that computers will not bring the children any closer to God; however, it appears that monetary considerations also play a major role in his decision. The Shaykh is vigilant that the school be run on a shoestring budget. There are no frills or after-school activities, and teachers earn a paltry starting salary of LE100 per month. Unlike public sector teachers whose salaries are supplemented by monthly bonuses and incentives, teachers at Al-Fath receive only two annual bonuses of LE25 for the religious holidays Ramadan and Bairam. Some teachers complain that their salaries are unreasonably low, but the Shaykh refuses to increase them, arguing that the income generated by fees is needed for the association's other services.

Shaykh Mohammad strongly believes that children should grow up in an Islamically orthodox or religiously conservative environment. He determines

---

[54] During most of the 1990s the exchange rate of the Egyptian pound to US dollar was LE3.3 to $1. In 2001/2002 the pound devalued and the current exchange rate is LE4.5 to $1.

the school's Islamically oriented policies but depends on his senior administrative staff, three women in their mid to late 40s and all former Arabic teachers, to implement them. As Chairman of Al-Fath Association he spends most of his time supervising other activities and rarely visits the school. The Shaykh considers it imperative that children master the Quran and the Arabic language, comport themselves in a decent, religiously sanctioned manner, and avoid activities that distract them from their religion. Along these lines, the school's formal policies include sex segregation of students, mandatory extra-curricular Quran classes, forbidding the use or possession of popular music cassettes or videos, and enforcing Islamic school uniforms for female students and teachers. Aspects of the state curriculum that the Shaykh considers superfluous, such as girls' physical education and English language instruction, are underemphasized. However, a number of factors, including the agency of students and teachers themselves, result in ongoing negotiations and shifts in school policy over the issues of what constitutes an acceptable Islamic upbringing. Due to space limitations we will concentrate on only two specific issues concerning girls' socialization: uniforms and physical education (P.E.) classes.

When Al-Fath school opened in 1981, the school uniform for girls from the first grade onwards consisted of a long white *hijab* bordering on a *khimar* and ankle-length gray smock. In 1994, when news of the new uniform regulation order reached Shaykh Mohammad, he initially refused to change the school's uniform policy, convinced that he, not the government, was religiously in the right. However, when faced with the very tangible possibility of the MOE taking over his school's administration, he reluctantly acquiesced and eliminated the headscarf for girls at the primary level. Nevertheless, with the parents' cooperation, the *hijab* remained mandatory for girls at the middle school stage. Initially, teachers, parents and even some students felt a sense of indignation against the government for what they perceived as its unjust interference in the school's internal policy and their private lives. Eventually, however, many students— followed by staff—began modifying their own style of dress in a gradual process of what I have called "downveiling."[55]

Backed by the law, the overwhelming majority of sixth to eighth grade girls were the first members of the school community to practice downveiling, and therefore act as agents of change. These girls aged 11–14 substituted their uniform *khimar* for a simple white scarf and, in an act of defiance against school policy, decided among themselves to replace the regulation gray smock uniform, which they described as "ugly" and "old-fashioned" (*balady*), for a more "normal" and attractive uniform of a tailored long

[55] Linda Herrera, "Downveiling: Shifting Socioreligious Practices in Egypt," *ISIM (International Institute for the Study of Islam in the Modern World) Newsletter* 6, 2000, pp. 1 and 32, and Linda Herrera, "Downveiling: Gender and the Contest over Culture in Egypt," in *Middle East Report* 219, 2001, pp. 16–19.

gray skirt and white or light gray blouse. Gradually, some members of the school staff also began downveiling. The most visible and controversial downveilers, as far as the students were concerned, were two senior administrators, second in command only to the principal and Shaykh Mohammad. These in-school disciplinarians and tacit role models gradually substituted their dark ankle-length skirts for slightly shorter cotton skirts, and, in gradations, replaced their thick polyester *khimars* which extended to their thighs, with shoulder-length scarves. Both women had begun sporting the *khimar* just prior to being employed at the school in the early 1980s, in part to show their commitment to working in an Islamic environment, but also because they could not justify wearing a lesser degree of clothing than the children under their authority. When the primary school children ceased to cover their hair and the girls in middle school downveiled on their own initiative, the need to dress religiously on a par with the students no longer existed. A number of other teachers, over time, also modified their dress to less concealing and more functional forms of Islamic dress.

The trend of downveiling has caused something of a crisis of moral authority at the school. A seventh grade student remarked, "Our school has really changed. In the beginning it was very strict and all our teachers wore the *khimar* or the *niqab*. Now a lot of our teachers who once wore the *khimar* wear very tight clothes with a little scarf," to which her friend added, "a very, very little scarf." An eighth grade girl complained that the vice-principal scolded her for wearing a uniform skirt that fit too snugly around her hips and for not buttoning her blouse to the neck and asked, "How can she comment on my appearance when she herself used to wear the *khimar*, took it off, and now only wears a scarf? She tells us not to wear tight clothing but she sometimes wears very tight skirts with sandals."

At the same time, however, students also complain when teachers steadfastly cling to more concealing and conservative forms of Islamic dress. The P.E. teacher Abla Hanan, for example, wears the *khimar* even while leading her class in exercises and overseeing their athletic training.[56] During a break in a morning P.E. class, a group of students commented to me on Abla Hanan's attire: "Just look at her." One girl remarked, "Have you ever seen anyone teach P.E. wearing a *khimar*? It's ridiculous." Although they may not be aware of it, Abla Hanan vigorously struggled to get the girls where they are today, in stretch pants playing basketball at an Islamic school.

Abla Hanan arrived as a new teacher of girls' P.E. eleven years ago and found all the girls out of shape, pale, and with no skills in any team sport. She immediately set out to bolster the girls' P.E. program by introducing

---

[56] "Abla," a title of Turkish origin, is a term of respect used for teachers or older female figures.

basketball, her favorite team sport. Shaykh Mohammad initially opposed her initiative, asserting that it was unsuitable for veiled girls to run and jump in view of male teachers and boys (boys in middle school can see into the girls' courtyard from their ground floor corridor). After a year of Abla Hanan persistently putting forward arguments in favor of girls' sports and after she had gained the support of parents who provided funds for installing basketball hoops in the girls' courtyard, the Shaykh relented. Abla Hanan immediately established a sixth and seventh grade girls' basketball team and began training them for a district-wide basketball competition. To her delight the school's team won first place and held their championship position for two consecutive years. Her second victory has been to make it acceptable for girls to change into stretch pants or jeans and a long t-shirt in lieu of their long skirts and blouses for P.E. class. In accordance with school regulations, however, they are still required to leave on their white scarves.

Shaykh Mohammad established Al-Fath Private Islamic School with the intention of creating a conservative orthodox Islamic environment in which students of middle class backgrounds could obtain their formal educational credentials. A number of factors, ranging from state intervention in school policy, youth culture, and the agency of teachers, students and parents, have all served to mediate his conservative, Islamically oriented policies. The case of Al-Fath demonstrates, in other words, how Islam and conceptions of Islamically correct practices are transformed as they are funneled—via human intervention—through the modern institution of the school.

As the next case will illustrate, Islam has also proved adaptable to other factors such as changes in the market and evolving consumption patterns of the new middle classes.[57]

Five star schooling: The commercialization of Islamic education

Prior to the mid-1980s, private Islamic schools, although profit-making enterprises, were not viewed as especially lucrative business ventures. They were often affiliated with philanthropic associations like Al-Fath Private Islamic School, or individuals involved in "social Islam." With the economic liberalization of the 1990s and subsequent proliferation of the private education market, a new genre of private Islamic school emerged, the "five star" Islamic school. The new luxurious private schools cater to affluent urban Muslims who may also support other Islamic capitalist ventures such as Islamic banks and investment companies, high quality

---

[57] See Galal Amin, *Whatever Happened to the Egyptians?* (Cairo: AUC Press, 2000), for a discussion of the new middle classes in Egypt and how social mobility has served as a powerful force for change.

Islamic publications, Islamic computer games and informational CD-ROMs, and upscale Islamic clothing boutiques.[58]

At the high end of the new private Islamic schools is Al-Bashaer School, an English language school that projects an image of cosmopolitan modernity.[59] The fees at Al-Bashaer are LE8,000 for the first year, and between LE5000–6000 for subsequent years depending on the educational stage. An Egyptian engineer and businessman Muhammad Fawzi Al-Qadi founded Al-Bashaer school in a new residential area inhabited largely by Egyptian professionals, New Maadi in 1994. The school, built on 2,850 square meters, offers large playgrounds, two mosques, small class sizes with a maximum class size of 23 pupils (it is licensed for a total of 700 pupils), science laboratories, a library, a theatre, medical clinic, resource rooms, two swimming pools (which are fenced off during the year and are only in use during the summer when the school sponsors a camp), a modern cafeteria, and ample sporting and extra-curricular activities. The school's showpiece is its computer lab which is fully internet accessible. It comes equipped with a full-time teacher, a young bearded man who sports a white prayer cap and gives courses on the use of the internet and oversees the school's website, http://www.albashaerschools.com.

Apart from its state of the art facilities, the school also projects its elite, cosmopolitan image through the realm of clothing, food, and transport. Students are required to wear a British style prep school uniform replete with a navy blue blazer with the school's insignia of two children, one male and one female jumping in front of a rainbow, embroidered on the lapel. The *hijab* is optional for girls from middle school. The custom named air-conditioned school buses can be found cruising the more affluent parts of Cairo. The school cafeteria offers lunch specials on Thursdays which alternate between different American fast food restaurants—McDonalds, Pizza Hut, and KFC.

The school prides itself on its mission of raising Muslim children for the 21st century, and its axiom is "Knowledge and Faith."[60] Its main aim, as stated in its bilingual English/Arabic brochure which has the school logo of jumping children on the left hand side of the page and an elaborate

---

[58] Dale F. Eickelman and J. W. Anderson, "Print, Islam, and the Prospects for Civil Pluralism: New Religious Writings and Their Audiences," *Journal of Islamic Studies* 8:1, 1997, pp. 43–62;.

[59] In language schools between two to four main subjects are taught in a foreign language, however the curriculum is still determined, and all textbooks provided, by the MOE.

[60] Like all general schools Al-Bashaer is officially open to children of all religions. During a visit to the school in 1999, I asked the vice-principal if non-Muslim children were eligible to join the school and she responded, somewhat tentatively, "Yes, they can attend the school, but they might object to some of the things we are doing because we advocate an Islamic spirit and do things that non-Muslims may not want to participate in." According to a teacher, only two non-Muslim children have attended the school, however they stayed for only a year.

Arabic calligraphic drawing of "In the Name of Allah" on the right side, is to develop in its students "a personality committed to religious beliefs and values and, simultaneously, to follow up and take part in the rapid progress of science and technology." It also attempts to foster a spirit of transnational tolerance and calls on children to "respect ... other cultures, beliefs and nationalities." However, like other Islamic schools, educators at Al-Bashaer discourage children from imitating certain aspects of "Western" culture which they consider inimical to Islam such as dating, dressing in immodest ways, and consuming music, film and other products of Western (i.e. American) popular culture. The English language, however, is considered an essential asset for success in the international business and scientific community and thus holds a central place in the school's program of studies.[61] Teachers try to talk with the mainly Egyptian student population in English as much as possible and the administration makes a concerted effort to hire native English speakers. Currently, a total of seven British and American women, all Muslim with the exception of one who is Christian, are on the staff of Al-Bashaer School. All female teachers must wear a uniform that is provided by the school for a fee and consists of a navy blue coat with a scarf or a navy jacket and skirt with a scarf.

As for Islam, it permeates the everyday life of the school in a variety of ways. Fifteen minutes are devoted each morning to teaching children Quranic recitation (*tajwid*) and meaning. All the children participate in the noon prayer which is preceded by *wudu'* (the ritual cleansing) and followed by a 10–15 minute religious discussion group in the mosque. Class teachers are encouraged to incorporate religion in their lessons in whatever way they can, and to instruct children to greet each other with "Salam Aleykom" and refer to each other as "brother" and "sister." Teachers also decorate their classrooms with religious posters in English and Arabic. Islam is also present in the realm of P.E. and sports. The school teams, or "houses" as they are called in the British system, are distinguished by color and name. Being an Islamic school, the houses are named after *al-khulafa al-rashidun*, (Prophet Muhammad's four successors) as follows: the Green Team, Abu Bakr Al-Siddiq; the Red Team, 'Umar ibn al-Khatab; the Yellow Team, Uthman ibn Affan; and the Blue Team, Ali Bin Abi Talib.

The school owner sometimes invokes Islam as a justification for financially penalizing teachers. Depending on their qualifications, teachers earn

---

[61] On the subject of the English language, the school brochure reads: "Since it is a language school, the pupil should be privileged in his use of the language (conversation/comprehension/knowledge) is [*sic*] full fluency so that on entering university anywhere all over the world, it will be easy for him to deal with the international references and to benefit from the international education. The pupil deals with the English language inside and outside the classroom. We do not only teach Mathematics and Science in English (as in most schools), but also communicate with the pupil in English."

between LE500 to LE1000 per month, a relatively high amount in relation to Arabic schools, however they rarely receive their full pay. The owner, backed by his administration, regularly docks a quarter day's pay for any number of minor infractions such as not wearing socks, since, he argues, socks are a requirement in Islam.[62] One teacher explained that the owner runs the school with the businessman's sense of cost efficiency and uses whatever justification necessary—Islamic or other—for cutting operating costs. Many of his profits are being used towards expansion of the business; he anticipates building a separate high school in the coming year.

Al-Bashaer school, by combining cosmopolitanism, English language training, and emphasis on modern technology, within an Islamic atmosphere, has found an eager market among new groups of affluent urban Muslims.

As this chapter attempts to demonstrate, Islamization and education have been intertwined in a dialectical process whereby each influences and transforms the other. As Islam is adapted as a political language and cultural form to the institution of the school—mediated by the exigencies of state policies, human agents, and shifts in the market—both education and Islam undergo change.

Islamization represents a process that is fraught with contradictions and colored with nuances and infinite variety. At times it has served as a regressive force and contributed to an atmosphere of repression and fear. In the 1980s, for example, Islamist teachers commonly used coercive tactics to influence students towards greater religiosity and sympathy for their political causes. The state adapted aggressive measures to thwart educational Islamization and was successful in eliminating, to a large extent, political extremism in schools. However, it was far less successful in controlling people's desires for cultural manifestations of Islam. The immense public outcry and ongoing struggles over the *hijab* and *niqab* are cases in point. Although highly contested, the uniform regulation served as a catalyst for the relaxation of Islamic dress among certain circles of women, as evidenced by downveiling. Yet as the example of the P.E. teacher/basketball coach demonstrates, the factor of steadfastly choosing more concealing types of dress does not necessarily reflect a conservative gender outlook.

In the wake of economic liberalization in the 1990s, a range of new markets and consumption patterns emerged within Egyptian society including new types of elite Islamic language schools. Islam was adapted to a cosmopolitan educational environment to fulfil the aspirations of a globetrotting Muslim community. However, in the name of cost

---

[62] Interview with a teacher from Al-Bashaer, Mar. 19, 2002.

efficiency, Islam was sometimes reduced to its most banal form as when teachers were financially penalized for not wearing socks.

Formal education, because of the state's attempt to control its content, monitor, and administer it, provides a particularly compelling site for uncovering the ways in which Islamization occurs at the institutional level, is negotiated, and changes over time. Schools, in other words, serve as stages for shifting cultural practices and politics and reflect broader changes in society. Multiple factors, including state policies, the agency of students, parents, and teachers, and changes in the market, converge in complex ways to mediate between education and Islamization.

Part III

RE-ISLAMIZATION
IN EUROPE

8

THE GROWING ISLAMIZATION OF EUROPE

Oussama Cherribi

"... Islam is truly a world religion, increasingly visible in Europe and the United States as well as Asia, Africa, and the Middle East. Muslims are very much part of the mosaic of Western societies, no longer foreign visitors but fellow citizens and colleagues."[1]

Muslims are no longer outsiders in Europe. Three main developments have occurred in the Muslim communities of Western Europe over the past few decades. One is an ongoing process of institutionalization of the establishment of Islam in Europe, including the growth of mosques, Islamic schools, social, cultural, and even political networks. A second development is the emergence of Islamic religious leadership in Europe, in the form of imams as a major voice of the Muslim community on social issues of importance in European societies. I refer to these two developments as the Islamization of Europe.

A third development is the re-Islamization of Europe. By this, I refer to the re-Islamization of the secular Muslims in Europe. The emergence of Islamic religious leadership in the 1990s in Europe has also meant that the secular and often left-wing leadership of migrant organizations that represented Muslims in the 1970s and 1980s, have taken a back seat to religious leaders, who now appear to be the driving voice of the European Muslim communities. The secular elite had been not only the spokesmen of the migrant Muslim communities, but also the partners of government in the effort to integrate minorities, and mosques were seen by the same secular elite as reactionary places working for the agenda of the Islamic country of origin. At that time, imams were seen as reactionary and controlling, and working for the government of the country of origin, rather than working

---

[1] John L. Esposito, *Islam: The Straight Path,* 3rd edn. (New York: Oxford University Press, 1998), p. xvi.

for the migrants to obtain more legal rights in the society in which they lived. Nowadays, however, there is less division within these Muslim communities and the formerly secular leaders express agreement with the religious leaders that an Islamic identity is very important.

In this chapter, I discuss the key developments that have brought about the Islamization and re-Islamization of Europe, with examples from European countries and with reference to what lies ahead. Three main developments account for the Islamization and re-Islamization of Europe: the growth of the Muslim communities in Europe; the increasing visibility of Islam in the European public space; and the political mobilization of Muslims in Europe. In conclusion, I discuss these developments in light of the current concerns among the Muslim communities, as well as the concerns of political elites and the non-Muslim population in European countries.

THE GROWTH OF MUSLIM COMMUNITIES IN EUROPE

It is important to recognize that there is not one but many Muslim communities in Europe, with distinctive ethnic communities.[2] In Britain, Pakistani Muslims are the largest group, but there is a not inconsiderable presence of Moroccan, Algerian, and Gulf State Muslims in London, for example.[3] In Germany and the Netherlands, Turkish Muslims predominate, and among the Turkish Muslims there are at least three distinctive groups: Mili Gurus, Dianet, and Suleimangi. The Netherlands also has a considerable number of Moroccan Muslims and Surinamese Muslims. In France, there are four million Muslims and, as in Spain and Belgium, most of them are from the Maghreb, with small Turkish and African minorities.[4] Many Pakistani, Kurdish, and Muslims from former Yugoslavia have settled in Scandinavia. There are also smaller numbers of different ethnic Muslim groups in all of these countries. And there are also Muslim political refugees in these countries, many of whom are Kurds, or who come from Albania as well as the former Yugoslavia.

It is difficult to get accurate estimates of the actual numbers of Muslims in European countries, because not only do the estimates of legal

---

[2] Steven Vertovec, "Multiculturalism, Culturalism and Public Incorporation," *Ethnic and Racial Studies* 19, 1996, pp. 49–69; and Steven Vertovec and Ceri Peach, eds, *Islam in Europe: The Politics of Religion and Community* (London: Macmillan, 1997).

[3] See also Bernard Lewis and Dominique Schnapper, *Muslims in Europe* (London: Pinter, 1994); Jørgen Nielsen, *Muslims in Western Europe*, 2nd edn. (Edinburgh University Press, 1995); and Lars Pedersen, *Newer Islamic Movements in Western Europe*, Research in Migration and Ethnic Relations (London: Ashgate, 1999).

[4] France has a distinctive conception of citizenship that has led the country not to endorse the Council of Europe's Charter on the Recognition of National Minorities. This is because France argues that there are no national minorities in France, only citizens. See also Martin Schain and Martin Baldwihn-Edwards, "The politics of immigration: Introduction," *West European Politics* 17:2, 1994, pp. 1–16.

immigrants vary, but there is also little in the way of reliable information on the numbers of illegal immigrants. In Italy, for example, Caritas, the Catholic charity, estimated that there were half a million Muslims living in the country legally in 1999, although other estimates put the figure at one million.[5] Muslims are expected to outnumber non-Muslims in Europe by 2050. In many of the major European cities, however, given the low birth-rates among indigenous populations, Muslim schoolchildren will be in the majority within the next decade. This anticipated development has been the subject of a not inconsiderable number of news stories in various European media outlets in recent years.

European national governments focus on the Muslim populations within their own countries, and political elites privately express concern about the possible ability of the governments of Islamic states to mobilize that ethnic community. Ironically, the Gulf War and the Rushdie affair provided an opportunity for this fear among the general population in France, Britain, and the Netherlands, for example, to mark the beginning of the development of a broader Muslim identity. In the early 1990s, because of these events, young Muslim men and women were interviewed on radio and television programs in these countries and asked if they thought of themselves as Muslims or Europeans (i.e. French, Dutch, or British). One young man interviewed on Dutch television at the time told me, "I've never before asked myself this kind of question, but now I realize that they want me to be a Muslim. I am a Muslim."

THE INCREASING VISIBILITY OF ISLAM IN
EUROPEAN PUBLIC SPACE

Over the past three decades, Islam has become increasingly visible in European public space. Mosques, halal foods, Muslim customs and ways of dress, are all increasingly common in European countries. The first mosque in Europe was erected in the 12th century by the Moors, in Andalucia, southern Spain. The Alhambra mosque has been a magnet for the growth of Spain's Muslim community, which is largely concentrated in the south of the country. La Grande Mosquée de Paris was completed in 1926, and was a gift from the King of Morocco. Morocco was a French colony at the time and France accepted the gift as a gesture of friendship and in order to have an appropriate venue to receive the King when he visited the city. The largest and most elaborate mosques in Europe today that have been built in recent years, or that are planned in the near future, are also largely supported by funding from Islamic states. The grand mosque at Hyde Park in London, for example, was funded with support from the Gulf States. They are also funding the construction of one of the largest

5 HYPERLINK "http://www.news.bbc.co.uk", www.news.bbc.co.uk, Sept. 6, 2001.

mosques in northern Europe, on the outskirts of Rotterdam, which will be known for having the tallest minaret in Europe. The larger mosques in Europe can often serve as a venue to bring together the different ethnic Muslim communities on special occasions.

The smaller mosques, built with funding from the local communities, which usually cater to one particular ethnic Muslim group, are far more modest. They are often reconverted old buildings such as warehouses or garages. In the Netherlands, where there is the lowest unemployment rate in Europe, the police and temporary employment agencies even organize special sessions in mosques to inform people about employment possibilities and community projects. There has been a growth of these smaller local community-based mosques in Europe. With this have come a growth in support for Islamic schools and, more recently, a call for Islamic retirement housing, and pastoral work such as spiritual counseling for Muslim prisoners in Europe. Some European states now have introduced halal food for their defense forces, and day care centers and schools in some European countries provide lunches without pork for Muslim and vegetarian children.

Britain and the Netherlands have served as examples to other European countries in how to accommodate the Muslim communities. Major supermarkets in both countries, for example, have recently introduced major sections for halal foods. In both countries, there appears to be more willingness to accommodate cultural differences than in some other European countries. Take, for example, the decision of the city of Rotterdam in the late 1990s to open some of the public swimming pools for special times only to Muslim girls and women, and to organize special courses such as training in bicycle riding for Muslim women who are often wearing floor-length dresses.

The issue of women wearing the veil has been a prominent one in Europe, largely because of the way it developed in France. There, the issue of schoolgirls wearing the scarf is well known for dividing the country in the mid-1990s, and still today many Muslim girls and women teachers cannot wear scarves in schools because the school does not permit it. Scarves in schools never became an issue in Britain or the Netherlands, and there has been a more liberal approach to accommodating Muslim women in the workplace, as well as special circumstances for children in schools. In Britain, for example, Muslim women police officers are permitted to wear the scarf. In the Netherlands, the Muslim women checkout cashiers at the upscale major supermarket chain Albert Heijn wear a specially made scarf with a corporate logo.

The current challenge in the Netherlands is within the legal profession. A Muslim woman courtroom clerk in early 2001 was prohibited from wearing a scarf on the job, and her challenge to this decision resulted in an overruling of the judge by the legal profession's Committee on Equal Rights. But the dispute is not yet entirely resolved and continues to split women in the profession. Even the most left-wing feminist women who would normally support a woman's right to choose on this issue, argue that the traditional symbol of justice (a woman wearing a blindfold so that she is totally impartial in making legal judgments) will lose its efficacy if women judges are wearing scarves.

In both Britain and the Netherlands, there are also Muslims represented at the highest levels of national government. There are Muslim members appointed to the House of Lords and elected to the House of Commons in Britain. There are even more elected members to the Dutch Parliament's equivalent of the House of Commons (the Tweedekamer), with seven Muslims spread across four political parties: the Liberal Party (VVD) has two, the Social Democratic Party (PvdA) has three, and the Greens have one. By contrast, in France there are no Muslim representatives in the Assemblée Nationale or in the Senate, Germany has only one Muslim member of the Bundestag in the Green Party, and Spain has none. Although Belgium has no Muslim members in the Assemblée Nationale, there are some Muslims in the separate regional parliaments in the French and Flemish parts of the country.

Despite Germany's major role in driving the process of European integration, within its own borders it has been slower than Britain, the Netherlands, Belgium, or France in integrating its Muslim populations. Muslim children's dietary restrictions, for example, specifically the cultural aversion to *schweinfleisch*, which is a staple German food, continue to be perceived by average Germans as a serious problem. Even political and media elites perceive this as a problem, based on the interviews I conducted with German members of the Bundestag in July 2001. (In the well known restaurant Die Eins in Berlin, over lunch with a German MP, I discovered little else but pork on the menu so I ordered what was described as a tomato with cheese, only to later discover minced pork hiding beneath a blanket of cheese!) The call for Islamic schools is perceived as an even more serious problem by even the left-wing political elites in Germany, and only now is Germany being forced by its courts to treat Muslim requests for Islamic schools in the same way that the country provides for Jewish and Christian schools. One of the Social Democratic Party (SPD) MPs with whom I spoke described the current state of the country as fearing not only the growth of the Muslim community, which is largely Turkish, but also the growing needs that community has, such as schools, which will ultimately cost the state money at a time of severe economic difficulties.[6]

One policy expert described the Germans as "ten years behind the Dutch" in terms of policy and accommodation of minorities, and the

[6] Interview July 19, 2001.

accommodation of Muslims in particular.[7] For example, the success of the Turkish Mili Gurus in the Netherlands is in large part explained by the entrepreneurial leadership of the group, who are networked in Dutch society and especially in politics and the press. In Germany, however, despite the fact that there are more Turkish entrepreneurs than in Holland, and therefore they potentially have more economic power, they move in an isolated circle and have no network in the civil society. They believe that the press and the politicians are against them in Germany, and they are probably right. The Germans have not stimulated minorities to be active in politics even at the local level, and until very recently the minorities and in particular the Turkish were entirely excluded from German citizenship. The Netherlands, by contrast, gave immigrants without Dutch citizenship the right to vote and to stand for elected office at the local level as early as 1986, and it has long been easier to obtain Dutch citizenship than German citizenship. A Dutch political analyst, Brieuc-Yves Cadat, however, argues that there is still a problem with citizenship in the Netherlands because one can have rights at the local level but is simultaneously denied them at the national level.[8] In 2001, Germany finally changed its citizenship requirements to make them more liberal, following the Dutch approach.

THE ROLE OF MEDIA AND NEW TECHNOLOGY

"Imams on-line" are a relatively new phenomenon and became common in the late 1990s in different European countries. Many of these websites are in several languages. They have encouraged interaction between younger people, who are the regular users of computer technology, and religious leaders who are able to answer questions on-line about rituals, problems of assimilation and integration, as well as personal issues concerning marriage or sexuality. The new interactive technology has not made the imam an agony aunt, but has given him more access to new audiences.

Local cable television in European cities, and local radio in Europe, is another means by which Muslim communities discuss issues of importance and Muslim religious leaders seek to maintain their support and attract new followers. Call-in local radio programs give the Muslim community an opportunity to interact with local imams. Imported Muslim programs on videotape from Islamic countries are often broadcast on local cable television because the local communities do not always have the resources to produce their own programming. On the same cable system in

---

[7] Interview Aug. 15, 2001 with Gijs von der Fuhr, a policy expert who advises the German Bureau for Policy on Foreigners (Auslaendersbureau) in Berlin, and who also works as a policy adviser and press officer at the Amsterdam Center for Foreigners. He also happens to be a third-generation German immigrant to the Netherlands.

[8] Interviewed Jul. 4, 2001.

Amsterdam, for example, one can find programming direct from Turkey, Morocco, Saudi Arabia, or London. On many of the live call-in programs made in Islamic countries and broadcast on European cable channels or via satellite, I have observed that many of the callers are European Muslims, which means that there is a not unimportant transnational dimension to the audience and to interpretations of Islam.

There are also newspapers throughout Europe that cater to Muslim populations. These range from the most established and widely read Arabic newspapers such as *Al Hayat*, printed in London via satellite with a special European edition, to the special newspapers produced in cities for different Muslim language communities.

In short, new technology and traditional media have meant that the visibility of religious leadership has moved from the private sphere of the mosque to be much more visible and accessible in the public sphere. This has made religious leadership more accessible to Muslim publics as well as more visible to non-Muslims.

One of the problems in many European cities has been the call for prayer, which comes five times a day, via loudspeaker from the mosque, and which has generated considerable anger among the nearby non-Muslim residents. New technology has been used by the Muslim community in some countries to get around this problem. During Ramadan in early 2001, the webmaster of a special Dutch site,[9] for example, gave people the opportunity to log on and provide their mobile phone numbers in order to receive the calls for prayer via a SMS text message. This was a very popular development, and it did not go unnoticed in the press. The most widespread SMS message went out at the time of the official sunset, so that Muslims could begin their meals.

THE POLITICAL MOBILIZATION OF MUSLIM COMMUNITIES

Research in the United States and Western Europe on social movements and mobilization has generally concentrated on national politics and collective action.[10] Little attention, however, has been paid to the mobilizing activities of immigrants or Muslims in European societies. I distinguish between two types of mobilization here. One is in an effort to achieve legislative or policy goals, or specific material requests. This type of mobilization is less spontaneous and more dependent upon social networks and resources to accomplish goals. Another type of mobilization is what Pierre

---

[9] HYPERLINK "http://www.maroc.nl", www.maroc.nl.

[10] For an excellent review of the theoretical approaches taken in this research see Sidney Tarrow, "National Politics and Collective Action: Recent Theory and Research in Western European and the United States," *Annual Review of Sociology* 14, 1988, pp. 421–40.

Bourdieu has termed "sudden mobilization."[11] Sudden mobilization is in response to an unexpected event or decision, and it may or may not be aimed at achieving some legislative or policy goal.

Mobilization with specific policy goals

France and transit visas. One example of this type of mobilization was in the mid-1980s, prior to the Schengen agreement, which enabled citizens to travel without borders or visas between a number of European countries. Mobilization of Moroccans, Tunisians and Algerians occurred because France imposed a transit visa requirement on all non-European citizens living in Europe, who wanted to travel through France. There were petitions signed, and demonstrations in front of the French embassy in a number of European countries, and threats to take France to the European Court of Justice. After some months, France removed this transit visa restriction.

Building a mosque and community in the Netherlands. The Mili Gurus Turkish community in Amsterdam, known as the most extremely conservative group of Turks because they support the Turkish Refah (Welfare) Party, provides another example of mobilization with specific policy goals. In the 1980s, the community purchased a large building with fenced-in parking that had been an auto sales and repair dealership, at a time when property in that part of the city was quite reasonably priced. They proposed to renovate the area to construct a new mosque and an apartment complex for Turkish Muslims. The City Council was entirely opposed to this proposal because they did not want to encourage a "Turkish ghetto" within an area that was already perceived as an "ethnic ghetto." After lobbying at the national and local level, the Turkish Mili Gurus entrepreneurs sought cooperation with a major Dutch housing association and agreed to make part of the proposed apartment available to Dutch residents. Because of the established reputation of the Dutch housing authority, and their agreement with the Turkish on this proposal, the City finally agreed to go ahead with the project, after nearly a decade of debate.

Three main consequences emerged from this struggle to establish the Ayasofia mosque and the apartment complex. One is that the term "Ayasofia" has become a kind of brand name in the community. The Ayasofia mosque is not only a place to worship, but there is also a café inside, a restaurant, workshops, an employment agency, a travel agency and a grocery store. A second consequence is the visibility of the leader of and spokesman for the Mili Gurus community, Haci Karager, who appears to be a tolerant and well-integrated example of Turkish entrepreneurship in Dutch society, and far from the stereotype of Mili Gurus "extremism." He has been invited to Germany by politicians and policymakers to serve as an example

---

[11] Pierre Bourdieu, *La Distinction* (Paris: Minuit, 1979).

for the moderate face of Turkish Mili Gurus Islam. Finally, a number of Dutch local political personalities ended their political careers because they stood firmly against the proposal, and ultimately lost.

Germany and Islamic schools. Whereas Islamic schools have not been an issue in some European countries such as Britain and the Netherlands where there are many, other European countries do not want this development. In 2000, Muslims in Germany used the courts to attempt to obtain rights to have Islamic schools. The German Basic Law (constitution) permits religious schools for Christians and Jews, but the political establishment has been unwilling to open this opportunity to Muslims. Although this has not yet been resolved, the expectation is that Muslims will win this right. This issue is one that recently propelled the MG Turks in Germany to form their own Islamic political party.[12]

Sudden mobilizations

Well-known examples of sudden mobilizations in the early 1990s include the protests surrounding the Rushdie affair in Britain and other European countries, and the demonstrations surrounding the issue of the scarf in France in that same period. In the Rushdie affair, most Muslims who were demonstrating in Britain and other countries were against the publication and sale of his book *The Satanic Verses*. In the case of the scarf in France, Muslims initially demonstrated for personal freedom and against a decision taken by a school to prohibit a Moroccan girl from wearing a scarf. The more general Muslim perspective was that the right to wear a scarf should be seen as akin to the right to wear a necklace with a cross or the Star of David. In what follows, I discuss some other examples of sudden mobilizations in Belgium, Britain, the Netherlands, and Germany.

Belgium: Bringing communities together. An example of sudden mobilization is the public response to the horrific torture and murder of a number of young girls in Belgium, by a pedophile serial killer, in the late 1990s. One of his victims was a Moroccan girl. A series of public demonstrations took place, known as the "white march" movement, against the "dirty hands" of the government and justice system, which had been found to be corrupt and incompetent in investigating these murders. At the Moroccan girl's funeral in Brussels at the largest mosque in Belgium, there was a silent demonstration where thousands gathered together. Those in the mosque included parents and families, dignitaries, politicians, and even the King of Belgium. They displayed a united force between the Muslim community and the Belgians against this horrific act. The dead girl's older sister, wearing a white headscarf, addressed the gathering in poetic and fluent French, and the event was broadcast live across Europe. The impact

---

[12] HYPERLINK "http://www.kranten.nl", www.kranten.nl, Sept. 5, 2001.

of this event extended to and was augmented by the arrival of the girl's body in Tangiers for burial, where hundreds of mourners lined the streets. Many Europeans followed this on television.

The sudden mobilization of the public against the Dutroux murders was aimed at achieving justice and a prosecution of the accused, which in fact has not yet happened. The older sister who spoke at the funeral has since become a cultural icon in Belgium. She has published a book, appeared on many television talk shows, and written for a number of newspapers and magazines. Some political observers have suggested that this highly visible and powerful event of the funeral of a Muslim girl, in which the Muslim community expressed solidarity with the French-speaking Belgian community, actually contributed to the subsequent disappearance of the extreme-right French-speaking party from the regional parliament of the French-speaking community in Belgium.

Britain: Race or religion? Another sudden mobilization occurred in the form of violent protests in the summer of 2001 in England. In the final week prior to the June 7, 2001, British general election, the news reported "race riots" in Oldham and neighboring working-class towns where "Asians" and "British people" lived side by side. Asian (Pakistani) young men and teenage boys overturned cars and set fire to houses and businesses, to protest against racial discrimination and racial harassment in the neighborhoods. In one of the national television news items reporting the event, a local spokesperson from the extreme-right British National Party (BNP) gave his view of the problem, which contrasted sharply with the views of the young Asian men who also spoke in the television news story. At that stage, close to the time of the event itself, this was generally referred to in the news media as a "race" problem.

What was most remarkable about this sudden and violent mobilization of young Pakistani Muslim men against the local racism they claim confronts them and their families on a daily basis, is what the event accomplished electorally for the BNP rather than for the Muslim community. Less than one week after these so-called "race riots," the vote for the BNP in the general election in the two constituencies in that area was unusually high.[13] The BNP claimed that was because citizens wanted to protest against the Labour government's handling of immigration and the way the local council had handled these local problems. But others suggested that the BNP stoked the local conflict in the weeks leading up to the election in

---

[13] BBC Online (See note 15), Jun. 8, 2001: "Following recent racial tension in Oldham, there was a significant increase in support for two British National Party candidates who scored their best ever showing in a parliamentary election. In Oldham East and Saddleworth, won by Labour's Phil Woolas, they scored 5,091 votes. In Michael Meacher's Oldham West and Royton, they recorded 6,552, pushing the Liberal Democrats into third place, and coming to within 500 votes of the Conservatives." http://www.bbc.co.uk/manchester/vote2001/oldham.shtml.

order to provoke this violent event and send fearful voters running into the arms of the right-wing anti-immigrant parties:

The people of Oldham are clearing up after two nights of rioting in the town. Petrol bombs and bricks were thrown at police officers and cars set on fire in the worst race related violence in Britain for 15 years. Greater Manchester police have condemned the violence during which twelve people were arrested and 25 treated in hospital for minor injuries. At a press conference, the police dismissed claims that they have lost the confidence of the local community, stressing that activity by right wing extremists had stirred up racial tensions in Oldham. Chief Superintendent Eric Hewitt of Greater Manchester Police said: "There is no doubt that the presence of the National Front and British National Party in recent weeks would seem to be a deliberate ploy to exploit our racial situation and it has struck a chord of fear among all our communities, not just Asians." He added that the BNP and the National Front were both recruiting in the town but there was nothing to suggest that they were breaking the law or inciting racial hatred with their leaflets. …[He said] there would be no stepping down of their zero tolerance policy in Oldham despite criticism of their "heavy-handed" dispersal of Asian youths in the Glodwick and Westwood areas. Richard Knowles, Liberal Democrat leader of Oldham council, also blamed right wing extremists for exploiting the town's racial tensions. He said: "The BNP and the NF are legal but their methods of canvassing support are very different to most political parties. They are vile racists, there is no two ways about it." He admitted there had been racial tensions in Oldham for some time but added: "There is a very small minority of people trying to manipulate events to their own ends and we are wise to their intentions and will not allow them to spoil Oldham's name."[14]

Racial fighting between gangs of South Asians and whites, and the police, continued sporadically throughout the month of June in England's northern towns. On June 27, 2001, the Prime Minister publicly condemned the BNP for stirring up racial tensions in Burnley:

Prime Minister Tony Blair has condemned the "hideous influence" of the British National Party following the race-related riots in Burnley. Mr Blair told the Commons it was "totally unacceptable" for organisations to stir up race hatred in towns like Burnley and Oldham, which had earlier also been rocked by rioting. Answering an MP's question on the riots during which white and Asian youth clashed with police, Mr Blair said: "There can be no excuse whatever for attacks on the police or acts of racist violence."[15]

Up to this point, most of the news coverage and political observers had used the term "race" when describing these problems. That same week, however, on the BBC's late-night current affairs program *Newsnight*, when the mild-mannered looking leader of the BNP was interviewed at length by the probing and notoriously hard-hitting journalist Jeremy Paxman, the BNP leader repeated more than once that this was "not an

Asian problem" but rather "a Muslim problem" (his emphasis). He noted that it was not the Hindus in the area, but the Muslim Pakistani young men who were particularly violent, and mentioned that the home of one mixed Hindu-British family had been attacked. When Paxman then asked how he would feel if one of his children wanted to marry a Muslim, the BNP leader replied that he would not approve, and that his view would also be the view of many other average British families as well as most Muslim parents. He also made the point in that interview that since he had been elected leader of the BNP, the Party no longer called for the automatic repatriation of all immigrants to their home countries, and therefore the party can no longer be described as racist or extreme, in his view. He indicated too that the BNP intends to stand candidates in every constituency in the country in the next British general election within five years.

Another example comes from Glasgow, Scotland, in August 2001, where Kurdish political asylum-seekers were housed just next door to a notoriously poor working-class housing estate. One young Turkish Kurdish man was found murdered, and another Iranian asylum-seeker was stabbed in an unprovoked attack:

Yesterday around 150 asylum seekers were joined by 400 anti-racist protesters, trade unionists and members of the public at an emotionally charged vigil in the city. Race campaigner Aamer Anwar laid the blame for Mr Yildiz's death at the door of the city council and the Home Office, claiming the policy of placing asylum seekers in some of Britain's most deprived areas was fatally flawed. He said: "The majority of people in Glasgow are outraged at what happened on Saturday night and what is happening in this community. When you send 4000 asylum seekers to one of the most deprived areas in the country and do not provide the resources, this is what happens."[16]

The Netherlands: Minorities in conflict. A problem for the Muslim community in the Netherlands emerged in the public sphere on May 3, 2001, when imam El-Moumni from the largest mosque in Rotterdam made an impromptu statement on *Nova*, the major late evening current affairs program.[17] He had agreed to be interviewed on tape for the program because they were planning to do a story on the problem of crime and Moroccan teenage boys. Moroccan boys had been the subject of some press attention as troublemakers, because they had been stealing and pickpocketing, pouncing on bikini-clad girls in swimming pools, and even beating up some

---

[16] ITN Online, Aug. 7, 2001: http://www.itn.co.uk/news/20010807/britain/06glasgow_murder.shtml.

[17] See Oussama Cherribi, "Imams and Issues: The Politics of Islam in the European Public Space" (Paper presented at the annual meetings of the American Political Science Association, San Francisco, Aug., 2001). This topic of political mobilization in the Netherlands was the subject of a lecture I gave on July 16, 2001 at the Wissenschaftskolleg zu Berlin at the Humboldt Foundation funded workshop on "Muslim Identities in the Public Sphere" organized by Dale Eickelman.

homosexual schoolteachers. The imam was reluctant to be interviewed as he had never before been interviewed by the Dutch news media, but after encouragement from the board of governors of his mosque he agreed to be interviewed on the understanding that he would see the tape and agree to it before broadcast. That was not the way it turned out, however. Asked an unexpected question about his opinion on homosexuality, he described it as a sickness. This became the focus of the story.

This is a highly contested issue involving two contested minority groups that have experienced years of discrimination in the country. It has been a continuing news story that involves big names, celebrities, and political personalities. Imams from the largest cities in the country, from various origins including Turkish, Surinamese, Moroccan, and Pakistani, declared their support for imam El-Moumni and declared publicly that they too believed in what he said. The 3rd May report on *Nova* had a snowball effect and soon all the media from the right to the left were discussing this issue and its various digressions. Since El-Moumni's statement, the topic was in the news almost every day in one form or another, for the subsequent two months.

A consequence of this event is the mobilization of the Muslim community and its various subgroups, in particular Moroccan and Turkish. Within the Muslim community there is also now the emergence of more critical reflection and debates on the possibility of a future for a different kind of Islam, a more liberal Islam. There is also more public debate between the Muslim community and the homosexual community. Never before were (straight) Muslims and (non-Muslim) homosexuals so often mentioned within the same sentence, or seen together on the same platform debating their personal beliefs. The event also generated greater mobilization among the already highly organized homosexual community.

Germany: Self-imposed segregation? In 1986, a gang of extreme-right young men walking through the Turkish area of Kreuzberg 36, Berlin, grabbed the headscarves off of a number of Turkish women. The Turkish community was in shock over this. The men decided to organize in order to protect their wives and children. A number of Turkish young men, who had been trained in the martial arts, began patrolling the area to protect women and children. They modeled themselves on the Guardian Angels in New York and Protectors of the Nation of Islam in Chicago, and came to be known as the "36 Boys." Some of the young men in the community learned from this experience, however, that they could not only work together effectively to protect women and children, but they could also use their strength for other purposes, such as drug trafficking or robbery.

Over the past decade, the Kreuzberg 36 area has become even more of an ethnic enclave. It reflects the norms and practices of Turkish society some twenty years earlier. Women nowadays, for example, often walk several paces behind men. Segregation is more visible and tensions are running high.[18] This contributes to a fear among the top levels of the political elite in Germany, who meet in the Reichstag, which is not far from Kreuzberg, that there is now even less potential for integration in the country.[19]

MOBILIZATION IN COMPARATIVE PERSPECTIVE

These are, of course, not the only examples of mobilizations that have occurred among Muslim communities in Europe in recent years. Think of Bosnia, for example. While nothing compares to the devastation in Bosnia, there have been other eruptions of violence. There were Muslim demonstrations in southern Spain in the summer of 2000, for example, against the burning of mosques and attacks on Muslim businesses, stemming from violent interaction between Muslim and non-Muslim communities. Recent survey research among various immigrant groups in Spain (comparing North Africans, Latin Americans, Asians, and sub-Saharan Africans) also found that North Africans were more likely to claim to have been victims of aggression or personal conflicts with Spaniards or with other immigrants.[20] These examples raise questions about Muslim identity and the perceptions of the Muslim communities in European societies, and the conditions under which mobilization occurs.

Both types of mobilization that I have discussed above bring the attention of the wider national, and sometimes international, public to the local Muslim community. Sudden mobilization potentially puts more pressure on public officials to solve a problem in a reasonable period of time. The amount of media attention only adds a greater urgency to finding a solution. Media attention, as the Belgian and Dutch examples have shown, can also build reputations and potentially creates heroes not only for the Muslim community, but also for the wider national community. Interestingly, the British news coverage of the "race" problems in northern cities avoided using the word Muslim. It was only the extreme-right BNP that described these events as "a Muslim problem," for self-serving purposes.

Some of these examples have raised connections between Muslim mobilization and the mobilization of extreme-right groups or political parties in Europe. In some countries, the anti-immigration sentiment and ethnic tension has been "largely unexploited at the party political level," while in others, it has been "to a greater extent channeled" into the party system.[21]

---

[18] See also Ruud Koopmans, "Germany and Its Immigrants: An Ambivalent Relationship," *Journal of Ethnic and Migration Studies* 24:4, 1999, pp. 627–47.

[19] Interview with SDP MP, Jul. 19, 2001.

[20] Juan Diez Nicolas and Maria Jose Ramirez Lafita, *La Voz de los immigrantes* (Madrid: IMSERSO, 2001).

[21] Anders Widfeldt, "Scandinavia: Mixed Success for the Populist Right," *Parliamentary Affairs* 53:3, 2000, p. 499.

CONCLUSIONS

Concerns of the non-Muslim communities

Amidst the ongoing processes of European integration, the introduction of the common single currency, and the enlargement of the European Union to the East, there is also a concern about the threat to the European way of life posed by the ongoing processes of Islamization and re-Islamization in Europe. Economic, social, and religious rationales lie behind a fear of Islamization. There are examples of this in every European country, among the political elite as well as the public.

These concerns include the population growth among second and third generation Muslim immigrants and the impact of this on the demographics of Europe's major cities; the distinctive clothing worn by Muslims now increasingly visible in the public sphere; the growth of Islamic schools and European Muslim media outlets; the influence of Islamic countries on European Muslim populations, including the fear of possible terrorism and espionage; the violence among Muslim youngsters; and even the treatment of Muslim women by Muslim men. There is also concern about the threat of illegal immigrants, most of whom are from sub-Saharan Africa, who regularly come ashore from Morocco, Algeria, and Tunisia onto the coasts of Europe, as well as Albanians crossing into Italy, or Kurds from Turkey and Iraq who have been among the most visible in the most recent regular influx of political refugees who are also practicing Muslims. This is in addition to the fact that European communities express concern about the sheer numbers of legal immigrants. The anti-immigrant Danish People's Party, for example, in August 2001 published a full-page ad in a quality national newspaper in which the names of 4,371 legal immigrants who had just become Danish citizens were printed.[22]

While these types of concerns are the rhetorical bread and butter of extreme anti-immigrant parties,[23] there is increasing evidence that they are shared by the center-right, the moderate center, and even the left. The Bishop of Bologna recently called for the Italian government to give preference to Catholic immigrants over Muslim immigrants, because Muslims pose a threat to the country's Christian way of life. Jeremy Paxman, one of Britain's most well-known television journalists, writes about the average Englishman's concern that Pakistanis and other immigrants will come to outnumber them in London and other major English cities:

---

[22] http://www.4371.dk.

[23] Dietrich Thrandhardt, "The Political Uses of Xenophobia in England, France and Germany," *Party Politics* 1:3, 1995, pp. 323–45, and Uwe Backes and Cas Mudde, "Germany: Extremism without Successful Parties," *Parliamentary Affairs* 53:3, 2000, pp. 457–68.

By 1998, it was white children who had become a minority at local-authority secondary schools in inner London and even in the suburbs they made up only 60 percent of the secondary-school population. Over a third of inner London's children did not even have English as their first language.[24]

The French in Marseilles fear that the city will be taken over by the North African immigrants. And the Germans are concerned about the growing population of Turks in their country. A SPD German Member of the Bundestag recently expressed to me his concern that Berlin has the largest population of Turks outside Turkey (with 300,000) with some two million in Germany overall, and described this as a "massive" Islamic presence in the nation's capital.[25]

Some scholars have argued that these fears are a result of perceived irreconcilable differences between the Muslim culture and the European culture based on Christian values. Eatwell goes so far as to describe this as "racism" dressed up as "reasonableness" based on the idea of "irreconcilable cultural differences":

Even racism can be dressed up in the language of majoritarian reasonableness ("its only natural that most people in France do not want Muslim girls attending schools in traditional garb, a symbol of female oppression"). In sophisticated contemporary propaganda, racism based on hierarchy ("blacks are stupid") is replaced by the concept of irreconcilable cultural difference[.][26]

Alongside these concerns is the fact that when Muslims do appear in the news in Europe, it tends to be because of negative events. Research in the United States on the coverage of African-Americans in the news has suggested that there is a stigmatization that triggers racial fears and tensions and can create distorted perceptions of the African-American community among the wider public.[27] It is an open question as to whether the treatment of Muslims in the European news media would have similar consequences.

Concerns of the Muslim communities

Spain is one European country in which extensive survey research has been conducted that takes account of the opinions of the Spanish public about immigrants as well as the opinions of the immigrants themselves.[28] Only 3 percent of immigrants named religious culture as the most important obstacle to integration in Spanish society.[29] The study also shows that in

---

24 Jeremy Paxman, *The English* (London: Penguin, 1999), p. 8.

25 Interview Jul. 19, 2001.

26 Roger Eatwell, "The Rebirth of the 'extreme right' in Western Europe?" *Parliamentary Affairs* 53:3, 2000, p. 411.

27 Robert M. Entman and Andrew Rojecki, *The Black Image in the White Mind: Media and Race in America* (University of Chicago Press, 2000).

28 Juan Diez Nicolas and Maria Jose Ramirez Lafita, *La Immigracion en Espana* (Madrid: IMSERSO, 2001), and *La Voz de los immigrantes*.

29 Diez Nicolas and Ramirez Lafita, *La Voz de los immigrantes*, p. 106.

terms of self-perception of the degree to which they are integrated in Spanish society, North Africans, who are largely Muslim, rank themselves at approximately the same level as Asians. These two groups are in between Latin Americans, who perceive themselves to be the most integrated, and (sub-Saharan) Africans, who perceive themselves to be the least integrated in Spanish society.[30]

One of the less discussed concerns that the Muslim communities in Europe must have is the lack of influence they are able to exert over the mainstream news media. For example, the recent conflict in the Netherlands between imams and the homosexual community, the latter of whom were supported by the established political parties and the government, led Muslims to no longer trust the Dutch media to report their perspective in an objective fashion.[31]

Otherwise Muslims are noticeably missing from certain circles. Michel Foucault, one of France's major thinkers, has said, "the question of Islam as a political force is an essential question for our epoch and for the years to come[.]"[32] Despite the importance of the issue of Islam in the 21st century, *Le Monde de l'education* in July/August 2001, in a special issue identifying "21 thinkers in the world to understand the 21st century," fails to name even one Islamic thinker.

Another concern is the description of the Muslim communities as the "underclass" of the European societies in which they live. There are, of course, exceptions, and numerous examples of wealthy entrepreneurs and an emerging middle class, just as among African-Americans in the United States. But for the most part, many Muslims are among those with the lowest incomes and the largest families in their countries. Joppke argues that while being part of the welfare state is

an asset for first-generation immigrants ... it becomes a liability for second- and third-generation immigrants, whose home is the receiving society, but whose lasting exclusion from its national community makes them vulnerable and stigmatized minorities.[33]

The examples discussed in this chapter point to the establishment of the transnational *umma* (the community of believers) in European countries in which Islam is a minority. These examples include the emergence and increasing visibility of Islamic leadership in European public spheres, the institutionalization of an Islamic infrastructure (with mosques, schools,

---

[30] Ibid., p. 99.
[31] Cherribi, "Imams and Issues."
[32] Michel Foucault, *Dits et Ecrits III* (Paris: Gallimard, 1996), p. 708.
[33] Christian Joppke, "How immigration is changing citizenship: A comparative view," *Ethnic and Racial Studies* 22:4, 1999, p. 645. See also Christian Joppke, *Immigration and the Nation-State: The United States, Germany and Great Britain* (Oxford University Press, 1999).

and welfare arrangements for Muslims), as well as the political mobilization of Muslim communities, and they all serve as symbols to further the
development of an Islamic identity. The socio-genesis of this Islamic identity has not only to do with these processes within the Muslim community,
but also with the tendency of the media and the indigenous population to
stereotype immigrants from Islamic countries as a group having a religious identity that is more important than their various ethnic identities.

Muslims perceive the processes of Islamization and re-Islamization as
a way to achieve religious citizenship, and see this as an advanced form of
citizenship in democratic European multicultural societies. Recognition of
Muslim customs and holidays in the Islamic calendar, alongside Christian
customs and holidays, is a stepping-stone to this more advanced form of
citizenship. This type of recognition exists in limited ways in only some
European countries. This emphasis on rights is not intended by Muslims to
compete with Christians, but rather is understood as the realization of freedom of religious belief and equality among citizens.

EPILOGUE: LIFE IN EUROPE SHORTLY AFTER
SEPTEMBER 11, 2001

The horrific terrorist attacks in New York and Washington DC that killed
thousands of innocent civilians from around the world, and like an earth-
quake shattered the structural foundations of some of the world's most
prime real estate, also had the consequence of pulling the rug out from
under Muslim communities and individuals in Europe who now, sud-
denly, appear to be outsiders. The number of hate crimes in the US in the
week following the terrorist attack numbered nearly 400, and although
there are no comparable figures available for the European Union countries, there is much news about harassment of Muslims (verbal abuse and
spitting have been most common), as well as physical attacks on individuals, mosques, and Islamic schools.

The outward contempt for Muslims, and the new suspicion under
which Muslims in Europe appear to be held, does not appear to be limited
to coming from non-Muslims with low education or non-cosmopolitan
backgrounds. One young and attractive (designer scarf donned) Turkish
woman commuting daily from eastern Holland to Amsterdam, for example, who studies law and Arabic at the University of Amsterdam, was ver-
bally harassed on the train by what appeared to be "a 30-something
intellectual male." This is one of many such examples across Europe. One
of the most interesting comments I have heard from many is that Muslim
women, identifiable by their headscarves, are being singled out for verbal
abuse.

The fact is that despite the many aforementioned conversations I have
had with mainstream parliamentarians from various European countries,

in which they expressed their concerns about the growth of the Muslim communities in their countries and the impact it could have on, for example, the German, French, Belgian, Dutch, or British ways of life, rarely were these kinds of statements ever made public in the press. Now, however, there is open discussion by European politicians, media, and public alike of possible "Fifth Columns" operating within European countries and the new security threats from within. In the days following the attacks, political elites and the media in the US and UK appeared to be well ahead of continental Europe in regularly reminding people that Islam is a tolerant and peaceful religion and the vast majority of Muslims are law-abiding citizens who love the democracies in which they live and deplore violence.

In response to these horrific terrorist attacks, Muslim religious leaders in Europe mobilized politically in their various national and transnational networks to send messages of condolence to the US and to express to their national governments and the European Union that Islam is a peaceful religion and deplores these terrorist actions. There are two problems, however. One is that there is the occasional example of the European Islamic religious leader in one or another country, who uses extremist rhetoric in sermons, leaflets, or public statements to support the terrorist attacks, and this, of course, attracts a great deal of attention in the news. In Britain, for example, the quality newspaper *The Independent*, known for its objectivity, notes that two "self-appointed" London-based sheiks who "praised the terrorism as a justified attack on a crazy superpower" have been criticized by Muslim leaders in the UK who have been "horrified" by these provocative comments.[34] The Muslim Council of Britain said: "We are used to responsible comments from them, but in this climate where there are attacks on mosques, assaults on Muslims, these kind of remarks are highly dangerous."[35] While this was reported in an objective manner in the quality press, this type of story is one with which the British tabloids have a field day.

A second problem is that in contrast to the public statements of the vast majority of Muslim leaders in Europe who denounce the terrorist acts, there are some isolated examples of Muslim children and teenagers in Europe reacting to the attacks with celebration, like the now infamous and censored images of youngsters in Palestine smiling, cheering and celebrating the attacks with their few adult minders. Although most Muslims in Europe deplore this type of response to the tragedy, these images have set in motion a discussion in the European public spheres about the extent to which Muslims in Europe may have an understanding of a rational justification for the terrorism or have empathy with why these attacks were carried out.

---

[34] Ian Burrell, "Anger at clerics' extremism as race attacks rise: British Muslims," *The Independent*, Sept. 20, 2001, p. 5.
[35] Ibid.

Let me conclude with an example from the Netherlands, a country on the Continent reputed for its tolerance and multiculturalism, with more Islamic schools than any other European country. On September 18, 2001, at the official opening of the Parliament, the Queen's Speech focused on the tragic disaster and emphasized Dutch support for the United States and the victims. Normally the color orange is prominent among the political and diplomatic guests at this important event because it is the color of the House of Orange. But to express my solidarity with the victims of this tragedy that day, instead of orange my tie was red, white, and blue, with the Stars and Stripes of the American flag. The reaction of most of my parliamentary colleagues was one of mild amusement, but one Member of Parliament from an extreme right-wing Christian party was outrightly hostile and suggested to me that such a symbolic gesture had no place at this royal event.

My symbolic gesture of solidarity that day led to an article with a photograph in a quality national newspaper, in which I offered my comments on the attacks including that "no religion or belief can justify these horrible acts," that "terrorists are the friends of no one," and I later said in a radio interview that "we are all New Yorkers now."[36] I also said that there is a double moral standard among Muslims in many countries who expressed support for these attacks because at the same time they are fascinated by American popular culture and films, they often enjoy American imported fast food, and they wear American designer labels.

I had many positive responses to this article from the Dutch public and members of the press, some of whom mentioned being pleased that a person with a "Muslim background" took such a "strong pro-western stand." It is obviously the fact that I am of Muslim background that makes my comments noteworthy. At the same time, there was a major discussion going on in the country, fuelled by questions from the media and daily news, in which some other prominent Dutch Muslims said that they understood why Muslims might believe the causes of the attack to be "American hegemony and foreign policy," but only later mentioned that they condemned the attacks.

The Muslim communities of Europe are under direct observation now, not only for security reasons. The news media in the Netherlands, at least, are playing up these discussions within the Muslim communities, and the consequences of this for public impressions of these communities are unknown. Comparatively little is said in the press, however, about those fundamentalist Christians in the country and in Europe who believe that these attacks were meant to happen because of the so-called "permissive American society."

The events of September 11, 2001 caused a fracture in the world of Muslims in Europe. It will be difficult, to say the least, and it will take a

---

36 Frits van Veen, "De dubble moraal van de Moslims" [The double moral standards of the Muslims], *De Volkskrant* Sept. 19, 2001, p. 3.

long time, to be able to return to the path of social integration. Such a path is based on a certain level of trust and acceptance within and between different social communities. Although I began this chapter before September 11, 2001, with the view that Muslims are no longer outsiders in Europe, the way the world has changed since that fateful day may mean that Muslims in Europe in the foreseeable future become increasingly isolated and stigmatized, as opposed to integrated and respected. That said, I remain optimistic. This is not only because of my conversations with many Muslims in Europe, including those from different Arab and Asian countries as well as Turkish Mili Gurus, who emphasize their admiration for democracy and human rights and their appreciation for being able to practice their religion in open societies, but also because of my conversations with many non-Muslim European political elites who have confidence in the European Muslim communities and believe in working together to confront and conquer the difficult challenges ahead.

9

THE HOLY GRAIL OF MUSLIMS IN WESTERN EUROPE

REPRESENTATION AND THEIR RELATIONSHIP WITH THE STATE

Dilwar Hussain

This chapter will look at the relationship that exists between the Muslim communities in most countries of Western Europe and their respective governments. There is a wide diversity of models upon which such relationships are based. In Spain, the Muslims have an agreement with the King, while in Austria there is official recognition of the Muslim community, and in France there is a strict notion of *laicité*, or secularity, restricting not only the relationship between the state and religious bodies, but the whole notion of visible religion in public life. This chapter will attempt to explore firstly the formal relationships that exist in different countries,[1] or the lack of such a relationship, and will also try to look beyond the relationship *per se*, to examine the reality of such relationships. An example of this may be seen in the difference between Muslim representation in the UK and Belgium. In the case of the former, there is no official recognition of Islam. However in recent years, especially since the inception of the Muslim Council of Britain (MCB), Muslims have been able to meet frequently with government officials and air their views on a wide range of subjects and have successfully lobbied the government on a number of issues. In the case of Belgium, where there is legal recognition, various attempts have been made at setting up a representative council of Muslims. There have been accusations of certain individuals being purposefully excluded from the process as a result of their particular religio-political views, leading to the initiatives either collapsing or producing an atmosphere of tension and mistrust. This brings us to another aspect of this chapter, which is to look at the whole notion of

---

[1] It is to be expected that in such a survey there will be some disparity in the amount of information given on each country. Indeed some countries will not be covered as their Muslim communities may be considered too small or research on such communities may be quite scant.

representation, and to raise some of the implications this may have on the Muslim community.

The types of organizations formed by Muslims in Europe tend to fall into the following broad categories, which are not always mutually exclusive:

—mosques;
—grassroots membership organizations that deal with general needs as well as preservation and propagation of Islamic values;
—single-issue organizations, e.g. relief organizations, publishing groups.;
—service organizations, e.g. Islamic centers, research bodies;
—representative councils, federations, and umbrella bodies.

Some of these are entirely local in nature, whereas others are influenced by transnational movements. Still others are influenced or sometimes directly run by departments of Muslim governments, e.g. the Diyanet (Religious Office) of Turkey. The focus here will be on those organizations that claim to be representative bodies, or those that are federal or umbrella bodies by nature. We will also look into the specific philosophy and historical background behind each country's treatment of its minorities, but will not dwell too much on the Muslim migration patterns, and demographic specificities within each country.

Estimates of the number of Muslims residing in Western Europe range from 10 to 15 million. As most countries in the EU do not have reliable census data on their Muslim communities, the overall figure is an estimate. It is, in fact, a misnomer to use the term "Muslim community" in reference to a Europe-wide phenomenon, as there is very little in the way of organization and communication between Muslims in different countries. Indeed, this is at times the case even within a single state. The ethnic diversity of Muslims in Europe is very wide, with almost every ethnic group found in the Muslim world being represented in some proportion. There are also a small number of "converts" of indigenous European origin. The largest single groups are Turks, Algerians, Moroccans, and then Pakistanis. The countries with the highest Muslim population are France, Germany, and then the UK. Migration patterns vary widely from country to country. In some places, e.g. Spain, Muslims have a long historical legacy and presence, while in others, e.g. the UK, Muslims started to arrive (albeit in small numbers) in the 19th century. In other countries, e.g. Sweden, Muslims arrived after the Second World War, when there was a labor force shortage. Two of the countries with the largest populations of Muslims, Britain and France, both have a long colonial legacy with the Muslim world, whereas countries like Sweden were never colonial powers.

The states of Europe also have varying traditions in terms of their relationship with religious bodies. This diversity also impinges upon the language that is used. Consider the word integration. It can mean very different things depending upon one's cultural background. The French notion of integration could almost be called assimilation in the British context.

Religion and state

Religion has been a contentious and sensitive issue in Europe. Since the establishment of Christianity in the Roman Empire there has been a parallel development of religion and state. The evolution of Christianity shows that it incorporated the hierarchies of society and took on an almost state-like apparatus, giving rise to a differentiation of societal authorities along sacred and secular lines, which would be far reaching. The relationship with the state has been varied, but often estranged. Although the legitimacy of the monarch came from the Church, the monarch was also the head of the Church, giving rise to a complex interplay of influence and shaping of each other. Naturally, this sometimes led to great tension between state and clergy. In addition to this, the reality of the different Churches and denominations meant that there was intra-Christian rivalry, at times culminating in religious wars. Perhaps it was because of these complexities and tensions that the concept of the Enlightenment spread so rapidly in Europe. Modernity brought with it the break with religion and the desire to compartmentalize it, creating the secular societies so characteristic of the West. Thus, a European Values Survey in 1990 showed that less than one-quarter of people found it acceptable that their Church should express views on government policy.[2] Each country has its own specific experience of dealing with faith, usually shaped by its particular political, ideological and social history. Some states have a national Church, whereas others are neutral or laic. The Protestant Churches, not having a central body like Rome, have tended to take on a greater degree of national flavor and often have close association with the state. However, the common points between states are a separation between Church and state and a declared tolerance of religion, although the degrees of separation and tolerance vary from country to country.

Religious freedoms are not only enshrined in the constitutions of the various European states, but are the subject of a number of articles in international treaties. The European Treaty for the Protection of Human Rights and Fundamental Liberties, the International Treaty Concerning Civil and Political Rights, The Universal Declaration of Human Rights, The European Convention on Human Rights, and the Declaration on the Elimination of all Forms of Intolerance and Discrimination Based on Religion and Philosophy of Life all deal with the matter of religious freedom. This freedom is construed to be one of not only holding a faith, but also of being

---

[2] Quoted in: Ole Riis, "Religion Re-Emerging: the Role of Religion in Legitimating Integration and Power in Modern Societies," *International Sociology* 13:2, June 1998, p. 263.

able to behave according to the precept of the faith—and indeed, of being able to reject faith altogether. Limits may be placed on these freedoms for public benefit, but such limits must be based on the Constitution or the Treaties that the state is party to.[3] Tariq Ramadan points out that there are at least five fundamental freedoms (or rights) generally available to Muslims in Europe:[4]

—right to observe most of the major practices;
—right to knowledge;
—right to found organizations;
—right to form representative bodies;
—right to appeal to the law.

The relationship between religion and state can be structured in many different ways. Shadid and Koningsveld have suggested the following broad categories[5] that are modeled on a continuum:

1. Complete fusion
2. Union—usually expressed in one of the following three sub-categories:

a. Recognition
b. Official state religion
c. Partial recognition

3. Separation—subdivided into three:

a. Total indifference
b. Hostile separation
c. Sympathizing tolerance

It may also be useful to add here the "pillarization" model that was found, until quite recently, in the Netherlands. Of course it is very difficult to neatly compartmentalize the behavior of people, let alone states, and perhaps with time (as the categories are meant to be in a continuum) states may move slightly from one sub-category to another.

Islam and Europe

Despite the long history between Islam and Europe—one could point to Muslim rule in Spain for almost eight centuries, significant historical presence in parts of France, Italy, and Austria, as well as trade and diplomatic relations between various European and Muslim states—it is perhaps true to say that Islam is seen as an alien interjection into European society.

---

[3] For a more detailed discussion see W. A. R. Shadid and P. S. van Koningsveld, *Religious Freedom and the Position of Islam in Western Europe* (The Hague: Kok Pharos, 1995).

[4] Tariq Ramadan, *To Be a European Muslim* (Leicester: Islamic Foundation, 1999), pp. 135–7.

[5] Shadid and van Koningsveld, *Religious Freedom*, pp. 20–1.

Over the last twenty years, the presence of Islam has become much more visible; mosques, headscarves, and beards have accompanied a growing second, third, and fourth generation who seem to be more confident in their expression of faith. European society is therefore trying to understand, study, and fathom this "new" presence of an "alien" culture, which is at times seen as a problem, at other times as a threat, and often as just another socio-religious phenomenon.

The historical conflict between Islam and Europe cannot be detached from this and perhaps to some degree can be used to explain the current tensions and suspicions that exist. Montgomery Watt identifies four main features of the Medieval European image of Islam:[6]

—Islam is a false religion and is a perversion of the truth;
—Islam spreads by the sword;
—Islam is a religion of self-indulgence and permissive behavior;
—Muhammad is the Anti-Christ.

Watt further implies that these distortions continue to influence some European thinkers today. Charles Husband, writing within the British context, adds to this:

... that historically derived stereotypes of Islam and "the Orient" are continuously latent within British popular culture and learning.[7]

The effect of such stereotypes has been to see Islam as a threat[8] and a problem. This feeling has perhaps become even more heightened after the collapse of the Soviet Union and the effective replacement of Communism as the political "Other" with Islam and predictions of the "clash of civilizations." Having said this, it would be unfair to make this a one-sided affair. There are stereotypes of Europe in the minds of many Muslims. For some Muslims the notion of Europe conjures up images of a society that is less moral and religious than Muslim societies. The early Muslim families that migrated to Europe felt very eager to 'protect' their offspring from the liberal morality of Europe. The tensions stemming from a colonial experience also added to this. Furthermore, many Muslims are:

... now discovering an unaccustomed way of being Muslim which is not analysed by the Islamic tradition. It is a matter of fact that Muslim theology offers, up to the present, no systematic formulation for a minority status. However this situation is

---

6 Montgomery Watt, *Muslim-Christian Encounters* (London: Routledge, 1991).
7 Charles Husband, "The Political Context of Muslim Communities' Participation in British Society," in *Muslims in Europe*, ed. Bernard Lewis and Dominique Schnapper (London: Pinter, 1994), p.80.
8 See Jochen Hippler and Andrea Lueg, eds, *The Next Threat: Western Perceptions of Islam* (London: Pluto Press with the Transnational Institute, 1995), and John L. Esposito, *The Islamic Threat: Myth or Reality?* 3rd edn. (New York: Oxford University Press, 1999).

changing due to the increasing number of Muslim minorities in the democratic context.[9]

The result of such influences was to create barriers of trust and meaningful communication between the early migrants and the wider European society.

A minority in Europe

It is important to consider the place of minorities in the different states in Europe. Shaped by diverse historical factors, some of which have been briefly mentioned above, the states have adopted various attitudes and ways of dealing with their minorities. Shadid and Koningsveld have identified three major differences in this regard between the states:[10]

The relationship between political and religious authorities.
Extent of decentralization of political power.
The legal status of migrants in the host country.

These differences impact upon the type of integration policies and structural models used to cater for minorities. Despite some countries claiming (until quite recently) that they are not officially countries of immigration (e.g. Germany), all the states considered here have considerable numbers of immigrant communities, most of whom arrived in Europe after the Second World War due to "push-pull" factors. Despite the initial expectation, both from the migrants and European states, that there would be a short phase of residency followed by a return to the place of origin, this obviously did not happen to any significant degree. On the contrary, families joined the workers and became established in Europe, exploding the "myth of return." Our interest here is in the Muslim migrants that came in this era. It should also be noted that some small communities of Muslims did exist long before the mass migration. Such communities could be found mainly in Britain, France, Germany, and Austria. A very recent factor in Muslim migration has not been work related, but pertains to political refugees. Muslims from various countries including Bosnia, Eritrea, Somalia, and more recently Kosovo have arrived in European states, sparking off a new debate about the acceptability of and service provision for these new migrants.

On the whole there have been three main models by which EU states have tried to deal with migrants:[11]

---

[9] Jocelyne Cesari, "Muslim Representation in a European Political Context," *Encounters: Journal of Inter-Cultural Perspectives* 4:2, Sept. 1998, p. 150.

[10] W. A. R. Shadid and P. S. van Koningsveld, *The Integration of Islam and Hinduism in Western Europe* (The Hague: Kok Pharos, 1991), p. 19.

[11] Han Entzinger, "A Future for the Dutch 'Ethnic Minorities' Model?" in Lewis and Schnapper, *Muslims in Europe*, pp. 19–20.

1.   the "Guest worker" model, where migrants are seen to have a temporary presence, which is primarily used in Germany, but also in Austria and Switzerland in some modified form;

2.   assimilation model, where migrants are seen to be permanent and therefore strategies are employed for individual integration into the culture of the state and the formation of "communities" of migrants is discouraged. France is the primary example of such a country;

3.   ethnic Minorities model, in which there is room for the preservation of cultural identity and some degree of pluralism is institutionalized. This model tends to be followed in the Scandinavian countries as well as in the UK.

Each of these models has its own distinct advantages and disadvantages, its own lobbies and academics. There does seem to be some feeling now that the Guest worker (Gastarbeiter) model is a denial of the reality of settlement and does not allow for adequate policy formation to deal with this reality. The French Assimilation model has behind it the fear of "the contradictions inherent within a political system giving priority to the existence of separate communities over individual integration." France has "based its policies on principles which categorically reject the formation of separate communities and favour their withering-away within secular society."[12] The vision then is to incorporate minorities not as communities, but as individuals, who directly form a contract with the state. This is so that the identity of the Republic can be maintained and so that the isolation of ghettoes can be eliminated. Some French academics seem to view with displeasure the establishment of "ethnic minorities" across the Channel and feel that this will be a disaster for British society. The reaction of the Muslims in the UK to *The Satanic Verses* affair and recent disturbances between Asian and White youths in inner city areas are hailed as examples of the failure of the British model. The American experience is seen in much the same light. However, one needs only to walk the streets of Paris, Marseilles, or Lyon to realize that *de facto* ghettos do exist in France, as Oliver Roy notes:

"Gallicization", while continuing to observe religious practice on an individual basis, would seem to be the end result of the process of integration for groups which are socially and economically assimilated. On the other hand, a new kind of ethnic identity, a characteristically American kind, which in the place of attachment to a specific national and religious identity takes the form of shared fellowship as a subculture within the dominant culture, seems likely to prevail among the young Arabs (and Blacks) of the urban zones, who are casualties of the integration process.[13]

12   Gilles Kepel, *Allah in the West* (London: Polity, 1997), p. 5.
13   Olivier Roy, "Islam in France: Religion, Ethnic Community or Social Ghetto," in Lewis and Schnapper, *Muslims in Europe*, pp. 54–5.

Habermas describes the Ethnic Minorities or "Multicultural" model as follows:

In multicultural societies, the equally protected coexistence of lifeforms means ensuring for each citizen the opportunity to grow up, and have his or her children grow up, in a cultural world of his or her own origins without being insulted because of this by others; the opportunity to come to terms with this culture—as every other—to perpetuate it in its conventional form or to transform it; and also the opportunity to turn his or her back on its imperatives out of indifference or to break away from them in a self-critical manner, to live henceforth spurred on by having made a conscious break with tradition or even to live with a split identity.[14]

This model is also not without its critics both within and outside the states professing it. There are those such as Lord Tebbit in the UK who feel it is dangerous to have different communities living side by side. Others are more critical of the disparity between privileges that are granted to some ethnic minorities and not to others:

The Race Relations Act, 1976, is designed to outlaw some form of this differential treatment, though by failing to explicitly recognise religious identity and religious discrimination, it itself contributes to a new form of religious inequality, namely the inequality in law between those religious groups that the courts recognise as ethnic groups and those that they do not. So that, while Sikhs and Jews are recognised as groups against whom unlawful direct racial discrimination may be proven and penalised, Muslims and Rastafarians are ruled out from such legal protection.[15]

Perhaps an important factor in how a nation treats its minorities is rooted in the self-image of that nation. Germany historically had a notion of blood descent that forms the nation, perhaps due to the legacy of the Germanic tribes that were so influential in European history. It may be for this reason that Germans could not accept for so long that a foreigner (Ausländer) could be a citizen. Furthermore, German nationalism was partly formed in the defense of its realm against Napoleon, an external force, whereas French identity was forged in the struggle against its own Monarchy, ruling class, and religious establishment. For France it is therefore the Republic and the notion of Republican Unity, the pride in the culture where all are equal, that defines the self. The UK has long been a country of "migration," invaded by many different groups of people who each left something of their traditions, culture, and language. It has also had a diverse experience of Christian religious traditions and has had perhaps the broadest contact with other cultures through colonialism, factors that have forged a nation of polite pragmatists.

---

[14] Jürgen Habermas, "Struggles for Recognition in Constitutional States," *European Journal of Philosophy* 1:2, 1993, p. 143.
[15] Tariq Modood, "Establishment, Multiculturalism and British Citizenship," *Political Quarterly* 65, 1994, p. 57.

While the Muslim communities in the various states of Europe are at very different stages of development, it must be remembered that in European history it has taken many generations, if not centuries, for religious groups to adapt and find their place in society. It is true that we are in a world of rapid changes today; nonetheless, Muslim minorities must be given the chance to adapt and come to terms with their surroundings in a way that allows them to feel they are a part of Europe. Tariq Modood is critical of measures that force secular identities upon religious minorities and writes against what he terms "radical secularism":

For radical secularism cannot be secured without illiberal measures; and the communalism that such a policy may provoke will be due less to the traditions of groups such as Muslims (though that won't prevent victims from being blamed) than to the exclusionism implicit in radical secularism.[16]

Community-state relations

France. The first sentence of the French constitution states: "France is an indivisible and laique Republic." It is perhaps the notion of laïcité that is the single most significant factor when discussing the relationship between the French state and the Muslims in France. As Danièle Hervieu-Léger writes:

In the case of France, it seems that one of the most decisive changes that have occurred since the beginning of the 1980s has been the transformation of a society in which cultural homogeneity seemed assured within the normative space defined by the great republican referents, to a multi-cultural society ... The question of Islam, which has become the second religion in France after Catholicism—ahead of Protestantism and Judaism—constitutes the highly sensitive point of crystallization of a problem that is much more vast: the question of the relation between particularity and universality in the very definition of French identity.[17]

Jocelyne Cesari looks at this from a slightly different perspective:

... Islamic membership introduces confusion between the public and private spheres. Islam cannot be confined to the mosques and private worship as Catholicism has been. The social dimensions of Islam are still significant for the majority of French Muslims and that is why they refuse to limit the expression of their faith to the mosques and why they maintain a lot of rules which regulate their social life even if these are shocking for the French majority. Islam has changed the balance between three major "pillars" of French political life: unity, respect for religious pluralism and liberty of conscience.[18]

---

[16] Ibid., p. 73.

[17] Danièle Hervieu-Léger, "The Past in the Present: Redefining Laicité in Multicultural France," in *The Limits of Social Cohesion*, ed. Peter Berger (Boulder, CO: Westview Press, 1998), p. 39.

[18] Cesari, "Muslim Representation," p. 154.

The history of France is embedded in the long struggle between the French Kings and the Roman Catholic Church. With the collapse of the Ancien Régime and the Revolution of 1789, society became strictly secularized. The citizen now related to the political authority directly and the religious legitimacy for the monarchy was not seen to be necessary. The constitution of 1791 granted the freedom to practice religion, but this was not an issue of public concern; there would be no "State Religion." The new authorities had by now seized much of the land owned by the Catholic Church and distributed the monies amongst the citizens. This led to a deep schism between the Church and the Republic, which was further exacerbated when the Constitutional Assembly repeatedly refused to acknowledge Catholicism as a state religion. As a compromise, Bonaparte signed a concordat with Rome in 1801 that acknowledged Catholicism as the religion of the majority of the French. The degree of tension between Church and state can be seen in a statement of Pope Pius X in which he referred to Émile Combes, the Premier of France, as the "Satanic Monsieur Combes."[19] What had effectively happened was the separation of France into two distinct groups—the religious and secular—with these ongoing struggles being labeled "The War of the Two Frances." It was perhaps in order to appease the growing tensions between clerical France and laique (laic) France that the Separation Law of 1905 was brought in (this did not apply to the three constituencies of Haut-Rhin, Bas-Rhin, and Moselle in the Alsace-Lorraine region). Although the clergy, with the backing of Rome, initially opposed this, the law found support among liberal Catholics in France. The result was that religious institutions previously under state control were released and became an entirely private affair. This only calmed some of the tension between the two Frances, the rest of which eventually subsided with the eruption of World War I and the threat of an external enemy against whom an alliance had to be forged.

The French colonial experience, especially with Algeria, was somewhat bloodier than many others and represents a long phase of tension and violence between Algeria and France. The French mode of colonization was also different in that there was a strong drive to impose French language and culture on the colonies. This can be seen in contrast to the British method in India that started with trade and was somewhat more subtle in exporting its influence—political, social, and legal.

The public perception in modern day France seems to be that if Muslims are allowed to form communities then they will be left in ghettos and these will be a threat to the identity and security of the nation, a sentiment that the far right party of Le Pen has played on. It is against this background that the Muslim migration needs to be looked at and the consequent concerns over the reappearance of religion in the public

---

[19] Hervieu-Léger, "The Past in the Present," p. 44.

sphere. The presence of the Harkis[20] in the early part of the 20th century led to the establishment, with help from the French government, of the Paris Mosque in 1926 as a goodwill gesture. This institution became (and remains) an important contact point between the government and the Muslim community, at least in the eyes of the government. In 1982, the Mosque was handed over to the Algerian government (by the outgoing rector Si Hamza Boubaker who had been in the position since 1957), which officially ran it until 1992. It is thought that despite the official handover, the Algerian government still has much influence over the mosque.

The interior minister allowed foreign citizens the right to form associations in 1981, leading to a large number of institutions, some of which were perhaps already in operation, eventually registering openly. Among these were the Union des Organizations Islamiques de France (UIOF) established in 1983 in Paris, the Fédération Nationale des Musulmans en France (FNMF) established in 1985 in Paris, and the Union des Jeunes Musulmans (UJM) established in 1987 in Lyon. The first two are national umbrella bodies that were set up to represent Muslims in France. The UJM is mentioned here because of its important role among Muslim youth and the debates it has started on the topic of integration and electoral participation. The UOIF is formed from a mixed ethnic group of Algerians, Moroccans, and Tunisians and has some 200 organizations as affiliates. The FNMF was inspired by the Muslim World League's (MWL) Paris office and has about 70 affiliated organizations.[21] Two other organizations that deserve mention in this context are the Foi et Pratique (Jama'at Tabligh) and the Union Islamique en France (UIF), a branch of the Milli Gorus. There has been extensive foreign government intervention in the politics of the Muslim community. The Algerian government has usually worked through the Paris Mosque, the Moroccan government through the Amicales des Travailleurs et Commerçants Marocains, the Saudi government through the Muslim World League (MWL), and the Turkish government through its Diyanet Office in France.

Prior to the 1988 elections, the Paris Mosque expressed support for the right-wing party of Chirac. However, as it happened, the left-wing party of Mitterrand came into power and decided to snub the Paris Mosque. It also perhaps looked at the possibility of the FIS winning power in Algeria and wanted to distance the Muslim community in France from possible influence. In 1990, the Interior Minister Pierre Joxe decided to establish links with a new body and set up the Conseil de Réflexion sur l'Islam en France (CORIF), a body whose legitimacy was contested by many Muslim groups. The declared intention by Joxe was "to help to manage as well as

---

[20] Those (of Algerian origin) who fought on the side of the French against Algeria.
[21] Tariq Ramadan, *Muslims in France: The Way Towards Coexistence* (Leicester: The Islamic Foundation, 1999), p. 35.

possible the concrete situations created by the practice of the Muslim religion in France."[22] The CORIF had some transient success in dealing with burial plots for Muslims and announcing the dates for Ramadan. When the right-wing government came back into power in 1993, it re-established support for the Paris Mosque and the CORIF dwindled away. In 1993, the Paris Mosque launched a new initiative called the Conseil Représentatif des Musulmans de France. This council, however, lacked the support of the UOIF and the FNMF—a significant factor given that both of these organizations achieved a heightened prominence during the "veil affair." In 1995, another attempt was made to form a representative body, pitted against the Paris Mosque, called the Conseil Supérieur des Musulmans de France. However, this body split up after only a few months. In 2001 new attempts were initiated to set up a representative group. The only real success stories, so far, in the representation of Muslims' interests have been in the case of single issues such as the campaign against *The Satanic Verses*, when an ad hoc coordinating body was set up consisting of the UOIF, FNMF, and the Paris Mosque, or in the case of the scarf affair when informal coordination occurred.

The UK. The UK contains perhaps the most diverse Muslim community in Europe. This diversity is not only present in the Muslim community but also in the history of the UK. The Celts, Romans, Germanic tribes (Angles, Jutes, Saxons), Danes, and Normans among others have invaded the British Isles and left their mark. Of course, the UK itself is not a single country but England, Scotland, Wales, and Northern Ireland, the historical tensions between which are well known and are not without their modern day implications. Although English is originally a Germanic language, French was for some time the official language of England leaving the English language with a distinct Latin influence. Add to this the vast expanse of the British Empire in colonial times and the arrival of migrants subsequent to colonialism and one is able to see that the UK has a unique history of diversity. The religious traditions of the UK are also quite diverse and, at the same time, very interlinked with the establishment. Henry VIII broke away from the Catholic Church in 1534 and formed the Church of England (which developed in a typically British manner—blending Catholic and Protestant influences). Henry VIII became the head of the Church and established it as the official religion of the UK. This position has been maintained and the monarch today is the "Defender of the Faith." This does not mean that all other Christian denominations simply died away. Most still remain, and today relate to each other with relative harmony despite long phases of conflict in the past. The public have responded to this diversity of faith by making it into a very private affair. Ronald Blythe once wrote:

---

[22] *Le Monde*, Mar. 17, 1990, quoted in Kepel, *Allah in the West*, p. 190.

As for the English churchman, he goes to church as he goes to the bathroom, with the minimum of fuss and with no explanation if he can help it.[23]

The privileged status of the Church of England (and the Presbyterian Church in Scotland) has meant that there are automatic seats for the clergy in the House of Lords and that parliament is the ultimate legislative authority for the these two established Churches. It can also have some say in the appointment of clergy, but gives no direct funding. Funding is, however, available for buildings of historical value and local government can give certain grants to religious bodies.

All of this has been arranged in the UK in the absence of a written constitution as found in other countries. In the UK it is the various Acts of Parliament that form the "constitution." This is an important distinction, for the Acts are more fluid and adaptable than a formal constitution. It also means that although there have been many reforms of the legal system, there have been few upheavals as far-reaching as the Constitutional Reforms of other European states. The Magna Carta was one such upheaval and it is from those feudal days that the division between local and central government has evolved.[24] The UK does not have a system of "recognition" of religion as found in other EU states such as Germany or Belgium. Instead the relationship is a complex one governed by various Acts that may be of relevance to the minority concerned. The Jews and Sikhs are recognized as ethnic groups and are therefore protected when it comes to discrimination. There are also some limited provisions for Jews to observe elements of Jewish law in personal matters. Citizenship has been quite easy to obtain in the UK as compared to some other countries in Europe and most people from the minorities residing in the UK today are British citizens.

With the arrival of larger numbers of migrants in the 1960s and 70s, a very pronounced debate started to take place as to the position and status of these migrants. The tone of the debate in the early stages was very similar to that in other parts of Europe. Should these minorities be sent back? Would they take away jobs from British people? Would they be an economic burden? Perhaps the most vociferous participants in the debate were Enoch Powell of the Conservative Party and Roy Jenkins of the Labour Party. They naturally stood poles apart. It was within this debate that the British notion of multiculturalism was crystallized:

... a flattening process of uniformity, but cultural diversity, coupled with equal opportunity in an atmosphere of mutual tolerance.[25]

---

23 Ronald Blythe, *The Age of Illusion: Glimpses of Britain Between the Wars 1919–1940* (Oxford University Press, 1983).

24 See Jørgen Nielsen, "Islam, Muslims, and British Local and Central Government" (CSIC Papers, Birmingham: CSIC, 1992).

25 Roy Jenkins, *Essays and Speeches*, 1967. Quoted in Phillip Lewis, *Islamic Britain: Religion, Politics and Identity among British Muslims* (London: I. B. Tauris, 1994), p. 3.

Despite the reservations expressed by Roy Jenkins in the aftermath of *The Satanic Verses* affair, and some criticism as mentioned before from the Right, Left, and the minorities, the notion remains in currency, although a close examination may show signs of evolution and adaptation. Most people in the UK including the "ethnic minorities" seem to be quite proud of their multicultural arrangement. Perhaps this took root more easily in the UK due to the distinct lack of a strong British identity. The British do not seem to be as visibly proud of their "national" identity as are, say, the Americans or French. Recent events have also led to a rise in increasing local awareness, or devolution, with the establishment of the Welsh, Scottish, and Northern Ireland Assemblies. All of this has led to an ongoing debate on what it means to be British. Interestingly, elements from the "ethnic minorities" are also engaging themselves in this debate. A recent survey conducted by the Policy Studies Institute showed that 66 percent of Pakistanis said that they think of themselves "in many ways" as being British. At the same time 90 percent also said the same regarding being Pakistani. It seems, therefore, that what is evolving among the Pakistanis (and most likely other ethnic minorities) is a sense of hybrid or hyphenated identity (British-Pakistani).[26] This point is mentioned here because so far it seems to be a unique situation among Muslims in Europe and will no doubt play an important role in the dynamics of representation and relationship with the state.

Coming onto the Muslim organizations, the first major initiative in the post-Second World War period was the establishment of the Islamic Cultural Center and the Mosque Trust in 1944 and the subsequent opening of the London Central Mosque at Regents Park in 1977. The trust was composed of Muslim Ambassadors and High Commissioners from 13 Muslim countries, establishing a strong relationship between the Mosque and some governments in the Muslim world (especially the Saudi and Egyptian). Although this was not a representative body as such, it has been a significant player in the eyes of the state and is often consulted on matters of importance to the Muslim community. The first attempt at representation and coordination came from the Union of Muslim Organizations (UMO) established in 1970 with the representatives of 38 organizations.[27] This number grew over the subsequent years, but the UMO was unable to attract the support of some of the larger organizations that became established. It also tried to lobby the national government, perhaps unwisely, at a time when most decisions related to Muslims occurred at a local level. It was also perhaps a premature move, the Muslim community not being in a settled enough position to realize the importance of such a

---

[26] Tariq Modood *et al.*, *Ethnic Minorities In Britain* (London: PSI, 1997).

[27] M. Manazir Ahsan, "Islam and Muslims in Britain," in *Islam, Muslims and the Modern State: Case Studies of Muslims in Thirteen Countries*, eds. Hussin Mutalib and Taj ul-Islam Hashmi (New York: St. Martin's Press, 1994), pp. 374.

step.[28] The early issues of concern to Muslims in the UK, and in fact across Europe, were typically: planning permission for mosques, educational facilities for children, and provision of *halal* food. It was in the pursuit of such needs at a local level (as well as the campaign such as the one against Ray Honeyford in Bradford[29]) that Muslims began to acquire experience of dealing with the government and lobbying for their needs. In 1984, two other attempts were made to form coordinating bodies, the Council of Mosques and the Imams and Mosques Council. The former was inspired by the Muslim World League, and the latter brought together some of the Brelwi Imams and mosques among others. Both organizations, working in opposition, played a prominent role in local projects especially on educational matters.

But it was not until the hysteria caused by *The Satanic Verses* in 1988 (and onwards) that the more representative coordinating bodies were formed. *The Satanic Verses* affair was indeed a milestone in the history of Muslim organizations in the UK.[30] It was the single external force that was able to galvanize Muslim opinion and bring it (almost) together. The UK Action Committee on Islamic Affairs (UKACIA) was set up in 1988 with broad-based representation primarily to lobby against the publication and ask for its withdrawal. However, it did continue to work long after the events had died down and lobbied the government with regards to Kashmir, Palestine, the Gulf War, and the War in Bosnia. Nonetheless, there were subtle differences among Muslims *vis-à-vis* this affair and the Muslim Institute (formed in 1972) seemed to voice the most radical view. It had aligned itself very closely with Iran and criticized some of the other bodies for their "weak response" (not only during *The Satanic Verses* affair but also during the Gulf War). The Council of Mosques was also a very prominent actor at this time, often working alone, often with the UKACIA.

In 1992, The Muslim Parliament was set up by the Muslim Institute, the name being chosen to attract media attention. The Muslim Parliament remained a radical and highly vocal entity for a few years until the death of its founder and main activist Kalim Siddiqui. It ad a separatist view towards the future of Muslims in Britain and called for the formation of parallel institutions as it felt Muslims would have little success in influencing the establishment. The UKACIA, due to its broad base, had to tread very carefully. It soon realized that it could only speak on issues where there was unanimity of opinion. This often caused problems when

28 Jørgen Nielsen, *Muslims in Western Europe* (Edinburgh University Press, 1995), p. 47.
29 Philip Lewis, *Islamic Britain: Religion, Politics and Identity among British Muslims* (London: I. B. Tauris, 1994), pp. 153–64.
30 See M.M. Ahsan and A.R. Kidwai, eds, *Sacrilege Verses Civility: Muslim Perspectives on The Satanic Verses Affair* (Leicester: Islamic Foundation, 1991). Also, Ziauddin Sardar and Merryl Wyn Davis, *Distorted Imagination: Lessons from the Rushdie Affair* (London: Grey Seal Books, 1990), and Philip Lewis, *Islamic Britain*.

speaking out on foreign affairs, e.g. the Gulf War, as the Islamic Cultural Center, which had leanings toward the Saudi government, was one of its main affiliates. The experiences of the UKACIA eventually led to the search for a new type of organization that would be not just a committee, but would be more closely knit and could establish a link between the Muslim community and the government. To this end the National Interim Council for Muslim Unity (NICMU) was set up, which eventually led, after some years of extensive consultation, to the establishment of the Muslim Council of Britain (MCB).

The MCB was launched in November 1997, in London, with the backing of around 250 affiliate organizations[31] with the following aims:

—to promote cooperation, consensus and unity on Muslim affairs in the UK;
—to encourage and strengthen all existing efforts being made for the benefit of the Muslim community;
—to work for a more enlightened appreciation of Islam and Muslims in the wider society;
—to establish a position for the Muslim community within British society that is fair and based on due rights;
—to work for the eradication of disadvantages and forms of discrimination faced by Muslims;
—to foster better community relations and work for the good of society as a whole.

Although the MCB is perhaps the most representative of the bodies available, it would be untrue to say it is representative of the whole Muslim spectrum.[32] It will be interesting to see how this umbrella body develops in the future. It is true to say that it has been able to create a significant impact in the short time that it has been in existence. It has met with the Ministry of Health, the Home Office, and has facilitated regular meetings with the Foreign Minister and leaders from the Muslim community. It has also been able to facilitate receptions with the Prime Minister.[33] It has also spearheaded a number of campaigns. such as the inclusion of a question on religious affiliation in the National Census (2001) and a recent initiative directed at affecting political party policy prior to the General Elections. This was coupled with its encouragement to Muslims to participate in the

---

[31] It should be noted that many national organizations are represented by more than one of their larger branches, as local organizations, and therefore the actual number of different organizations would be less than this.

[32] Some of the notable organizations as yet to be fully involved are: the Shia organizations, the Muslim Parliament, the Hizb al-Tahrir and al-Muhajiroun, Q-News, and the Imams and Mosques Council.

[33] See the MCB web site: www.mcb.org.uk.

electoral system and vote intelligently for their interests.[34]

Another aspect to the relationship between Muslims and the state in the UK is the presence of three Muslims in the House of Lords and two in the House of Commons. There have also been a significant number of Muslims involved in local government as councilors, estimated to number over 200. One of the Lords, Nazir Ahmed of Rotherham asked for a prayer room to be set aside in the House of Lords. He, and the others Lords and MPs, have also been invited extensively to gatherings of the Muslim community and have facilitated the hiring of a room in the House of Lords for a monthly public debate and discussion.[35] This direct political involvement is a recent development and though it has attracted very mixed and at times cynical reactions from Muslims, time will tell how this affects the Muslim community. It should be mentioned that all of these figures have entered the political system via the established political parties (in this case all those mentioned are from the Labour Party). Attempts at setting up separate Muslim political entities have had little or no support from the wider Muslim community, as could be seen in the case of the Muslim Parliament and the Islamic Party of Britain,[36] which have both dwindled considerably in recent times.

Germany. As mentioned before, the traditional German concept of nationhood placed great emphasis on blood descent and less on territory. One could find the roots of this emphasis in the migration of the Germanic tribes that laid the ground for post-Roman Europe. Up to the time of the Second World War, the central idea for German nationality was one of Volksgenossen (national comrades). Differences were felt between those who were Deutsche (citizens of German descent), Reichsdeutsche (citizens of non-German descent) and Volksdeutsche (those of German descent but living outside Germany).[37] On the religious level, it was the merging of countries with different confessions that formed Germany. The constitution of Germany, called the Basic Law, therefore guarantees that "freedom of belief, conscience and of religious confession and world-view are inviolable," and that the state must, "guarantee the undisturbed practice of religion." The history of Christianity in Germany is a notable one. It is from this region that the legendary Charlemagne began his conquest of Europe, creating a vast empire in the name of Christendom. For centuries, the political locus of the Holy Roman Empire hovered around the north, much of

---

[34] See the Votesmart website: www.votesmart.org.uk.

[35] The Islamic Society of Britain's London branch organizes a monthly meeting which is attended by Muslim and non-Muslim participants.

[36] This party set itself up as a Muslim political party and placed a candidate in Bradford for the General elections. However it managed to attract very few votes from the Muslim community.

[37] Habermas, "Struggles for Recognition," p. 151.

which is modern Germany. Yet it was in Germany in 1517 that Luther sparked off the Reformation with his "protest" movement. The ensuing religious tensions between Catholics and Protestants left indelible marks on the history of Europe. In Germany, distinct regions formed, those in the south and west favoring Catholicism while those in the central region and northeast became Protestant. This did not lead to an easy accommodation, for during Bismarck's time the Prussian Empire engaged in a vociferous anti-Catholic campaign, the Kulturkampf, fuelling the estrangement between the two branches of Christianity. In modern Germany, Church and state are separate, although historically a special relationship has existed between the state and communities that have the status of Körperschaft öffentlichen Rechts (publicly recognized corporation). The state is not a laicist state as France, but regards itself as religionsneutral, that is, it does not take a stance on religious affairs. However there is very good cooperation between the churches and regional states, especially in the field of education and welfare. Approximately 80 percent of publicly funded nursery schools, a number of hospitals, and some welfare organizations are run by churches. Among those who fall under the category of "publicly recognized corporation" are the Lutheran and Catholic Churches, Judaism, and a number of smaller Christian groups. Such a status enables the community to deal with the central government and the Länder (local government), leading to advantages such as a tax benefit scheme in which the state collects a tax, Kirchensteuer, from members of the community and, after deduction of an agreed administrative charge, hands this over to the corporation. There are also further advantages including state subsidy, a voice on religious education matters, and representation in public institutions such as the media, hospitals, and prisons.

The Germanic states have been in contact with Muslims since the 16th and 17th centuries when Ottoman Turks attempted to expand their territories through the Balkans; two sieges were held in Vienna in 1529 and 1683. It was the latter incident that, after the retreat of the Ottoman army, left behind many Muslims, some of whom decided to settle. Diplomatic relations were established between Berlin and Constantinople in the 18th century, and by the 19th century trading treaties were set up between the two cities. These developments encouraged the crossover of citizens between the Ottoman and German states. In 1930, the German Muslim Association was formed, followed by the Berlin branch of the World Muslim Congress in 1932.[38] These early organizations were able to bring together large sections of the Muslim community, perhaps due to the very small numbers present. This degree of unity has not been achieved among Muslims to the present day.

---

[38] M. Salim Abdullah, "Muslims in Germany," in *Muslim Minorities in the West*, ed. Syed Abedin and Ziauddin Sardar (London: Institute of Muslim Minority Affairs, 1995), p. 68.

By 1951, the Muslims in Germany were able to establish a forum called the Geistliche Verwaltung der Muslimflüchtlinge in der Bundesrepublik Deutschland (Spiritual Administration for Muslim Refugees in the Federal Republic of Germany). In 1986, the German Islamic Council was formed with the cooperation of the World Muslim Congress, the Nurculuk Movement, and the Friends of Islam. Another attempt was soon made to form the Islamic Working Group in Germany, which eventually led, in 1994, to the formation of the Zentralrat der Muslime—"Central Council of Muslims in Germany" (ZMD). This council currently has around 20 organizations and networks affiliated to it, representing some 700 mosques and communities. It is also composed of a broad ethnic mix, including German converts. So far the ZMD has shown perhaps the most promising signs of being accepted by the German authorities, but none of these organizations are currently officially recognized as they are not thought to be representative of the whole Muslim community. The following groups are also very influential within the grassroots of the Muslim community and may be potential participants in one of the existing bodies or on their own in the aim of representation: Diyanet Isleri Turk Islam Birligi—"Turkish-Islamic Union of the Agency for Religion" (DITIB), set up by the Turkish Government; Avrupa Milli Gorus Teskilati—"Association of the National Vision in Europe" (AMGT); and the Verband der Islamische Kultur Zentren— "Union of Islamic Cultural Centers" (VIKZ), the network of the Sulaymanci Movement.

The role of the Turkish state in the politics of the German Muslim community is a very significant one and cannot be ignored. Its work in Germany aims to counteract some of the "fundamentalist tendencies" found among the Turkish Islamic Activists and, as some would add, to try to retain a hold over its Nationals. It also makes a strong contribution to the debate on German citizenship and dual nationality, which is a topical issue at the moment.[39] The Turkish community in Germany is known for attachment to Turkey and this creates a complex interplay of influences over the community. The DITIB brings in religious teachers from Turkey in an attempt to keep the religious connection with the Turkish state alive. This has been challenged by both the AMGT and the VIKZ who have opened local centers for the training of *hocas* (Imam).

Although the Muslim minority in Germany has not been able to achieve a formal status of recognition, giving rise to a loss of negotiating power with the state amongst other disadvantages, the very presence of the community has had an impact on the German perception of minorities and their treatment. Until the late 1980s, the common perception was that German society was not one of immigration and that the Gastarbeiter

---

[39] The law was changed in 2000 to allow easier access to German citizenship, and to allow dual citizenship for those below 18 years age. However, the number of applications have not been as great as initially anticipated.

would eventually "return home." Due to this, Islam has mainly been regarded as a foreign issue, rather than a domestic one by the German government. However, the changes in policy post September 11th 2001, swept this attitude away. The claims of those organizations seeking recognition have been mainly that they wish to have a level playing field on which they are recognized as legitimate actors on the German scene. The main requests have therefore been for easy access to citizenship, the right to dual nationality, and recognition as a religious community. Given that Islam is the second largest religion in Germany, with around three million followers, this is seen by many to be a rightful claim. Another issue of serious concern for campaign has been provision for religious education and education in general. As churches run around 80 percent of kindergartens in Germany,[40] many Muslims are not willing to send their children to such institutions and there have been calls for facilities to cater to the needs of Muslim children. Other issues include provisions for Islamic burials. *Halal* slaughter provision was also a big concern for the Muslim community, but this was granted in 2001.

The German State has tried to grapple with the reality of immigration in a paradoxical manner, by not acknowledging its existence and yet trying to assimilate and integrate, or at times repatriate by offering financial incentives for those who leave. The stigma of being "foreign" and "guest worker" lives with the immigrant communities, many of whom reciprocate by refusing to integrate into a system that, to them, obviously does not want their presence. In the view of Faruk Sen (writing before the changes to citizenship laws)[41] this is a serious problem for democratic societies:

Although migrants—"foreigners" as they are called in Germany—are required to pay taxes and obey the law, and their lives are as affected by government decision-making as any other resident, they have no say or very little say in the decision making process ... If a substantial number of permanent residents cannot vote, the legitimacy of the political decision-making process is impaired. It must be noted that the existence of such disenfranchised groups in significant numbers throughout Europe undermines democracy.[42]

But the notion of Gastarbeiter is now being challenged and the debate has turned towards citizenship and *Multikulturelle Gesellschaft* (multicultural society) and its relative merits as well as the possibility of the right to vote for non-citizens. The current center-left government has given out some sympathetic vibes towards the minorities indicating its desire to create policies for a multi-ethnic Germany. A recent report released by the

---

[40] Faruk Sen, "Islam in Germany," *Turkish Daily News*, May 4, 1999.
[41] While this statement was written before change to the law, the relatively low uptake of citizenship is something that needs careful examination and many of the implications still seem to be present.
[42] Ibid.

Interior Ministry argued the need for further immigration due to the declining workforce and aging population. It will be interesting to see how this develops and what impact it will have on the Muslim community.

The Netherlands. The Netherlands has had its fair share of conflicts with other European states and its history has placed it at odds with England, France, Spain, and more recently Germany. There has also historically been a long ideological and political struggle between Catholics and Protestants leading to the concept of *Verzuiling* or "pillarization" as a means to manage religious diversity. This concept involved the stratification of society along the lines of different communities, each having their own methods of schooling and minor social sub-structures. This concept developed around the end of the 19th century and was in full force by the middle of the 20th century. The latter part of the 20th century saw the use of this concept dwindling, with it coming to an end around 1983 from when laicist influences started to take root. Modern day Dutch society therefore contains remnants of the legacy of pillarization with quite a strong sense of *laicité*, though not perhaps as strong as in France. The emphasis in pillarization was on three main issues: religious freedom, equal treatment (hence if the government was to subsidize places of worship for one "pillar" it would be expected to do so for the others as well), and freedom of education. Pillarization meant implicit recognition for all groups; hence this has not been such an important issue in the Dutch Muslim discourse.

Contacts between the Dutch and Muslims date back to the time of the Crusades and the later diplomatic and trade relations established with Turkey and Morocco in the 16th century. After that came the Colonial Era with colonies in Indonesia and Suriname. The first group of Muslims, Indonesians, arrived around 1950, and a mosque, funded entirely by the state, was opened for them in 1956.[43] The migration of Surinamese and Turks followed this in the 1960s and 1970s, the migrants being initially viewed as "guest workers."

The Scientific Council for Government Policy (WRR), an advisory body to the Prime Minister, reported in 1979 that the myth of return should be abandoned and policy to encourage the immigrants' social and economic integration should be developed, in order to build better community relations. There also seemed to be a general feeling, based on guilt, that forced return would be unethical considering the workers had come from areas that were previously under colonial rule. Such a policy was expressed in the Note of Minorities of 1983, in which the Government explained that members of minority groups living in Holland would have equal opportunities and full chances of development. It would also take

---

[43] A. van Bommel, "The History of Muslim Umbrella Organizations," in *Islam in Dutch Society: Current Developments and Future Prospects*, ed. W. A. R. Shadid and P. S. van Koningsveld (The Hague: Kok Pharos, 1991), p. 126.

into account the culture, religion, and background of minorities in the creation of a multicultural society.[44] This was to be extended even to those who were not nationals, including also the right to vote. The other immediate advantages were the subsidies for mosques, education, Islamic schools, and airtime on national television. (This right is derived from the Broadcasting Act of 1967, which caters for "associations with a spiritual root.") After an uninterrupted residency of five years, migrants are able to become Dutch nationals upon payment of a fee. The strategy of the government seems to have given certain real advantages to the Muslim community. But with unemployment being high among some immigrant groups, their image seems to be getting worse.

The first attempt at forming a coordinating body came in 1973 with the formation of a local group in Utrecht, the Werkgroep de Moskee (Mosque Working Group). This group involved Muslims from different backgrounds and one its first major activities was the celebration of Milad an-Nabi, to which many VIP and dignitaries were invited as well as representatives of others Muslim organizations. This meeting prompted the founding of the Nederlandse Islamitische Sociëteit (Dutch Islamic Society) in Amsterdam, with the intention of uniting all Muslims. A similar initiative was undertaken at the national level in 1974, with the setting up of a working group from many different nationalities. This group eventually set up the Federation of Muslim Organizations in the Netherlands (FOMON) in 1975. The FOMON dealt with a wide range of community needs including arrangements for sites for mosques, halal food, burial, and education. With the growth of Islamic organizations in the 70s, the FOMON called a national conference in 1980 to broaden its affiliates. This led to the founding, in the following year, of a new group, the Muslim Organizations in the Netherlands (MON). However, this new organization ended up being ineffective and remains a paper organization, as is the Netherlands Islamic Parliament (NIP). During the 80s, the number of Turkish groups grew rapidly, bringing onto the scene the Turkish Islamic Cultural Federation (TICF) that was established in 1979 and works closely with the Diyanet organization, the Islamic Foundation in the Netherlands (ISN), established in 1982; the Netherlands Islamic Federation (NIF)—the Milli Gorus, established in 1981; and the Islamic Center in the Netherlands (ICN)—the Sulaymancis, established in 1972. The Turkish organizations are represented on an advisory council to deal with the Dutch Government. Two Moroccan coordination groups exist (that oppose each other): the Union of Moroccan Muslim Organization (UMMON), established in 1978, and the Dutch Federation of Moroccan Islamic Organizations (NFMIO), established in 1990.

The Surinamese and Pakistanis have tended to organize more at a local level with organizations that have loyalty to various international Sufi

---

[44] Shadid and van Koningsveld, "Institutionalization and Integration of Islam in the Netherlands," in *The Integration of Islam*, p. 92.

Turuq. The three national bodies that exist, the Foundation for the Welfare of Muslims in the Netherlands, the World Islamic Mission in Amsterdam, and the International Muslim Organization in The Hague, do not seem to have much to do with relating to the Dutch state as of yet.

The latest attempts at creating a representative body incorporating Muslims from different national backgrounds resulted in 1989 in the formation of the Islamic Council in the Netherlands (an unsuccessful venture) and in 1990, the formation of the Islamic Foundation for the Promotion of Integration (ISBI). As can be seen, the pursuit of coordinating groups in the Netherlands, and perhaps many other countries in the EU, has been hampered by the national/ethnic lines along which most of the organizations seem to prefer to work. This is not the only frustration of Dutch Muslims, however, as Abdul Wahid van Bommel expresses:

When the Muslims do not offer representation to the Government, they are asked why they do not organise themselves collectively. For years, the oft repeated question was, "With which Muslim organisation can we go into discussion?" When subsequently, after extensive preparations, a Federation is founded, the response is that such a form of organisation is "alien to Islam, and authoritarian". When various government bodies were approached with requests for subsidies, the response was often "Why don't you get help from those rich oil states?" When in reality any of these countries send help, this is regarded as some kind of conspiracy "to establish a grip on the Muslim community".[45]

Denmark. The Danish constitution of 1848, while expressing the principle of Freedom of Religion, supports the Evangelical-Lutheran Church as the National Church (Folkekirke) and has since incorporated it as one of the departments of the state. It is fully funded by the government, 80 percent of expenses coming from national and local taxes and 20 percent from direct grants, and 91.5 percent of the population are registered members.[46] This close cooperation between the Church and the state is further demonstrated in the regular prayers that are said by the clergy for Royal Family and nation. Religious communities are managed through recognition in three ways.[47] Currently eight other Christian denominations are recognized as well as the Jews. The second category is that of those groups which are officially unrecognized, but for whom there is some legal provision and empowerment. The third category is that of those communities which are not seen as religious, e.g. the Moonies.

Despite the relatively small number of Muslims in Denmark, whose presence is a result of mainly labor migration, they form the second largest

---

[45] Van Bommel, "The History of Muslim Umbrella Organizations," p. 134.

[46] Shadid and van Koningsveld, *Religious Freedom*, p. 11.

[47] See Lars Pedersen, "Islam in the Public Discourse in Denmark," in *Muslims in the Margin: Political Responses to the Presence of Islam in Western Europe*, eds W. A. R. Shadid and P. S. van Koningsveld, (The Hague: Kok Pharos), 1996, p. 204.

religious group. The Islamic Cultural Center in Copenhagen, established in 1974, is the oldest mosque (its trustees are the local ambassadors of Saudi Arabia, Morocco, Egypt and Pakistan).[48] In addition to this center, the two largest groups are among the Turkish community: the Diyanet and the Milli Gorus. There are also some smaller organizations among the Pakistanis.

The issue of representation in Denmark is quite peculiar in that the Government's perception is that the only real advantage of recognition would be to grant priests the right to perform marriages. This has been addressed by the permission in 1969 for priest of unrecognized religious communities to perform marriages, hence granting a *de facto* recognition. On this basis, it has been indicated that no new religions will be granted official recognition. This however does not correlate with the Muslim community's views on the matter. Many community leaders feel that the matter is more complex than this and express that their needs are not understood. They wish to be placed on a par with other religions and do not wish to be discriminated against.[49]

Belgium. Belgium has been traditionally subject to many different cultural influences, perhaps the strongest of which have been French and Dutch. Belgium broke away from Dutch rule in 1830 and established its own sovereignty in 1831. The dual influences of the Netherlands and France remain to this day in the languages spoken in the Flanders and Wallonia regions. The Belgian legal system is based on the Napoleonic system, and although there was a laicist movement in the 19th century, it did not take root in Belgium as it did in France. The country is largely Roman Catholic and the Belgian State has given recognition to the Catholic Church, the Reformed Church, the Anglican Church, and the Jews. There is, of course, religious freedom for non-recognized religions, but in Belgium recognition implies that the religion concerned has a significant input in education in schools and that the clergy are paid by the state.

Belgium has a significant history of immigration, especially for labor, for which Muslims started to arrive in the 1960s, mainly from North Africa; they were joined later in the 1970s by Turks. Although there are a number of mosques and Muslim organizations,[50] of particular interest is the Islamic Cultural Center of Belgium (ICC), which has become the *de facto* representative of Muslims in Belgium. The land for the center was handed over to King Faisal in 1967 as a gift in exchange for donations he had made. The mosque was then established with the support of the

---

[48] Lars Pedersen, *Newer Islamic Movements in Western Europe* (Aldershot: Ashgate, 1999), p. 43.

[49] See Pedersen, "Islam in the Public Discourse," p. 205.

[50] Among the Turks there are mainly the Diyanet and Milli Gorus and the Amicales among the Moroccans.

Muslim World League and the board of trustees chaired by the ambassador of Saudi Arabia. After the establishment of the mosque, some Belgian politicians started to call for the recognition of Islam as the Muslim community had grown larger than the Jewish or Anglican communities. Another factor was the expectation that Muslims would settle in Belgium and that this recognition would ease the process. Some have also suggested that the debate around recognition was perhaps raised to place Belgium in favour with the oil-producing countries with which it was negotiating contracts.[51] The law recognizing Islam was passed in 1974, but to this day no organization has fulfilled the criteria for being the representative body. There are possibly three reasons for this:

—the Muslim organizations found it difficult to assemble themselves and agree upon a representative structure;
—the state had placed strict criteria for membership as it did not want any "fundamentalists" on such an assembly;
—during the 80s, the image of the Muslim community, locally and internationally, started to change. International events such as the Iranian revolution, events in Lebanon, and the war between Iran and Iraq had changed the mood of public opinion to one that was very suspicious of Islam.

The Cultural Center therefore became the only point of reference that the government was willing to deal with, albeit on a temporary basis. In 1977, Muslims from different national groups set up the Culture et Religion Islamique (CRI) to rival the Cultural Center, which they accused of being manipulated by foreign governments. The Jama'at Tabligh also set up the Federation of Mosques and Islamic Cultural Association in 1985, which was designed to be an umbrella body to challenge the Cultural Center. In 1989, the ICC stated that it was not truly representative of the Muslim community, and in consultation with a cross-section of the community decided to form a committee to arrange for elections for a new body. The Minister of Justice was meanwhile preparing to set up the Superior Council of Muslims and asked for the elections of the ICC's committee to be stopped. When the ICC did not heed this request, it was discharged following a public disavowal of its competence and lack of representation. A Provisional Council of Elders was set up on which three seats were allocated to the ICC (which were not taken up); this council was given the mandate to set up a representative council. The Council of Elders proved to be ineffective, but in the meantime the ICC and others from the Muslim community had gone ahead with the "cancelled" elections and formed the Conseil Supérieur des Musulmans de Belgique. The

---

[51] See Nielsen, *Muslims in Western Europe*, p. 70, and also Albert Bastenier, "'Islam in Belgium," in *The New Islamic Presence in Western Europe*, ed. Tomas Gerholm and Y. Georg Lithman (London: Mansell, 1988), p. 140.

government refused to recognize this body, as it did not represent the Turks[52] and was too "Islamist."[53] After a long period of debate and discussion, in 1994 the Minister of Justice decided to accept an assembly of 17 people as interlocutors, in which the Milli Gorus were excluded from putting a candidate forward to the assembly. This assembly also eventually became ineffective.

Spain. Spain is one of the few countries in Europe that had a historical presence of Islam on its soil for some significant period of time. For much of this, from 711 when Muslims arrived in Spain to 1492 when the last communities were expelled, Muslims ruled most of what is Spain today as well as some of the neighboring areas. Naturally, during such a long period of presence, Islam blended into its European surroundings, giving rise to an Arab-Iberian culture. Although this period is hailed by many Muslim historians as a high point of Islamic, and indeed European, civilization, the European collective conscience seems to be somewhat ambivalent to it, perhaps especially so in Spain. However, despite the fact that the few Muslims who did remain in Spain were forced to convert or practice their faith in secret until the last century, this memory has not remained entirely suppressed. The newer Muslim presence as a result of migration for work and education has brought Islam onto the discussion table again. Another factor in this may be the significant landmarks left by Andalusian rulers in parts of Spain, which have been a constant reminder of the historical reality. The Muslim community is quite diverse, mainly formed of Moroccans, Algerians, Pakistanis, Arabs from various states, Iranians, and Africans. There are also a number of Spanish coverts that see their conversion to Islam as a rediscovery of their past.

What is very prominent in people's minds, however, is the five centuries of strong relationship with the Catholic Church, which officially ended when the constitution of 1978 declared Spain to be a non-confessional and laic state. However, it also allowed room for the state to cooperate with the Church in order to guarantee the rights of citizens to religious freedom. This cooperation was to be actualized through the establishment of an agreement with the religious bodies as mentioned in the Organic Law of Religious Liberty. It was this principle that led, in 1992, to the King of Spain signing official agreements with the Protestants, Jews, and Muslims (represented by the Spanish Islamic Commission).[54] In order to conclude the agreement it was stipulated that each community should have a certain number of adherents registered in the Register of Religious Bodies, to show that the creed was established in the country. The Spanish Islamic

---

[52] In fact it was only the Diyanet that did not participate; the Milli Gorus did.

[53] Johan Leman and Monique Renaerts, "Dialogues Among Authorities and Muslims in Belgium," in *Muslims in the Margin*, pp. 174–5.

[54] For the full text of the agreement between the King and the Muslim community, see *Encounters: Journal of Inter-Cultural Perspectives* 2:2, Sept. 1996, pp. 155–67.

Commission was formed to meet the criteria of the agreement and is itself an amalgamation of two bodies that were noted in the Register: the Union of Spanish Islamic Communities and the Spanish Federation of Islamic Religious Bodies.

The appendix to the agreement lists a preamble stating the purpose behind the agreement and then 14 articles that actually deal with the issues. Some of these are:

—Protection extended to archives and documents of the Commission;
—Provision for burial;
—Provisions for Imam and religious teachers;
—Provisions for performing marriages;
—Provisions for religious welfare in the Armed Services, prisons, and hospitals;
—Provision for Islamic education in schools as well as the right to set up schools and universities;
—Certain tax exemption on literature, donations, and mosques;
—Provision for unpaid leave from work between 1.30pm and 3.30pm on Fridays and one hour before sunset in Ramadan;
—Provision for those in employment to substitute national holidays with the following events from the Muslim calendar: Hijra, Ashura, Milad an-Nabi, Isra, 'Id al-Fitr, and 'Id al-Adha. Students are not required to attend school on these days;
—Measures for the conservation and promotion of the Islamic historic and artistic heritage in Spain;
—Provision for *halal* food.

It will be interesting to see how this very progressive agreement is implemented in the long term and how this will be negotiated between the state and the Spanish Islamic Commission. Spain is also a country that is recently coming to terms with its European partners after having been isolated for so long. The consequent interplay of mutual influence with respect to treatment of minorities will be another important factor to look at.

Despite the above agreement, there is some feeling of alienation among the Muslim community. Muslims are still seen as a foreign phenomenon as expressed by Montserrat Abumalham:

The group of "invisible Muslims" [those of mixed family origin] perceive a kind of ignorance among the Spanish born about their religion but especially, and more importantly to them, about their culture. Their complaints refer to the scant treatment the Arab-Islamic culture is given in the text books comparing, for example, to the classical culture of Greece and Rome ... They equally regret the fact that despite speaking proper Spanish and having no external features capable of distinguishing them from most Spanish people, they are asked every time why their names are so strange.[55]

Italy. The very close and complex historical relationship between Italy and the Roman Catholic Church is well known and needs little reference. The new Concordat of 1984, however, means that Catholicism is no longer the state religion and that state subsidies for the salaries of clergy have been stopped. Nonetheless, people are able to contribute a percentage of their income tax towards the Church and they are also entitled to tax deductions from donations. There are provisions for religious care in the army, in hospitals, and in prisons, as well as the teaching of Catholicism in schools and the freedom to establish Catholic schools. Canonical marriages are also valid in a civil context. In the same year, similar agreements were signed with other denominations including Methodists.

Italy is also one of those countries in which Muslims have had a historical presence, at least in the south. The Arabs arrived in Sicily towards the end of the 7th century and ruled it for almost two hundred years from the 9th to the 11th century, being pushed out by the Norman invasion. There have also been contacts between Italy and the Muslim world during the Italian Colonial experience in Africa, particularly Libya. These factors, together with the memory of the Crusades, when Muslims often attacked the south of Italy, have meant that both have tended to see each other as old enemies.

The current presence of Islam is quite recent, most migrants arriving into Italy from the 1980s onwards. This has been something of a culture shock for the Italians, as they have traditionally exported migrants to other parts of the world. The current Muslim population, made up of those who primarily came for educational and economic advantages, is very mixed, with the largest group being Moroccans. There are many Sufi orders as well as the Jama'at Tabligh, the Union of Muslim Students (USMI), some other smaller centers, and also a group of Muslim converts. In terms of representation there are two important elements:[56] the Islamic Cultural Center of Italy, based in Rome, and the Union of Communities and Islamic Organizations in Italy (UCOII). The Islamic Cultural Center (and Central Mosque) was founded in 1985 and has been supported by the Muslim World League; as is usual with these initiatives the board of trustees is composed of Muslim ambassadors. The UCOII was formed in 1990 and incorporates, among others, the USMI and the Islamic Center of Milan. The UCOII intends to be the official representative of Islam to the state, an identity that is yet to be carved out despite its efforts in liaising with official bodies.

---

[55] Montserrat Abumalham, "The Muslim Presence in Spain," in *Muslims in the Margin*, p. 86.

[56] See Stefano Allievi, "Muslim Minorities in Italy and their Image in Italian Media," in *Islam in Europe: The Politics of Religion and Community*, ed. Steven Vertovec and Ceri Peach (London: Macmillan Press, 1997), pp. 211–23.

Sweden. Sweden has traditionally been a mono-religious country of Lutheran Christian background, which is still reflected in the 95 percent following of the Lutheran Church. Its people have also been very homogenous and the traditional slogan has been "one nation, one people, one religion." It was only in 1873 that the law allowed people the right to belong to other Christian denominations, who could previously be expelled on the ground of belonging to the wrong faith,[57] and in 1951 that full freedom of religion was accepted. However, the post-Second World War period in Sweden has seen perhaps the greatest change, due to immigration, of any Western European country. Especially since the 1960s, Swedish society has been rapidly liberalized and has, on the whole, become highly secularized, although individually the people seem to have deep religious sentiments. The Freedom of Religion Act itself is so secular that it refers only to a very strict notion of what is religious. Therefore separate laws deal with matters of clothing, food, marriage, and so on.

The neutrality of Sweden in both World Wars and also its lack of a colonial legacy have given it a unique position in the eyes of the international community. With the arrival of immigrants in the 1960s, some major debates relating to immigration took place. This eventually led to the establishment of an Immigration Board and in 1975, a multicultural policy was adopted to deal with migrants. The Swedish multicultural policy is based on three objectives: full equality between all, freedom of culture for migrants, and cooperation between majority and minority.[58] Religious diversity is seen as something to be welcomed, hence religious groups are given state funding after they reach a certain size. As in the Netherlands, non-citizens are able to participate in elections and attainment of citizenship is also relatively easy: permanent settlement can be granted after one year of legal residency, and after five years full citizenship can be attained. In dealing with the minorities the Swedish government has resisted working with the governments of the country of origin, hence the Diyanet and other embassies have less influence among the Muslim community in Sweden.

The Muslim community is very cosmopolitan, the largest groups being from Iran, Turkey, Iraq, Lebanon, Bosnia, Ethiopia, Syria, and Somalia. There are also a small number of converts. The Lutheran Church is state funded through a Church Tax. For other religious bodies, if they are able to establish a federal structure with a list of members and procedures for appointment of leaders, then once the membership reaches a certain number the body is entitled to state funding. Muslim organizations have

---

[57] A. Sander, "The Road from Musalla to Mosque: The Process of Integration and Institutionalization of Islam in Sweden," in *The Integration of Islam*, p. 63.
[58] Nielsen, *Muslims in Western Europe*, p. 82.

thus been quite well funded. However, this has lead to federations splitting once the required size has been met, in order to attract further funds.

Sweden has dealt with multicultural education in a rather novel manner. Since the mid-70s the state actively recruited teachers from minorities and developed a programme that enabled non-Swedish speaking children to join the school system in their parental language, along with special classes to teach Swedish. As the child grows through the school system, the Swedish-taught component increases and the parental language is gradually phased out.

The attitude of the state in creating room for migrants needs to be balanced by the public view of Islam. The media has been quite instrumental in portraying Islam as a danger to Swedish values; this, coupled with the low level of educational attainment among some immigrants and high levels of unemployment, has meant that the overall public image tends to be quite negative.[59]

Among the Muslim organizations present, the Islamiska Förbundet I Sverige (the Swedish Islamic League) based in Stockholm is perhaps the most organized and has the widest network. It has a large center and has a number of groups affiliated to it, including a youth and student group.

The Swedish state has taken steps, utilizing its neutral image, as a broker of understanding between Islam and Europe. The high-profile conferences organized in 1996 and 1997 on Euro-Islam allowed a much needed dialogue to take place between representatives of European states, Muslim and non-Muslim academics, and representatives of some Muslim organizations.

Austria. Austria is yet another country that had historical encounters with Islam. During the 16th and 17th centuries there were ongoing attempts by the Ottomans to expand westwards into Europe; the infamous sieges of Vienna in 1529 and 1683 and the subsequent defeat of the Ottomans were instrumental in creating a lasting image of the "Islamic threat" or the "Turkish peril." This was, of course, particularly felt by the Germanic states, especially Austria, or the Hapsburg Empire as it was then. The retreat of the Ottomans left behind a number of soldiers, some of whom settled in small communities. As time went by, trade and diplomatic relations were established between the Germans and the Ottomans and the relationships began to improve. In 1874, a law was passed that recognized some aspects of Muslim family law. In 1878, the Austro-Hungarian Empire annexed Bosnia-Herzegovina and in order to cater to the Muslims there it allowed the application of Islamic family law in the courts, necessitating the translation into German of Hanafi family law codes in 1883. In 1912, the law of 1874 was expanded to recognize the Hanafi Madhhab and

---

[59] Sander, "The Road from Musalla to Mosque."

those who followed it as a religious group.[60]

In the 1960s, Muslims, mainly Turks, migrated to Austria for work and in 1962, a group of Bosnian Muslims set up the Moslemischer Sozialdienst (Muslim Social Service). This group queried the viability of recognizing the Muslim community under the law of 1912 and started to campaign for this. Eventually in 1979, it was accepted that the law could apply to the new migrant communities and a National Assembly was set up to coordinate the affairs of the Muslims. The Muslim Social Service became the executive of the Assembly and a Mufti was appointed. Some of the benefits of this recognition have been limited access to broadcast media, provision for Islamic education in schools, and certain tax benefits for the Muslim community. Another important organization is the Islamic Center in Vienna, established in 1979 and run by Muslim ambassadors.

The current religious composition of Austria is 85 percent Catholic, 6 percent Protestant, 1 percent Muslim and 0.1 percent Jewish. Among the Muslims, the largest group are the Turks and there is some presence of the Milli Gorus, Sulaymancis, and Diyanet.

Muslim representation in Europe

The issue of representing Muslims in order to communicate with the state has been placed very high on the agenda of some associations and groups in Europe—some would say unnecessarily high. It has been an issue that has at times led to some very adventurous maneuverings, perhaps more befitting of a Hollywood movie than of the reality it bears upon. Many of the states in Europe have asked for a single voice to refer to as an interlocutor in order to deal with Muslims' demands and needs. This seems like a reasonable request, given that it would be very confusing, not to say ineffective, to attempt to address a multitude of requests and opinions from perspectives as diverse as the Muslim community can have. However, upon closer examination it may look like a very unrealistic demand. At least the reality has shown that, on the whole, Muslims in Europe have been quite inept at forming representative coordinating bodies that are fair and democratically run. Spain and Austria, the two instances where this has seemed to work and has resulted in "recognition," have their own particular conditions that have helped. Perhaps the Muslim community is quite small, or largely dominated by one ethnic group, or the historical presence of Muslims has played a role. But even in these cases it is important to ask how representative the bodies that have been recognized really are? It is really up to the Muslim organizations in Europe to think about their present needs and future aspirations and carve out their own agenda, rather than defensively respond to an external

---

[60] See J. Waardenburg, "Religion and State," in *The Integration of Islam*, p. 38, and Nielsen, *Muslims in Western Europe*.

one all the time. The crucial question that needs to be addressed is what do Muslims want in Europe and from Europe?

Pitfalls have occurred in the process of trying to negotiate their rights. Often attempts to form uniting bodies, on the contrary, disunite the Muslim community further, with different groups vying for the limelight and position of authority. The best models of success have been found in those organizations that were formed as ad hoc groups to deal with a single issue of common concern. The desire to appear favorable to the state has also led some organizations to "tone down" their criticisms in order to seek favour for long-term ambitions. The demographic realities of Muslim migrants living in Europe are important factors affecting the ability of Muslims to work together on the basis of the concept of *umma* (community). The communities are usually formed of people from very diverse national or ethnic backgrounds, each with their own linguistic and cultural heritage that they are proud of. There are many differences of *fiqh* (law), approaches to Islam, and even creed. There are, of course, other reasons: the desire to attain a taste of power among the powerless, a prominence in the community, to have one's moment of glory, or to even achieve some financial reward. This can be seen not just on the personal level but also on the collective, organizational level. Often the larger players within umbrella bodies vie for position to promote their own agenda. Another pertinent factor (albeit with positive dimensions as well) is the difficulty in organizing a religion that is so devoid of hierarchy. Any Muslim can set up a mosque, or train to become an Imam, or establish a group of followers. There is no Church, Synod, or Diocese that directs the Muslim community. These are some of the internal problems along the path of representation.

External factors are no less significant. Some Muslim leaders have accused the state of using the need for a single voice as a delaying tactic, or an excuse. When Michael Howard, British Home Secretary in 1994, called leaders from the Muslim community to a meeting, he rejected their request to legislate against religious discrimination on the basis that he could only negotiate with a representative organization that could express a single voice. It was later pointed out that it was he who had invited the leaders and must have thought they were representative to have done so.[61] It is also pointed out that it took Muslims in Austria almost 17 years of lobbying to have a law, one that was already passed, be recognized. Another accusation, which appears to be not without justification, is that the state chooses who to accept and who not to. This can be seen in the case of France and Belgium, both of whom tried to impose representative councils upon the Muslim community and also tried to exclude certain individuals they considered to be fundamentalists. In this way it appears that the state has

---

[61] Vertovec and Peach, *Islam in Europe*, p. 32.

taken upon itself to decide what Islam is or should be. This would seem to be a rather shortsighted approach that could risk deepening the feelings of isolation and alienation that many immigrants already feel. It should also be noted that when the path to democratic representation is closed or even constricted, it could push the insecure to seek refuge in radical gestures (and vice-versa). There is also the important dynamic between the sentiments (and indeed agenda) of foreign Muslim authorities and the priorities and needs of local Muslim communities. As has been shown, a number of important centers across Europe have direct foreign representation.

There are other, more transient problems that the umbrella bodies, and indeed other Muslim organizations, in Europe have faced, such as:

—Lack of familiarity of surroundings and political acumen in dealing with the state;
—Financial constraints;
—Discrimination from the host society;
—Lack of effective leadership;
—Lack of direct political or economic power with which to negotiate.

It is true that as communities go through the process of settlement they will have a hierarchy of needs that they will strive to satisfy. For a relatively new Muslim community that is still struggling with where to pray and what type of food to eat, it is unrealistic to expect that they will be able to create elaborate structures to lobby even for their very dire needs. The initial phase of disorientation that comes with the change of surroundings needs to be overcome. This is not just a matter of a few years but could take generations.

It seems that in the desire to represent and coordinate themselves, Muslims have largely attempted to work with the state, forgetting the opportunity to also work within the state. It is, of course, true that this is not always possible, for example, where public opinion is very alienating, or where citizenship is difficult to obtain. Nonetheless, where possible, minorities can learn much by participating directly in political parties and making the whole society their concern rather than just their own parochial interests. Similarly, there is a tremendous opportunity for working outside the state, within the arena of civil society. All this, however, requires some shift in the Muslim psyche. Are they prepared to admit that Europe is their home and their future? Can they become European? Not only is this an emotional challenge, but it also requires some legal endeavor, *ijtihad*, from Muslim scholars to arrive at a new *fiqh* construct to deal with the contemporary challenges of living in Europe as a minority, while remaining faithful to the sources of Islam.[62]

Finally, there can, at times, be a serious disparity between statements, granting of rights, and recognition in theory, and what actually happens in

---

[62] See Tariq Ramadan, *To be a European Muslim*. Also Jørgen Nielsen, *Towards a European Islam* (Basingstoke: Macmillan, 1999).

reality, in the day-to-day occurrences of people's lives. This is not to trivialize the benefits that can be accrued from formal recognition in some states, whereby equal opportunities policies can be formed that can have far reaching effects. But the point is that all this takes political will power and that means a change in attitudes and removal of stereotypes. This is the crucial challenge, after which recognition, changes in the law, and other such advantages would be quite easily acceptable. Tariq Ramadan goes further to express that the law (of France in this case) is not the real problem today:

On the one hand, Muslims are not aware of the content, scope and even consequences of the law, and, on the other French politicians or academics have [only] an elementary knowledge of Islam as a religion and way of life ... Despite all passionate debates and mutual misunderstanding, the Constitution offers to Muslims an important element of manoeuvrability to fulfil their religious obligations. Laws, however, are not the chief problem today: the State Council, for instance ... has stated that wearing the scarf is not in contradiction with the Constitution. This is one example among many others: it would appear then, that French laws are less on edge concerning Islam than are French politicians.[63]

The search for recognition and representation by Muslims in Western Europe has largely been as elusive and disappointing as the search of the medieval knights for the Holy Grail! What should be borne in mind, however, are the very complex histories and philosophies of the different states in Europe. There is, of course, much in common, but what differentiates is perhaps as much of a consideration, if not more so. It is this cultural specificity that Muslims need to be aware of when they relate to their new European homelands. There is much diversity among Muslims and, despite the common bonds that tie them together, it is difficult to see them as a homogenous community in each country, let alone across Europe. One such difference is the way the state is perceived. Muslims who have become accustomed to living under authoritarian regimes are not well versed in the art of organizing within civil society. A difference can be perceived between Muslims arriving from Eastern Asia (including the Indian sub-continent), where civil society has been present (though perhaps not as pronounced as in Europe), and the Arab world or Turkey, where there is a long tradition of totalitarian rule in which even many Muslim organizations and movements have been banned. The new generations that have grown up in Europe present another dimension to the Muslims' community. For those Muslims who had no chance of organizing themselves outside the state in their inherited traditions, the state has always played an exaggerated role in their lives. This too impinges on

---

[63] Tariq Ramadan, *Muslims in France*, p. 19.

the current discussion. At a time when some would say that society seems to be moving away (albeit very slowly) from the concept of nation state to civil society, the whole debate on recognition by the state and the question of the relationship with the state needs to be analyzed very carefully. This is not to deny that there are very real, immediate needs of Muslim communities that perhaps do need recognition and change in law and policy. Martin Luther King said, "the law does not change the heart but it restrains the heartless," and it is in this context that changes to the law need to be seen. Laws and official decrees will give some minimum protection, but they will not always change the attitude of people—perhaps the very people that have to interpret and implement the law. But it is not only European law that needs to be addressed, Muslim *fiqh* also needs to face the challenge of being in the new European context. Issues that relate to minority status, citizenship in non-Muslim territories, participation in authority, and public life have begun to be addressed, but they need further elaboration.[64] Other debates have also been refocused as a consequence of Muslims living in the West—such as gender issues, dealing with people of other faiths, and dealing with secularism. It would not be an exaggeration to say that by looking in the mirror of Western liberalism and feminism, Muslims have begun to challenge the age old traditional practices of many of the eastern countries with respect to the lack of prominence given to women in society. This is perhaps more a cultural phenomenon than an Islamic issue, but at times it becomes hard for some to distinguish between the two. Muslims have also begun to encounter people of many diverse faiths (and indeed no faith) as fellow students, co-workers, and neighbors. How are these people to be perceived? Are they viewed as "people of the Book," as some Muslim scholars in history expanded this notion to include Hindus and others? What implication does this have on social interaction, marriage, etc? In terms of secularism—how can Muslims engage with political orders that often see religion as a divisive force, or at least one that should be kept private? Is secularism a useful model for dealing with the reality of the multi-religious societies of today? Furthermore, the debate surrounding tradition, modernity, and post-modernity, that not only affects Muslims but also underpins much of Western thought, deserves precise and meticulous analysis by Muslim thinkers.

What Muslims in Europe face is a civilization that seems to have a different *Weltanshauung*, or worldview. Some would respond to this by saying that there is therefore no hope for a common future, but this neglects the degree of tolerance, openness, and understanding that both

---

[64] The European Council for Research and Fatwa (Al-Majlis al-Urubi li'al-Ifta' wa'l-Buhuth) which involves Yusuf al-Qaradawi, Faisal Mawlawi, and some European Muslim scholars, has been meeting annually since 1996 to tackle some of these issues. In the UK there have also been some initiatives by Zaki Badawi of the Muslim College in London and the late Syed al-Darsh of the UK Shariah Council.

European society and Islam are capable of showing. It is the false perceptions and stereotypes that both Muslims and Europe have of each other that need to be addressed. What is needed therefore is multidimensional dialogue in order for Muslims to understand Europe and for Europe to understand Muslims. To go beyond the discourse of "tolerance" and approach "respect" and to go beyond mere "co-existence" and think about "pro-existence."

10

MUSLIM MINORITIES IN EUROPE

THE SILENT REVOLUTION[1]

Jocelyne Cesari

Introduction

As late as the 1960s, Western Europeans still regarded Muslims as aliens who belonged somewhere "out there," beyond the pale of familiar culture and community. This view persisted in spite of a long history of diverse contacts with Islamic countries. Despite Muslims' growing and enduring presence, they were considered migrants by definition. Western European governments differentiated them by their economic status, their race, and their nationality—not by their social or cultural norms.

Islam first emerged as a social issue between Muslim communities and their host societies in Western Europe when European governments changed their immigration policies in response to the 1972–74 recession. Governments introduced family reunification—a plan permitting immediate family members to join migrant laborers in the host country—while at the same time abruptly suspending policies to admit new male workers. Family reunification increased the contact point between Muslims and their hosts: children entered schools, women appeared in daily life, and families gained visibility. Muslim immigrants increasingly demanded recognition of their religious practices, provoking debate among European societies and, occasionally, violent clashes between immigrants and "native" Europeans. Committed to establishing *masjids* (prayer rooms), mosques, and Islamic community organizations, a new generation of Muslims refused to practice their religion covertly or with a sense of shame, as their parents had done. While the social status of their fathers or grandfathers was defined by their economic roles, this "second generation," born and educated in Europe, forced Western European governments and societies to confront the cultural and political consequences of migration.

[1] Special thanks to Susannah Vance for her help in rewriting this chapter.

Unfortunately, Western clichés too often provide the chief framework for coping with this unprecedented situation. The presence of Muslims in Europe is commonly perceived as a cultural or terrorist threat. With this reductive and biased point of departure, many reflections on Islam in Europe fail to reach any enlightening conclusion. The very question that many of these analyses seek to answer—"Do Muslims fit into European societies?"—presupposes a radical opposition between Islam and the West. This opposition formed the basis of Orientalism, which has implicitly informed many subsequent theories on Islam and politics, such as Samuel Huntington's theory of the "clash of civilizations."[2] Orientalism is characterized by a substantialist approach to religion and a linear vision of history; the politics of the Islamic world, according to this view, are inherently theocratic and recidivistic.[3] A survey of the current scholarship on politics and Islam in the Arab and Muslim world often reveals a similar perspective. Rationalized language disguises a normative and value-laden approach, which tends to disparage the political legacy of the Muslim world while equating the Western political tradition with moderation, democracy, and human rights.[4]

Scholarship on Muslims in Europe falls prey to the same essentialist approach that characterizes political analyses of the Arab world. This approach involves a totalization effect: it mistakenly supposes that all immigrants of Muslim origins are devoutly religious and observe all the principles of Islamic law. It thereby overlooks the variations in Muslim belief and practice resulting from the impact of migration, as well as the influence of the pluralistic environment of Western Europe. Considering Muslims as an undifferentiated whole legitimates the view of Islam as a threat, prevalent in much European scholarship on Muslim minorities.

Centering on this recurring theme, explanations of the Muslim "threat" vary from one country to another. In France, various experts and journalists focus on the negative influence of Islam in the suburbs. These accounts have produced a kind of moral panic over the imagined rise of home-grown Muslim extremists. In the autumn of 1995, French police killed Khaled Khelkhal, the chief suspect in a terrorist bombing campaign. This incident provoked widespread public debate about the phenomenon of alienated young French Muslims joining violent Islamist groups. In Great Britain, the Runnymede Trust supported the publication of a report on Islamophobia in 1997. The report, describing "the prejudice and discrimination" Muslims encounter in everyday life, reveals the prevalence of narrow-minded and

---

[2] Samuel Huntington, *The Clash of Civilizations and the Remaking of World Order* (New York: Simon and Schuster, 1996).

[3] Baudouin Dupret, *Interpréter l'islam politique; une approche diachronique de la matrice coranique* (Université Catholique de Louvain, CERMAC, 1994).

[4] Jocelyne Cesari, *Faut-il avoir peur de l'islam?* (Paris: Presses de Sciences-Po, 1997).

xenophobic attitudes towards Muslims in Britain.[5] In Germany, Heitmeyer's book Verlockander Fundamentalismus, which implicitly equated Islam with violent and subversive activities and branded Muslim youth as "at risk," generated heated public debate.[6]

This kind of vision implies three major misperceptions. Firstly, it neglects the important transformations in Islamic identity under way among the generations born or educated in the West. These Muslim youths are involved in a quite new secularization process, which is repositioning Islam into the private sphere. Secondly, this essentialist vision does not take into account the fact that different cultures and ethnic boundaries affect both the meaning and the content of Muslim identities. Sectarian, ethnic, and nationalist groupings, in many cases, play a more prominent role in Muslim identity than any abstract notion of a universal brotherhood of believers, or *umma*. Finally, these analyses are often founded upon an artificial and misguided opposition between Islam and modernity. This opposition prevents analysts from understanding that references to Islamic law, or to the vocabulary of Islam in general, do not signify archaic attitudes, but instead demonstrate the capacity of this culture to reconcile its religious traditions with issues of social and political modernization.[7]

Islam as a transnational religion

In Europe, and in the West more generally, claims asserting an antagonism between Islam and modernity are situated within a broader debate about the "return of religion." The modern notion of religion as a system of personal belief, disconnected from the political and social realms, sheds little light on either the social function of Islam historically or the new forms of religiosity in Europe. One should not forget that the Western notion of the separation of church and state is not only relatively new, but also under intense scrutiny and debate today. This concept has artificially compartmentalized religion, doing violence to its nature and reinforcing a static, reified conception of religious traditions, rather than revealing their dynamic inner nature. According to this post-Enlightenment perspective, any religion whose doctrines do not conform with the relegation of spirituality to the private sphere appears to be retrogressive.

Increasingly, however, this approach is no longer dominant. Rather than examining how Islam can fit into a modern European context, it is more constructive to rephrase the question. What new forms of interaction between religion and politics are developing today, both in the Arab-

---

5 Runnymede Trust Report *Islamophobia: A Challenge for Us All* (London: Runnymede Trust, 1997).

6 Wilhelm Heitmeyer, *Verlockender Fundamentalismus* (Frankfurt-am-Main: Suhrkamp, 1996).

7 François Burgat, *L'islamisme en face* (Paris: La Découverte, 1996).

Muslim world and in those societies where the separation of church and state originated? In a period when the basic values of Western societies, such as individualism, science, and progress, are being called into question, when modernity and Western world are no longer synonymous, Third World societies are now addressing modernization and other pressing social issues in their own cultural languages. The use of Islam in the political and social arenas in Islamic countries demonstrates this quest for cultural authenticity. In European societies, the return of religious references to social and public life serves as another example of the growing tendency to blend religious and political meanings.

To explain this greater mobility of meanings, it is necessary to articulate a new conceptual framework to overcome the separation of politics and religion.[8] In fact, the two spheres are characterized by similar social and symbolic processes, and many scholars are currently examining how beliefs circulate from one realm to the other. Despite their similarities, religion, unlike politics, requires the legitimization of tradition. The strong role of tradition in the transmission of religious beliefs produces two consequences: on the one hand, dogmatic rigidity, and on the other, the control of consciousness and behavior. This control may be exerted simultaneously in two directions: it extends outward from the religious community, expanding the influence of religion in society; at the same time, it works within the community, reinforcing the barriers that separate the group's members from the rest of society. Depending upon their social and cultural contexts, religious communities exercise widely varying combinations of external and internal ideological control. The distinction between internal and external controls sheds light on the relationship between religion and politics. Religious groups defining membership *extensively* link their traditions with political and social processes and translate their doctrines into a broader public mission, while groups defining membership *intensively* emphasize the bond among members and the individual's spiritual experience.

This perspective allows us to draw a critical distinction between the workings of Islamist movements in the Arab-Muslim world and those in the West. So-called fundamentalism in Muslim countries refers to an extension of Islamic references to different social, cultural, economic, and political spaces which were formerly secular, at least since independence. Islamization in the Western context, on the other hand, operates on the intensive level, reinforcing the primacy of Islam in members' lives, often to the detriment of other social bonds. The minority condition of Muslims in the West is the chief factor producing these different emphases. For many Muslims in Europe, whose parents or grandparents emigrated from countries where Islam is the state religion, or at least the religion of the majority of the population, the

---

[8] Danièle Hervieu-Léger, *La Religion pour mémoire* (Paris: Cerf, 1993), and Patrick Michel, *Religion et politique. La grande mutation* (Paris: Albin Michel, 1994).

experience of life as a minority in a context of political and cultural pluralism is a novelty. In their efforts to practice Islam in Europe, they confront problems previously unexamined by the Islamic tradition: Muslim theology has not yet provided a systematic formulation of the religious implications of minority status. As the ranks of Muslim minorities in the West swell, however, many Muslim theologians are approaching this issue today.

Since the development and institutionalization of Islam in Europe necessarily involves interaction between Muslim minority groups and governments and religious organizations in the Middle East and North Africa, any examination of this subject must be linked with an analysis of cultural globalization. The improvement of communications and transportation, as well as the striking growth in recent international migrations, have contributed to new forms of ethnic groups, often labeled "transnational networks." In this shrinking world, it seems that nobody leaves forever. Technological developments constantly provide new and more efficient means of keeping in touch. Increasingly, people identify simultaneously with different nations and cultures, and manage activities and loyalties that cross national boundaries. The term "diaspora," whose meaning is extrapolated from its historical connection with the Jewish condition, may be useful in analyzing these new phenomena. A group must possess three main traits to comprise a diaspora: the awareness of ethnic identity; the existence of group organizations; and the persistence of relations—whether monetary, political or psychological—with the homeland.[9]

"Diaspora" refers to the ongoing ties, bridging both time and space, which ethnic groups maintain with their countries of origin; therefore, a diaspora may be considered as a specific sort of transnational network. Religion is an important aspect of these transnational networks and activities, since it increases the necessity for international circulation and mobility. In the case of Islam, diverse needs and activities—from the demand in Europe for religious leaders and teachers from the Middle East and North Africa, to the funds that Muslim-majority countries donate to religious organizations in Europe—contribute to the movement of people and money across the borders of nation-states.

Thus, mobile dynamics establish the autonomy of social groups in the international relations field. These social groups do not strive to assert themselves as collective actors in a transnational space; instead, private interests push them into this unintended role. Family reunions, marriage arrangements, and business activities, for example, are usually motivated by individual or family interests, but these activities often entail international mobility. Private decisions affect not only visiting rights, family

[9] Sheffer provides a more extensive definition of diasporas. Gabi Sheffer, "Whither the study of ethnic Diasporas? Some theoretical, definitional, analytical and comparative considerations," in *The Networks of Diasporas,* ed. Georges Prévélakis (Paris: L'Harmattan, 1996), pp. 37–46.

groupings, and monetary flows, but also religious, linguistic, and cultural models, indirectly producing a collective result on the international scene.

A glimpse into the complex interaction of local, national, and international groupings characterizing Islam in Europe reveals some of the short-falls of current scholarship on the subject. Because of the importance of transnational networks for the European Muslim community, any analysis that stresses Muslims' obligations to the host society, to the exclusion of international influences, fails to provide a balanced view. The adaptation of Islam to the democratic context is a two-dimensional activity, involving both the status of Islam in the countries of origin and the status of ethnicity in the different host countries.

Developments in the status of Muslim minorities hinge equally on the political and cultural climate of the *dar al-Islam*—the Muslim world as traditionally defined—and that of the European countries.

The emergence of a post-migration religious minority

The core dynamics of Islam in Europe are characterized by conflict, nego-tiation, and compromise—between the ethnic and religious ties, between the host country and the country of origin, and among Muslim minorities of different ethnic and national backgrounds. These processes, producing controversy and challenging the status quo in both Europe and the Middle East/North Africa region, disprove stereotypical views of Islam as anti-democratic and resistant to political and cultural change.[10]

One dynamic driving minority Islam in Europe might be described as a conflict between the specific bonds of ethnic and national groupings, and the universal bond of Islam. Islamic organizations and social movements in Europe are often anchored in ethnic and national ties derived from the country of origin, rather than the transnational *umma*. These ethnic ties often endure over generations, qualifying European Muslims' ties with the "homeland" as a diaspora, even though individual Muslims frequently deny the strength of their communal bond with the country of origin. North African immigrants are mostly likely to evince this discrepancy between real and perceived ethnic and nationalist ties. Families of Algerian descent, even if they do not describe themselves as devoted to Algeria, brave political violence and unrest to visit their families frequently. Attachment to the homeland often takes the form of family ties, rather than an overt nationalist bond: families of immigrant descent send home remit-tances, trade goods through the black market in the country of origin, and search for potential spouses for their children through family networks in North Africa. Other forms of attachment are more explicit and less

---

[10] Jocelyne Cesari, *Être musulman en France, associations, militants et mosquées* (Paris: Karthala, 1994), and *Être musulman en France aujourd'hui* (Paris: Hachette, 1997).

intertwined with family relationships, such as the growing number of satellite dishes in North African communities in France, allowing households to receive Arab television channels.

The challenge of establishing an institutional framework for Islam, as well as the strength of family and cultural ties, contributes to the tendency toward ethnic and national factionalism among Muslims in Europe. When first-generation migrants in France launched the first public calls for Islamic worship spaces, they made their demands independently, with no assistance from organizations and governments in the countries of origin. It soon became clear, however, that the difficult task of creating of a network of Islamic institutions in France would require scholars, teachers, and funding from the Middle East and North Africa. Imams recruited to manage mosques in Europe usually accept the offer, because these positions allow for more economic security and political stability than they could hope to attain at home. Also, their position as religious authorities living in Europe often allows them a safe space in which to oppose political regimes in the Middle East and North Africa. Immigrant circles in Europe frequently serve as sounding boards for political dissent that would normally be prohibited in the countries of origin. The Berber rights movement, initially suppressed in both Algeria and Morocco, first gained a foothold in France; Germany, similarly, has provided fertile ground for the Turkish Islamist movement. Both the political agendas of religious leaders in Europe and the influence of funding, often donated from one "home country" to its nationals abroad, accentuate ethnic and national divisions among Muslims.

Today, however, many young Muslims are attempting to combat this tendency toward factionalism. While previous generations accepted the primacy of ethnic and national ties in the practice of their religion, Muslims in Europe today often feel that these networks conflict with the universal bond of Islam. European Muslims of North African descent are among the most likely to experience this sense of conflict. Since their countries of origin do not offer widespread access to Islamic education, North African Muslims in Europe often seek intensive training in the Islamic tradition in Saudi Arabia or Egypt, rather than in their parents' homeland. Islamic ties, for these young Muslims, refer exclusively to the concept of *umma*, or community of believers. They express their transnational Islamic identity not just through their espousal of an orthodox Islam, free from the "taint" of national or ethnic traditions, but also through their sense of solidarity with their "brothers" abroad. The outcry of Muslims all over Europe during the controversy in Britain surrounding Salman Rushdie's novel *The Satanic Verses* attests to this solidarity, as did their concern for the plight of Muslims affected by the Gulf War and ethnic conflict in Yugoslavia.

In the face of these developments, the question of whether the religious group should reinforce or transcend ethnic bonds has become the most contentious issue surrounding organized Islam in the West. This debate has given rise to fierce competition among religious leaders seeking to impose their own conception of the community in different European countries. Some of them intend to maintain a relationship with the home-lands and a sort of ethnic partition of the religious community, while others defend a global view of Islam.[11] It is illusory to think that European Islam can cut itself off from the influence of different Muslim groups' countries of origin. Therefore, the main issue on the agenda should be to find conditions under which European Muslims may both assert their specificity as a minority, and form a legitimate part of the *umma*.

As well as a tension between ethnic and broader religious loyalties, a complex triangular interaction among Muslim minority groups, their receiving countries in Europe, and their countries of origin also develops. Homeland governments frequently try to manipulate the presence of their nationals in Europe to their advantage, in an attempt to improve relations both with individual host countries and with the European Union. At the Barcelona Conference of November 1995, for example, North African governments used the migration issue as a bargaining chip, demanding more benefits from the Euro-Mediterranean policy.

A similar relationship of bargaining and compromise has taken shape between Germany and Turkey. The Turkish state made no attempts to intervene in the affairs of its nationals in Germany during the first wave of migration, in the 1970s. After the military coup of September 1980, how-ever, it established a European annex of the Directorate for Religious Affairs in Ankara, the Dyanet Isleri Turk Islam Birigli.[12]

The dynamics of conflict and compromise visible among European Muslim groups today have dovetailed with social change in the Middle East and North Africa to combat traditional perceptions of Islam as an inherently anti-democratic and static worldview. Commonplace views among Western scholars hold that Islam condones unequal relationships between believers and unbelievers and between men and women, and that it is intolerant of diversity and political dissent. In cases in which Islamist groups are actually prominent players in electoral politics, such as in Egypt, Jordan, and Algeria, skeptics often speak of these groups as "hijacking democracy." As more Muslim countries begin to experiment with democratization, however, they are disproving stereotypes about Islamic society. Muslim scholars and political thinkers have condoned many techniques of modern democratic political organization—such as elections, representation, parliamentary rule, and the separation of powers—as compatible with Islam as they under-stand it. They have also embraced key values such as freedom, equality, individual responsibility, and accountability, despite the fact that general

[11] Jocelyne Cesari, *Géopolitique des Islams* (Paris: Economica, 1997).
[12] Valérie Amiraux. "Transnationalism as a Resource for Turkish Islamic Associations in Germany" (Seminar Paper MIG/25, Florence: European University Institute, 1998).

principles are confined to the framework of the Shariah.[13] Viewing these developments, some commentators have argued that the prevalence of autocratic governments and the lack of opportunities for democratic input in many Muslim-majority states may be attributed more to political impediments than to any inherent tendency of Islamic society.[14]

The settlement of Muslims in democratic societies plays a key role in changing the terms of this debate. The "transplantation" of Muslims into Europe, necessitating interaction with a largely non-Muslim environment, is crystallizing the social and cultural questions surrounding the role of Islam in modernity. Historically, the influx of Muslim populations to the West represents a unique challenge: Islamic law, elaborated chiefly between the 8th and 9th centuries, did not examine the possibility of Muslim minority communities resulting from voluntary migration, since Islamic society dominated the cultural, political, and economic realms during this period. Muslim minority groups are contesting traditional views of Islam as a social system by repositioning the relationship between religion and the public sphere. This process involves the individualization and privatization of Islam.

The emergence of a Muslim individual

Their status as members of a post-migration religious minority affects the ways in which contemporary Muslim youth identify with religion. "First-generation Islam," hampered by an uprooted sense of national identity and a weak organizational structure, is increasingly giving way to new forms of religiosity, characterized by individualism, secularism, and privatization. This emergence of a Muslim individual is partially the consequence of the migration process. Exile implies changes in the ways religious beliefs and practices are transmitted from one generation to the next. Among North African immigrants, the gap between the values of the first generation and the values of their children is more pronounced than among other immigrant groups.[15] As part of working-class French society, the parents have struggled to maintain the cultural system of their birth country, while their children have been socialized more by French institutions, such as schools and social workers. In general, as well, the first generation failed to pass along Arabic language skills to their children, and abandoned many North African

---

[13] Ahmad S. Moussali, "Discourses on Human Rights and Pluralistic Democracy," in *Islam in a Changing World: Europe and the Middle East*, A. Jerichow and J. Baek Simonsen (Richmond, Sy: Curzon Press, 1997), pp. 45–90.

[14] Yvonne Yazbeck Haddad, *Islamists and the Challenge of Pluralism* (Washington, DC: Center for Contemporary Arab Studies and Center for Muslim-Christian Understanding, 1995).

[15] Hélène Malewska-Peyre, *Crise d'identité et déviance chez les jeunes immigrés* (Paris: La Documentation française, 1982).

cultural habits. The growth of a "vernacular" Islam in Europe is the most interesting sign of this change: increasingly, public discussions, sermons, and literature are conveyed in the local European language. As the cultural legacy associated with the country of origin diminishes, non-first-generation Muslims begin to conceive of their religion less in terms of family and tradition, and more in terms of individual belief.

This social adaptation process of Muslim minority groups has placed Islam within the three interrelated paradigms of secularization, individualization, and privatization, which have until recently been distinctive characteristics of Western societies. Secularization refers to the decreasing functionality of religion in the structural differentiation of society. Individualization means a sharpening of self-consciousness, privileging personal choice over the constraints of religious tradition. Individualization is often associated with privatization: religion is increasingly confined to the private sphere, and religious values and rules are not placed at the center of one's personal orientation to life, but are conceived as a kind of annex or compartment. Like French Christians, many Muslims now identify most strongly with their religion during large festivals and at birth, marriage, and death. A related pattern, often referred to as consumerism, affects European Islam as it does other religions, especially among young people. Like buyers, people are increasingly choosing which tenets and rules of their religion they will recognize and which they will ignore. The inculcation of Western values through the educational systems certainly has an influence and can explain the emphasis on critical debate and reflexive questioning.[16]

But individualization, as well as reflexive questioning, can also be associated with collective and social identification with religion. In other words, strict observance and fundamentalism are also the outcome of individual choice. This tendency toward individualization explains why one generation evinces two seemingly opposite trends: a wholesale abandonment of Muslim attachments, and the attraction to Islam as a global symbol of resistance to Western political and cultural imperialism.[17]

Privatization of Islam

For these young people to define themselves as Arab or Muslim represents a symbolic assertion that is not always connected with their everyday lives. Usually, they have adopted the most important values of French society, such as liberty and equality. As they absorb the mores of the host

---

[16] Alistair Rogers and Steven Vertovec, *Muslim European Youth: Reproducing Ethnicity, Religion Culture* (Aldershot: Ashgate Ltd, 1998).

[17] Jocelyne Cesari, *Musulmans et Républicains. Les jeunes, l'Islam et la France* (Brussels: Complexe, 1998).

country, they often grow more critical of the situation in their family's country of origin, and suspect that their relatives consider them too westernized. Due to these tensions, the decision of young people to define themselves in France as Arab or Muslim indicates less a feeling of nostalgia for their country of origin than a response to their situation in France. Often, it is a reaction to discrimination. The relationship between these youths and French society is unequal, because their families' countries of origin are considered poor. In the case of North African immigrants, this inequality is also a consequence of colonial history. The more the relations between the groups are unequal, the more migrants are evaluated through pejorative ethnic categories. Even if these second-generation Muslims automatically obtain French nationality (according to the *jus soli*), they are still defined and considered as Arab or Muslim.

This negative perception produces different and opposite reactions among North Africans. The majority consider Arab and Muslim identity as positive, despite their negative connotations in the French context. In others words, they manage a semantic reversal: the more their Islamic and Arab origins are despised, the stronger their identification with them. But this identification with the Muslim or Arab world does not mean that they live as Muslims or Arabs; it is a more symbolic allegiance. At the same time, because this cultural identity is derived from values transmitted through the family, it is also a very emotional and passionate identity. This identification with the Muslim world is not limited to their parents' country, but extends to the worldwide Muslim community, especially involving solidarity with and interest in struggles such as the Palestinian cause and conflicts in Bosnia and Chechnya. The focus on the Muslim world was particularly significant during the Gulf War, during which many European Muslims felt solidarity with the Iraqi people, while at the same time wishing not to be suspected of disloyalty toward France.[18]

Young Muslims often feel an affinity to both their families' values and the French cultural system. This coincidence of values is not hypocritical or deceitful, but an attempt to manage different loyalties. Attempts to juggle the two value systems are easier when young people's identification with France is rooted in the local communities where they were born and educated. A more abstract "French" identity, focusing on political values such as liberty and democracy, is more likely to produce ideological conflict with young people's feelings of loyalty toward their countries of origin. Identification with their local context is often more meaningful for young Muslims than is French nationalism.

---

[18] Jocelyne Cesari, "La guerre du Golfe et les Arabes de France," *Revue du Monde Musulman et de la Méditerranée*, no. HS, 1991, pp. 125–29. During the Gulf War, this mistrust clearly appeared in the attention paid to them by the French political class and within public opinion because their loyalty to French institutions was questioned.

Although the new generations are not always practicing believers, they do frequently respect Islamic rules and values. Most define themselves as believers and have a positive perception of Islam. This attests to their desire to remain within their parents' community. To them Islam signifies, above all, important rites and episodes of family life, such as feasts and holidays. Meaningful occasions create a rupture with the space and time of the dominant social environment. This emphasis on festive moments, rather than on the daily practice of Islam, is due in part to the fact that most second-generation Muslims in Europe have not received a real religious education, either inside or outside their families.[19] This lack of religious education within the family can be explained by their parents' attitude towards Islam during the first period of migration. During that time they neglected Islamic prescriptions, because they did not consider themselves to be permanently settled in French society. Moreover, within the traditional rural family in North Africa, religious grandfathers or uncles are more involved in children's religious education than their parents. This important role of the extended family cannot be duplicated in France, and the migrant family is often unable to undertake the responsibility of religious education, particularly if it has been separated and then reunited by the migration process.[20]

To describe their relationship with Islam, young European Muslims often distinguish between practicing religion and believing religion. Islam forms part of their cultural legacy within the private sphere, serving as a source of ethical and moral values, but it has no direct influence on their social and public behavior. This discrepancy between the private and public functions of religion is especially acute for the upwardly mobile. Individuals thus demonstrate their autonomy from the group, and act as mediators between the content and the application of Islamic law. In this way, they express their inventiveness and liberty. This profound change in the practice of Islam is related to new forms of religiosity within modern societies. The believer no longer obeys the norms legitimated by tradition or institutions, but instead chooses among "salvation goods" according to preference.[21] An individual logic thus moderates the collective dimension of membership of the Islamic community. The attitudes of second-

---

[19] For certain age groups over 25 there were no Quranic schools when they were children. The situation is now different because the development of Islamic associations in France since the early 1980s was accompanied by the foundation of numerous Quranic courses. The majority of mosques established during this period provided religious education for children.

[20] These two stages refer to two periods. In the first, the North African migrant came to France alone: he married in his home country and often went back to meet his wife and his first children. In the second period he let his family come to France and new children were born there.

[21] Françoise Champion and Danièle Hervieu-Léger, *De l'émotion en religion. Renaissance et traditions* (Paris: Le Centurion, 1990).

generation parents toward the religious education of their children reflect this logic of consumerism: they selectively pass on to their children the tenets of Islam they consider important, preferring a liberal education. This trend is most prevalent among well-educated parents.

But the individualization of Islam is constrained by two firm religious prescriptions: circumcision and the prohibition of intermarriage. Muslims in Europe attach great meaning to circumcision. Although this requirement is not one of the "five pillars of Islam," it is considered a strong shaping force of the identity of the community. In a non-Muslim society, it acts as the ultimate sign of attachment to their origins. The restriction of marriage to non-Muslims, another important outward symbol of Muslim identity, is more complicated in its application. According to Islamic law, only women are barred from marrying non-Muslims; a man may marry any woman, as long as she is a member of the "people of the Book" (Christians, Jews, Muslims). When men choose not to marry non-Muslim women, their opposition is justified not by religious arguments, but by cultural ones: they contend that there would be a cultural incompatibility between husband and wife and a risk of domination of one by the other. Even so, the latest national statistics from France show a growing number of marriages across religious boundaries among young Muslim men.[22] Among women, given the greater taboo, sexual relationships and cohabitation with non-Muslim men occur more frequently than does intermarriage. Women who are financially autonomous, and thus able to exert independence from their families, are the most likely to become involved with non-Muslims. These relationships rarely result in marriage, however, since this would call the woman's Muslim identity into question, and might lead her family to disown her.

Most Muslims born and educated in France try to find some coherence between their parents' values and those of French society. That explains why, even if they are not always strict in their practice of Islam, they still prize this part of their family legacy. The emphasis they place on privacy in their relationship to Islam constitutes a radical break with the status accorded to religion in their parents' countries of origin. But individuality can also be associated with so-called fundamentalism.

---

[22] Jocelyne Streiff-Fenart, *Les Couples franco-maghrébins en France* (Paris: L'Harmattan, 1989). Two social circles seem to favor intermarriages: university and associations. It should be noted that it is impossible to get precise information about intermarriages in France because official statistics only provide information about weddings between foreigners and nationals. There is no measure of exogamy among the French-born generations because it is illegal to officially differentiate people according to religious or ethnic origin. It is possible to state that between 1974 and 1985, the number of marriages between North Africans and French people doubled, rising from 2,703 from 5,189, thereby outstripping the marriages between Italian and French or between Portuguese and French. François Munoz-Perez and Michèle Tribalat, "Mariages d'étrangers et mariages mixtes en France," *Population* 3, 1984, pp. 427–62.

Islam as a new form of citizenship

The Islamist trend among young European Muslims is very recent. Although they still represent a small minority, a growing number of young people have become stricter in their respect of Islamic rules. As they grow acquainted with the texts and practices of orthodox Islam, they often distance themselves from the religious habits of their parents, which they perceive as superstitious. They distinguish these customs from what they call "the real Islam." Displaying impressive initiative, they either learn on their own or seek the help of young students who come from Arab countries and are often committed to various offshoots of the Muslim Brotherhood, to *al-Nahdah* of Rashid Ghannushi in Tunisia, or to Algerian Islamist movements like the Islamic Salvation Front (FIS) and Hamas. For these young religious leaders, Islam cannot be reduced to ethics or confined to privacy. Instead, it informs social behavior and can even justify collective action. Although some of them are involved in opposition groups contesting the regimes of their home countries, they do not use Islam to disseminate political propaganda among young Muslims in Europe. Instead, they intend to preserve Islam among young people and to prevent their assimilation.

For young people, Islam is a credible alternative to the prospect of unemployment, drugs, alcohol, or delinquency. It allows them to recover some personal dignity and to project a better image of themselves. They seek to reaffirm their identity and to live according to Islamic teachings. Contrary to one widely held opinion, this phenomenon is not exclusively an expression of opposition to the West, but is also a positive affirmation of self-confidence among young Muslims. Young people are often turning to an Islam purified from the accidents of its traditional readings. For the more educated among them, it is no more an Islam of the Moroccan, Algerian, or Pakistani countryside, but instead a return to the basics of Islamic teaching through immediate contact with the sources, the Quran and the Sunnah. Islam in the West should have a specific and appropriate actualization; this is the message the young are clearly conveying.

In order to achieve this "Islam of the West," scholars are reflecting on the legacy of the Quran and the Sunna, in order to re-examine the relevance of the concepts of *Dar al-Islam* and *Dar al-Harb.* These terms, literally meaning "house of Islam" and "house of war," are used in the classic texts to distinguish between Muslim and enemy territories. The term *Dar al-Harb* is not appropriate to describe the condition of Muslim citizens in secularized democracies: most of them, or their ancestors, migrated voluntarily to these countries, and for the most part they live there peaceably. That is why the opinions of *ulama* (religious scholars) in the Muslim world on the situation of Islam in Europe have evolved. The condition of large populations of Muslims permanently settled in Europe has forced scholars to reconsider their previous admonitions to distance themselves from society, not to take the nationality of a Western society, and to keep in mind that they must "go back home" as soon as possible. All of these statements, presented as *fatwas* in the past, do not correspond with social realities today. A considerable number of *ulama* have come to the conclusion that Muslims in Europe should be able to organize their futures according to the tenets of Islam in their adopted countries.[23]

Since developments in Europe inform many of the new trends in Islamic thinking, it is necessary to analyze Islamic renewal movements in relationship to the European context. It is impossible to understand the behavior of young Muslims in Europe today without bearing in mind the strong influence that their European environment exerts on their beliefs and opinions. One prevalent trend in Europe has particularly encouraged Islamic renewal among young people: the challenging of previously accepted notions of progress and modernity. For some young Muslims, religious membership fills the gap left by weakened institutions, such as schools, political parties, and trade unions, which had traditionally strengthened social solidarity and projected an image of progress. Economic recessions further challenge the mythos of social mobility and reinforce young adults' impression of something missing in their European environments, a gap which only religion can fill. These social realities are prompting young people of other creeds, as well, to turn to religion. For young people in search of collective identity, Islamization may serve simply as a source of solidarity, rather than a belief system requiring strict practice. Following in the footsteps of past social movements, such as the civil rights and anti-racist demonstrations of the 1980s in France, some young people today are using Islam as a vector for collective action and protest.

The Islamization of European political cultures

Immigration and citizenship laws, while crucial, are not the only factors impacting the status of minority groups in European countries; policies dictating the status of religion in the public domain play an equally important role. A cursory comparison of the immigration policies of France and Germany would seem to indicate that France accords more respect and openness to newcomers than Germany. In the 1960s, Germany implemented a *Gastarbeiter* (guest worker) policy: permitting migrant workers to enter in response to a labor shortage, the German government granted them only provisional residence permits. This precarious legal status, combined with the German policy of privileging of blood-based over territory-based citizenship criteria, makes it very difficult for the migrant workers of the 1970s and 1980s to gain citizenship today. In response to the obstacles they have met, immigrants have organized associations, often under the auspices of their country of origin, to represent their cause before the German

[23] Cesari, *Musulmans et Républicains*.

government. In France, on the other hand, where *jus soli* is applied, the children of migrants rapidly become nationals, and therefore citizens.[24]

When one examines the structures accommodating ethnic and religious diversity in Europe, however, the seeming openness of France's immigration procedures belies other social policies that inhibit the cultural integration of minorities. Political culture in France is built upon the idea of the individual as the basic social unit. Social solidarity is thus based on the equality of individuals. Ethnic and religious ties should, according to this perspective, play no role in the public sphere. The nation is conceived of as a framework for individual emancipation. That is why France adopted a policy of equal treatment and punishment of all discrimination, while carefully avoiding the recognition of group rights. This perception of group-based religious identity as a threat to France's secular culture may explain the nervousness with which the public reacted to Muslim demands that France permit the wearing of the headscarf in public schools.

The political traditions of the Netherlands and Britain, unlike that of France, accord respect to particularistic identities and have historically recognized ethnic and religious communities within the public sphere. While France emphasizes the integration of individuals, Britain accords primacy to processes of collective bargaining and collective integration. Civil society, rather than the state, develops the mechanisms of social solidarity. The political process in Britain is based not on the absolute equality of individuals, as in France, but on civil ethics, such as mutual respect and fairness. This emphasis favors pragmatic solutions accommodating the concerns of different social groups. At the same time, however, it also implies that British society is more tolerant of inequality among ethnic and religious groups on the national level. In Germany, more diversity is permitted in the public sphere than in France, and more formal organization of religious and ethnic groups is required than in Britain. On the one hand, the German political system holds that any group forming part of German society should have a right to representation in public; if particularistic ties are recognized as part of society as a whole, this view contends, all members will maintain a stable identification with society. This, by the way, is one of the reasons for the hesitation of the German public to admit new groups: integration into German society takes usually one to two generations longer than in other European countries. On the other hand, the German system requires more systematic and centralized organization of minority groups, in order to avoid too much heterogeneity and therefore inequality.[25]

These models, reflecting the shape and dynamics of their respective civil societies, are now changing under the influence of the Muslim

---

[24] Jocelyne Cesari, *L'Islam en Europe* (Paris: La Documentation française, 1995).

[25] Werner Schiffauer, "Islam as a Civil Religion: Political Culture and the Organization of Diversity in Germany," in *Debating Cultural Hybridity: Multicultural Identities and the Politics of Antiracism*, ed. P. Werbner and T. Modood (London: Zed Books, 1997).

presence. In all of Western Europe, the appearance of Islam has introduced a heated debate on religious freedom, tolerance, and the acceptable limits of the public expression of faith. The different position accorded to religion in each state's conception of social membership, however, has made for very different interactions between Islam and the "secularized West" within Europe. In France, the "headscarves affair" challenged widely held assumptions that *laïcité* prohibits public displays of religious affiliation. In Britain, Indian and Pakistani Muslim groups are contesting race-oriented policies that brand them as "blacks" or "Asians," rather than Muslims. Similarly, in Germany, Turkish Muslim groups seek to form representative bodies authorized by German legislation, which will advocate their interests as German Muslims rather than as alien "Turks." Thus, the "Islam question" galvanizes the most controversial social debates endemic to each European country: the status of religion in France, the status of ethnicity in the UK, and the status of nationality in Germany.

In France, this debate concerns the content of secularity, or *laïcité*: membership of the Islamic community creates confusion over the boundaries between the public and private spheres, which have appeared to be stable since the passage of a law declaring the separation of church and state in 1905. Islam, whose doctrines emphasize the social and communal facets of religious belief, cannot be confined to homes and places of worship, as Catholicism has been. Islam has disrupted the balance among three major "pillars" of French political life: unity, respect of religious pluralism, and liberty of conscience. Recent decades have witnessed a shift in the sources of social conflict: while until the 1960s, most internal strife in France stemmed from workers' demands for economic and social rights, the battleground today has shifted into the cultural realm. As religious and ethnic minorities demand the right to collective recognition in the public sphere, the French political ethos of individualism is unequipped to respond to this new dimension of social conflict.

From now on, each country in Europe must face up to a new challenge: the institutionalization of Islam within the present framework of legislation. Different initiatives have been taken: CORIF in France (Council for Reflection on Islam in France), the Supreme Council of Muslims in Belgium, and national organizations in Britain and in the Netherlands, charged with overseeing the building of mosques, the employment of imams, and the availability of *halal* meat. But these attempts to organize European Islam have until now been relatively unsuccessful, because of the national, ethnic, and doctrinal cleavages dividing Muslim populations. Does this factionalism perhaps reflect the anxiety of a Western culture attempting to impose its own standards, without really taking into account either the demands of immigrant Muslims or the process of religious transformation in transplanted Islam? Admittedly, the transition phase inaugurating a uniquely European Islam is in evidence everywhere, but the social and cultural dimension of religious belonging tends to be overrated, and European Muslims are still far from a confessional Islam, focusing chiefly on ritual and cult. The future of European Islam hinges on the way young Muslims in Europe today will live their beliefs, and how they will eventually reinterpret Islamic doctrines to accommodate their needs.

Finally, one must consider the ways in which the construction of the European Union could influence the form and the content of Islamic expression. The 1986 stage of European unification initiated visa requirements for nationals of North African countries, and through the approval of the Schengen agreements by Italy, Spain, and Portugal in 1990 and 1991, the borders separating Europe from its southern and eastern neighbors were reinforced. At the same time, social issues such as the controversy surrounding the Gulf War and the publication of *The Satanic Verses* in Britain brought European Muslims together in protest, provoking hostile reactions from Europeans who, for the first time, viewed Europe's immigrant Muslims as a unified whole. All these events led to both questioning of the significance of Muslims' collective presence in Europe and radicalization of European Islamic identity. Some commentators fear that this trend in Europe could feed on, and contribute to, the radicalization of Islam under way on the other side of the Mediterranean.

Pluralism as an issue

How to adopt a European nationality while retaining one's sense of ethnic origins and faith is not a new issue in the Netherlands or Britain. It is new, however, in France and Germany. Indeed, the problem of national identity and multiculturalism remains a contested issue. This debate concerns not only countries with a tradition of assimilation, but also countries where multiculturalism is politically recognized.

In the past, culture has been defined as a kind of luggage packed with goods from home, which one may either decide to keep or alternatively replace with new goods offered by the host country. Superficial features of the country of origin, such as clothing, food, rituals, and more importantly, language, are usually tolerated rather than encouraged in Europe's host countries. As a consequence, the proclaimed multicultural society, which was intended to grow out of the freedom of cultural choice, has remained an undefined entity. The politically proclaimed freedom of cultural choice has led to a paradoxical situation. European societies emphasize, at the same time, tolerance of cultural diversity and implicit normative assumptions of the superiority of mainstream cultural norms, values and models. "We," as representatives of the dominant collective community, create the "others."[26] At the

---

[26] Wuokko Knocke, "Problematizing Multiculturalism: respect, tolerance and the limits to tolerance," *Nora: Nordic Journal of Women's Studies* 2:5, 1997, pp. 127–36.

political level, the space reserved for the development of multiculturalism has been managed and defined by mainstream power holders. Religious communities, as important as these may be, are segregated into ethnic niches. Public funding, as well as administrative rules and regulations, have served as instruments for controlling religious minority groups from above. In the Netherlands, for example, the superior status of the dominant culture is taken for granted, while other cultures are viewed as problematic.[27]

Moreover, the situation of Muslims in the West is quite different from the status of other religious minorities (migrants or indigenous converts) who, however ethnically diverse, possess a shared Judeo-Christian culture. Muslims find themselves in a Western cultural context where they are often regarded as completely "other," just as Jews were in the past. Ignorant attitudes among Europeans, who often equate Islam with extremism and terrorism, contribute to this stigmatization; so, too, does Europeans' failure to appreciate the extent to which Islam is part of a Judeo-Christian-Islamic tradition. Despite its monotheism and prophetic tradition, Islam has been grouped with "foreign religions" in Western scholarship, university curricula, libraries, and bookstores. While there are significant differences among the three "Semitic" faiths, there is also a common theological outlook and shared ethical monotheism, which can serve as a source of mutual respect and confirmation, rather than confrontation. Many Europeans interpreted the demonstrations, violence, and threats that accompanied the Salman Rushdie affair to indicate the presence of radical Islamic networks with international connections; this view reinforced stereotypes about militant Islam and raised questions about national security and immigration policies. That is why the traditional debate over the "assimilation" of Muslim populations is often perceived as a question of whether such assimilation will entail a sacrifice of national interest.[28]

All of the controversies surrounding Islam in Europe center on moral pluralism: what is the moral basis for a shared public culture? Is agreement on common social and cultural values possible?[29] Europe's rapidly growing Muslim population is defying the capacity of public policy to draw the limits of tolerance, and hence, challenging the operative public values of European societies.[30]

---

[27] Philomena Essed, "Black Women in White Women's Organizations: Ethnic Differentiation and Problems of Racism in the Netherlands," *Resources for Feminist Research* 18:4, 1991.

[28] John L. Esposito, "Contemporary Images of Islam in the West" (Conference on Europe and Islam, Ortega y Gasset Foundation, Toledo, Apr. 11–13, 1996).

[29] Jean Leca, "La démocratie à l'épreuve des pluralismes," *Revue française de Science Politique* 46:2, 1996, pp. 225–79.

[30] Bhikkhu Parekh, "Cultural Pluralism and the Limits of Diversity," *Alternatives* 20, 1995, pp. 431–57.

INDEX